Florida Overview Map

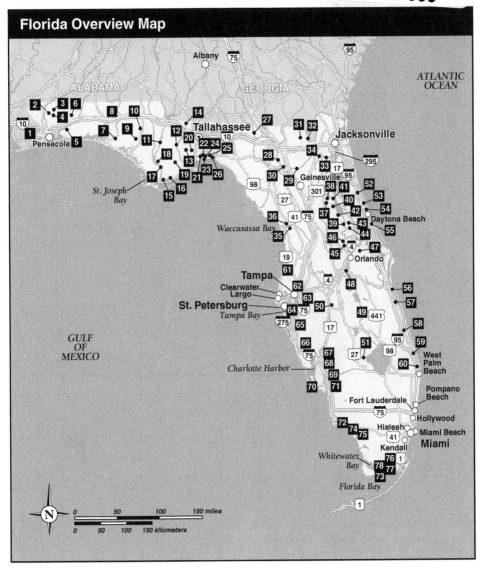

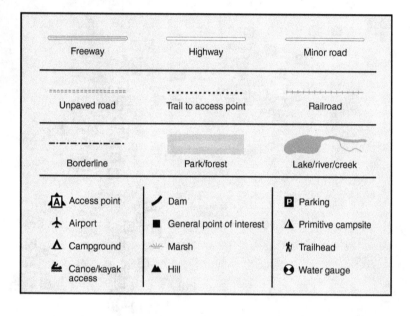

Freeway	Highway	Minor road
Unpaved road	Trail to access point	Railroad
Borderline	Park/forest	Lake/river/creek

Access point	Dam	Parking
Airport	General point of interest	Primitive campsite
Campground	Marsh	Trailhead
Canoe/kayak access	Hill	Water gauge

OVERVIEW MAP KEY

OTHER MENASHA RIDGE PADDLING GUIDES

The Alaska River Guide

Canoeing & Kayaking Georgia

A Canoeing & Kayaking Guide to Kentucky

A Canoeing & Kayaking Guide to the Ozarks

Canoeing & Kayaking New York

Canoeing & Kayaking South Central Wisconsin

Canoeing & Kayaking West Virginia

Carolina Whitewater

Paddling the Everglades Wilderness Waterway

Paddling Long Island and New York City

OTHER BOOKS BY JOHNNY MOLLOY
FOR MENASHA RIDGE PRESS AND WILDERNESS PRESS

60 Hikes Within 60 Miles: Nashville

60 Hikes Within 60 Miles: San Antonio & Austin, 1st–3rd Editions (with Tom Taylor)

A Canoeing & Kayaking Guide to the Streams of Kentucky (with Bob Sehlinger)

Backcountry Fishing: A Guide for Hikers, Backpackers, and Paddlers

Best Tent Camping: The Carolinas

Best Tent Camping: Colorado

Best Tent Camping: Georgia

Best Tent Camping: Kentucky

Best Tent Camping: Southern Appalachian & Smoky Mountains

Best Tent Camping: Tennessee

Best Tent Camping: West Virginia

Best Tent Camping: Wisconsin

Day & Overnight Hikes: Kentucky's Sheltowee Trace

Day & Overnight Hikes: West Virginia's Monongahela National Forest

Five-Star Trails: Chattanooga

Five-Star Trails: Knoxville

Five-Star Trails: Roanoke and the New River Valley

Five-Star Trails: Tri-Cities of Tennessee and Virginia

Land Between the Lakes Outdoor Recreation Handbook

Top Trails: Great Smoky Mountains National Park

Top Trails: Shenandoah National Park

Waterfalls of the Blue Ridge

CANOEING
& KAYAKING
FLORIDA

3RD EDITION

JOHNNY MOLLOY

MENASHA RIDGE PRESS
Your Guide to the Outdoors Since 1982

DEDICATION

THIS BOOK IS FOR ALL THE PADDLERS OF FLORIDA—*those on the waters of the Everglades, the kayakers on the crystalline spring runs of the Ocala National Forest, the casual floaters on the Chipola, the float fishermen on the Withlacoochee, the canoe campers on the Peace, those floating the entire length of the Suwannee River, and those plying the tidal waters of the Tomoka on a Sunday afternoon— may you keep stroking the waters of the Sunshine State.*

Canoeing & Kayaking Florida

Copyright © 2017 by Johnny Molloy

All rights reserved
Published by Menasha Ridge Press
Distributed by Publishers Group West
Printed in the United States of America
Third edition, first printing

Project editor: Ritchey Halphen
Cartography: Tommy Hertzel, Steve Jones, and Johnny Molloy
Cover design: Scott McGrew
Text design: Alian Design; adapted by Annie Long
Cover and interior photos: © Johnny Molloy, except as noted
Copyeditor: Kerry J. Smith
Proofreader: Laura Franck
Indexer: Ann Weik Cassar / Cassar Technical Services

Library of Congress Cataloging-in-Publication Data

Names: Molloy, Johnny, author.
Title: Canoeing & kayaking Florida / Johnny Molloy.
Description: Third Edition. | Birmingham, Alabama : Menasha Ridge Press, [2016] | Series: Canoeing & kayaking | "Distributed by Publishers Group West"—T.p. verso. | Includes index.
Identifiers: LCCN 2016018876 | ISBN 9781634040303 (paperback) | ISBN 9781634040310 (e-book) ISBN 9781634042079 (hardcover)
Subjects: LCSH: Canoes and canoeing—Florida—Guidebooks. | Kayaking—Florida—Guidebooks. Florida—Guidebooks.
Classification: LCC GV776.F6 M65 2016 | DDC 797.122—dc23
LC record available at lccn.loc.gov/2016018876

 MENASHA RIDGE PRESS
An imprint of AdventureKEEN
2204 First Avenue S., Suite 102
Birmingham, AL 35233
800-443-7227, fax 205-326-1012

Visit menasharidge.com for a complete list of our books and for ordering information. Contact us at our website, at facebook.com/menasharidge, or at twitter.com/menasharidge with questions or comments. To find out more about who we are and what we're doing, visit blog.menasharidge.com.

DISCLAIMER Paddling is an assumed-risk sport. The decision to run a river can be made only after an on-the-spot inspection, and a run should not be attempted without proper equipment and safety precautions. Neither Menasha Ridge Press nor Johnny Molloy is responsible for any personal or property damage that may result from your activities. By using any part of this guide, you recognize and assume all risks, and you acknowledge that you are responsible for your own actions. While every effort has been made to insure the accuracy of this guidebook, river and road conditions, along with phone numbers, websites, and other information, can change greatly from year to year.

CONTENTS

ACKNOWLEDGMENTS

Thanks to all the people with whom I floated a Florida river while researching this book: First and foremost, thanks to my wife, Keri Anne, for paddling the Sunshine State with me from the St. Johns River in the north to the Everglades in the south; to John Cox for accompanying me on the St. Marys; Chris Phillips on the Suwannee; Aaron Marabel on the Santa Fe; Brian Babb on the Tomoka; Kevin Thomas on the Shoal and the Yellow; and to Wes Shepherd on the Ochlockonee and Sopchoppy. Thanks to Holly Berman for paddling too many rivers to mention. And thanks to Hans Hollmann and Jeff Cochran for accompanying me down the Peace River, on the Suwannee, and in the Everglades.

Thanks to Old Town for providing me with an excellent canoe and kayak, to Kelty for their fine tents, and to Silva for a reliable compass. Thanks to Steve "Devo" Grayson for hitting the Everglades on numerous occasions, and to Tom "Take-a-Break" Lauria too. Thanks to Mike and Pam Hoehn for their help on the Apalachicola River. Thanks to John and Barb Haapala for helping wherever possible. Thanks to Miss Helen on Fisheating Creek, to the Clearwater Seven and their offspring for floating the Weeki Wachee with me, and to Bill "Worldwide" Armstrong for floating the Turner River. Thanks to Roger and Pete for floating down to and then giving me a ride on the Wacissa, to Jim Bob Cooter for floating the Estero, to Vivian "Snook" Oliva for loving paddling places all over the country, and to Meredith for providing a refuge and a friendly face.

Much appreciation to the editors at Menasha Ridge Press for their assistance and skill in updating this edition. Finally, thanks to all the outfitters who ran shuttles and answered a lot of irritating questions.

—*Johnny Molloy*

PREFACE

Welcome to the third and newest edition of *Canoeing & Kayaking Florida*. The state of Florida has an abundance of water; therefore, it is only natural that native Floridians and transplants alike paddle and ply the waterways of this aquatically blessed state. Of course, Florida's aboriginal Indians and subsequent settlers used the creeks, streams, and rivers long before the first plastic kayak or fiberglass canoe took to this watery paradise. Recreational paddling took off in the early 1970s, when the state of Florida established a paddling-trail system borne of paddlers discovering the many destinations here. For various reasons, this state-sanctioned trail system lost momentum but has since revived. Building on the state's efforts and adding their own discoveries, paddling enthusiasts Elizabeth F. Carter and John L. Pearce brought together the rich and varied streams, creeks, and rivers of Florida. Together, they penned the very first incarnation of this book, *A Canoeing & Kayaking Guide to the Streams of Florida, Volume I*. Their guide covered the north-central part of the state as well as the Panhandle. I used this excellent book for years on almost every river it detailed, never dreaming that I would get the opportunity to update and add to it. This was followed by *A Canoeing & Kayaking Guide to the Streams of Florida, Volume II*, written by Lou Glaros and Doug Sphar. Their book covered the southern half of the state. Paddling grew steadily in Florida due in part to these excellent guidebooks, the establishment of paddling clubs, the positioning of outfitters on rivers, and population growth.

Since then, paddling in Florida has blossomed further. More people began exploring new waterways, not only in new kayaks made of varied plastics but also ultralightweight canoes easy to paddle and transport. The rise in the variety and use of recreational kayaks has contributed to the continuing growth of paddling's popularity here.

Paddling grew in importance with me as I began making regular excursions to the Florida Panhandle, paddling all the major rivers there. Next, I pointed south, to the Everglades, ultimately seeing the need for and then writing the definitive book for those taking self-propelled boats there, titled *A Paddler's Guide to Everglades National Park*. I later wrote several other hiking and camping guides to Florida, including a paddling adventure narrative that detailed my journey from the uppermost Suwannee River to the Gulf of Mexico, where I jumped into a sea kayak and paddled the Gulf all the way to the Florida Keys. That book, *From the Swamp to the Keys: A Paddle Through Florida History*, cemented in my mind the fact that the state truly is a unique and nearly limitless paddling destination that deserves national attention.

Later, I grabbed the opportunity to revise and combine Volumes I and II of *A Canoeing & Kayaking Guide to the Streams of Florida* into a single guidebook. I refloated previously covered rivers, checked access points, and paddled new waterways to highlight additional opportunities for Florida canoeists and kayakers. And in the course of paddling, I eliminated some old paddle destinations, such as the Braden River, simply because the accesses had been eliminated and/or they were simply overwhelmed by urbanization. I subsequently added more-wilderness-oriented rivers to the book, such as the Econfina River of Taylor County, now a National Recreation Trail, and the New River, which snakes through Tates Hell State Forest.

Other new destinations involved developed paddling trails such as Graham Creek and the East River, part of the Apalachicola Wildlife and Environmental Area, a preserved estuarine swath of the lower Apalachicola River in the Panhandle.

This latest edition of *Canoeing & Kayaking Florida* includes still more new waterways to explore. In this updated guide, you will find a wealth of information to execute paddling adventures all over the Sunshine State. Things change over time, paddling accesses open and close, outfitters come and go.

The rebirth and expansion of Florida's paddling-trail program, as well as the addition of county and city blueways, has brought forth more paddling destinations with accesses—places such as Shell Creek in Charlotte County and Blue Creek in Lake County. Paddlers are seeing waterways large and small as paddling destinations; hence,

the addition of rivers such as the Caloosahatchee, St. Johns, and Apalachicola, along with stillwater paddles, such as secluded Stagger Mud Lake. Today's paddlers desire more there-and-back destinations, eliminating a shuttle, even if they paddle up and downstream on a river, ply tidal waterways, or travel lakes. Paddlers also want to explore places with wild, undeveloped banks, such as North Fork Black Creek in Jennings State Forest. To that end, I've added paddles that wander through national and state forests, wildlife refuges, and/or public water-management lands. Finding and paddling these destinations was a real treat and adventure, a venue to view God's glory in and around Florida's waterways.

Along the way, I got lost in the car, lost in the boat, rained on, sunburned, scraped ice off the canoe in the morning, jumped in the water after a blazing afternoon in the kayak,

A HIKER BRIDGE SPANS HICKEYS CREEK.
(See Trip 69, page 271.)

got bit by no-see-ums near the coast and away from the coast, got bit by troublesome mosquitoes nearly everywhere, cut my foot on oyster bars, got stopped by headwinds in the Everglades, fell onto a cypress stump, crashed into logs, got stuck in shallows, knocked a fishing pole into the water, dragged my boat over logjams, fought waves on the St. Johns, and couldn't find a campsite when I needed one. But I also saw azaleas bloom on the Sopchoppy; shot the shoals on Sweetwater Creek; turned a lazy bend on the New River and saw a bear; saw more springs than you can imagine on the Suwannee and other rivers; met new faces around every turn, making new friends along the way; saw smiles on the faces of those peering into the clear waters of the Weeki Wachee River; enjoyed a great campfire and a better dinner alongside the Peace River; explored the majesty of lower Alexander Springs Creek; and came to understand why the Loxahatchee is a federally designated Wild and Scenic River. All in all, it was a great experience. I am humbled to be a part of this book, which I hope will, in its updated and improved state, continue to serve the worthy paddlers of Florida.

Over the years, I have paddled more than 4,000 miles of Florida waterways. This guidebook is the product of paddling and scouting those waterways, miles and miles of driving, shuttling, and loading and unloading boats ad infinitum, along with myriad hours of map work, researching, and writing. During the process, fond memories were made. And I hope you will make memories of your own while canoeing and kayaking Florida.

USING THIS GUIDE

First, a brief **overview** introduces each river profiled in this book.

Second, a list of **topographic maps** that can be used for a particular section of river is provided. Topo maps are listed in the order in which the river flows. Unless otherwise noted, all maps are located on the Florida Index of the United States Geological Survey (USGS). Topos are available at outdoors and sporting-goods stores, at many public libraries, and online (in both digital and hard-copy formats) at websites including store.usgs.gov, topozone.com, and mytopo.com. A number of online sources, including the USGS, offer topos at no cost as well as for purchase.

Third, the river segment profiled is in most cases labeled and identified by the section **put-in,** followed by the section **take-out.** For example, the first segment of the Perdido River is Three Runs to Muscogee Landing (page 16). Note that a few paddles are loops or out-and-back routes; thus, they have a single access point.

Fourth, an **at-a-glance box** lists basic river data, including class, length, time, gauge, level, gradient, and scenery.

Class, or river difficulty, has been adapted from a system developed by American Whitewater and is rated Class I–VI. For detailed information on the rating system, see Appendix B (page 303).

Length lists the river miles traversed between the put-in and take-out. Where the route is a loop or an out-and-back, that information is noted here as well.

Time provides conservative estimates of how long the paddle will take to complete without allowing for lunch, fishing, playing, napping, or otherwise dawdling. Wind, currents, and tides can alter these times.

Gauge indicates whether the method of gauging the river is visual, obtained by phone, or obtained online. If the gauge is visual, you literally have to look at the river to determine whether it is runnable or not.

Level indicates the flow rates at which a particular river can be run. Most Florida rivers can be run year-round. "N/A" means that a specific number is unavailable. Government agencies like the USGS measure river flows at gauging stations throughout the country. This information is collected and recorded hourly. You will find websites and phone numbers listed in the discussion of river gauges following. You will also encounter "paddler's gauges" painted on bridge piers and rocks; although not reported on websites, they are used by many canoeists and kayakers.

Gradient is the average drop of the river in feet per mile. For example, 2 means that the river drops at an average rate of 2 feet per mile. Note that the difficulty of a river's rapids is not determined only by gradient. Some rivers drop evenly over continuous rapids of roughly the same difficulty; others alternate between long pools and drops that are steeper than the gradient would indicate. Many Florida rivers have swift currents that sweep through fallen trees around unseen bends, adding to the difficulty. **Scenery** is ranked on an *A–D* scale: *A* indicates remote wilderness areas with little sign of civilization; *B* indicates more-settled (but still beautiful) pastoral countryside; *C* indicates lots of development (cities or industrial areas); and *D*, unfortunately, indicates pollution, rundown buildings, and other forms of landscape abuse. The quality of the scenery along a river often changes. For example, the Hillsborough River within Hillsborough River State Park is considered *A* but becomes *C* on its lower reaches, where houses are common.

Fifth, a **Description** of the specific section of the river is provided.

Sixth, **Shuttle** lists detailed driving directions to both the put-in and the take-out. (Loops and out-and-back routes require no shuttling and are designated instead with "Directions.")

Seventh, **Gauge** shows which gauges are needed to determine river runnability. Again, note that gauges are not available for some streams.

Finally, **maps** detail each river included in this guidebook. They include put-ins, take-outs, and mileage segments, plus features of interest such as bridges, landing areas, rapids, and confluences with other rivers, creeks, and streams. These maps will aid you in finding your way, but they are no substitute for detailed USGS topographic maps, public-land maps, or digital maps.

USING RIVER GAUGES

The Water Resources Division of the USGS measures water flow on most rivers in the United States at frequent intervals; the US Army Corps of Engineers and various power companies collect similar information. These flows are recorded in cubic feet per second (cfs) and are available to paddlers.

The key variable is the height of the river at a fixed point. Gauge houses, situated on most rivers, consist of a well at the river's edge with a float attached to a recording clock. The gauge reads in hundredths of feet. Rating tables are constructed for each gauge to get a cfs reading for each level.

This information can be useful for paddlers who are planning a trip. In Florida, however, most rivers can be paddled year-round because they are spring-fed or tidal, or they simply have slow rates of fluctuation—a product of being fed by low-lying, swampy drainages, rather than faster-draining hills and highlands of other states. But because droughts and excessive rainfall occur in Florida, gauges can be useful. You don't want to drag down a droughty, low river, nor do you want to take a harrowing paddle down a flooded one. This gauge information can be obtained quickly at various websites, along with recent rainfall information. Paddlers should make use of this data. Gauges are listed for Florida rivers where they exist. In most instances, the minimum and maximum runnable flow rates have not been established for a particular river. But if you float your favorite river time and again, you can record the flow rates and water levels each time you paddle the river and establish your own flow rates and levels at which you like to paddle the waterway.

WATER-LEVEL SITES

Real-time water levels for Florida can be found at waterdata.usgs.gov/fl/nwis/rt. At this in-depth USGS website, hundreds of gauges for the entire country are updated continually, and graphs showing recent flow trends are available at the touch of a mouse. This is the greatest thing for paddlers since dry bags were invented.

FRIENDLY ADVICE

✧ **WEATHER** Florida lives up to its nickname with plenty of sunshine, but paddlers will need to consider other facets of Florida weather, especially seasonal variations. General weather patterns are discussed below for three geographic regions: the Panhandle, Central Florida, and South Florida.

The Panhandle has four distinct seasons, though the climate is very long on summer, where highs regularly reach the 90s and thunderstorms pass through on most any afternoon. Nights can be uncomfortably hot. Fall finds cooler nights and warm days with less precipitation than summer. Winter is variable. Highs push 60°F. Expect lows in the 40s, though subfreezing temperatures are the norm during cold snaps. There are usually several mild days during each winter month. Precipitation comes in strong continental fronts, with more persistent rains followed by sunny, cold days. Snow is very uncommon, though not unheard of. The longer days of spring begin to warm into the 70s, often straying into the 80s, and can vary wildly.

Central Florida is drier and warmer than the Panhandle. It is far enough south to attract snowbirds escaping the cold of the north. Winter is generally pleasant and dry. Daytime highs push 70°F, yet the region is far enough north that a cold snap can bring afternoon highs down to the 50s and occasional temperatures below freezing.

Spring is an excellent time to enjoy waterways of the central part of the state. The days are warm and clear, often topping 80°F, yet nights remain cool enough to enjoy a campfire. Mornings are still crisp, and insects are not bothersome. Then the days really warm up and frequent thunderstorms result, beginning in June. Daytime highs can exceed 90°F during the long, humid summer, although temperatures will be a little lower at the nearby coastline. Fall is very nice too. The thunderstorms subside and cool fronts clear the skies.

South Florida has a near-tropical climate with two distinct seasons, wet and dry. Snowbirds flock to this area during winter. Winter temperature readings at Fort Myers and other cities can register as the nation's warmest, though cold fronts will punch down this far south, cooling things down. Rain occasionally accompanies the fronts, though infrequent storms will drift in from the Gulf. But, overall, winter is also the dry season. The rainy season starts in May and lasts through September. Brief but heavy downpours inundate the area, adding to the extreme humidity. The Gulf side does not get as strong or frequent breezes as the Atlantic, resulting in some sweltering summer days.

✧ **INSECTS** During the warm months, mosquitoes, sand gnats, and yellow flies can be a source of discomfort. Mosquitoes are usually confined to shady, wooded areas and are at their worst just at dusk and in the early morning. Commercial insect repellents containing 30% DEET are effective in discouraging them. Yellow flies are usually present on hot, still days. They are rarely a problem after dark. They, too, are repelled by most commercial DEET products, but it may take a stronger formula, and every piece of exposed skin must be treated. Sand gnats, or no-see-ums, are a great reason why quality tents have fine netting on the doors and windows. The bothersome gnats are most common in marshy areas near the coast, but are occasionally encountered inland. Insect repellent does not deter them as easily, but application of something oily to the skin sometimes will.

✧ **REPTILES** Six species of poisonous snakes are found in Florida. They are the Southern copperhead, cottonmouth, coral snake, and three varieties of rattlesnakes: the timber rattler, pygmy rattler, and Eastern diamondback rattler. The cottonmouth frequently lounges on deadfall trees, and its coloration makes it difficult to spot, so exercise caution when negotiating downed trees or making portages. The coral snake and diamondback are most apt to be found near campsites, especially around logs and thick brush. Use common sense when walking in the woods, never climb on or step over logs without checking for snakes, and avoid walking through stands of palmetto palms or dense underbrush.

Alligators, not surprisingly, maintain a serious presence in Florida waterways. If you are reasonably quiet, your chances of seeing alligators on most Florida streams are excellent. Usually as soon as they see you, they will slip into the water and swim away. If they do not, avoid approaching or annoying them in any way. In some more-populated areas where alligators have become accustomed to people, they are no longer shy and may be more daring than you would like. To avoid troubles, do not swim in areas where alligators live, and do not feed or harass them.

✧ **CAMPING** Try to camp on public lands where possible. If not, attempt to get permission from the landowner. Minimize your impact as much as possible when camping on Florida's rivers.

Sandbars are your campsites of choice when they're available. They have fewer insects and no poison ivy, and they generally help you avoid the possibility of camping on private property. If no sandbar is available, look for a clearing in the woods on high ground.

BEACH CAMPING AT ITS BEST: HIGHLAND BEACH, EVERGLADES NATIONAL PARK

Camping in a swamp is definitely a bad idea. Bugs and/or rising water could make you miserable.

If possible, avoid camping at boat ramps or other access points. A quiet dirt road leading to the river may turn into the local party spot after dark.

Either bring your own drinking water or purify streamwater to make it safe to drink.

Mosquitoes can be fierce at night, so a bugproof shelter is necessary for a good night's rest.

Finally, obtain camping permits where necessary for such destinations as Everglades National Park and certain water-management-district lands, such as the Suwannee River.

❖ KNOWING YOUR RIGHTS ON THE RIVER

Florida's navigable rivers, lakes, and tidelands are held in a public trust that imposes a legal duty on the state to preserve and control them for public navigation, fishing, swimming, and other lawful uses. The Public Trust Doctrine protects the public status of navigable water bodies in Florida.

A waterway is navigable if, at the time Florida became a state, in 1845, it was used or was capable of being used (by canoes as well as other boats) as a highway for waterborne trade or travel conducted by the customary modes of that period. Navigability does not require year-round capacity for navigation, but it does require such capacity in the water body's ordinary state. Artificial water bodies (that is, canals) or waterways rendered navigable through improvement by dredging are not legally navigable.

In Florida, the boundary of navigable freshwater lakes and rivers is the ordinary high-water line. The public has the right to make all lawful uses of sovereignty lands up to this boundary line, including use of the shore or space between ordinary high- and low-water marks. By the same token, landowners' rights to prohibit trespassing on their land along creeks, if they so desire, are also guaranteed. Therefore, access to rivers must be secured at highway rights-of-way or on publicly owned lands if permission to cross privately owned lands cannot be secured.

In granting you access to a river, landowners are extending you a privilege. In Florida, many paddling destinations pass through populated areas, with houses and docks and such. Don't betray landowners' trust if they invite you to launch canoes or kayaks or camp from their shores. Don't litter, drive through newly planted fields, or climb on a dock or into someone's backyard.

You will run into landowners who are hostile to paddlers. They may resent people driving hundreds of miles for the pleasure of floating down a river, or they may even feel that they own the river you want to paddle. Happily, you'll also encounter landowners who are welcoming, friendly, and approachable. Appreciate this goodwill, and don't abuse it.

In general, paddlers risk trespassing when they portage, camp, or even get out for a quick lunch break. If you are approached by a landowner when trespassing, by all means be cordial and understanding and explain your predicament (in the case of a portage or lunch break). Never knowingly camp on private land without permission. If you do encounter a perturbed landowner, don't panic. Keep cool and be respectful.

Landowners have the right to keep you off their land, and the law will side with them unless they inflict harm on you, in which case they may be both civilly and criminally liable. If a landowner points a gun at you, fires warning shots, or assaults or injures you or a boater in your group, you are certainly

EVERGLADES NATIONAL PARK

Six of the seven trips in Part Nine (page 281) lie entirely or partially within Everglades National Park. The following information is good to know before you go.

You must pay an admission fee at the main park entrance on FL 9336 in Florida City. Call 305-242-7700 or visit nps.gov/ever/planyourvisit/fees.htm for the latest information. No fees are charged at the Everglades City entrance off County Road 29.

An overnight trip in the park requires advance planning. To get started, visit nps.gov/ever /planyourvisit; click "Brochures" for general trip-planning information as well as overnight-specific information.

Wilderness permits, required for backcountry camping, are available only in person at the Flamingo Visitor Center (239-695-2945) and the Gulf Coast Visitor Center (239-695-3311) and may be obtained up to 24 hours before your trip.

Before you make your backcountry-trip request with park staff, have alternative routes planned; this way, if campsites are already reserved, you'll have a backup plan ready. Once your permit is issued and the park regulations are explained to you, you must pay a permit fee.

Be aware of heavy-use periods. The general paddling season in Everglades National Park runs from November through April. Insects, thunderstorms, and occasional hurricanes conspire to keep the Everglades backcountry nearly deserted May–October. When the first north breezes cool and clear the air, reducing insects, paddlers turn their eyes southward to the Everglades. A few campsites begin to fill on weekends, but the crowds really pick up around the holidays.

The period between Christmas and New Year's is the Everglades' busiest. Expect full campsites and plan alternative trips. After this, weekends can be busy, but you can nearly always get into the general vicinity of where you want to go. Plan your trip during the week for the most solitude.

The next big crowds come around Presidents Day weekend in February. The last big hits come during mid-March, when college students flock to the Everglades for overnight trips. Again, get to the ranger stations early and you should be able to get ahold of some campsites. As the weather warms up in April, visitation tapers off, dying by the end of the month.

within your rights to protect yourself. Further, the landowner has no right to detain you as if holding you for law enforcement. In turn, landowners have the right to protect themselves from paddlers who threaten them verbally or physically.

Confrontations between belligerent paddlers and cantankerous landowners are to be avoided, that's for sure. Although the chances of such showdowns may be rare, paddlers nonetheless should know their rights and the rights of landowners. Judges don't like

trespassers any more than they like landowners who harass trespassers.

✧ **FEES AND PERMITS Florida State Parks** charge entrance fees of varying amounts. Because these fees are subject to change— and because they inevitably change between editions of a print book—it's best to check with the parks directly for the most up-to-date information. Go to floridastateparks.org and search for a specific park at the top of the page; select the park from the pop-up menu to be taken to its homepage. Call the phone number listed there or click "Hours & Fees." For camping information, click "Stay the Night" on the main homepage.

Florida State Forests charge fees for day use, camping, lodging for hunters, and the use of off-road vehicles, among other fees. Visit tinyurl.com/floridastateforests for the latest information.

The Florida Fish and Wildlife Conservation Commission provides information on fishing and hunting permits and regulations at its website, myfwc.com.

✧ ROADS Access roads used to reach the waterways in this guidebook range from congested interstates cutting through big cities to potholed sandy swaths snaking through sloppy swamps. Others, such as national-forest roads, will be somewhere in between. Generally speaking, the more urbanized a stream is, the higher the likelihood you will be traveling paved roads on your shuttles. Consider weather in your shuttle process. Poor access roads may have deep sand pits in dry weather and wet bog holes during the rainy times.

✧ LEAVING CARS UNATTENDED In writing this and other books, I've parked all over the state of Florida, often for days at a time and not always with the best results. (I once had my laptop stolen from my car in a national forest north of Florida.)

Use your intuition when deciding where to leave your vehicle. If you can't arrange for someone to look after your car, paying a small parking fee is worth the peace of mind. National, state, and county parks with on-site rangers are good choices for leaving your vehicle overnight. Also check with fish camps and liveries—many of these provide shuttle services and safe places to park. Private businesses sometimes allow overnighters to park

in their lots as well; just be sure to ask permission and offer to pay. When you're parking on day trips, leave your car near the road rather than in the woods and out of sight.

✧ PADDLING SKILLS Don't assume that the paddling skills you've developed will qualify you for everything Florida waterways have to offer. Many streams here are twisting, fast, and loaded with obstructions. They may also be miles from a road through sand hills or swamp. Five miles on a straight, spring-fed river is very different from 5 miles on a narrow, cascading stream with 15 pullovers, or in a sweeping current pouring through a fallen tree. Read the trip descriptions carefully before you set out.

Other waterways in this guidebook are tidal. Be aware of the tides before you set out! Otherwise, you may be paddling against a very strong current or, worse yet, you may get stuck trying to paddle where there is no water.

FLORIDA RIVERS AND CREEKS

GEOLOGY

The state of Florida is a landmass that occupies a minor portion of the Florida Plateau. Attached to the continental United States, this plateau is a partially submerged platform about 500 miles long and ranging from 250 to 400 miles wide. It has existed for millions of years and is one of the most stable places on the crust of the earth.

Over the millennia, Florida has submerged and resurfaced from a series of ancient seas. The Coastal Lowlands are the most recent land-masses to have emerged from the sea. They consist of those areas that surround the hills of the Highlands in the northern and western sections of the state, and they make up the flatlands that are known as South Florida.

The aforementioned **Highlands** are geologically much older than the Coastal Lowlands, and they reach their highest point at about 345 feet above sea level in the greater Yellow River watershed. Because the Florida peninsula is narrow, especially in the northwestern Panhandle, it is often less than 50 miles from a high point of 300 feet above sea level to the Gulf of Mexico. The resulting gradient, combined with the terraces and ledges that have been left on the landscape with the recession of the seas, has produced the unique geological phenomena that have made North Florida rivers a paradise for canoeists.

North Florida includes the **Western Highlands,** the **Marianna Lowlands,** the **Tallahassee Hills,** and the **Central Highlands.** In geographic terms, this includes an area beginning at the Perdido River on the Alabama–Florida line and continuing south to an imaginary line

drawn from New Port Richey on the west to Orlando on the east.

For the purposes of this book, the lower half of the Florida peninsula has been partitioned into four regions: the **Atlantic Coast,** the **Southwest Gulf Coast,** the **Central Highlands,** and the **Everglades.** Among these areas, less than a day's drive separates the beauty and solitude of the Everglades from the stretches of whitewater on the Hillsborough River. Dark and mysterious cypress forests, high, pine-covered bluffs, and the open expanse of a coastal marsh can all be experienced in a single day of paddling. The unique natural history of the lower half of the Florida peninsula makes this enjoyable paddling possible. The rivers and streams within each of these regions share generally similar geology and natural communities.

The streams of the Atlantic Coast drain a long, narrow region that was ocean floor before glaciers covered North America. An ancient dune line forms a ridge that isolates

PADDLING FLOTILLA

the coastal drainage area from the St. Johns River drainage. The low elevation of this region—less than 50 feet above sea level—means generally sluggish stream flow. As these streams approach the ocean, they develop broad, funnel-shaped mouths known as estuaries. In estuaries, fresh water mixes with salt water and ocean tides assume control of the water dynamics. The estuaries of Florida's central Atlantic Coast feature grassy marshes, whereas mangrove swamps are characteristic of the southern Atlantic Coast.

Upstream plant communities often comprise hardwood swamp forests with cypress, oaks, and maples, or cabbage-palm hammocks with palms, oaks, and wax myrtles. Alligators and otters are frequently seen upstream, but the manatee enjoys the estuary. The estuaries also provide great birding. The heron, egret, anhinga, and osprey are at home here. Ducks fly in when the weather turns cold up north.

The Southwest Gulf Coast has a number of major stream systems that pierce the interior of the peninsula. Tampa Bay alone is the terminus of four major streams: the Hillsborough, Alafia, Manatee, and Little Manatee. The nearby Peace River constitutes one of the largest drainage basins of Florida. A notable feature of the streams of the Southwest Gulf Coast is an underlying layer of limestone. On streams such as the Hillsborough and Alafia, this limestone spices up a day of paddling with stretches of Class II whitewater. Streams of the region typically have origins in interior highlands and upland plains. These areas are generally characterized by pine flatwoods and palmetto prairies; however, hardwood swamp forests with oak and cypress often are found in the immediate stream valley. A diverse selection of wildlife unfolds along the way. The distinctive call of the pileated woodpecker is frequently heard, as is the knocking noise it makes pecking for insects. The shadowy form of the owl is seen fluttering through the forest canopy. Limpkins and ibis feed in the marshes and swamps that the streams pass through.

A region of highlands and upland plains lies north of Lake Okeechobee and inland between the two coasts. The streams in this region drain lands that in some places exceed 150 feet above sea level—stratospheric by Florida standards. This beautiful countryside presents a completely different image of Florida from the palm-studded beach scenes of tourist brochures. Central Highlands forests are heavy with pines, and complement areas where oak and hickory predominate. Fleeting glimpses of deer darting through brush are not uncommon, and wild turkey can sometimes be seen. Curious raccoons and playful otters, as well as alligators, make a living along these streams. Groups of turtles basking on downed tree trunks slide into the water as a canoe glides by.

There is only one Everglades. A unique combination of ancient events created this wonderful ecosystem—an environment that exists nowhere else on this planet. In fact, the Everglades is an International Biosphere Reserve and a World Heritage Site. The Everglades is a sheet of water that flows imperceptibly south from Lake Okeechobee into Florida Bay. The underlying base of this drainage is a plain of oolitic limestone, which was formed from the sediment of an early sea. The gradient of this plain is so gentle that water only drops 15 feet over the 100-mile journey to Florida Bay. The limestone is covered with peat soils that support the vast freshwater sawgrass marshes for which the Everglades is famous. Along the coastal extreme of the Everglades, grass prairies give way to mangrove forests. The western extreme of the

Everglades has vast stands of cypress forest known as strands.

The Everglades is justly famous for bird-life, and early in this century the Everglades supported a plumage industry that decimated many wading bird species. Wildlife regulations and changing fashions ended this practice. The Everglades is home for rare and endangered animals. The crocodile and the Florida panther are making a last stand here. This unique habitat also supports the Everglades kite, reddish egret, roseate spoonbill, Florida mangrove cuckoo, and Everglades mink.

WATERSHEDS OF FLORIDA

Florida's watersheds are generally small compared with those in many other states. Think about the shape of Florida: it is 465 miles at its widest and 447 miles at its longest. Florida encompasses 54,090 square miles, making it the 22nd largest state by area. Its highest point, 345 feet, is in Walton County, its lowest point anywhere that borders the Atlantic Ocean. The maximum width of Florida is deceptive, however, as it actually runs in an east–west line across the Panhandle to the Atlantic. Its maximum length from north to south can be deceptive, too, for anywhere a person stands in Florida, he or she is never too far from the ocean. This fact is important in analyzing Florida's watersheds. In most parts of the state, there simply isn't enough land to drain before any given waterway hits the salty sea.

The largest river by volume in Florida is the Apalachicola. But this river primarily drains Georgia and Alabama, not the Sunshine State. In terms of length, the St. Johns is the longest river that flows entirely in Florida. The Suwannee, which originates in Georgia, is the longest river in this guidebook and has a larger drainage acreage than the St. Johns.

Most streams of the Panhandle form their own drainages extending from their sources in Alabama and Georgia to the Gulf, or they meet in bays just before the Gulf, such as the Yellow–Shoal–Blackwater River complex. Moving east, the Choctawhatchee captures the Panhandle west of the Apalachicola. The rivers of the Big Bend, such as Ochlockonee, Econfina, and Steinhatchee, form their own watersheds. Northeastern Florida has an interesting phenomenon: two rivers draining one great swamp with one river heading to the Gulf and the other to the Atlantic. Here, the St. Marys leaves the Okefenokee Swamp and heads to the Atlantic Ocean, additionally forming the boundary between Florida and Georgia, while the Suwannee heads southwest to the Gulf, absorbing other rivers in this guidebook, such as the Santa Fe and Withlacoochee.

Heading into the peninsula of the state, we begin to see rivers with drainages located entirely in Florida, all heading to the coast. An especially interesting drainage layout starts in the Green Swamp of Central Florida. Here, the Ocklawaha, Withlacoochee (South), Hillsborough, and Peace Rivers head their respective ways, with all but the Ocklawaha aiming for the Gulf. The Ocklawaha flows into the St. Johns, which flows into the Atlantic Ocean.

Farther south, the Everglades extends its huge influence despite development of the entire eastern Everglades that is now part of the South Florida metroplex. Most rivers here flow into the Gulf or join the slow sheet flow of the Glades on its inevitable journey south and west. Rivers of the lower Atlantic Coast, such as the Loxahatchee, break east through

THIS CANOE WAS PULLED UP WELL
ASHORE IN ANTICIPATION OF HEAVY
RAINS ON THE OCHLOCKONEE RIVER.

OUTSTANDING FLORIDA WATERS

An Outstanding Florida Water (OFW) is a body of water designated as worthy of special protection because of its natural attributes. This designation is applied to select waters and is intended to protect existing good water quality. Most OFWs are areas managed by the state or federal government as parks, including wildlife refuges, preserves, marine sanctuaries, estuarine research reserves, certain waters within state or national forests, Wild and Scenic Rivers, or aquatic preserves. Generally, the waters within these managed areas are OFWs because the managing agency has requested this special protection.

Florida OFWs featured in this guidebook include all or part of the following waterways: the Aucilla, Blackwater, Chipola, Choctawhatchee, Econlockhatchee, Estero, Hillsborough, Myakka, Ochlockonee, Ocklawaha, Perdido, Rainbow, St. Marks, Santa Fe, Shoal, Silver, Suwannee, Tomoka, Wacissa, Wakulla, and Wekiva Rivers, along with Spruce Creek.

SPRING-FED RIVERS

Many of Florida's waterways are spring fed or their flow is aided and enhanced by springs. Paddle trips included in this book that begin at a spring source include Salt Springs Run, Juniper Creek, the Ichetucknee River, the Weeki Wachee River, and Rock Springs Run, to name a few. In other places, springs will flow into or on the edge of the river, as occurs in many places on the Suwannee River.

Florida's springs are among the most beautiful and unusual phenomena that paddlers are privileged to see. There are over 300 major springs in Florida—more than in any other state in the United States and more

the Atlantic Ridge of the East Coast and meet the Atlantic Ocean.

than any other country in the world. They are the natural outflow of water from an underground water system and vary from tiny rivulets trickling from the ground to deep caverns far below the surface of crystal-clear pools.

Most of Florida's springs lie along major rivers and are concentrated in the western part of north Florida. Some of the springs have been incorporated into state parks, national-forest recreation areas, or privately owned tourist attractions and drinking water enterprises. Over time, the state has acquired springs for protective and recreation uses, such as Weeki Wachee Springs, Silver Springs, and Rainbow Springs. Many more of them remain hidden away in areas not yet touched by development. These secluded gems of blue and green and silver are the special reward for those who paddle a boat to see them.

For paddlers, spring-fed waterways are a reliable boating bet. Spring-fed streams offer a constant or slightly variable flow that can be counted on during dry and wet weather. In these situations, there is little need to call ahead or check flow rates on websites to see if the riverway can be paddled.

Where springs occur on the waterways described in this guide, every effort is made to describe their location, appearance, and the name by which they are most commonly known. Springs do change; high water may obscure them and extreme dry weather may reduce their flow. Some have been purchased privately and are fenced from public access—even from navigable water. In many cases the land around a spring may be private property, but paddlers may enjoy the spring from their boat.

TIDAL RIVERS

With Florida having so much coastline, it is only natural that many of the state's streams and rivers would have a tidal component. This aspect in which freshwater ecosystems change to saltwater adds to the biodiversity of your paddle on such waterways as Pellicer Creek and Turner River. These tidally influenced destinations are governed both by the changing flow of water into and out of their estuarine regions and the absolute flows heading downriver. Take the time to learn the tides before you set out on your trip! A good Internet resource is the website freetidetables.com.

Tides can be your enemy or friend. Low tides can leave you stranded in the tidal mudflats, and high tides can make your return paddle to the put-in a strong-arm battle. Tides may cause discomfort or delay, but they can be dangerous in other situations. Be careful around man-made canals; a strong pull will take you where you don't want to go or ram you into a tree lying half-submerged in the water. The biggest problem with tides comes when cutting corners in rivers. You will be paddling in one direction and the tide will be flowing perpendicular to your direction, catching the nose of your craft and turning you over before you know what happened. Watch for direction flow in the water ahead of you, such as ripples and eddy lines, and adjust your speed and direction.

Tides can be a directional indicator as well. If you know the general times of tidal variation in your given area, you can tell in which direction the ocean lies and vice versa. Use the tides to your advantage while traveling the rivers described in this guidebook.

RECOMMENDED RUNS

With thousands of miles of paddling possibilities in the Sunshine State, it's sometimes hard to know where to begin. The following paddling recommendations will help get you started. Note that some of these runs are shorter segments within featured paddles.

NOVICE MOVING-WATER PADDLES

28 Suwannee River: Suwannee Springs to Suwannee River State Park (p. 123)

32 St. Marys River: Thompkins Landing to Traders Hill (p. 148)

36 Rainbow River: K. P. Hole Park to County Road 484 (p. 165)

49 Arbuckle Creek: Lake Arbuckle to Arbuckle Creek Road (p. 205)

50 Peace River: Brownsville to Arcadia (p. 214)

GREAT PADDLING TRIPS FOR CHILDREN

30 Ichetucknee River: Ichetucknee Springs to US 27 (p. 141)

39 Alexander Springs and Alexander Springs Creek: Alexander Springs to 52 Landing (p. 173)

47 Econlockhatchee River: CR 419 to Snowhill Road (p. 201)

60 Loxahatchee River: River Bend Park to Jonathan Dickinson State Park (p. 240)

70 Commodore Creek Canoe Trail (p. 274)

OVERNIGHT PADDLING– CAMPING TRIPS

4 Blackwater River: Chessher Bridge to Deaton Bridge (p. 26–28)

11 Apalachicola River: Hickory Bluff Landing to Bloody Bluff Landing (p. 66)

12 Ochlockonee River: Lake Talquin Dam to Ochlockonee River State Park (p. 73)

38 Ocklawaha River: FL 40 to County Road 316 (p. 169)

73 Everglades National Park: Flamingo to Everglades City (p. 286)

FASTWATER PADDLES

7 Choctawhatchee River: County Road 36 to AL 27 (p. 38)

9 Econfina Creek of Washington and Bay Counties: Scott Bridge to Walsingham Bridge (p. 50)

13 Sopchoppy River: Forest Highway 13 to Forest Road 329 (p. 77–78)

40 Juniper Springs and Juniper Creek: Juniper Springs to FL 19 (p. 177)

51 Fisheating Creek: Burnt Bridge to Palmdale (p. 216)

SINGLE-CAR PADDLES

(no shuttle required)

43 Stagger Mud Lake (p. 184)

56 Turkey Creek: Goode Park to Turkey Creek Sanctuary (p. 230)

68 Shell Creek: Hathaway Park to Shell Creek Preserve (p. 269)

69 Caloosahatchee River and Hickeys Creek (p. 271)

76 Nine-Mile Pond Canoe Trail (p. 292)

PADDLES ON OR NEAR SPRINGS

28 Suwannee River: FL 51 to Branford (p. 129)

29 Santa Fe River: US 27 to FL 47 (p. 139)

37 Silver River: Silver Springs State Park to Ray Wayside Access (p. 167)

45 Wekiva River and Rock Springs Run: Kings Landing to Wekiva Island (p. 192)

61 Weeki Wachee River: Weeki Wachee Springs to FL 595 (p. 246)

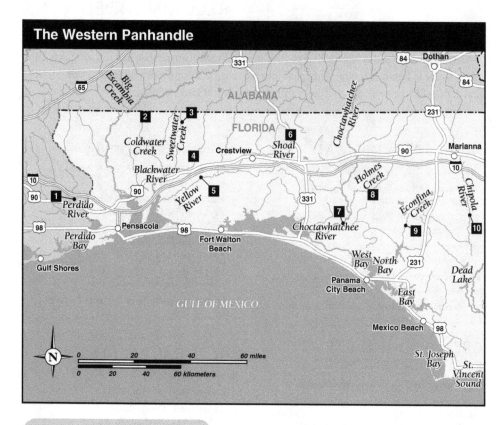

The Western Panhandle

1 PERDIDO RIVER

✧ **OVERVIEW** Located about 15 miles west of Pensacola and forming the Alabama–Florida state line, the Perdido River comes to be in south Alabama where Dyas Creek meets Perdido Creek. The upper course of the Perdido is clear and easy to follow despite the name's Spanish meaning of "lost"; however, the river's name derives from Perdido Bay, where it reaches the Gulf of Mexico in seemingly hidden passages.

The Perdido makes for a fun and friendly paddling river, except for its uppermost headwater segments near Dyas Creek, where shallows and fallen logs can be problematic. The remote river courses southeast beside overhanging cypress and juniper banks in addition to oaks on higher ground. An aerial view of the Perdido reveals a pattern of straight sections alternating with big bends where gravel and sandbars find a home.

Under normal flows, the Perdido River runs shallow. Water tint varies from very clear to toffee- or butter-colored where siltation occurs, despite very little farming or industrial activity along the stream. These alluring sandbars draw in sunbathers and picnickers while deep holes provide swimming opportunities.

As the Perdido meanders toward the Gulf, streams from Alabama and Florida add their flow. The primary tributary is the River Styx (see page 88). Private hunting clubs claim much of the Alabama side of the Perdido, while Perdido Wildlife Management Area, a cooperative public hunting area managed by the Florida Game and Fresh Water Fish Commission, occupies much Sunshine State shoreline. Paddlers who camp should honor posted private property.

These wild shores and limited access points provide a haven for wildlife from bears to hogs to deer and turkeys. Alligators will be seen sunning and anglers can vie for bass, bream, and catfish.

✧ **MAPS** Perdido River Paddling Trail map; Seminole, Barrineau Park (USGS)

A Three Runs to Muscogee Landing

Class	I
Length	27
Time	Varies
Gauge	Phone, web
Level	210
Gradient	2.8
Scenery	A

1A **DESCRIPTION** Unfortunately, river access on this section is limited by rough roads or lack of public landings. Paddlers can travel 5.0 miles from Three Runs Landing to Old Ferry Landing, but a four-wheel-drive vehicle is needed to access it. Fillingim Landing is 12.0 miles distant from Old Ferry Landing, and Muscogee Landing is 10.0 miles from Fillingim Landing.

Unless you like pulling your boat over logjams of brittle and unforgiving red cedar don't start any higher than the Three Runs area. Starting at Three Runs Landing, the river is 50 feet wide, with heavily forested banks 6–8 feet high. The water tends to be shallow, and there may be some obstructions, but it is an easy section, and maneuvering is not difficult. There are large gravel bars on the insides of most of the curves. The forests on either side are hunting preserves, and it is a remote area with no public access. Schoolhouse Branch enters from the east about midway between Three Runs Landing and Old Ferry Landing.

The river continues to be remote beyond Old Ferry and varies between straight sections with clearly defined banks to gentle curves. Several creeks, including West Fork of Boggy Creek and McDavid Creek, flow in from the east, and the river becomes wider. Fillingim Landing is part of the Perdido Wildlife Management Area (WMA). The day-use-only area has a floating dock for paddlers and picnic tables. This is the official start of the designated Florida paddling trail. Wildlands continue on both sides, and there are frequent sandbars and gravel banks. It is 4.0 miles from Fillingim Landing to the Pipes Landing, also within the Perdido WMA.

The Perdido retains its shallow, winding characteristics with sandbars on the insides of turns and alternating straight sections with deeper water. There are a number of places where the presence of old pilings in the river indicates the location of former bridges. Just before reaching Muscogee Landing, the Perdido River divides around an island. The river narrows at this point and runs swiftly, giving a touch of excitement to the run. It is 5.5 miles from the Pipes Landing to the Muscogee Bridge.

◇ **SHUTTLE** To reach the Muscogee Landing take-out from Pensacola, take US 29 North 7.6 miles to Muscogee Road/County Road 184. Turn left on CR 184 and follow it west 4.8 miles to River Annex Road, just before the bridge over the Perdido River. Turn right (north) on River Annex Road and, in 0.5 mile, reach Adventures Perdido River, an outfitter with a private launch and pay access.

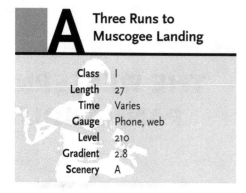

THE SUN SETS ON A
NORTHWEST FLORIDA day

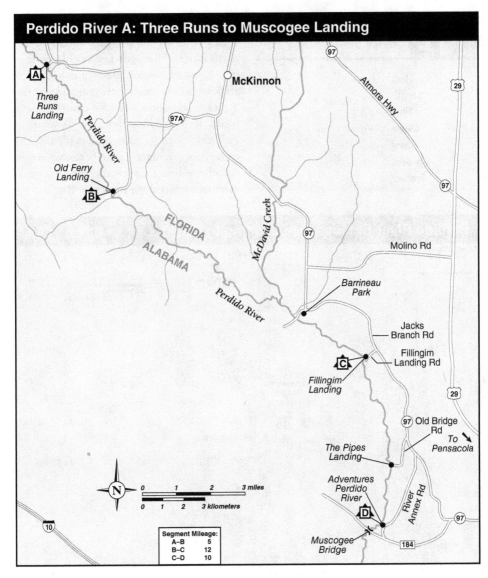

Perdido River A: Three Runs to Muscogee Landing

Segment Mileage:

A–B	5
B–C	12
C–D	10

To reach the uppermost access from Pensacola, travel north on US 29 for 11.4 miles. Turn left (west) on Barrineau Park Road and proceed 8.7 miles to FL 99. Turn right (north) on FL 99 and continue 6.8 miles to the junction with FL 97A. Turn left (west) and continue 2.8 miles until the paved road makes an abrupt turn to the right (north). Turn right and travel 1.5 miles to the first intersection with a graded road, South Pineville Road. Turn left (west) on South Pineville Road and continue 2.3 miles, crossing two creeks along the way. Look for a left turn onto sandy Three Runs Road to reach the Perdido River.

 GAUGE Web. The relevant USGS gauge is Perdido River at Barrineau Park. The minimum runnable level is 210 cfs.

B

Muscogee Landing to US 90

Class	I
Length	8.5
Time	4
Gauge	Web
Level	210
Gradient	1
Scenery	A

1B **DESCRIPTION** Swimmers and sunbathers are attracted to the sizable sandbar on the north side of Muscogee Landing. Enjoy this one, as campsite-size sandbars downstream are fewer where the river deepens and widens. Typically, one shore will have clearly defined banks while the other shore will be swampy. Paddling campers can find sandbars big enough for overnighting, but be choosy in this 8.5-mile section. Large swaths of the east bank continue as part of the Perdido WMA.

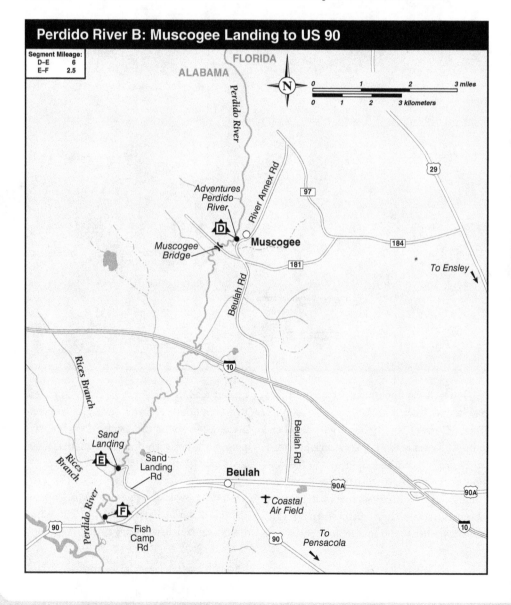

Perdido River B: Muscogee Landing to US 90

Segment Mileage:
D–E   6
E–F   2.5

FLORIDA
ALABAMA

Perdido River

0   1   2   3 miles
0   1   2   3 kilometers

29

Adventures Perdido River

River Annex Rd

97

D

Muscogee Bridge

Muscogee

184

181

To Ensley

Beulah Rd

Rices Branch

10

Sand Landing

E

Sand Landing Rd

Rices Branch

Perdido River

Beulah Rd

Beulah

90A

90A

Coastal Air Field

F

90

Fish Camp Rd

90

10

To Pensacola

The distance from Muscogee Landing to I-10 is a little more than 2.0 miles. Watch for a drop in the river just below the interstate. Here, the Perdido dashes betwixt old bridge pilings. An exception to the generally wider and deeper nature of the river occurs about 0.5 mile below the interstate highway. Logjams sometimes occur here, as the river narrows and flows swiftly through the more confined area. Then the channel narrows further as it splits around an island—either side is navigable.

The Perdido widens and deepens downstream of the isle, attracting motorboats. The shoreline remains forested, and quiet sloughs provide additional opportunities for exploration. Sand Landing is the recommended take-out and is the official end of the state-designated paddling trail. Sand Landing is 2.5 miles below the I-10 bridge and 6.0 miles from the outfitter on River Annex Road. From Sand Landing, it is 2.5 miles to the Ruby's Fish Camp take-out.

Below US 90, the Perdido becomes tidal and begins to finger off into sloughs and bayous. This area is frequented by large motorboats as well. The east bank along the lower Perdido from US 90 to Hurst Landing, an 8.0-mile trip, is now owned by the Florida Conservation Association and offers attractive scenery. Hurst Landing is the last public access before you reach Perdido Bay, a large body of water that is subject to waves and high winds and not recommended for paddling unless you are an experienced sea kayaker.

◇ **SHUTTLE** To reach the take-out from Exit 5 off I-10 near Ensley, take US 90A West 4.4 miles until it merges with US 90 West. Stay on US 90 for 2.2 miles and then turn right onto Ruby's Fish Camp Road, just before the bridge over the Perdido River. Ruby's Fish Camp, a private landing, offers parking and launch facilities.

To reach the Muscogee Landing put-in from Pensacola, take US 29 North 7.6 miles to Muscogee Road/County Road 184. Turn left on CR 184 and follow it west 4.8 miles to River Annex Road, just before the bridge over the Perdido River. Turn right (north) on River Annex Road and, in 0.5 mile, reach Adventures Perdido River, an outfitter with a private launch and pay access.

◇ **GAUGE** Phone, web. Call Adventures Perdido River at 850-968-5529 for the latest river conditions. On the web, the USGS gauge is Perdido River at Barrineau Park. The minimum runnable level is 210 cfs.

2 COLDWATER CREEK

◇ **OVERVIEW** The Blackwater River and its tributaries, one of which is Coldwater Creek, together provide miles of paddling pleasure. Coldwater Creek is the westernmost of these Blackwater River State Forest streams and is a state-designated paddling trail. The swift, narrow, and sometimes steep stream courses for 20 miles through wild terrain. Paddlers will work through the speedy current while dodging fallen trees, sandy shallows, cypress knees, and tree stobs. Paddlers will need a modicum of skill while navigating the obstacles and staying in the primary current.

◇ **MAPS** BLACKWATER RIVER STATE FOREST, McCLELLAN, SPRING HILL (USGS)

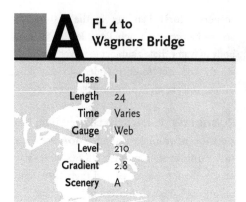

A FL 4 to Wagners Bridge

Class	I
Length	24
Time	Varies
Gauge	Web
Level	210
Gradient	2.8
Scenery	A

2A **DESCRIPTION** The upper part of this waterway, from which you put in at the FL 4 access, is technically the East Fork of Big Coldwater Creek. The stream varies from 25 to 30 feet wide at the beginning to 40 to 60 feet wide farther down. The banks are up to 8 feet high; some have colorful variations of pipe clay. There are some obstructions in the water, but they are not hazardous.

Pass under the Jernigan Bridge and an alternate access at 4.0 miles. The access is the site of Coldwater Recreation Area. There is an improved campground with tables, running water, and restrooms. This is also the spot where most of the liveries start their canoe and kayak rentals, and this section may be crowded from late May to early September.

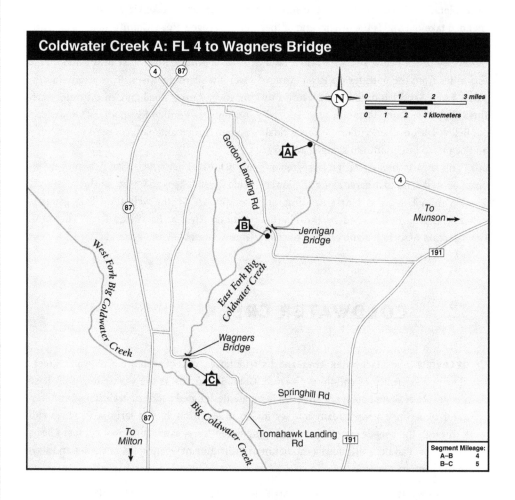

Coldwater Creek A: FL 4 to Wagners Bridge

Gordon Landing Rd

Jernigan Bridge

To Munson →

West Fork Big Coldwater Creek

East Fork Big Coldwater Creek

Wagners Bridge

Springhill Rd

To Milton ↓

Big Coldwater Creek

Tomahawk Landing Rd

Segment Mileage:	
A–B	4
B–C	5

As the creek flows downstream from the Jernigan Bridge, it occasionally narrows to 20–30 feet wide and may be somewhat deeper in these spots. For the most part, it is wide, shallow, and clear, with many large sandbars. There are also two or three places where the stream runs over slight drops caused by cypress roots or rocks in the waterway. This adds a touch of spice to an otherwise leisurely trip. Take out at Wagners Bridge on Springhill Road.

◇ **SHUTTLE** To reach the take-out from Munson, take CR 191 south 7.7 miles to Springhill Road. Turn right on Springhill Road and follow it west about 5.5 miles to Wagners Bridge over Coldwater Creek. Parking here is limited to just a couple of cars, as the adjacent land is owned by outfitters.

To reach the put-in from Munson, travel west on FL 4 for 5.0 miles to the bridge across the East Fork of Big Coldwater Creek—this will be the second bridge, the first having been the bridge across Juniper Creek. The access road is located on the southwest side of the bridge.

◇ **GAUGE** Web. The relevant USGS gauge is Big Coldwater Creek near Milton, Florida. Minimum runnable level is 210 cfs.

B Wagners Bridge to County Road 191

Class	I–I+
Length	9
Time	5
Gauge	Web
Level	210
Gradient	2.5
Scenery	B+

2B DESCRIPTION The upper part of this section is heavily populated by tubers and on warm summer days may be congested. Fortunately, the confluence with the West Fork of the Big Coldwater occurs less than 1 mile downstream from the Wagners Bridge put-in, resulting in a much wider waterway. The West Fork is paddleable from FL 87, a distance of just more than 1 mile.

Shortly below the confluence of the two creeks is Party Island, a white-sand island in the middle of the river. This is a favorite stopping place for picnicking and swimming. At the southernmost end of the island, the river branches, its widest part flowing right and a small stream flowing almost due left.

Adventures Unlimited is located at Tomahawk Landing, 4.0 miles below the put-in for this section. Facilities include a private campground, launch area, and boat-rental outfit. Kayaks and canoes may be rented and shuttles arranged for a fee. There is also a fee for launching private boats and for parking.

It is 2.5 miles from Adventures Unlimited to the Old Steel Bridge. The remains of a bridge are here and the area is used as an access since it has been acquired by the state forest. This is an alcohol-free zone. After leaving the state forest, this lower section of the Coldwater begins to lose its feeling of remoteness. It is also wider and shallower, and there are areas where sawgrass grows along the banks as it becomes more influenced by salt water. The creek continues 3 miles beyond

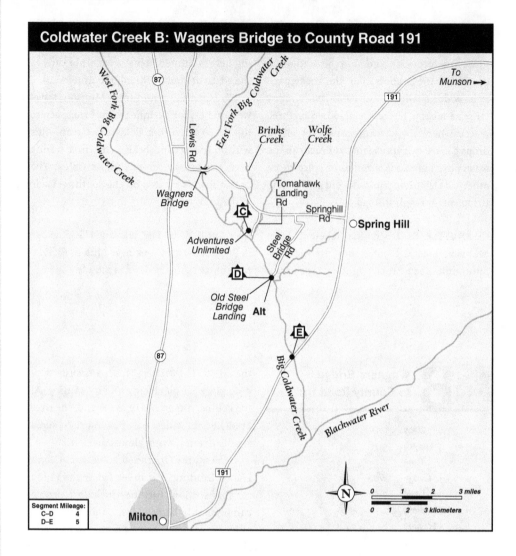

Coldwater Creek B: Wagners Bridge to County Road 191

Segment Mileage:
C–D 4
D–E 5

CR 191 to its confluence with the Blackwater River. It is an additional 10.0 miles down a broad, tidal river to the city of Milton.

✧ **SHUTTLE** To reach the take-out from the intersection of FL 4 and CR 191 in Munson, take CR 191 south about 12.0 miles to the bridge over Coldwater Creek.

To reach the put-in from Munson, take CR 191 south 7.7 miles to Springhill Road. Turn right on Springhill Road and follow it west about 5.5 miles to Wagners Bridge over Coldwater Creek. Parking here is limited to just a couple of cars, as the adjacent land is owned by outfitters.

✧ **GAUGE** Web. The relevant USGS gauge is Big Coldwater Creek near Milton, Florida. Minimum runnable level is 210 cfs.

3 SWEETWATER CREEK AND JUNIPER CREEK

◇ **OVERVIEW** Kayakers and canoeists usually paddle these two tributaries of the Blackwater River together, starting on Sweetwater Creek, then taking it to Juniper Creek. Trips of varied lengths can be undertaken, with access points on the creeks as they flow through the Blackwater River State Forest. Paddlers theoretically can run Juniper Creek above FL 4, but the narrow waterway is overhung with branches and littered with fallen logs, making for a difficult endeavor. There is no access to Juniper Creek at the FL 4 bridge. However, paddlers can put in at the FL 191 bridge, downstream of FL 4 and paddle Juniper Creek a little under 2 miles to meet Sweetwater Creek.

However, the best upriver put-in on the Sweetwater is at Sandy Forest Road, a little more than 2 miles downstream of FL 4. Paddlers can still enjoy the shade of a canopied stream for 2 miles before reaching the confluence with more-open Juniper Creek.

The best experience on Sweetwater and Juniper Creeks will be had by somewhat skilled paddlers who understand these fast waterways should be respected. Check the gauges before paddling, avoiding high water. While on the streams, keep an eye peeled downriver for sweepers, strainers, and other obstructions.

◇ **MAPS** BLACKWATER RIVER STATE FOREST MAP, MUNSON, SPRING HILL (USGS)

FL 4 to Indian Ford Bridge

Class	I–I+
Length	13
Time	6
Gauge	Phone
Level	Call outfitter
Gradient	3.3
Scenery	A

3 **DESCRIPTION** Beginning at FL 4, Sweetwater Creek may have many pullovers, unless the shallow, fast, and narrow waterway has been cut clear by previous paddlers. Lower water means more snags. Rapids and shoals sing past small sandbars beneath shady trees.

It is 2.0 miles from FL 4 to the Sandy Forest Road Bridge. Sweetwater Creek retains its attractive characteristics during the 2 remaining miles to the confluence with Juniper Creek. The two streams' convergence creates a wider waterway bordered in big, white sandbars, attracting water lovers when the weather is warm.

Red Rock Recreation Area is 5.0 miles below Sandy Landing Bridge. Red Rock got its name from the 40-foot-tall sandstone bluff on the east bank just below the bridge. This is the mightiest bluff among the Blackwater River tributaries. The stream continues to be wide and swift, with very large sandbars on either side.

It is 6.0 miles from Red Rock to Indian Ford Bridge. Watch for canopied Alligator Creek entering the east bank about a mile from Indian Ford Bridge, making for a cool stopping spot on a hot day. Below Indian Ford,

Sweetwater Creek and Juniper Creek: FL 4 to Indian Ford Bridge

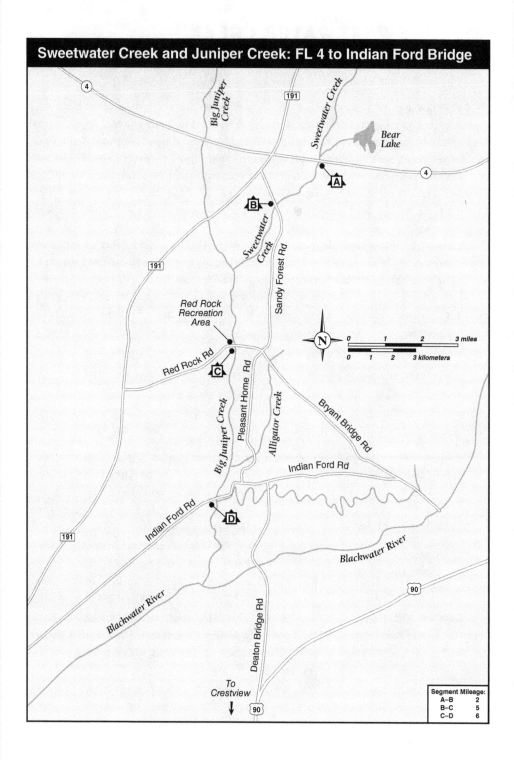

Segment Mileage:	
A–B	2
B–C	5
C–D	6

Big Juniper Creek can be choked with fallen trees and is not recommended.

◇ **SHUTTLE** To reach the take-out from Crestview, drive 20.8 miles on US 90 West to Harold and turn right on Deaton Bridge Road, crossing the Blackwater River to reach Indian Ford Road. After 5.5 miles, turn left on Indian Ford Road and follow it 1.7 miles to the bridge over Juniper Creek. Access is on the west side of the bridge.

To reach the put-in from Crestview, take I-90 West to Milligan and, after 4.3 miles, bear right on FL 4 where the road forks. Take FL 4 West 16.4 miles to the bridge across Sweetwater Creek. This access is about 1 mile east of County Road 191.

To reach the FL 4 put-in from the Indian Ford take-out, backtrack east on Indian Ford Road and, after 1.0 mile, turn left to head north on Pleasant Home Road. Keep north as Pleasant Home Road becomes Sandy Forest Road, which reaches Munson Highway/ CR 191 in 9.9 miles. Turn right on CR 191 to reach FL 4. Turn right on FL 4 and take it 1.2 miles to the put-in.

◇ **GAUGE** Phone. Call Adventures Unlimited at 850-623-6197 for the latest stream conditions.

4 BLACKWATER RIVER

◇ **OVERVIEW** The headwaters of the Blackwater River originate primarily in south Alabama's Conecuh National Forest. As a result, there is virtually no development or agricultural activity to spoil the purity of the water. There are no real springs in the area, but some of the tributaries flowing into the Blackwater have such clarity that they look like spring runs.

A reflection of its tributaries—Coldwater, Sweetwater, and Juniper Creeks—the Blackwater River flows swift and shallow, bordered by beautiful sandbars. Despite its name, the Blackwater River is really a dark reddish color where it's deep but clear in the shallows. But because it's darker than nearby waterways—due to tannins in its waters—the name "Blackwater" stuck.

A state-designated paddling trail, the Blackwater River flows nearly 50 miles through hilly woodlands and wild protected lands, much of it in the Blackwater River State Forest. These public banks make paddle-camping trips desirable along the Blackwater River. In addition to sandbars, overnighters can enjoy the developed campground of Blackwater River State Park.

Red cedars grow rife along the Blackwater, intermixed with red maple, cypress, and oak; stands of planted longleaf pine are frequent on the higher ground. Anglers occasionally catch black bass and small catfish from the streams, but the lack of aquatic vegetation greatly limits the fish population. A quiet paddler may see raccoons, skunks, opossums, perhaps even a turkey, bear, or deer. However, the scarcity of fish leads to fewer sightings of turtles, otters, or wading birds.

◇ **MAPS** Blackwater River State Forest map; Blackman, Baker, Munson, Floridale, Harold (USGS)

A Chessher Bridge to Cotton Bridge

Class	I–I+
Length	15
Time	8
Gauge	Web
Level	120
Gradient	3.3
Scenery	A+

4A **DESCRIPTION** The river itself is clear, shallow, and swift, with a fine sand or gravel bottom. The uppermost section of the Blackwater may have many pullovers. The banks are 5–6 feet high and heavily wooded with occasional small sandbars on bends in the stream. Expect to get out of your boat a few times in low water, but the solitude and wild surroundings are worth the trouble.

Blackwater River A: Chessher Bridge to Cotton Bridge

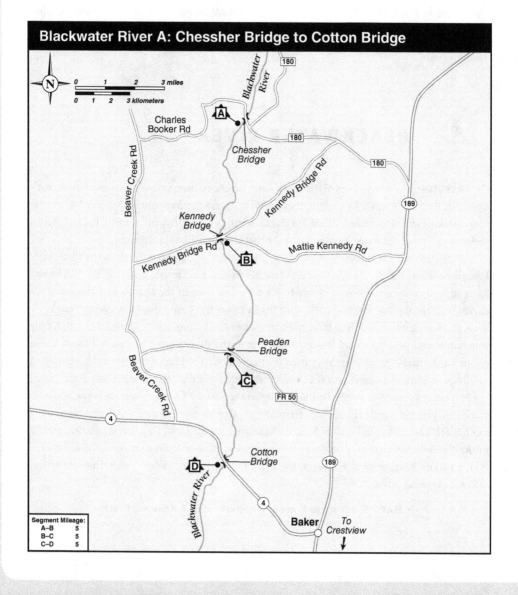

Kennedy Bridge is 5.0 miles below Chessher Bridge. Kennedy Bridge marks the start of the state-designated paddling trail for the Blackwater River and begins a fun, carefree paddle. The Blackwater flows mostly wide and shallow, though has slow, deeper sections. Sandbars suitable for campers can be found throughout the run.

Peaden Bridge is 5.0 miles below Kennedy Bridge. Below Peaden Bridge, the Blackwater remains wild and undeveloped. Wide, shallow sections dominate the river, though there are a few deeper segments. Take out at Cotton Bridge on FL 4.

✧ **SHUTTLE** To reach the take-out from Crestview, take I-90 West to Milligan and, after 4.3 miles, bear right on FL 4 where the road forks. After 4.0 miles, make a sharp left to stay on FL 4, heading west-northwest, and drive 4.2 miles farther to reach Cotton Bridge. A developed public boat landing is on the west side of the bridge.

To reach the uppermost put-in from Crestview, follow the directions in the first sentence above, but instead of turning left on FL 4, keep straight (north) on FL 189 North. After 11.9 miles, turn left (west) on CR 180 and follow it 6.5 miles to Charles Booker Road. Turn left on Charles Booker Road a very short distance to reach the Chessher Bridge over the Blackwater River.

✧ **GAUGE** Web. The relevant USGS gauge is Blackwater River near Baker, Florida. The minimum runnable level is 120 cfs.

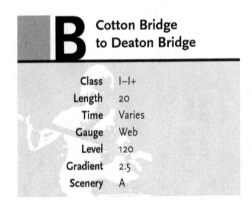

B Cotton Bridge to Deaton Bridge

Class	I–I+
Length	20
Time	Varies
Gauge	Web
Level	120
Gradient	2.5
Scenery	A

4B **DESCRIPTION** The Blackwater River is already broad at Cotton Bridge yet continues to widen as it works its way downstream to Bryant Bridge. Sheer clay banks alternate with huge, alluring white sandbars that beckon paddlers to stop. Below FL 4, tributaries add their flow as the Blackwater drifts through occasional private lands yet remains wild in appearance if not in fact.

Bryant Bridge, 12.0 miles below Cotton Bridge, can be very busy, since paddling liveries use it, as well as swimmers and other water lovers. Expect crowds on summer weekends. The Blackwater curves west and changes character a short distance below Bryant Bridge. Still and quiet sloughs, fed by tributaries of the Blackwater, increase in number as the river reaches the state park. Deaton Bridge is a common day-use area, so it may be crowded here as well on weekends.

From Bryant Bridge, it is 8.0 miles to Deaton Bridge at Blackwater River State Park. This full-facility state park includes a very nice tent-camping area. If you plan to leave your car overnight at the state park, call ahead (850-922-6007) for the latest arrangements. Cars may not be left overnight in the parking areas near Deaton Bridge.

Below the state park, the Blackwater continues to widen with more frequent sloughs that are now covered with sawgrass. It is 2.0 miles to the confluence with Sweetwater–Juniper Creek and 7.0 miles to the confluence with the Coldwater. It is

14.0 miles to the roadside park at the city of Milton. The broad, slow nature of the river and the advent of motorboat traffic usually discourage paddlers from proceeding below Deaton Bridge.

✧ **SHUTTLE** To reach the take-out from Crestview, drive 20.8 miles on US 90 West to Harold. Turn right on Deaton Bridge Road and follow it north 3.4 miles to Deaton Bridge at Blackwater River State Park. There are accesses on both sides of the bridge. A fee is required to park here (see "Fees and Permits," page 6).

To reach the put-in from the take-out, backtrack on Deaton Bridge Road to US 90. Turn left (east) on US 90 and drive 16.8 miles. In Milligan, make a sharp left onto FL 4, heading northwest. After 4.0 miles, make another sharp left to stay on FL 4, heading west-northwest, and drive 4.2 miles farther to reach Cotton Bridge. A developed public boat landing is on the west side of the bridge.

✧ **GAUGE** Web. The relevant USGS gauge is Blackwater River near Baker, Florida. The minimum runnable level is 120 cfs.

THE BLACKWATER RIVER MAKES A BIG BEND.

Blackwater River B: Cotton Bridge to Deaton Bridge

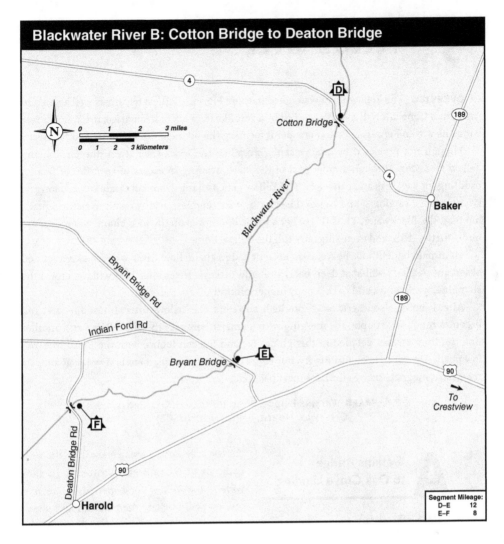

N

0   1   2   3 miles
0   1   2   3 kilometers

4

D

Cotton Bridge

189

4

Baker

189

Blackwater River

Bryant Bridge Rd

Indian Ford Rd

Bryant Bridge

E

90

To Crestview

Deaton Bridge Rd

F

90

Harold

Segment Mileage:
D–E   12
E–F   8

5   YELLOW RIVER

◇ **OVERVIEW** The Yellow River watershed harbors Florida's loftiest terrain as well as hills in Alabama's Conecuh National Forest. Fed by a veinlike network of tributaries, the Yellow River winds its way to Pensacola Bay, at one point forming the boundary of Eglin Air Force Base.

Though not protected by a large state forest like the Blackwater River, the fast-moving Yellow meanders through a quiet part of the state, availing in excess of 50 miles of quality paddling for kayakers and canoeists. The Yellow gets its name from tan sands spread along its river bottoms, sandbars, and banks. The clearer water and less acidity result in richer aquatic life than the Blackwater. Thus the richer aquatic life moves up the food chain, whereby more birds, turtles, fish, and even alligators call the Yellow home.

Mammals benefit too. Beavers are entrenched in the Yellow River watershed. Quiet and observant paddlers will spot deer, bear, and wild turkeys. River birch and willows crowd the shoreline, while pines and oaks occupy higher ground.

After keeping a southerly tack from its headwaters, the Yellow turns almost due west and becomes much wider upon the merging with its major tributary the Shoal River, still another fine paddling stream detailed in this guide. Beyond the confluence with the Shoal, the Yellow pushes 30 miles to end in Blackwater Bay. This lowermost segment is very broad and is a motorboat magnet, losing allure for most paddlers.

◇ **MAPS** Watkins Bridge, Wing (Alabama), Oak Grove, Crestview North, Baker, Holt (USGS)

A   Watkins Bridge to Oak Grove Landing

Class	I–I+
Length	23
Time	Varies
Gauge	Visual, web
Level	N/A
Gradient	2
Scenery	A

5A DESCRIPTION The AL 55 bridge marks the highest upstream paddlers can reasonably start on the Yellow River. The waterway twists and turns past banks ranging from water level sandbars to 20-foot-high bluffs. These sandbars are found on the inside of bends while deeper waters are on the outside of these curves. Five Runs Creek enters from the west bank about 6.0 miles downstream. Its flow widens the Yellow for a period before narrowing again, where there lies a rocky shoal. Downstream, more narrow spots speed the current, forcing novice paddlers to make quick decisions, especially around a mile above the AL 4 bridge. This section can be divided into two shorter paddles, as there is an access at AL 4. It is 13.0 miles from AL 55 to AL 4 and 10.0 miles from AL 4 to County Road 2.

Below the AL 4 bridge, the Yellow continues to twist and turn, creating sandbars on the inside of bends while high banks are still frequently seen. The current remains strong, pushing the paddler downstream, but that same current can push the paddler toward obstacles along some of the tightest curves. Primitive private accesses bring locals to the

Yellow River A: Watkins Bridge to Oak Grove Landing

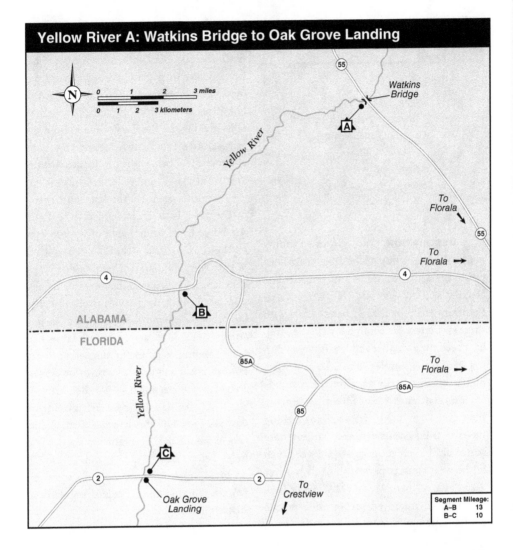

river for fishing, swimming, and other water fun. However, a lack of public accesses keeps the remote section lesser paddled.

◇ **SHUTTLE** To reach the take-out from the intersection of US 90 and FL 85 in Crestview, travel north on FL 85 for 13.1 miles to the junction with CR 2. Turn left (west) on CR 2 and continue 4.6 miles to the bridge across the Yellow River. Access is from the Oak Grove Landing boat ramp, complete with a picnic area.

To reach the put-in from Crestview, keep straight on FL 85 at the intersection with CR 2, heading north and then east for 12.1 miles to reach the Florida–Alabama line. Drive 0.8 mile farther, now on Third Street in Florala, Alabama, and turn left on Fifth Avenue, which becomes AL 55. Drive 9.2 miles northwest on AL 55 to the Watkins Bridge over the Yellow River. The access road, just before the bridge, may be potholed.

◇ **GAUGE** Visual, web. The Yellow is normally floatable year-round. However, to check if the river is flowing at normal levels, the USGS gauge is Yellow River near Oak Grove, Florida.

B Oak Grove Landing to Little Gin Hole Landing

Class	I
Length	27
Time	Varies
Gauge	Visual, web
Level	N/A
Gradient	1.5
Scenery	A

5B **DESCRIPTION** Oak Grove Landing marks the beginning of the state-designated paddling trail. The river becomes deeper and cloudier as it flows toward US 90. The variation from steep banks to low sandbars with some swampy areas continues with the sandbars becoming smaller and less frequent during the first 15.0 miles. Bluffs up to 40 feet high are occasionally seen on the east side and may continue for 0.25 mile or more along the bank. There are myriad streams feeding the river from both sides, and campsites are scarce until a few miles above US 90. Much of the west bank is part of the Yellow River Water Management Area (WMA). Silver Lake Landing, an improved access off a private road, occurs just more than 8.0 miles down this section. There are several houses along the east bank at this point.

About 2.0 miles above US 90, the large sandbars resume, and there is ample camping space available on most of them. Reach a big island dividing the river just downstream of the US 90 bridge. The Louisville and Nashville Railroad trestle is located on the south end of the island and was considered the upper end of navigability of the Yellow back in the days when this part of Florida was as much linked by water as by land.

Below US 90, the riverbanks lower and sandbars become infrequent. Thick woods cloak the subdued shorelines. Watch for the noisy I-10 bridge about 4.0 miles below US 90 (no access). The confluence with the Shoal River is less than 3.0 miles downriver from here. Just before meeting the Shoal, the Yellow River divides into numerous fast channels, making the Shoal—flowing in from the east—difficult to identify among the many channels. It is below this confluence that the Yellow turns west and widens considerably.

From this point on, the left, south, bank of the river is restricted property of Eglin Air Force Base, while much of the property on the right bank is part of the Yellow River WMA. The public lands of Yellow River WMA alternate with private inholdings of houses and cabins with their own private accesses. Motorboats become more common in this stretch. The final access point, Little Gin Hole Landing, is on the military reservation, however, and requires a permit for access. To get a use permit, call 850-882-4165. If you don't feel like getting a permit but you do want to paddle this lower section, simply take out at the nice boat ramp on US 90, 17.0 miles below FL 2. It is 10.0 miles from US 90 to Gin Hole Landing. You can access an Eglin public use map, updated regularly, at jacksonguard.com.

Most paddlers avoid the Yellow River below Gin Hole Landing. That said, the state-designated paddling trail extends all the way down to Broxson and the FL 87 bridge, 28.0 miles downstream. It can be a worthy float if you don't mind the motorboats. Below the FL 87 bridge, the tidal portion of the Yellow River devolves into mazelike channels. A map-enabled GPS is recommended here. Be apprised big Blackwater Bay can blow up into big waves when the winds are howling.

✧ **SHUTTLE** To reach the put-in from the intersection of US 90 and FL 85 in Crestview, take FL 85 South across the Shoal River and,

Yellow River B: Oak Grove Landing to Little Gin Hole Landing

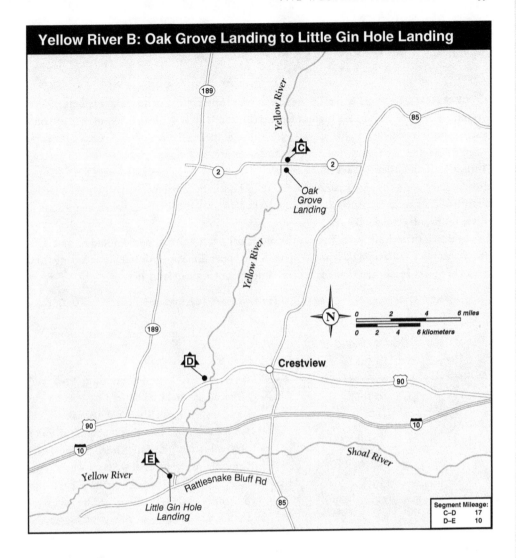

after 5.8 miles, turn right (west) onto Rattlesnake Bluff Road. Follow the road about 4.8 miles and look for a two-track sand road look for a two-track sand road leading right (north) to Gin Hole Landing, 0.3 mile to the Yellow River. (There may or may not be a sign on a tree at the turn.)

To reach the put-in from the intersection of US 90 and FL 85 in Crestview, travel north on FL 85 for 13.1 miles to the junction with County Road 2. Turn left (west) on CR 2 and continue 4.6 miles to the bridge across the Yellow River. Access is from the Oak Grove Landing boat ramp, complete with a picnic area.

⟡ **GAUGE** Visual, web. The Yellow River is normally floatable year-round. But to check the river to see if it is at normal levels for any given time period, the relevant USGS gauge is Yellow River at Milligan, Florida.

6 SHOAL RIVER

◇ **OVERVIEW** The Shoal River, the Yellow River's little brother and primary tributary, also originates in some of Florida's highest terrain (Britton Hill, at 345 feet, is Florida's high point and is within the Shoal's drainage system). Formed at the confluence of Big Swamp Creek and Gum Creek, the Shoal works west for the first 15 miles, picking up major tributaries such as Turkey Creek and Pond Creek along the way. The Shoal turns southwest near aptly named Bends Creek and runs nearly parallel to the Yellow until the Shoal meets another major feeder branch—Titi Creek. Here, the Shoal runs west again until it delivers its waters to the Yellow River near Rattlesnake Bluff.

Draining these hills leaves the tan-colored Shoal a fast-moving, sand-bottomed, and shallow waterway. Civilization has caught up with the upper Shoal west of DeFuniak Springs and north of Mossy Head, and there have been some disputes about launches.

◇ **MAPS** NEW HARMONY, DORCAS, CRESTVIEW NORTH, CRESTVIEW SOUTH, HOLT (USGS)

A County Road 1087 to US 90

Class	I
Length	17
Time	9
Gauge	Visual, web
Level	N/A
Gradient	2.5
Scenery	A-

6A **DESCRIPTION** Not surprisingly, the uppermost Shoal flows narrow and shallow, twisting and turning among occasional sandbars and higher banks. It can be broken into two segments, using an access site at the Pond Creek Bridge, 7.0 miles downstream. A plethora of swift, slender, and clear tributaries add flow to the Shoal, though some of them enter the river as sloughs.

Crowder Cemetery Road bridges the Shoal about 4.0 miles downstream. The steep banks here make access difficult along the slim watercourse. Two miles farther downstream,

the Pond Creek Bridge on Laird Road still offers access and may be your best bet for farthest upstream paddling on the Shoal.

You'll meet Pond Creek about 2.0 miles downstream of the Pond Creek Bridge. Pond Creek is as wide as the Shoal where they meet, significantly widening the Shoal below the confluence. There used to be access at the FL 393 bridge, but this is no longer the case. The Shoal flows swiftly here and gains volume from additional tributaries. Sandbars can be found on the bends, but be apprised there are numerous river straightaways too.

Below FL 393 the Shoal continues its westward ways. Interestingly named tributaries Poverty Branch, Steves Wash Branch, and Painter Branch add their flow before the Shoal bends south at Beech Branch. The river then continues south to US 90 and the Ray Lynn Barnes boat launch.

◇ **SHUTTLE** To reach the take-out from Crestview, take US 90 East 3.7 miles to the

Shoal River A: County Road 1087 to US 90

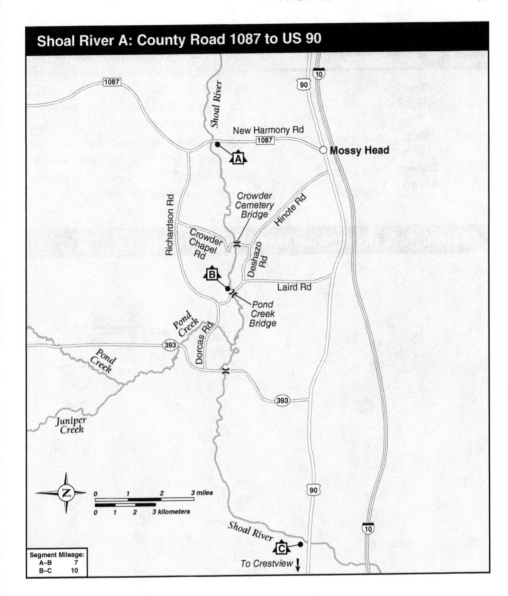

bridge over the Shoal River and the Ray Lynn Barnes boat launch, to the left (north) before you cross the bridge.

To reach the put-in from Crestview, continue east 12.0 miles on US 90 to Mossy Head. Turn left (north) on New Harmony Road/CR 1087 and follow it 3.7 miles to the bridge over the Shoal River. The access road is before the bridge on the west side.

◇ **GAUGE** Visual, web. The best way to determine water level is in person. However, the Yellow River is normally floatable year-round. But to check the river to see if it is at normal levels for any given time period, the USGS gauge is Yellow River in the town of Milligan, Florida.

B US 90 to Gin Hole Landing

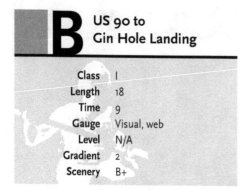

Class	I
Length	18
Time	9
Gauge	Visual, web
Level	N/A
Gradient	2
Scenery	B+

6B **DESCRIPTION** Below US 90, the banks of the Shoal rise higher and the river widens. This section can be broken into two segments, from US 90 to FL 85, 10.0 miles, and FL 85 to Gin Hole Landing, 8.0 miles. Where the river bends you will find sandbars large enough for your average camping party. Much of the land along the Shoal here was purchased by Okaloosa County for watershed protection, keeping the banks wild. Float

Shoal River B: US 90 to Gin Hole Landing

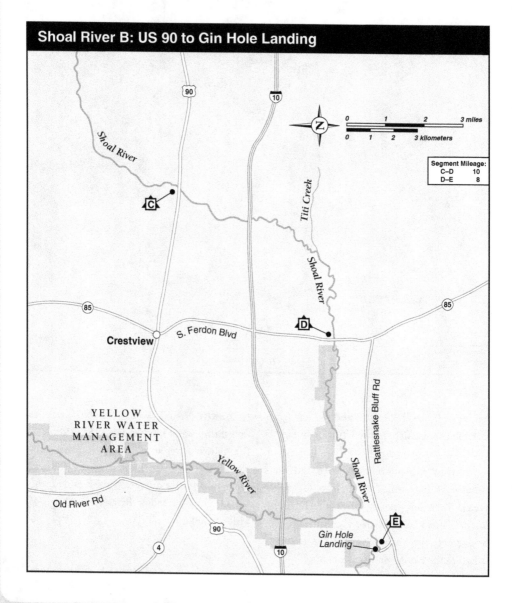

Segment Mileage:
C–D   10
D–E   8

beneath the I-10 bridge (no access) a little under 3.0 miles from US 90. The riverbanks lower even more downstream of I-10.

Titi Creek adds its flow to Shoal River about 3.0 miles below I-10. Despite the addition of 35-foot-wide Titi Creek, the Shoal River actually narrows here to 60 feet. To compensate for its narrowness, the Shoal flows very fast for a distance, then ultimately widens. Sandbars can still be found downstream of Titi Creek. Watch for sloughs and overflow ponds filled with reeds and lily pads where the water stills. Increased accesses both public and private decrease the wild nature of the Shoal.

Below the FL 85 access, the banks of the Shoal lower enough to become downright swampy in spots. The river becomes very narrow just above its confluence with the Yellow then splits into multiple channels, many of which run under complete tree cover. Some of these slender channels may have strainers and/or sharp turns in them, so be on the lookout. Interestingly, where the Shoal and Yellow meet is a confluence of multiple channels from both rivers, instead of two big rivers meeting. Gin Hole Landing is about a half mile below this confluence, situated on the left (south) bank of the Yellow River, within the confines of Eglin Air Force Base. This last access point, Gin Hole Landing, being on the military reservation, requires a permit for access. To obtain a permit, call 850-882-4165.

⟡ SHUTTLE To reach the take-out from the intersection of US 90 and FL 85 in Crestview, take FL 85 South across the Shoal River and, after 5.8 miles, turn right (west) onto Rattlesnake Bluff Road. Follow the road about 4.8 miles and look for a two-track sand road look for a two-track sand road leading right (north) to Gin Hole Landing, 0.3 mile to the Yellow River. (There may or may not be a sign on a tree at the turn.)

To reach the put-in from Crestview, take US 90 East 3.7 miles to the bridge over the Shoal River and the Ray Lynn Barnes boat launch, to the left (north) before you cross the bridge.

⟡ GAUGE Visual, web. The best way to determine the water level is in person. However, the Shoal is normally floatable year-round. To determine if the river levels are normal for any given time period, the USGS gauge is Shoal River near Mossy Head, Florida.

7   CHOCTAWHATCHEE RIVER

⟡ OVERVIEW The Choctawhatchee River flows more than 170 miles from its headwaters in Barbour County, Alabama, to Choctawhatchee Bay near Fort Walton Beach, Florida. The third-largest river in Florida in terms of water volume discharge, the river flows for 96 miles in the Sunshine State. Together with the 50 floatable miles in Alabama, paddlers wanting a long adventure can have a great camping trip on the Choctawhatchee. Additionally, day-trippers can tour differing sections of the river that deliver a variety of experiences over its entire length. Improved accesses in Alabama and Florida make adventures on the Choctawhatchee even easier to execute. In addition, much of the riverbanks in Florida, more than 57,000 acres altogether, are publicly held as part of the Choctawhatchee Wildlife Management Area, comanaged with Northwest Florida Water Management District.

The flood-prone nature of the Choctawhatchee has discouraged development along much of its banks. Up Alabama way, a narrower river features high limestone banks, rocky shoals, and rapids. After entering Florida, a now wider river has fewer rapids and shoals but becomes more remote, with huge sandbars overlooking the yellowish-tan waters. Above the water, flood-plain forests vie with upland hardwoods and pine stands. Elsewhere, marshes and swampy wetlands hold sway. Bear, turkeys, and deer are found in the wildlife corridor, along with otters, songbirds, waterfowl, and raptors.

By the time the Choctawhatchee reaches Florida, it is a sizable river. Alabama feeders include Judy Creek—a paddleable stream, the East Fork of the Choctawhatchee, the Little Choctawhatchee, and the Pea River, a fine touring river in its own right. In Florida, Wright Creek, Holmes Creek, and many springs, highlighted by Blue Spring and Morrison Spring, add further flow.

⟡ **MAPS** Ewell, Pinckard, Daleville, Clayhatchee, Bellwood, Geneva E (Alabama); Izagora, Hobbs Crossroads, Prosperity, Caryville, Hinsons Crossroads, Ponce De Leon, Red Bay, Millers Ferry (Florida) (USGS)

A County Road 36 to AL 92

Class	I–I+
Length	22
Time	Varies
Gauge	Visual, web
Level	N/A
Gradient	4
Scenery	B

7A **DESCRIPTION** CR 36 is generally regarded as the uppermost put-in. Here, the shallow West Fork Choctawhatchee River stretches 50 feet, bank to bank. You will soon experience your first rock-strewn rapids that slow to a pool. This pool–rapid–pool series continues downstream, making it a fast-moving, fun event at the right water levels.

Judy Creek enters the Choctawhatchee 3.5 miles below CR 36. Paddlers can start at the Judy Creek CR 36 access at higher water levels to tackle its rocky rapids during the 2.0-mile run from CR 36 to its meeting the Choctawhatchee. The river shallows below Judy Creek, exposing more sand bottom, as

well as additional rock shoals. Just upstream from the AL 27 access, known as Browns Crossroads, watch for a 2-foot drop over a rocky ledge, especially if you are in a loaded boat. Run this 2-foot drop on the extreme left and do not be scared to portage if you are unsure of your ability to run the rapid. From Judy Creek's confluence with the Choctawhatchee, it is 2.5 miles to AL 27, and a total of 6.0 miles from CR 36 to AL 27.

A fast shoal speeds you beyond the AL 27 bridge. Rapids continue with frequency until the West Fork meets East Fork of the Choctawhatchee. Float under the bridge at Bagwells Crossroads, about 3.0 miles down from the AL 27 bridge. It offers additional access. Paddle another mile to meet the East Fork, where the current is lively on the now 100-foot-wide Choctawhatchee.

A steady, strong current overwhelms the drop-and-pool nature of the West Fork, though a few small shoals sing below 10- to 15-foot-high banks. Pass under the US 231 bridge a mile below the East Fork–West Fork

Choctawhatchee River A: County Road 36 to AL 92

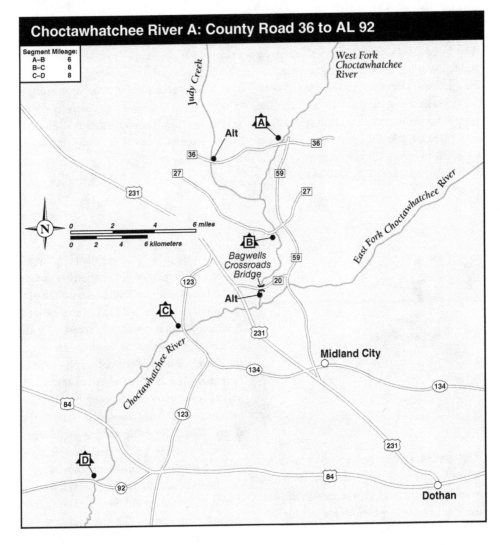

Segment Mileage:
A–B 6
B–C 8
C–D 8

confluence. Avoid using this area as a put-in/ take-out due to a rough access road and steep riprap leading down to the banks. Look on the south bank just below US 231 for a narrow limestone defile created by a tributary making a fern bordered waterfall as it enters the Choctawhatchee.

A railroad trestle crosses the river about 2.5 miles below US 231. Just downstream, a large sandbank on the northwest side is heavily used as a local river access. From the trestle it is another 1.5 miles to the AL 123 bridge and John Hutto Park in Newton. The park has camping,

water, and electricity and is an ideal access. It is a total of 8.0 miles from AL 27 to AL 123.

Watch for an old mill's pilings and caught debris just below the AL 123 bridge. Otherwise, a steady flow makes this section below AL 123 a fun run. High, sheer banks make campsites more difficult to find, however, although modest sandbanks make for stopping spots. The Little Choctawhatchee, a paddleable waterway, enters the river about 1.5 miles downstream from US 84. It is 2.0 miles farther to the AL 92 bridge. It is a total of 8.0 miles from AL 123 to AL 92.

◇ SHUTTLE To reach the lowermost take-out from downtown Dothan, Alabama, take US 84 West 14.5 miles to AL 92. Turn left on AL 92 and follow it 4.3 miles west to the access on the southwest side of the bridge over the river.

To reach the uppermost access from the intersection of AL 134 and CR 59 in Midland City, Alabama, take CR 59 north 12.2 miles to CR 36. Turn left on CR 36 and drive 0.4 mile to the bridge over the Choctawhatchee River.

◇ GAUGE Visual, web. Checking the river in person is the most reliable way to determine the water level. However, the Choctawhatchee is normally floatable year-round. The USGS gauge helpful in determining if the river is near average levels is Choctawhatchee near Geneva, Alabama. Stay off if the river is excessively above historical average.

B AL 92 to FL 2

Class	I
Length	29
Time	Varies
Gauge	Visual, web
Level	N/A
Gradient	1.8
Scenery	B

7B **DESCRIPTION** This section's multiple access points provide paddlers with routes of varied lengths. A long sandbar on the east bank at the AL 92 put-in draws in sunbathers, swimmers, and paddlers wanting an easy put-in. There is also a concrete ramp on the west side of the bridge. Sandbars are large and frequent for the next 3.0 miles, until the confluence with Pates Creek 3.0 miles downstream. High, sloping banks increase while sandbars decrease.

Four miles farther downstream, big Claybank Creek enters from the northwest. Downstream a mile, the Choctawhatchee splits around an island before coming to the AL 167 bridge. Access is on the right, north, bank. It is 9.0 miles from AL 92 to AL 167. The banks of the river rise at AL 167,

culminating in a quarter-mile-long, high, wooded bluff that lowers as the river bends to the left, where you will find a pair of sizable sandbars on the left bank. The Bellwood Bridge at CR 45 avails no easy access.

The Choctawhatchee resumes its winding ways below the Bellwood Bridge. These numerous bends do give rise to low sandbars that are good for stopping but poor for camping since they barely rise above the river. Watch for alligator-heaven Barnes Creek, 2.5 miles below Bellwood Bridge. About 6.0 miles downstream from AL 167, the river bends to the east, then south. Watch for a rock bluff on the west bank, then you come to the CR 41A boat ramp on the east bank. A big sandbar is just below this access on the left bank.

Continuing downstream, scan for sheer rock walls, rising 15 feet from the water's edge, covered in dripping ferns. High banks and almost no sandbars continue to AL 52 near Geneva. You will find a boat ramp at Geneva City Park just above the confluence of the Pea and Choctawhatchee Rivers, on the west bank about a half mile below the AL 52 bridge. It is 12.0 miles from AL 167 to the confluence.

The Pea River is a worthy day-tripping and overnight-paddling river. The Pea's volume

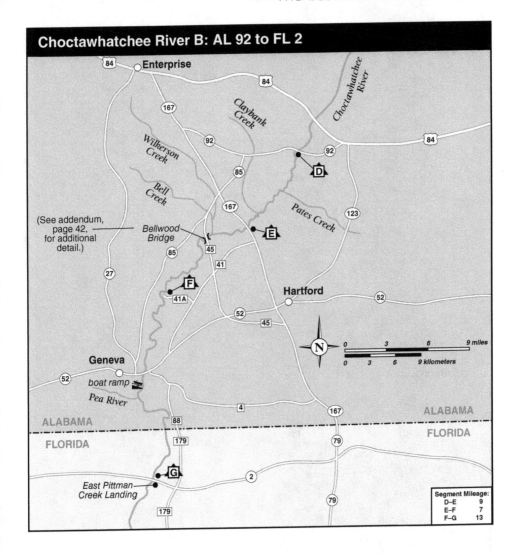

Choctawhatchee River B: AL 92 to FL 2

widens the Choctawhatchee to 300 feet, before the Choctawhatchee narrows again. Almost every major bend harbors an alluring sandbar, stretching below high and heavily wooded banks. From the Geneva access to the Florida state line the river flows for 5.0 miles, then winds 3.5 miles farther to ramp on the east bank of FL 2 after the bridge.

✧ **SHUTTLE** To reach the lowermost take-out from Exit 104 off I-10 in Caryville, take Waits Avenue 1.0 mile north to US 90. Turn right on US 90 and head east 0.5 mile to Wrights Creek Road/CR 179. Turn left on CR 179 and follow it north 13.9 miles to FL 2. Turn left on FL 2 and head west 1.4 miles to reach the East Pittman Creek boat landing, on your left before the bridge over the Choctawhatchee.

To reach the uppermost put-in from Hartford, Alabama, take AL 167 north 8.1 miles to AL 85. Turn right on AL 85 and follow it northeast 2.9 miles to West Main Street/AL 92 in Daleville. Turn right on AL 92 and follow it 0.3

Choctawhatchee River B Addendum

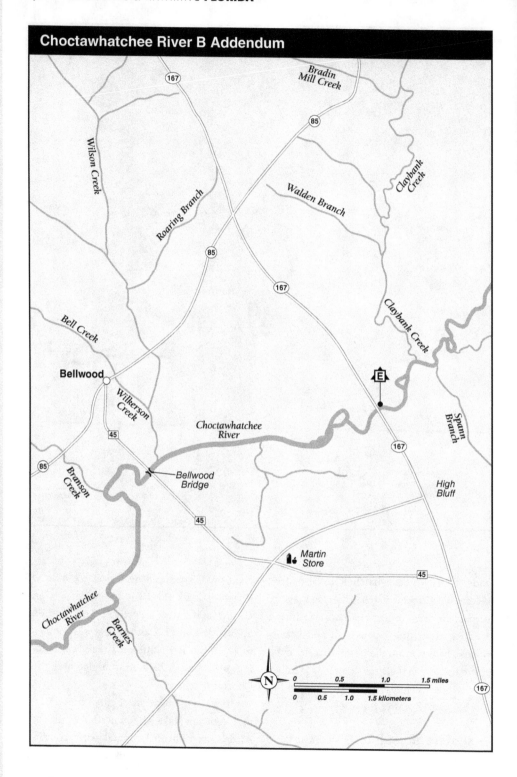

mile to the put-in on the southwest side of the bridge over Choctawhatchee River.

◇ **GAUGE** Visual, web. Checking the river in person is the most reliable method to determine water level. However, the Choctawhatchee is normally floatable year-round. A USGS gauge helpful in determining if the river is near average levels is Choctawhatchee at Caryville, Florida.

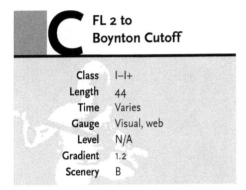

C   FL 2 to Boynton Cutoff

Class	I–I+
Length	44
Time	Varies
Gauge	Visual, web
Level	N/A
Gradient	1.2
Scenery	B

7C DESCRIPTION From here, Northwest Florida Water Management Lands occupy much of the banks. This section has several accesses for varying trip lengths and also makes an excellent paddle-camping trip. The next 10.0 miles below from FL 2, the steady current of the Choctawhatchee winds south past a wealth of huge sandbars, many of which exceed 10 acres in size. Look for animal tracks on these sizable sandy shores.

Thick, wooded banks guard the river from civilization. You will find a park with a ballfield at the old Curry Ferry site, 2.5 miles downstream from FL 2 on the east bank. Sandbars remain bountiful. Old Warehouse Landing is on the west side at the end of a Baker Landing Lane, 4 more miles downstream. Watch for Blue Spring on the west bank about 5.0 miles below Old Warehouse Landing, across from Cork Island. (Note that Cork Island is only a true island at higher flows, as its east channel will run dry). Blue Spring is the most northwesterly spring in the Sunshine State. The boat-only accessible upwelling has a deep, clear-blue vent, ideal for swimming. Find Camp Meeting Bay and Cerrogordo Landing on the west bank about a mile below Blue Spring, 11.0 miles below FL 2.

Work around the west side of Canebrake Island 3.0 miles downstream from the Camp Meeting Bay access. A few more bends lead you past a private ramp and a few houses on the east bank, then Wrights Creek enters from the east. Below the confluence, the river appreciably widens, the sandbars become fewer, and the current moderates. From the Wrights Creek confluence, it's less than 2.0 miles to US 90. At US 90, 17.0 miles below FL 2, the shallow, slow-moving Choctawhatchee stretches 300 feet across. A large boat ramp is found on the east bank just below the US 90 bridge. The town of Caryville is not too far east on US 90. Pass a pair of sandbars bracketing the I-10 bridge, 1 mile below US 90. Northwest Florida Water Management District Lands continue on most banks. Attentive paddlers will be able to discern old river channels and former islands among the low, heavily wooded banks where willows and river birch stretch over the water. Still other banks stand as swamp woods.

Watch for a rapid at the confluence with Gum Creek, 5.0 miles below US 90. Oxbow bends, old channels that have become sloughs, and high-water islands become common. Let the current lead you if unsure. The

Choctawhatchee River C: FL 2 to Boynton Cutoff

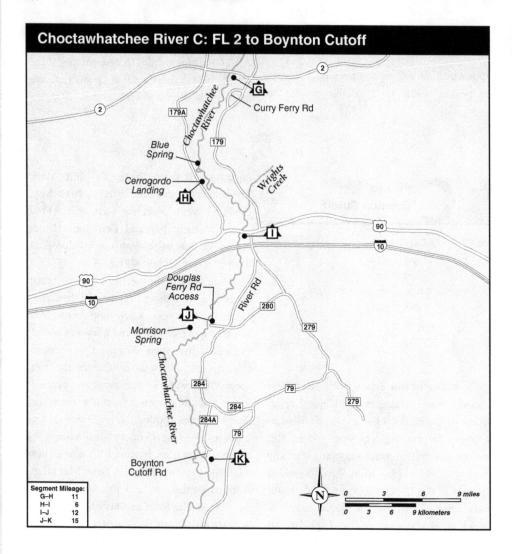

Segment Mileage:
G–H	11
H–I	6
I–J	12
J–K	15

river begins to widen again and the current slows as the landing at Douglas Ferry Road (CR 280) nears. This landing on the east bank, also known as Billy Lee Landing, is on the lower end of an island. It is 12.0 miles to this landing from US 90.

Beyond this landing, the Choctawhatchee flows strong and wide below deeply forested banks. The outflow of Morrison Spring enters the river from the west about 3.5 miles below Douglas Ferry access.

Paddlers have to head upstream a mile to find the 250-foot upwelling pool featuring three deep vents. This popular swimming, diving, and picnicking spot is now a Walton County park, and includes a canoe and kayak launch. The Choctawhatchee continues its oxbow bends, with visible old channels. Three miles downstream from Morrison Spring Run, spring-fed Sandy Creek enters from the west. Below Sandy Creek, a row of houses lines the west bank.

Come to an island created by Roaring Cutoff less than a half mile below the aforementioned houses. Roaring Cutoff, the west option around the island, is shorter. Public and private lands are interspersed. Look for signage before landing. About 3.5 miles downstream of Roaring Cutoff, the Choctawhatchee makes an extended southbound straightaway, with just a few bends, almost to Boynton Cutoff. A few houses can be spyglassed well back from the river.

At Boynton Cutoff, the main river has now rechanneled itself and follows the channel of Boynton Cutoff, rather than its old channel to the west (though at high water it undoubtedly flows down the west channel). The water flows swiftly in this vicinity. Watch past the next bend on the left for the take-out at the boat ramp on the east side of the river. Just to be sure, mark the Boynton Cutoff Landing in your GPS: **N30° 31.439' W85° 52.271'**.

After Boynton Cutoff rejoins the old channel of the Choctawhatchee River, the river widens noticeably and becomes a magnet for motorboaters. It is 7.0 miles downstream from Boynton Cutoff Landing to the FL 20 bridge. Paddlers continuing on to Choctawhatchee Bay can expect the heavily wooded, tidally influenced river to split into multiple channels before entering the open, brackish waters. A map-loaded GPS unit or smartphone would come in handy here.

◇ SHUTTLE To reach the Boynton Cutoff take-out from Exit 104 off I-10, take Pate Pond Road/CR 279 south 1.2 miles to River Road. Turn right (south) on River Road, which becomes CR 284, and follow it to 13.9 miles to Shell Landing Road/CR 284A. Turn right on CR 284A and follow it south 3.1 miles to a right turn onto Boynton Cutoff Road, which dead-ends after 1.3 miles at the Boynton Cutoff public boat ramp, just past a few houses.

To reach the FL 2 put-in from Exit 104 off I-10, turn left (north) on Waits Avenue. After 1.0 mile, turn right on US 90 and head east 0.5 mile to Wrights Creek Road/CR 179. Turn left on CR 179 and follow it north 13.9 miles to FL 2. Turn left on FL 2 and head west 1.4 miles to reach the East Pittman Creek boat landing, on your left before the bridge over the Choctawhatchee.

◇ GAUGE Visual, web. Checking the river in person is the most reliable method to determine its water level. However, the Choctawhatchee is normally floatable year-round. A USGS gauge helpful in determining if the river is near average levels is Choctawhatchee at Caryville, Florida.

8 HOLMES CREEK

✧ **OVERVIEW** Holmes Creek comes to be near Fadette, Alabama, and flows a short distance before entering the Sunshine State near Graceville. Although numerous tributaries add flow, Holmes Creek remains a diminutive and unnavigable stream until magnitude 2 Cypress Springs contributes its volume above Vernon, where Holmes Creek becomes an easily paddleable waterway. At normal flows, Holmes Creek exhibits a clearish-green tint. This clear water and a variety of vegetation make this state-designated paddling trail a photogenic stream.

Despite having high banks near its beginning and end, the middle part of Holmes Creek flows through low swamps, along which spin off sloughs and bayous aplenty, adding to the exploratory possibilities. Additional springs and tributaries add their flow to Holmes Creek, availing still more paddling avenues.

Pines and oaks rise from higher banks, as do magnolias and maples, while cypresses and willows spread on lower shores. Wildlife is present since much of the shore is in public hands as the Choctawhatchee River Wildlife Management Area (WMA). Don't expect much help from the flow as you paddle Holmes Creek. The stream gradient is minimal and the current seemingly nonexistent. A few houses occupy higher banks not in the WMA, yet remoteness still reigns on Holmes Creek.

Be apprised that most paddlers take out on Holmes Creek well above its confluence with the Choctawhatchee River, though the official paddling trail stretches to the confluence with the Choctawhatchee. Paddlers wishing to paddle the whole of Holmes Creek can take out on the Choctawhatchee.

✧ **MAPS** Poplar Head, Vernon, Millers Ferry (USGS)

Burnt Sock Landing to Strickland Landing

Class	I
Length	19.5
Time	Varies
Gauge	Visual, web
Level	N/A
Gradient	0.6
Scenery	A

8 DESCRIPTION Over the years, paddle accesses have opened and closed on Holmes Creek, and this trend continues, happily with more openings than closings these days. With the purchase and addition of streamside Northwest Florida Water Management Lands, landings on agency property should remain stable. Leaving Burnt Sock Landing, Holmes Creek is narrow, obstructed with occasional logs, and mostly canopied overhead. The water isn't nearly as clear as downstream. Holmes Creek winds quite a bit to reach the outflow of Cypress Springs a little more than 2.0 miles from Burnt Sock Landing. To visit Cypress Springs, turn right, northeasterly, up Cypress Creek and reach Cypress Springs after two-thirds of a mile. This upwelling emits 89 million gallons of water per day. Therefore, Holmes Creek clears, widens, and is fully navigable downstream. The run of Becton Springs enters on river right at 3.0 miles. This 40-million-gallon-per-day

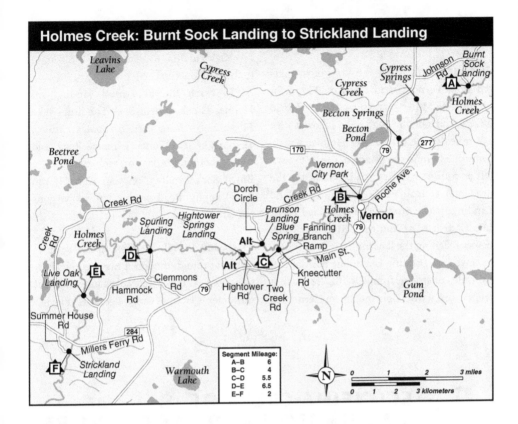

Holmes Creek: Burnt Sock Landing to Strickland Landing

Segment Mileage:	
A–B	6
B–C	4
C–D	5.5
D–E	6.5
E–F	2

spring adds more clarity to the water. Becton Springs is bordered by private property, but you can paddle the run to the upwelling. This upper run ends at the new bridge in Vernon after 6.0 miles.

Holmes Creek is wide at the Vernon access, with high banks and some houses for the first few miles. Fanning Branch boat ramp is 4.0 miles downstream. This is the site of Blue Spring. About 60 by 120 feet wide, and 7–10 feet deep, the spring emerges from a limestone cavity near the pool surface at the northeast end.

Holmes Creek alternates between high banks and swampy areas. Brunson Landing, on the right, is less than a mile downstream from Fanning Branch boat ramp. You can dock your craft at Brunson Landing then follow a short trail to a smallish spring here. Sloughs and backwaters become so frequent

that it is difficult to distinguish between them and inflowing branches and streams. It is also less than a mile down to Hightower Springs Landing, on the left bank. The creek continues its westerly meanderings, passing Spurling Landing in 3.5 miles. Holmes Creek then turns south to reach Live Oak Landing in 6.5 miles. The final 2-mile stretch passes under the CR 284 bridge before reaching Strickland Landing.

Paddlers wishing to continue down to the Choctawhatchee will find Shell Landing on the west bank 4.0 miles downstream and the last landing on Holmes Creek a half mile farther on the east bank—Potter Spring Road Landing. Make a few more bends and work around an island to reach the Choctawhatchee River. From the confluence, you can paddle a half mile up the Choctawhatchee to Boynton Landing, on the right bank. Otherwise, you have to float at least a few miles on the Choctawhatchee to take out.

⟡ **SHUTTLE** To reach the lowermost take-out from Vernon, head south on FL 79 for 7.1 miles to Millers Ferry Road/County Road 284. Turn right on CR 284 and follow it west 2.2 miles to the bridge over Holmes Creek. Continue beyond the bridge 0.4 mile to turn left on Summer House Road. Follow it to the dead end at Holmes Creek and Strickland Landing. (*Note:* Summer House Road turns into Catfish Alley and then River Road just before reaching the landing).

Live Oak Landing is a public boat launch 1.6 miles upstream from CR 284. To reach it from CR 284, turn right (north) on Hammock Road 1.4 miles west of the intersection of FL 79 and CR 284. After 1.0 mile, turn left onto Live Oak Landing Road and take it 0.6 mile to the public access.

To reach the uppermost landing on Holmes Creek—Burnt Sock Landing—take FL 79 North from Vernon about 4.1 miles. Turn right (east) onto Johnson Road and travel about 1.5 miles to reach the road to Burnt Sock Landing, on your right. If you pass Dauphin Road, on your left, you've gone too far.

⟡ **GAUGE** Visual. Holmes Creek is floatable year-round, though it may be low above Cypress Springs. A relevant gauge to check flow rates is Holmes Creek at Vernon, Florida.

9 ECONFINA CREEK OF WASHINGTON AND BAY COUNTIES

⟡ **OVERVIEW** This is one of the most challenging yet scenic paddles in the state. For starters, the upper half of the state-designated paddling trail features a gradient of 8 feet per mile! Most Florida streams have a gradient of less than 2 feet per mile. Draining hilly terrain, Econfina Creek and its tributaries have carved steep-sided drainages—canyons if you will—through which the stream speeds. And when you combine the steep gradient and 20-foot-deep chasms, it fashions a sometimes chaotic stream for experienced paddlers only.

The gullies are confined to the upper section, while the much easier lower section boasts an array of springs that enhances the aquatic beauty of paddling on the Econfina. The first-magnitude Gainer Springs group is the star of the show, while other upwellings will be found along the Econfina, namely Blue Springs, Williford Springs, Walsingham Spring, and Pitt Springs. Emerald Springs is noteworthy as it discharges from a 25-foot-tall limestone bank. Tubers favor this lower spring-rich section and can crowd the waters in summer.

Riverside bluffs can exceed 50 feet in height, and tributaries flowing into the Econfina produce true waterfalls as they spill into the river. Fern-draped limestone walls rival the waterfalls in beauty, and a float down the creek in spring will reveal blooming dogwoods, wild azaleas, and other plants commonly seen north of Florida. The cooler, moister canyon creates a favorable microclimate for beech, cedar, sweet gum, holly, magnolia, and red maple. Cypress finds its place along the water. The higher ground above the river is home to oaks and pines.

Luckily, these special lands have been acquired by the Northwest Florida Water Management District, and nearly the entire upper creek and much of the lower creek banks are bordered by public lands, keeping the setting natural. Additionally, accesses have been improved, and the sand roads—while still a little ragged—are in much better shape than in days gone by.

The upper Econfina is not only steep but also shallow. Paddlers should expect to encounter fallen trees and to pull atop logs, dash over and bang against rock ledges, and dance through sharp bends. Long kayaks are discouraged. This is not a stream to toy with in high water—the rapids, rocks, and strainers, combined with a very fast current, generate a hazardous combination. The Econfina's drainage-ditch character makes flash flooding more likely than your average Florida waterway. Smart paddlers will stay off the stream at high water or paddle early in the morning if thunderstorms are predicted.

With the expanse of public lands, Econfina Creek makes for a good paddle camping one-day option, as does the lower segment. Campers can use the primitive sites near Walsingham Bridge or pitch their tents along the Econfina. Paddling campers will need to get out of the boat to scout for campsites, since the high banks and a dearth of sandbars reveal no easy camps.

Don't get confused, by the way: this isn't the only waterway named Econfina in Florida. Another stream of the same name—also detailed in this guide (see page 109)—flows about 100 miles east of here in the lower Big Bend, east of St. Marks and west of Perry.

◇ MAPS COMPASS LAKE, CAP LAKE, BENNETT (USGS)

ECONFINA CREEK IS A NARROW WATERWAY.

A Scott Bridge to Walsingham Bridge

Class	I–I+
Length	11
Time	Varies
Gauge	Phone, visual, web
Level	2–4
Gradient	8
Scenery	A+

9A DESCRIPTION This upper section is recommended for canoes and short sit-on-top kayaks only—sharp turns and numerous obstructions require you to get out of the boat to surmount them. The Econfina is swift and shallow and averages 15–20 feet wide up here. Don't let the sandbars you see at first lull you into complacency, for quickly the Econfina begins slashing past fallen, partly submerged trees and over ledges of stone. It is early and the canyon isn't deep yet—only 4–6 feet high.

Econfina Creek of Washington and Bay Counties A–B: Scott Bridge to County Road 388

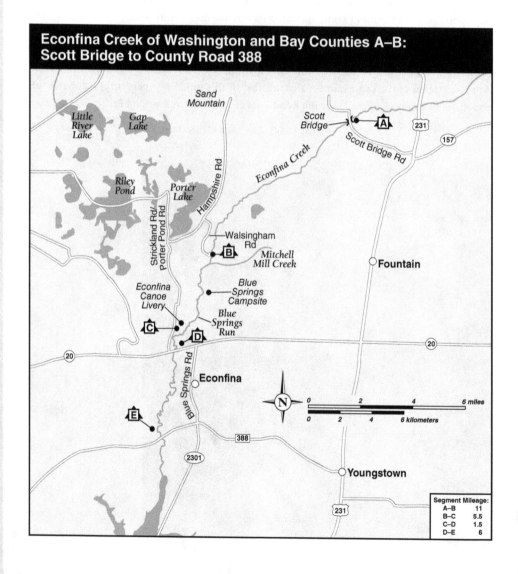

Segment Mileage:

A–B	11
B–C	5.5
C–D	1.5
D–E	6

A canopy rises over the waterway, which at times is barely wider than the boat. The creek drops alternately between slender steep sections with higher walls broken by brief segments with lesser drops. Try to look ahead as much as possible for creek-wide tree strainers, especially when navigating blind turns. Give paddlers in front of you and behind you adequate reaction room.

The narrow gorge gives way about 4.0 miles above Walsingham Bridge. Lower banks and a relatively wide and shallow stream mean a potential plethora of fallen trees, blocking clear channels. You may have to get out here and pull over limbs and logs, especially at lower water levels. However, parts of the remaining run to Walsingham Bridge will have deeper, steeper sections. Watch for an unnamed spring on the east bank contributing its volume to the Econfina.

The Florida Trail runs alongside the creek this entire section, allowing the added benefit of hiking and paddling. Along the way, the Florida Trail bridges Econfina Creek twice before reaching Walsingham Bridge. The water-management district has developed a few primitive campsites for overnighters. One of these is located by a spring boil in the middle of the river. Walsingham Bridge area has an excellent paddler's launch and primitive campsites.

✧ **SHUTTLE** To reach the lowermost takeout from downtown Panama City, take US 231 North 25.3 miles to FL 20. Turn left (west) on FL 20 and follow it 8.1 miles, bridging Econfina Creek near a good access, to reach Strickland Road. Turn right (north) on Strickland Road and follow it as it becomes Porter Pond Road. After 2.6 miles, Porter Pond Road doglegs left for 0.5 mile before heading north again, curving right after 0.3 mile, and then heading north yet again 0.3 mile farther. Drive another 1.3 miles, veer right on Hampshire Boulevard, and follow it 1.2 miles to Walsingham Bridge Road. Turn right (east) on Walsingham Bridge Road and, in 0.3 mile, turn right again to follow the road south. After 1.0 mile, Walsingham Bridge Road gradually bears left (east) to cross Econfina Creek. Once across Econfina Creek, follow the gravel road to the canoe/kayak launch.

To reach the Scott Bridge access, backtrack to FL 20 and head east to US 231. Turn left (north) on US 231 and drive 7.5 miles to reach Scott Road, which is just north of County Road 167. Turn left (west) on Scott Road and follow it 3.0 miles as it curves right to the bridge over Econfina Creek.

✧ **GAUGE** Phone, visual. Ideally, the Scott Bridge gauge should read 2–4 feet. At low water, expect more logjams. At 4–9 feet, be prepared for very fast water but fewer logjams. Stay off the river above 9 feet. Econfina Canoe Livery, at 850-722-9032, can provide general river conditions for paddlers.

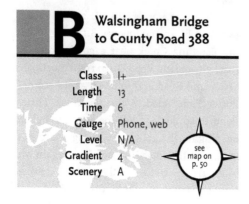

B Walsingham Bridge to County Road 388

Class	I+
Length	13
Time	6
Gauge	Phone, web
Level	N/A
Gradient	4
Scenery	A

see map on p. 50

9B **DESCRIPTION** From the Walsingham Bridge to Blue Springs, the run remains scenic, although it is not the gorge run of the upper section. Mitchell Mill Creek enters the Econfina just below Walsingham Bridge. Watch for small Walsingham Spring, on the west bank, about a quarter mile below the bridge, as well as an unnamed midriver spring a half mile below Walsingham Spring. Econfina Creek, now with lower banks than the upper run, widens further. Expect a few strainers. Private property and a few houses stand on the east bank 1 mile above Blue Springs, a recreation area that is now a reservation-only group campsite and can be used as an access only by those reserving the site.

Paddlers should look on river left for the 10-foot-wide run of Blue Springs. You can then paddle up the spring outflow for 150 yards and look left for the steps at the second split. The Blue Springs pool harbors a pair of underwater caves.

Downstream, the riverbanks lower still and the whole setting becomes more swamplike. The river leaves public lands temporarily, and a few houses appear. Ahead, watch for Williford and Pitt flowing in from the west bank. Williford is a group day-use area, and Pitt is a day-use area for everyone and includes a tube dock. Reach Econfina Canoe Livery on the west bank 2.0 miles below Blue Springs. The outfitter offers rentals, shuttles, and access, as well as parking. It is 1.5 miles downstream from the livery to the FL 20 access, which is on the east bank opposite Pitt Spring.

The section of river from FL 20 to CR 388 is 6.0 miles long. Most of the banks, alternating between swampy and high, are private land. Here, the creek is popular with tubers, and you may encounter a few motorboaters. Even though this section can be busy during the warm season, it has many springs that are attractive. The Ganier Springs group can be found less than a mile downstream of FL 20. Look for upwellings along both banks. You won't miss Emerald Springs, on the west bank, pouring forth from a 25-foot limestone bluff. Respect the resource and stay off the spring bluff.

Paddlers shy away from the water below the CR 388 bridge, since large motorboats are found along Econfina Creek, using it to access Deer Point Lake.

SHUTTLE To reach the lowermost access from downtown Panama City, take US 231 North 19.3 miles to CR 388 in Youngstown. Turn left on CR 388 and follow it west 7.8 miles to the bridge over Econfina Creek. The access is on the northwest side of the bridge.

To reach the Walsingham Bridge access, backtrack to Blue Springs Road/CR 2301, turn left, and follow it north 3.0 miles to FL 20. Turn left on FL 20 and follow it west 1.1 mile, bridging Econfina Creek near a good access, to reach Strickland Road. Turn right (north) on Strickland Road and follow it as it becomes Porter Pond Road. After 2.6 miles, Porter Pond Road doglegs left for 0.5 mile before heading north again, curving right after 0.3 mile, and then heading north yet again 0.3 mile farther. Drive another 1.3 miles, veer right on Hampshire Boulevard, and follow it 1.2 miles to Walsingham Bridge Road. Turn right (east) on Walsingham Bridge Road and, in 0.3 mile, turn right again to follow the road south. After 1.0 mile, Walsingham Bridge Road gradually bears left (east) to cross Econfina Creek. Once across Econfina Creek, follow the gravel road to the canoe/kayak launch.

◇ **GAUGE** Phone. Call Econfina Canoe Livery at 850-722-9032 for the latest river conditions. The lower river is spring fed and floatable year-round. A gauge of interest is Econfina Creek near Bennett, Florida. It can help determine if the river is at historical flow levels for any given period.

10   CHIPOLA RIVER

◇ **OVERVIEW** The Chipola River is born in southeast Alabama and flows southward into Florida, where 51 miles of the river are an official state paddling trail. The entire length of the Chipola from its headwaters to its mother stream, the Apalachicola River, is 80 miles. However, not the entire river flows above ground—at Florida Caverns State Park it moves under the earth. Beyond that, part of the waterway slows to become Dead Lake. The portion that is state paddling trail has segments that are a limestone-bordered, tree-flanked, fast-moving stream, while other sections are more riverine, wide, and slow flowing, with sporadic cliffs, caves, and bluffs. Along the way you will encounter several springs and the infamous Look and Tremble Rapid.

Despite originating in Alabama, the Chipola isn't navigable until just above the FL 162 bridge in northern Jackson County, where Cowarts Creek, Marshall Creek, and Hays Spring Run contribute their flow. More streams—including Waddells Mill Creek—pump the Chipola but the river subsequently dives underground at Florida Caverns State Park before emerging again just north of Marianna.

The immediate banks of the Chipola exude remoteness, but a view from overhead reveals the river wandering toward the Apalachicola through heavily populated agricultural lands, save for the segment near the Apalachicola River. At normal flows the river has a greenish hue but is subject to yellowing from the adjacent agricultural fields after heavy rains.

The banks of the Chipola change as you head downriver. High bluffs give way to sandy hills, which in turn yield to lowland swamps. This landscape variety leads to a variety of vegetation the paddler will see. Paddling anglers find their way to Chipola, vying for largemouth bass, bream, and catfish. Birders flock to the lower Chipola, especially the Dead Lakes area, downstream of the official paddling trail. Limited public lands make overnight trips more challenging, but a plenitude of put-ins and take-outs makes day trips viable throughout the waterway.

◇ **MAPS** COTTONDALE EAST, MARIANNA, OAKDALE, ALTHA WEST, CLARKSVILLE, FRINK (USGS)

A   Christoff Landing to Florida Caverns State Park

Class	I
Length	4.5
Time	2
Gauge	Phone
Level	N/A
Gradient	3.2
Scenery	A

10A   **DESCRIPTION** Most of the shore along this run is state-owned land, keeping the atmosphere wild. Christoff Landing, the uppermost public landing on the Chipola, is just below the confluence of Waddells Mill Creek and the Chipola, about 1.5 miles downstream from FL 162, a former access. The Waddells Mill Creek millpond comes to be from the outflow of second-magnitude Rockarch Spring. Waddells Mill is listed on the National Register of Historic Places.

The Chipola widens after the inflow of Waddells Mill Creek, resembling a slender lake for a half mile, then narrows again. Bends resume as the Chipola snakes through a low, swampy area, allowing the paddler close-up looks at the surrounding swamps and forests, mostly protected as Florida Conservation Lands. Bosel Spring Run, with its 50-foot pool fed by three main vents, flows into the Chipola's east bank about a mile above Florida Caverns State Park. Bosel Spring is about a quarter mile up the clear blue run from the Chipola.

Enter the state park and reach a boat ramp, near where the river goes underground. In prepark days, loggers dug a canal to float logs down the river from the sink to the Chipola's river rise. The half-mile-long canal, tree and debris choked, is now a wildlife preserve. The state park prohibits paddling through the old log canal.

SHUTTLE To reach the take-out from the intersection of US 90 and Jefferson Street/FL 166 in Marianna, take FL 166 North 2.7 miles to the entrance of Florida Caverns State Park, signed on the left. You must pay a fee to enter the park (see "Fees and Permits," page 6).

To reach the put-in, return to Marianna on FL 166 South, head west on US 90 and, in 1.6 miles, turn right (north) onto Penn Avenue, which turns into Bump Nose Road. At 5.2 miles, turn right onto Christoff Ferry Road to reach Christoff Landing after 0.3 mile.

GAUGE Phone. Call Florida Caverns State Park at 850-482-9598 for the latest stream conditions and other information.

Chipola River A: Christoff Landing to Florida Caverns State Park

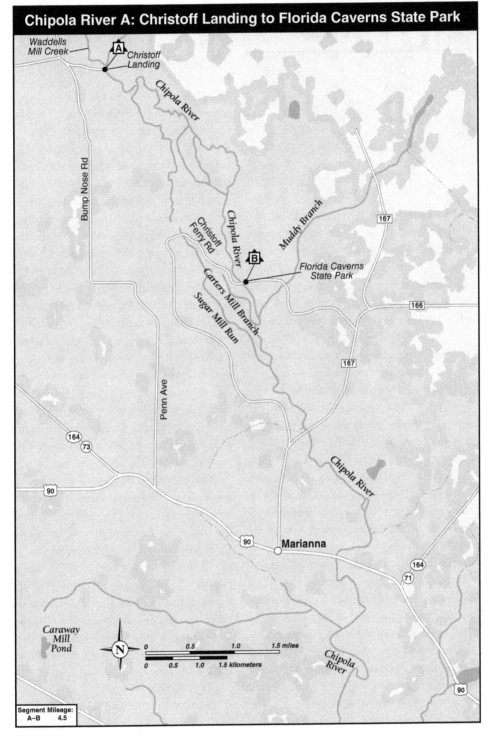

Waddells Mill Creek

A Christoff Landing

Chipola River

Bump Nose Rd

Christoff Ferry Rd

Chipola River

Muddy Branch

167

B

Florida Caverns State Park

166

Carters Mill Branch

Sugar Mill Run

167

Penn Ave

164
73

90

90   Marianna

Chipola River

164
71

Caraway Mill Pond

N

0   0.5   1.0   1.5 miles

0   0.5   1.0   1.5 kilometers

Chipola River

90

Segment Mileage:
A–B   4.5

B Yancey Bridge to Peacock Bridge

Class	I
Length	20
Time	Varies
Gauge	Phone, web
Level	N/A
Gradient	1.2
Scenery	B

10B

DESCRIPTION If you want to see the Chipola River rise, it is a 2.0-mile upstream paddle from Yancey Bridge. However, don't expect a dramatic sight. The Chipola seeps back up among trees rather than emerging from a singular locale. The run from Blue Hole Spring also flows into the river in this section, but having traversed almost 2.0 miles of swamp, the spring run loses its clarity and is not easily identified.

Heading downstream from the FL 166 put-in, the Chipola's banks remain low and swampy, despite seeing limestone shoreline. Sand Bag Springs flows in from the west bank about a half mile below FL 166. The Chipola flows under the US 90 bridge 2.0 miles down from FL 166, but there is no access. Unfortunately, this river section can be trashy due to heavy usage and flowing through Marianna.

The Louisville and Nashville Railroad tracks cross the Chipola about a mile downstream of US 90. Admire the high west bank, where a steep bluff harbors a cave, possibly enlarged by quarrying of limestone. The limestone wall continues along the west bank of the river for another half mile. Look in this vicinity for Alamo Cave, into which you can walk when the river is low. Dykes Spring enters the east bank shortly below the cave, flowing 75 yards from its upwelling. At 4.5 miles, after a quick series of bends, come to Hinson Conservation and Recreation Area.

It has a small canoe/kayak launch as well as hiking trails.

At 7.0 miles, aptly named Spring Creek, a major tributary of the Chipola, flows in from the east bank. The swift moving waterway is fed by one first-magnitude and several second-magnitude springs and is riddled with underwater caves, attracting divers to the 68°F water. A wealth of springs feed a dammed 4.0-mile-long lake, below which Spring Creek flows freely for 2.0 miles to meet the Chipola. This is an alternative put-in for a Chipola River trip that is well worth seeing but can be busy with tubers in summer. Paddlers trying to head upstream from the Chipola on Spring Creek will find the current very trying.

Instead of fighting up Spring Creek, savor a series of rocky rapids in the 1.0-mile downstream from the mouth of Spring Creek to the I-10 bridge (no access). The 10.0-mile float from Yancey Bridge to the access at County Road 280 (Magnolia Bridge) ends less than a mile downstream from the interstate on the southwest side of the CR 280 bridge.

The Chipola continues to sport several small rocky shoals below CR 280 underneath steep, sloping banks. The current is swift in the shoals but moderate to slow otherwise. Many islands break up the river, and you can usually take your pick around which side of the islands you want to go. Spring-fed and misnamed,s Dry Creek gives its waters to the Chipola 6.0 miles downstream from CR 280. Expect to see a few houses along this section of the Chipola. It is 10.0 miles from CR 280 to the take-out at CR 278.

✧ **SHUTTLE** To reach the take-out from the intersection of US 90 and Jefferson Street/FL 166 in Marianna, take US 90 East 3.1 miles to FL 71. Turn right and take FL 71 South

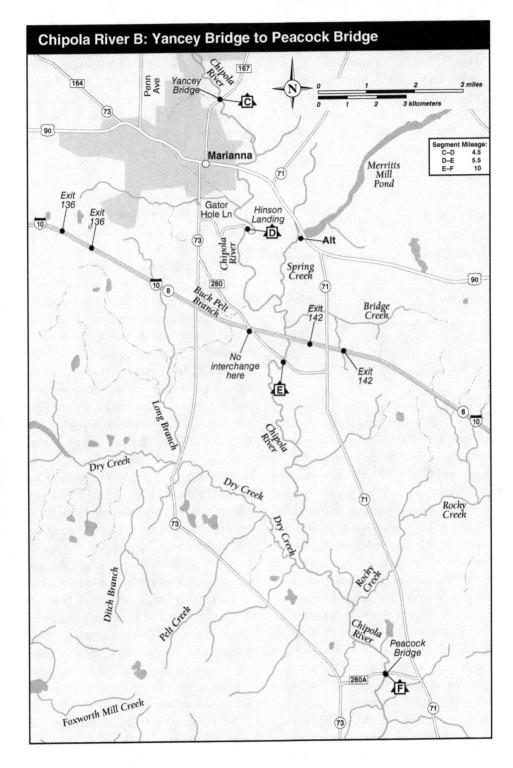

Chipola River B: Yancey Bridge to Peacock Bridge

164

167

Penn Ave

Yancey Bridge

Chipola River

73

90

N

0   1   2   3 miles

0   1   2   3 kilometers

C

Marianna

71

Merritts Mill Pond

Segment Mileage:
C–D   4.5
D–E   5.5
E–F   10

Exit 136

Exit 136

10

Gator Hole Ln

73

Hinson Landing

D

Alt

90

Chipola River

Spring Creek

71

Bridge Creek

10 8

Buck Pelt Branch

280

Exit 142

No interchange here

E

Exit 142

8
10

Long Branch

Chipola River

Dry Creek

Dry Creek

Dry Creek

73

71

Rocky Creek

Rocky Creek

Ditch Branch

Pelt Creek

Chipola River

Peacock Bridge

280A

F

71

Foxworth Mill Creek

73

8.9 miles to Peacock Bridge Road/CR 278. Turn right (west) on CR 278 to reach the access at Peacock Bridge in 0.7 mile.

To reach the put-in from the same intersection in Marianna, take FL 166 North 1.4 miles to the Yancey Bridge over the Chipola River. The boat launch is on the southwest side of the bridge.

◇ GAUGE Phone, web. Call Bear Paw Adventures at 850-482-4948 for the latest stream conditions. The Chipola is normally floatable year-round. A helpful USGS gauge to determine average river levels for any given period is Chipola River at Marianna, Florida. Do not get on the river if the gauge reads above 12 feet.

C Peacock Bridge to FL 71

Class	I–I+
Length	31
Time	Varies
Gauge	Phone, web
Level	N/A
Gradient	1
Scenery	A–

10C **DESCRIPTION** This section can be broken into runs of varying distances, with the addition of several public landings. The 8.0 miles from CR 278 to FL 274 is similar to the preceding 10.0 miles. This run can be shortened to 6.5 miles, exiting at Johnny Boy Landing. The soft limestone bottom for which the Chipola is known is evident on this section. Look for riverbed cracks and above-water formations, such as Table Rock, created during high flows carving the erosive limestone. Sink Creek adds its flow from the east bank shortly downstream of CR 278. The current speeds about 4.0 miles downstream, as shoals form. Johnny Boy Landing is on river left, the east bank, at 6.5 miles. The CR 274 bridge is 1.5 miles farther.

This 3.0-mile run from the CR 274 bridge to Lamb Eddy Run is one of the most popular paddles on the Chipola due to the presence of Look and Tremble Rapid, a limestone shoal that crosses the river a little below the CR 274 bridge. Who would think that one of the all-time best names for a rapid would be in Florida? Public lands border this shoal. At normal water levels, paddlers should shoot through near the east bank, but if the water is higher, head straight down the middle.

Below Look and Tremble Rapid, vertical limestone banks, averaging 6–8 feet, will border the Chipola. Lamb Eddy Landing is 3.0 miles below the CR 274 bridge. Limestone-bordered Tenmile Creek flows in from the west about 1.5 miles downstream from Lamb Eddy Landing. The banks gradually lower with only sporadic big bluffs. Fourmile Creek enters from the west 3.0 miles below Tenmile Creek. The current slows and the river deepens and broadens upon nearing FL 20. It is 10.0 miles from CR 274 to FL 20. FL 20 offers good access at a wayside park.

The FL 20 marks the end of the Chipola's journey through the highlands and begins its meanderings amid swamplands, despite the fact that elevated banks and limestone bottom continues. However, upon the inflow of Fox Creek from the east bank, lily pads and sloughs appear, with a corresponding increase in water-loving tupelo and cypress trees instead of oaks and pines.

Juniper Creek enters from the west 5.0 miles downstream of FL 20. The terrain becomes even swampier. Wildlife from alligators to waterfowl increases as the river

Chipola River C: Peacock Bridge to FL 71

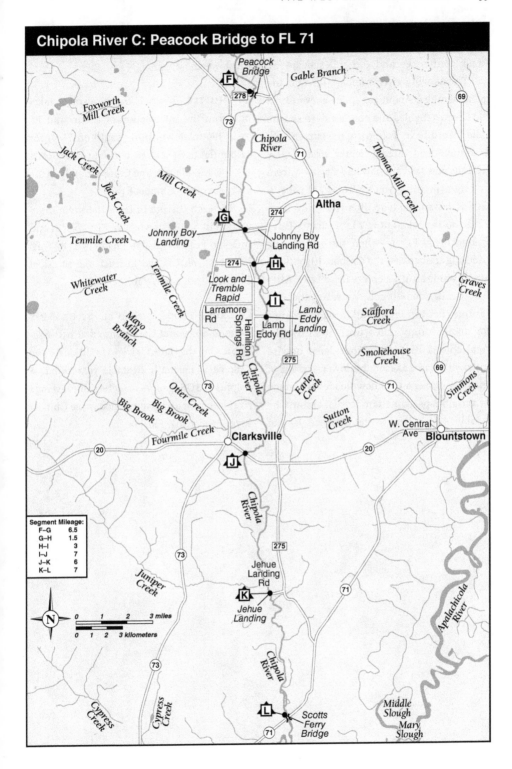

Peacock Bridge
Gable Branch
F
278
69
Foxworth Mill Creek
73
Chipola River
71
Jack Creek
Mill Creek
Altha
Jack Creek
Thomas Mill Creek
G
274
Johnny Boy Landing
Johnny Boy Landing Rd
Tenmile Creek
H
274
Tenmile Creek
Graves Creek
Whitewater Creek
Look and Tremble Rapid
I
Lamb Eddy Landing
Stafford Creek
Larramore Rd
Lamb Eddy Rd
Mayo Mill Branch
Hamilton Springs Rd
275
Smokehouse Creek
Chipola River
69
Simmons Creek
Otter Creek
73
Farley Creek
71
Big Brook
Big Brook
Big Brook
Sutton Creek
W. Central Ave
Blountstown
Fourmile Creek
Clarksville
20
20
J
Chipola River
Segment Mileage:
F–G	6.5
G–H	1.5
H–I	3
I–J	7
J–K	6
K–L	7

275
73
Jehue Landing Rd
Juniper Creek
K
Jehue Landing
71
Apalachicola River
N
0   1   2   3 miles
0   1   2   3 kilometers
73
Chipola River
Cypress Creek
Cypress Creek
L
Scotts Ferry Bridge
71
Middle Slough
Mary Slough

becomes swampier. Pass Jehue Landing on the left, a short ways below the Juniper Creek confluence and 6.0 miles below FL 20. The slowing river wanders off into frequent sloughs. About 3.0 miles above FL 71, the Chipola divides and enters a deep swamp called Ward Lake. Following the current will eventually lead directly to the bridge. Stay with the downstream flow and stay away from any signs pointing you toward Ward Lake. A GPS is reassuring here. It is 13.0 miles from FL 20 to the take-out at FL 71, Scotts Ferry Bridge. Below FL 71—where the official state paddling trail ends—the Chipola River flows amid swamps until it enters Dead Lake. After 8 or so miles, the Chipola comes together and resumes flowing south, still through swamps for another 10.0 miles until it meets the Apalachicola River. It is considered unwise to travel Dead Lake or the lower section of the river minus a GPS downloaded with topo or aerial maps, some tarot cards, and maybe a rabbit's foot. Due to the distance, lack of access, and lack of campsites, only intrepid and adventurous paddlers will want to tackle this lowermost section.

✧ **SHUTTLE** To reach the lowermost take-out from the intersection of FL 20 and FL 71 in Blountstown, travel south on FL 71 for 12.8 miles to the private boat launch at Scotts Ferry General Store and Campground, on the east side of the Chipola River.

To reach the put-in from the same intersection in Blountstown, take FL 71 North 15.6 miles to Peacock Bridge Road/CR 278. Turn left (west) on CR 278 to reach the access at Peacock Bridge in 0.7 mile.

✧ **GAUGE** Phone, web. Call Scotts Ferry General Store and Campground at 850-674-2900 for the latest river conditions. The Chipola is normally floatable year-round. A helpful USGS gauge to determine average river levels for any given period is the Chipola River near Altha, Florida.

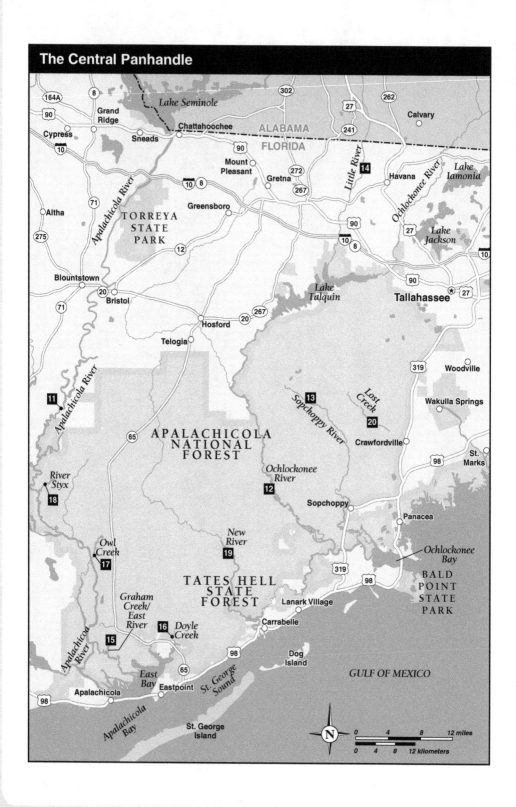

The Central Panhandle

11 APALACHICOLA RIVER

◇ **OVERVIEW** Once overlooked as a paddling destination, the mighty Apalachicola—which drains the also-mighty Flint and Chattahoochee Rivers—flows south from Lake Seminole, then brawls south over 100 miles to Apalachicola Bay. Much of the river's free-flowing journey traverses remote terrain, where overflow swamps and protected lands of the Apalachicola National Forest, as well as other public properties, conspire to keep the powerful waterway out of the public eye and enjoyed mostly by locals, who tour the river and utilize the floating houses you will see in places.

Yet paddlers have discovered this scenic gem, which has arguably the fastest current in Florida. I have paddled the river from the town of Chattahoochee over 100 miles to the town of Apalachicola and proclaim it a fine paddler-camping adventure. Sandbars and wooded public lands make finding campsites easier than in other places in the now highly populated Sunshine State. Numerous landings make shorter trips viable, however.

Fall through spring is the best time to paddle the Apalachicola—the temperatures are down, the motorboaters are mostly absent, and you can enjoy fall colors or spring's reemergence while on this wide waterway. The Apalachicola is wide throughout and open to winds and sun.

Upon leaving Hopkins Park in the town of Chattahoochee, the Apalachicola is already powering south, unleashed from Lake Seminole. On this upper stretch, the Apalachicola River passes under two busy roads and a power plant yet stays in relatively remote terrain. Then it speeds below the high bluffs of Torreya State Park, and later other highlands such as Alum Bluff, before rolling to Bristol. South of here, the river becomes even more remote, traversing vast segments of untamed terrain, especially below the confluence with the Chipola River. Side tributaries beckon, but the Apalachicola speeds on, passing a must-stop at Fort Gadsden Historic Site. The lowermost part of the river includes confluences with multiple tidal streams and channels, but if you stay with the Apalachicola River, you will end up at the historic seaside town of Apalachicola, a Florida paddling adventure of the first order under your belt.

Along the way you will see mile markers, wing dams, and dikes, vestiges of the attempt to make the river navigable. In our age, however, the Apalachicola River is a designated National Recreation Trail, or "blueway." An internet search will yield a downloadable guide to this blueway, noting scenic sights, ramps, and side streams. Try this big river out, and it will make you rethink the paddling possibilities of waterways big and small.

◇ **MAPS** APALACHICOLA RIVER BLUEWAY MAP; APALACHICOLA NATIONAL FOREST MAP; CHATTAHOOCHEE, SNEADS, ROCK BLUFF, BRISTOL, BLOUNTSTOWN, ESTIFFANULGA, ORANGE, DEAD LAKES, WEWAHITCHKA, KENNEDY CREEK, FORBES ISLAND, JACKSON RIVER, WEST PASS, APALACHICOLA (USGS)

A Chattahoochee to Estiffanulga Landing

Class	I
Length	42
Time	Varies
Gauge	Web
Level	44.0
Gradient	0.5
Scenery	A

11A **DESCRIPTION** The Apalachicola River is formed where the Chattahoochee and Flint Rivers converge, now submerged by Lake Seminole. The river then gushes from Woodruff Dam and is a huge waterway with a generally robust flow—Florida's largest by volume—even though the water comes from Georgia and Alabama. The banks are often woodlands, with sandbars on the insides of bends. The first big bluff comes below the I-10 bridge. Wildlife such as deer is abundant. Birdlife from songbirds to raptors hovers around the river corridor. Sandbars are abundant at lower water levels.

After 10.0 miles, float below the perched Historic Gregory House at Torreya State Park. Landings are well spaced along this section. Ocheesee Landing comes in a mile below the Gregory House. Pass beneath Rock Bluff before coming to Redds Landing on the west side of the waterway. Before reaching Bristol, paddle under the most impressive bluff of all: Alum Bluff. The landing in Bristol is off River Road.

◇ **SHUTTLE** To reach Estiffanulga Landing from the intersection of FL 20 and County Road 12 in Bristol, take CR 12 south for 8.4 miles, then turn right onto CR 333 and follow it 2.0 miles to turn right again on Joe Red Shuler Road and follow it 0.4 mile to the boat ramp.

To reach the uppermost put-in at Hopkins Park, from downtown Chattahoochee take US 90 West for 0.1 mile and turn left onto River Landing Road; then follow the road 0.4 mile to a ramp on the Apalachicola.

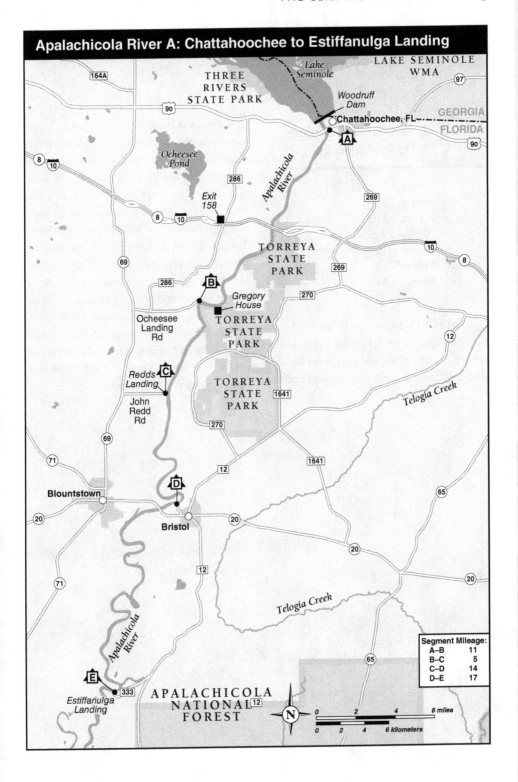

Apalachicola River A: Chattahoochee to Estiffanulga Landing

Segment Mileage:

A–B	11
B–C	5
C–D	14
D–E	17

GAUGE Web. The relevant USGS gauge is Apalachicola River at Chattahoochee, Florida. There is no minimum runnable level.

The maximum recommended runnable level is 44 feet.

B Estiffanulga Landing to Apalachicola

Class	I
Length	69
Time	Varies
Gauge	Web
Level	5.5
Gradient	0.5
Scenery	A+

11B **DESCRIPTION** A bluff rises below Estiffanulga, but generally the banks lower, the river bends more, and the shores become even more remote. Overflow swamps and low willowy banks become more common, keeping the corridor wild. Side channels along the main shore are more numerous. Civilization is reached at Gaskin Park, where the Chipola Cutoff links the Apalachicola with the Chipola River. Floating houses will be seen along the banks. Pass Sand Mountain, a large deposit of grains, 6.0 miles below Gaskin Park. The lower, main entrance of the Chipola River is passed 10.0 miles beyond Sand Mountain. Several alluring streams, including Kennedy Creek and Brushy Creek, flow forth from the national forest on the east bank. Hickory Landing is located 1.5 miles up Owl Creek, where there is a national-forest campground.

SANDBARS ADORN THE INSIDE BENDS OF THE APALACHICOLA.

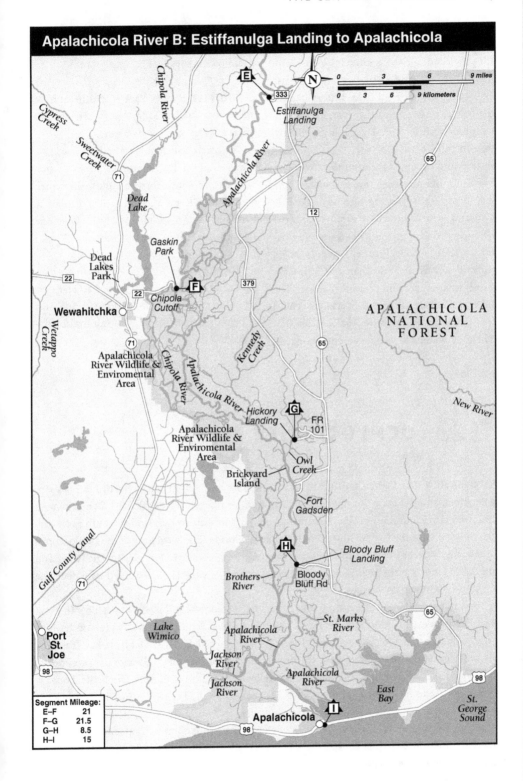

Apalachicola River B: Estiffanulga Landing to Apalachicola

Chipola River

Estiffanulga Landing

333

0   3   6   9 miles
0   3   6   9 kilometers

65

Apalachicola River

12

Cypress Creek

Sweetwater Creek

71

Dead Lake

Gaskin Park

Dead Lakes Park

22

22   Chipola Cutoff

F

379

Wewahitchka

APALACHICOLA NATIONAL FOREST

Kennedy Creek

65

71

Wetappo Creek

Apalachicola River Wildlife & Enviromental Area

Chipola River

Apalachicola River

New River

Apalachicola River Wildlife & Enviromental Area

Hickory Landing   G   FR 101

Owl Creek

Brickyard Island

Fort Gadsden

Gulf County Canal

H   Bloody Bluff Landing

Brothers River   Bloody Bluff Rd

71

St. Marks River

65

Port St. Joe

98

Lake Wimico

Apalachicola River

Jackson River

Jackson River

Apalachicola River

East Bay

St. George Sound

I

Apalachicola

98   98

Segment Mileage:	
E–F	21
F–G	21.5
G–H	8.5
H–I	15

Stop at Fort Gadsden Historic Site, 3.0 miles below the mouth of Owl Creek. Built in 1814 to encourage the Seminoles to ally with the British, the first fort was abandoned and later occupied by free blacks who rallied for the British cause in Spanish Florida. Two different forts sat on this site: the initial British fort and the American Fort Gadsden, built in 1818 and occupied through the Civil War. View bits and pieces of 1838 steamship boilers. Bloody Bluff Landing, also related to Fort Gadsden, is just a little high ground 4.0 miles below Fort Gadsden. Palms become a regular feature in the woods. Brother River enters 3.0 miles downstream, and then the St. Marks River merges 2.0 more miles down. The tides will affect the speed of the current at this point, 10 miles above Apalachicola Bay. The river widens to 700 feet across in places!

As you get closer to the mouth, houses begin to appear. The take-out is at Battery Park, in downtown Apalachicola.

✧ **SHUTTLE** Battery Park is within sight of downtown Apalachicola, near where the US 98/319 bridge crosses the river.

To reach Estiffanulga Landing from the intersection of FL 20 and CR 12 in Bristol, take CR 12 south for 8.4 miles, then turn right onto CR 333 and follow it 2.0 miles to turn right again on Joe Red Shuler Road and follow it 0.4 mile to the boat ramp.

✧ **GAUGE** Web. The gauge of interest is Apalachicola River near Sumatra. The best paddling conditions are found when the river is below 5.5 feet. There is no minimum runnable level.

12 OCHLOCKONEE RIVER

✧ **OVERVIEW** The Ochlockonee River is excellent for touring, is one of North Florida's longest rivers, and is a state-designated paddling trail for most of its length. The Ochlockonee's headwaters are found up in Worth County, Georgia. From there it meanders south for nearly 150 miles to meet the Gulf of Mexico near Panacea, Florida. The West Fork of the Ochlockonee and Barnetts Creek are its primary Peach State tributaries, while in Florida, Telogia Creek and the Little River are the main feeders. However, a host of creeks, rills, and streams feed the Ochlockonee along its journey.

In the headwaters above GA 93, the tapered Ochlockonee can be beset by willow thickets and fallen trees. At its mouth below Ochlockonee River State Park, it is wide and baylike: windy, tidal, and a motorboat haven. Touring paddlers will find the Ochlockonee from GA 93 to Ochlockonee River State Park the preferred paddling segment, despite the presence of dammed Lake Talquin along the way. For downstream of US 90 in Florida, the Ochlockonee is backed up for 19 miles through the man-made but very scenic Lake Talquin. The lake is long, with several arms created by backed up tributaries, including the Little River. Much of the shore is protected as Lake Talquin State Forest, with camping options. Trippers must portage the Lake Talquin Dam just above FL 20. However, your average paddler goes on floats either above or below Lake Talquin.

Once the river flows out of Lake Talquin, the distances between accesses lengthen. The Ochlockonee flows through Apalachicola National Forest and other public lands for 60 miles to Ochlockonee River State Park with only one bridge, sporadic house enclaves, and limited boat landings. The often-protected wild banks harbor both upland and lowland forests, and huge swaths of national forest make the Ochlockonee a rich wildlife corridor. I have actually seen a herd of wild pigs swim across the river here. The winding nature of the waterway creates a plethora of sandbars. Both developed and primitive campsites can be found. The river is a clearer yellowish color, different from its often blackwater brethren in North Florida, but the closer you get to the Gulf, the darker the river becomes, as tannins from the swamps and tributaries of the Apalachicola National Forest enter the watercourse.

The upper river in Georgia has privately held banks. Be discerning if you're choosing a campsite. In Florida, limited easements and Lake Talquin State Forest occupy significant shore, but below Lake Talquin, the huge Apalachicola National Forest provides vast swaths of publicly held banks with landings and camping opportunities abundant. However, river accesses are often downriver sloughs, referred to as lakes, and may be difficult to find without navigational aids. These lakes are actually arms or backwater areas of the river. A map-loaded GPS, national-forest map, and state-paddling-trail map will be invaluable to paddlers in making their way down the Ochlockonee.

⟨⟩ MAPS APALACHICOLA NATIONAL FOREST MAP; FLORIDA STATE PADDLING TRAIL, UPPER OCHLOCKONEE RIVER AND LOWER OCHLOCKONEE RIVER MAPS; CAIRO SOUTH, BEACHTON, CALVARY (GEORGIA), LAKE JACKSON, HAVANA SOUTH, MIDWAY, LAKE TALQUIN, BLOXHAM, WARD, SMITH CREEK, THOUSAND YARD BAY, SANBORN (FLORIDA) (USGS)

A   GA 93 to Old Bainbridge Road

Class	I
Length	29
Time	Varies
Gauge	Web
Level	13.5
Gradient	1
Scenery	B

12A DESCRIPTION Sane paddlers will begin their trips at the GA 93 bridge. Above that, too many willow thickets and fallen trees eliminate pleasantries from such paddles. But if the water is low, even the Ochlockonee below GA 93 can be a chore due to shallows and excessive vegetation, for the river flows serpentine through closely wooded banks obscuring nearby upland agricultural fields that can sometimes muddy the waters. Canoe and kayak campers seek sandbars found inside bends. Hadley Ferry Road crosses the river downstream, availing an access 9.0 miles downstream from GA 93. It is 10 more miles from Hadley Ferry Road to FL 12.

Below FL 12—where the state paddling trail begins—the river is surprisingly remote, despite having only one conservation easement along its banks. The shores are wooded with development-retarding swamps behind them, emitting darkish tannic water. The slowish current, despite numerous bends, makes it a long 15.0 miles to Old Bainbridge Road.

Watch for alligators galore about 4.0 miles down from FL 12, where tributaries link the Ochlockonee with Lake Iamonia to

Ochlockonee River A: GA 93 to Old Bainbridge Road

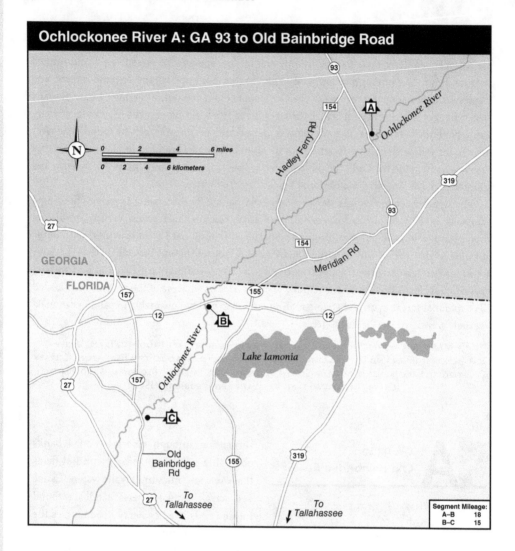

Segment Mileage:
A–B   18
B–C   15

the east. This creates a big swamp favored by the reptiles. Downstream, the crooked river is riddled with sandbars. Anglers and hunters may be seen at riverbank camps or angling on the Ochlockonee.

✧ **SHUTTLE** To reach the take-out from Exit 199 off I-10 just north of Tallahassee, take US 27 North 5.6 miles to Old Bainbridge Road/County Road 0361. Turn right (north) on Old Bainbridge Road and follow it 3.7 miles to a bridge over the Ochlockonee

River. There is a boat ramp on the northeast side of the bridge.

To reach the put-in from US 319 just north of I-10 off Exit 293, take US 319 North into Georgia. After 16.2 miles, turn left (north) on GA 93 and follow it 6.6 miles to the bridge over the Ochlockonee River. A boat ramp is on the northeast side of the river.

✧ **GAUGE** Web. The relevant USGS gauge is Ochlockonee River near Havana, Florida. The minimum runnable level is 13.5 feet.

B Old Bainbridge Road to Coe Landing

Class	I
Length	18
Time	10
Gauge	Web
Level	12.5
Gradient	1
Scenery	B

12B DESCRIPTION By Old Bainbridge Road, the river has become wider and less winding. However, it still has many turns and the potential for obstacles. There is some evidence of development in this section, which has both relatively straight and winding segments. It is 4.0 miles to US 27, a dual-lane highway with no good access to the river. Below US 27, the river runs very straight for 2.0 miles to just above the boat ramp at Tower Road. Directly above the boat ramp, the river makes an oxbow around a small island; the ramp is on the east bank. It is 6.0 miles from Old Bainbridge Road to the Tower Road boat ramp.

The slow-moving Ochlockonee twists and turns to the extreme along swampy banks below the Tower Road ramp. After the first 2.0 miles below Tower Road, the river becomes less twisting. Lake Talquin State Forest occupies much of the east bank and some of the west bank all the way to US 90. It is about a mile from the I-10 bridge to the US 90 bridge. It is 6.0 miles from Tower Road to US 90, where there is a boat ramp on the southwest side of the US 90 bridge.

The Ochlockonee widens below US 90, flowing under high banks. The river winds past a few houses then courses along the

A PADDLER TAKES TIME TO PHOTOGRAPH THE UNSPOILED BEAUTY OF THE OCHLOCKONEE.

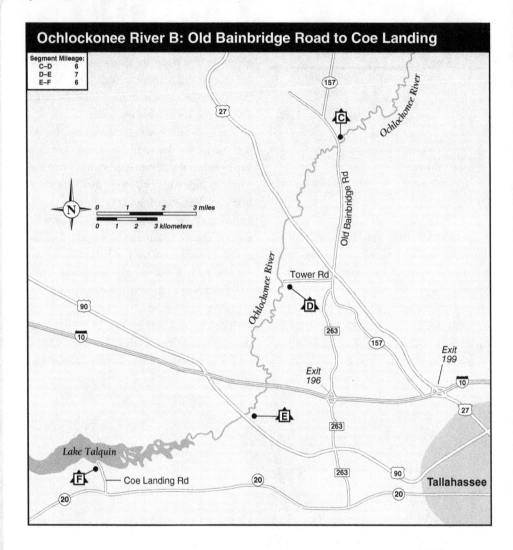

Ochlockonee River B: Old Bainbridge Road to Coe Landing

Segment Mileage:
C–D	6
D–E	7
E–F	6

lands of Lake Talquin State Forest and Joe Budd Wildlife Management Area. Near Lake Talquin, the shores are swampy. The island-dotted lake begins about 3.0 miles below US 90 and widens to a half mile in width before reaching Coe Landing, a Leon County park with a campground and, of course, a boat ramp, on the south bank. Such open waters on the roughly 10,000-acre lake can lead to waves and winds. The shore includes Lake Talquin State Park, which also has a landing. It is 6.0 miles from US 90 to the take-out at Coe Landing.

Lake Talquin widens and extends into fingers, continuing westerly for another 13.0 miles to end at the dam near FL 20. Consider the lake paddling yet another rewarding face of the Ochlockonee River. To continue on, however, you must portage the Lake Talquin Dam.

◇ **SHUTTLE** To reach the take-out from the intersection of US 90 and FL 20 in Tallahassee, take FL 20 West (which actually runs south, then west) 9.0 miles to Coe Landing Road. Turn right on Coe Landing Road and follow it 1.3 miles to the dead end at the public boat ramp on Lake Talquin.

To reach the put-in from Exit 199 off I-10 just north of Tallahassee, take US 27 North 5.6 miles to Old Bainbridge Road/CR 0361. Turn right (north) on Old Bainbridge Road and follow it 3.7 miles to a bridge over the Ochlockonee River. There is a boat ramp on the northeast side of the bridge.

◇ **GAUGE** Web. To determine if the river is at average flows, a helpful USGS gauge is Ochlockonee River near Havana, Florida. The minimum runnable level is 12.5 feet.

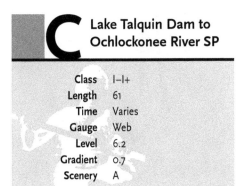

C Lake Talquin Dam to Ochlockonee River SP

Class	I–I+
Length	61
Time	Varies
Gauge	Web
Level	6.2
Gradient	0.7
Scenery	A

12C **DESCRIPTION** It's a great adventure to paddle from FL 20 down to Ochlockonee River State Park. Despite being dam-controlled, flow rates on this part of the river most often correlate with previous rainfall. A long, 250-foot-wide straightaway extends from the dam with houses on the east bank. The Apalachicola National Forest covers both banks just beyond the first river bend. Canoes and kayaks find their place among fishing boats, though fishing boats tend to be found near landings from which they embarked.

Rock Bluff Scenic Area, reached from Forest Route 390, rises on the east bank. It offers a rough access and primitive camping frequented by locals in trucks. At 3.0 miles on river right is Bradwell Landing, just a fishing spot and boat throw-in off FR 194. The national forest ends on the west bank and becomes posted, privately owned timberlands.

The Ochlockonee flows slowly in straight sections then bends repeatedly, narrowing on the bends, where you will also find sandbars and willows. Watch for more bluffs. Pass the signed historic Langston Ferry crossing at 12.0 miles. There is a memorial bridge over a small nearby slough. Cypress-dotted Telogia Creek feeds the Ochlockonee 15.0 miles below FL 20. At 16.0 miles, reach the Huey P. Arnold public boat ramp, on river right in Liberty County. Paddlers negotiate numerous bends for 2.0 miles before reaching Pine Creek Landing, a primitive camping spot and launch. It is 18.0 miles from FL 20 to Pine Creek Landing.

Below Pine Creek Landing, the willow-bordered river narrows and repeatedly bends, and is the most challenging segment since up Georgia way. Pass a bluff on river left, then reach Langston's Fish Camp Landing on river left, 4.5 miles downstream from Pine Creek on the east bank.

Below Langston Landing, the river divides into channels while making more willow-bordered bends. It is 4.0 miles from Langston Landing to the Forest Highway 13 bridge. A few houses pock the east bank. This is the first bridge over the Ochlockonee River since Lake Talquin Dam. However, FH 13 has no access, despite Porter Lake Landing being just a little west of the FH 13 bridge. However, reaching this landing requires paddling downstream from FH 13 for about 2.7 miles

Ochlockonee River C: Lake Talquin Dam to Ochlockonee River State Park

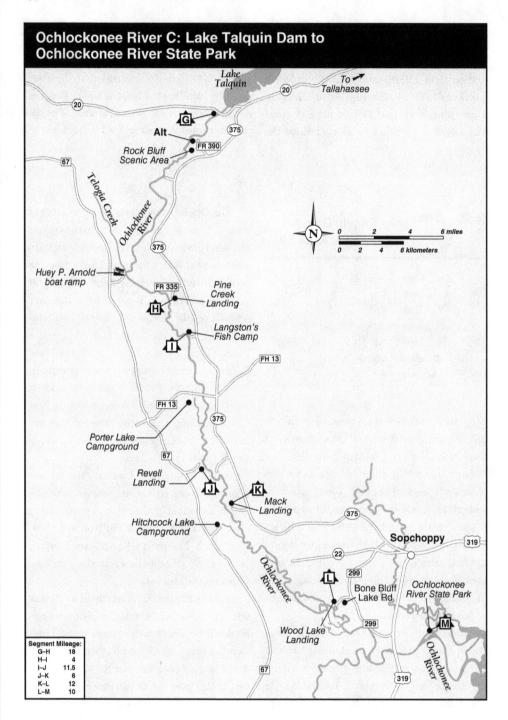

to the point where Porter Lake flows into the Ochlockonee and then paddling upstream to the campground landing. A GPS-enabled map shows the way. Here are the GPS coordinates for the entrance channel to Porter Lake: **N30° 09.462' W84° 40.302'.** En route up the channel to Porter Lake Landing, you will pass White-head Landing, which also has camping 0.5 mile from the Ochlockonee River. It is 1 mile farther up the channel to Porter Lake Landing.

Continuing downriver, you will pass near Revell Landing 6.0 miles downstream from FH 13. The landing is 0.1 mile up a slough on the west bank. Here are the GPS coordinates for the slough of Revell Landing: **N30° 07.686' W84° 40.230'.**

Ahead, the Ochlockonee splits and a smallish, sometimes brushy channel takes you through Mack Slough to Mack Landing, while the main river continues its winding ways. If you go through the Mack Slough channel, look for sawn limbs as guides. Here are the GPS coordinates for the entrance to the Mack Slough channel: **N30° 06.462' W84° 38.862'.** Mack Landing is 6.0 miles downstream from Revell Landing via the main river, while the river continues to alternate between wide, straight sections and narrow bends. It is 6.0 miles from Lower Langston Landing to Mack Landing.

Mack Landing offers a small campground on a bluff with a boat launch, 0.2 mile up from the main channel of the Ochlockonee River. In this era of satellites, we can use a GPS. Here are the coordinates for the slough of Mack Landing: **N30° 05.508' W84° 38.700'.**

Below Mack Landing, the river curves in wider bends, passing swampy banks. Hitchcock Lake access, on the west side of the river, is 2.0 miles downstream from Mack Landing. It is located 0.2 mile up a slough. The entrance to the slough is at **N30° 04.356' W84° 38.118'.**

Two miles below Hitchcock Lake Landing, Silver Lake Slough extends toward the community of Sanborn. Pinelands and swamps overlook the now-200-foot-wide river. Pass under power lines. Tate's Hell State Forest occupies some banks, along with the national forest. Pass the so-called Log Cabin auto- and river-accessible state-forest campsites on the west bank of Tate's Hell Forest, 6.0 miles down from Hitchcock Lake. The river ceases a long straightaway, then turns north before reaching the slough for Wood Lake Landing 3.0 miles farther on the east bank. It is 0.3 mile up a slough to the landing. Here are the coordinates for the Wood Lake slough entrance: **N30° 01.386' W84° 33.798'.**

The wide, now tidally affected river continues to bend, with dead sloughs and river cutoffs breaking off the main channel. Along the way you will pass Womack Creek Recreation Area, a state-forest camping option with picnic shelter, on the west bank 3.5 miles below Wood Lake, just after Womack Creek enters on the right. Downstream, the Crooked River enters on river right 6.0 miles below Wood Lake. It is also heavily influenced by the tide. Just below the Crooked River, pilings of an old wooden bridge stretch across the Ochlockonee. Look for a cleared channel toward the south bank as the Ochlockonee, in excess of 300 feet wide, turns east. Sawgrass and cattails line the now coastal waterway. Look for an island downstream after passing under the US 319 bridge. Head to the left of the island and, just before you reach the island, look left for a short channel leading to the boat ramp at Ochlockonee River State Park, 10.0 miles below Wood Lake.

✧ **SHUTTLE** To reach the lowermost takeout from Sopchoppy, take US 319 South 4.3 miles to the entrance to Ochlockonee River State Park, on your left just before the bridge over the Ochlockonee River. An entrance fee applies (see "Fees and Permits," page 6). The boat launch is about 1.5 mile ahead on your right, just off the park entrance road.

To reach the uppermost put-in from the intersection of US 90 and FL 20 in Tallahassee, take FL 20 West (which actually runs south, then west) 22.0 miles to the bridge across the Ochlockonee River. There is access on the west side of the river from a privately owned boat ramp. There is a fee for launching.

◇ GAUGE Visual, web. The best way to determine the water level is in person. However, the Ochlockonee is normally floatable year-round. A helpful gauge to determine average river levels for this section of the river is Ochlockonee River near Bloxham, Florida. The minimum runnable level is 6.2 feet. This gauge is below the Lake Talquin Dam.

13 SOPCHOPPY RIVER

◇ OVERVIEW The headwaters of the Sopchoppy River are found in the Apalachicola National Forest's Grand Bay Swamp. From there, the Sopchoppy flows for 50 miles—much of its uppermost waters almost impossible to paddle—to meet its mother stream the Ochlockonee River at Ochlockonee Bay. Lying almost completely within the boundaries of the Apalachicola National Forest, the Sopchoppy gathers as the East Branch and West Branch before merging north of the Bradwell Bay Wilderness, and becoming of interest to wilderness river-floaters. The river is noted not only for its continuous twists and turns but also extensive and unique cypress formations; high, mossy limestone banks; and a surprisingly swift current.

Paddlers on the Sopchoppy—a state-designated paddling trail—have to watch the water gauges carefully before paddling the river. Local rainfall leaves it a torrent in a gully or almost too low to go. No matter the water level, paddlers need also to watch for nonstop sharp turns and cypress knees presenting above water and underwater obstacles. The dark water is stained reddish-black from tannins. The high wooded banks are divided by occasional sandbars where paddlers break for a meal or pitch their tent. In addition, the Florida Trail parallels the Sopchoppy in places, adding a hiking possibility.

The uppermost run on Sopchoppy runs through the Bradwell Bay Wilderness. The protected untamed area is home to wild bears, deer and very big trees. The first 7.5 paddleable miles of the river flow through the wilderness.

Pines, palmettos, and live oaks wrap the high banks, while gums, cypresses, and titis rise in the moister margins. Mosses and ferns cover pale limestone walls. In spring, look for wild azaleas coloring the forest understory.

◇ MAPS APALACHICOLA NATIONAL FOREST MAP; BRADWELL BAY, CRAWFORDVILLE WEST, SOPCHOPPY, SANBORN (USGS)

Forest Highway 13 to Sopchoppy River Park

Class	I–I+
Length	23
Time	Varies
Gauge	Web
Level	11
Gradient	1.6
Scenery	A+

13 **DESCRIPTION** This is one of my favorite river paddles in the Apalachicola National Forest. Runs on the Sopchoppy River can be broken into varied segments, as there are numerous accesses. The upper river begins at the most southern edge of the Grand Bay Swamp, whose runoff forms the waterway. Adventurous and perhaps demented paddlers could attempt the Sopchoppy from the Forest Route 309 bridge upstream from the

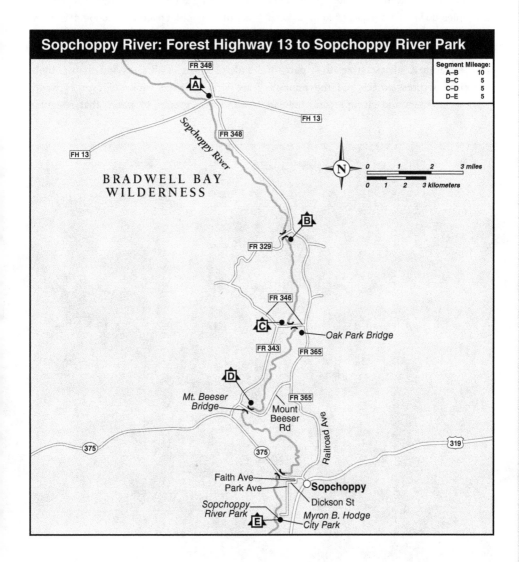

Sopchoppy River: Forest Highway 13 to Sopchoppy River Park

FH 13 bridge—the time-honored uppermost put-in—but high water and extensive bushwhacking are necessary. The river is wide but channeled at the FH 13 bridge. Start on the northwest side of the bridge and enter Bradwell Bay Wilderness. Moving rivulets finger off into a swampy area with low banks. Despite the swampy terrain, the current is easily detectable and eventually the fingers come together into a well-defined channel with banks from 1 to 3 feet high about 2.0 miles down. Pass adjacent to occasional pine–palmetto woods.

Very sharp twists and turns in a narrow streambed characterize this part of the river. Cypress knees and the remains of downed trees and stumps contribute to the obstructions that must be avoided. The constant curves and swift water leave little opportunity to scout, as immediate decisions are required in maneuvering. By 4.0 miles, the riverbanks have risen to 10 feet and the Sopchoppy is more manageable, with small sandbars in bends. The Florida Trail runs along the west bank. It is 7.5 miles from the FH 13 bridge to FR 329, where it leaves the wilderness.

Starting at FR 329, the middle Sopchoppy is a more popular paddling section. It is noted for the wide diversity of beautiful and unique cypress formations. In addition to a multitude of knees of all sizes and shapes, there are long, flowing banks of cypress wood, connecting groups of knees that resemble

THE AUTHOR PLIES THE LOWER SOPCHOPPY PAST A SANDBAR.

entwined serpents, monsters, gargoyles, or whatever the active imagination can envision. Monkey Creek enters from the west 1.5 miles below FR 329.

The sharp bends in the river are frequently obstructed by masses of cypress knees resulting in small shoals requiring fast maneuvering. Several small sandbars in this section beckon paddlers to stop. Pass under a power line a little before the FR 346 bridge, also known as the Oak Park Bridge. It is 4.5 miles from the FR 329 bridge to the Oak Park Bridge. Access is on the northwest side of the bridge, and a parking area for paddlers and Florida Trail hikers lies just west of the bridge.

From just above the Oak Park Bridge, the river begins to widen and the curves become gentler. High, limestone banks rise above live oak–dominated woods. Many a narrow island channelizes the Sopchoppy. Tributaries spill into the waterway, creating miniature waterfalls. Vertical banks and overhanging trees keep the river surprisingly cool during warm weather. A few houses appear. The river is deeper and easier to negotiate in this section but still requires some skill. Just before the Mount Beeser Bridge, the river leaves the national forest, and houses and other forms of encroachment appear. Small motorboats may also be seen near the end of this section. It is 4.5 miles from the Oak Park Bridge to the Mount Beeser Bridge.

Houses become the norm below the Mount Beeser Bridge. The Sopchoppy River's current begins to become tidally affected as it flows into marshier, coastal woods. It is 5.5 miles from the Mount Beeser Bridge to FL 375. However, this access is closed, so paddlers should continue another mile to the Sopchoppy River Park, on the left. The park has a boat landing, picnic area, and campground. You can paddle onward to the Sopchoppy's confluence with the Ochlockonee, but the experience is a disappointment compared with the upper reaches, due to extensive tides and heavy motorboat traffic.

✧ **SHUTTLE** To reach the lowermost takeout from the intersection of Rose Street and US 319 in Sopchoppy, take Rose Street six blocks (0.4 mile) west to Faith Avenue. Turn left (south) on Faith Avenue and follow it one block to Dickson Street. Turn right on Dickson Street and follow it one block to Park Avenue. Turn left (south) on Park Avenue and follow it 0.5 mile to Myron B. Hodge City Park, on the right, and a boat launch.

To reach the uppermost put-in from the same intersection in Sopchoppy, take Rose Street two blocks west to Railroad Avenue/ FR 365. Turn right and head north on FR 365 (also signed as Oak Park Road farther north) for 6.4 miles to FR 349. Veer left on FR 349 and follow it 1.7 miles; then turn left on FR 348 and take it 5.6 miles to FH 13. Turn left on FH 13 and follow it 0.2 mile to the bridge over the Sopchoppy River. Access is on the northeast side of the bridge.

✧ **GAUGE** Web. A helpful gauge to determine average river levels for this section of the river is Sopchoppy River near Sopchoppy, Florida. The minimum runnable level is 11 feet.

14   LITTLE RIVER

◇ **OVERVIEW** The Little River, a tributary of the Ochlockonee, is formed a few miles above FL 12 by the convergence of the Willacoochee and Attapulgus Creeks. It flows into the Ochlockonee at Lake Talquin. It is possible to put in at FL 12, but the access is poor and the upper section of the river is characterized by many pullovers and shallow water in all but the wettest seasons. Further, both sides of the riverbank are owned by private hunting clubs that not only discourage its usage but also make it somewhat hazardous during hunting season. This is also true of much of the lower, more runnable section, but the river is wider, deeper, and easier to maneuver, making a pleasant trip in the spring and early fall.

The Little River is like a miniature version of the Ochlockonee and is a very pleasant run. Very large alligators have been sighted here, and every sandbar is a tracker's paradise.

◇ **MAPS** QUINCY, LAKE TALQUIN (USGS)

US 90 to Lake Talquin

Class	I
Length	11.5
Time	Varies
Gauge	Visual, web
Level	N/A
Gradient	1.4
Scenery	A

14 **DESCRIPTION** It requires considerable skill to maneuver through the numerous obstructions on this section of the river, including stubborn logjams. There is usually a pleasant current, and the banks are intermittent swampy areas that are interspersed with some 20-foot-high bluffs. Several sandbars would make adequate campsites. I-10 crosses the river about 2.5 miles below US 90. It is 4.0 miles from US 90 to County Road 268. The CR 268 access is on the southeast side of the second bridge you reach, heading west from US 90.

Below CR 268, the river passes through parts of Joe Budd Wildlife Management Area. It widens and becomes both deeper and straighter. The sandbars disappear; the banks become high and heavily wooded. As the river nears Lake Talquin, it becomes swampier, with small bayous and sloughs off to the sides. When it flows into the Little River arm of the lake at 4.0 miles, the water becomes shallower, with many stumps showing above the water.

After entering the main body of the lake, paddlers should turn left (east) and remain on the north side of the lake. This is the upper portion of Lake Talquin; it is wide and may be windy. It is 2.5 miles from the confluence of Little River up the lake to High Bluff. High Bluff Recreation Area is part of Lake Talquin State Forest and has a good-quality tent campground. It is 7.5 miles from CR 268 to the take-out at High Bluff Landing.

◇ **SHUTTLE** To reach the take-out from the intersection of US 90 and US 27 in Tallahassee,

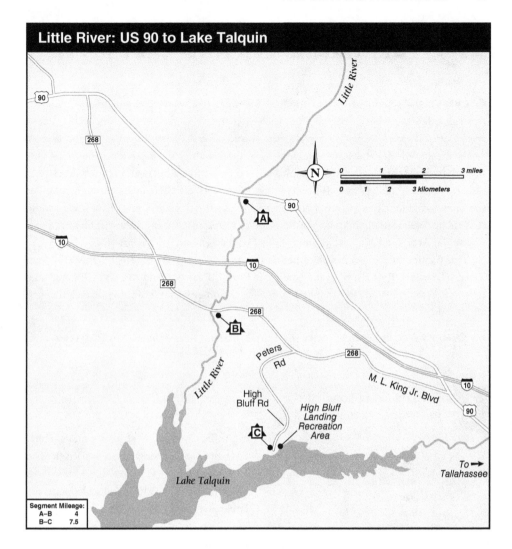

Little River: US 90 to Lake Talquin

Segment Mileage:
A–B   4
B–C   7.5

take US 90 West 9.6 miles, then turn left on East Brickyard Road/CR 268, which becomes M. L. King Jr. Boulevard in 3.0 miles. Continue west on M. L. King Jr. Boulevard/CR 268 and, in 1.8 miles, turn left on Peters Road, which swings sharply south and becomes High Bluff Landing Road after another 1.1 miles. The road dead-ends 3.9 miles later at High Bluff Landing Recreation Area, which has a boat landing and a campground.

To reach the put-in from the same intersection in Tallahassee, take US 90 West 18.3 miles to the bridge over the Little River.

◇ **GAUGE** Visual, web. The best way to determine water level is in person. A helpful gauge to determine average river levels for any given period is Little River near Midway, Florida.

15   GRAHAM CREEK AND EAST RIVER

◆ **OVERVIEW** Graham Creek and the East River are freshwater components of the lower Apalachicola Bay estuary. Located on Florida Fish and Wildlife Conservation Lands, These creeks are managed to protect the watershed and all the life within. Part of the greater Apalachicola Wildlife and Environmental Area, these waterways meander through the vast floodplain forests in the lower Apalachicola River delta. Black bears and other wild critters call this home. Paddlers call this a new opportunity to ply their boats through many of the waterways that extend throughout this region, for the Graham Creek–East River paddle route is but one of many marked paddle paths in the Apalachicola River Wildlife and Environmental Area Paddling Trail System. Trips here can extend from hours to days.

This particular trip begins on upper Graham Creek, then travels west to meet the East River. The wider East River heads southeast toward East Bay and the Gulf. Bikers, take note that Fish and Wildlife has installed bike racks on either end of this paddle, enabling a bike shuttle.

◆ **MAPS** Apalachicola Wildlife and Environmental Area Paddle Trail System map; Beverly, Jackson River (USGS)

Graham Creek Landing to Gardner Landing

Class	I
Length	7.5
Time	4
Gauge	Visual
Level	Tidal
Gradient	N/A
Scenery	A

15 DESCRIPTION This paddle trip leaves from the landing off County Road 65. Paddlers can head upstream, under the CR 65 bridge, and a mile east to the railroad bridge. Beyond the railroad bridge, you can head left, north, and up Deep Creek into Tates Hell State Forest. Most paddlers simply head west, downstream from the landing, enjoying the tupelo- and cypress-lined blackwater. The South Prong comes in from river right at 0.2 mile. Continue west for 2.5 miles. Here, Graham Creek meets the East River. The East meanders at first, and then the curves become gentler. Palms and oaks join the streamside forest mix. After 4.0 miles on the East River, work around an island just below the confluence with Caesar Creek. Stay to the left of this island to reach Gardner Landing after 4.5 miles on the East River.

◆ **SHUTTLE** To reach the take-out at Gardner Landing from Eastpoint (intersection of US 98 and FL 300), head east on US 98 for 3.7 miles, turn left (north) on FL 65, and follow it 12.0 miles to Gardner Road. Turn left on Gardner Landing Road and, at the split with Butcher Pen Landing Road (1.7 miles), head right across the railroad tracks to reach Gardner Landing.

Graham Creek and East River: Graham Creek Landing to Gardner Landing

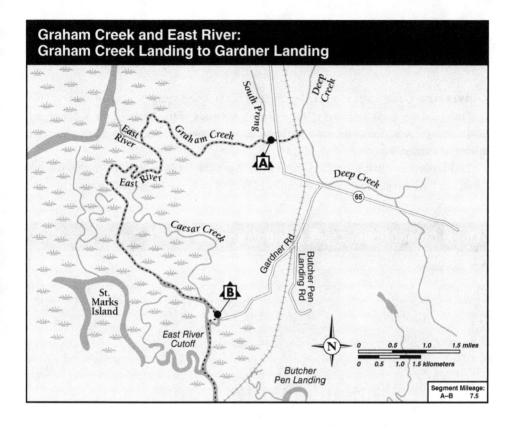

To reach the put-in at Graham Creek Landing, backtrack to FL 65, turn left (west), and follow FL 65 about a mile to the bridge over Graham Creek. The landing is on the southwest side of the bridge.

✧ GAUGE Visual. These coastal waterways hold enough water year-round due to downstream tidal influence.

16 DOYLE CREEK

✧ **OVERVIEW** Doyle Creek is a marshy tributary of the lower Apalachicola Bay estuary. This smallish tidal stream is also part of the extensive wetlands of the Apalachicola Wildlife and Environmental Area, whose waterways form an aquatic network of tidal veins pulsing through this remote area of Florida.

This is but one of many paddling routes in the Apalachicola delta. In fact, Whiskey George Creek and Cash Creek are within a few miles of Doyle Creek, availing paddling opportunities

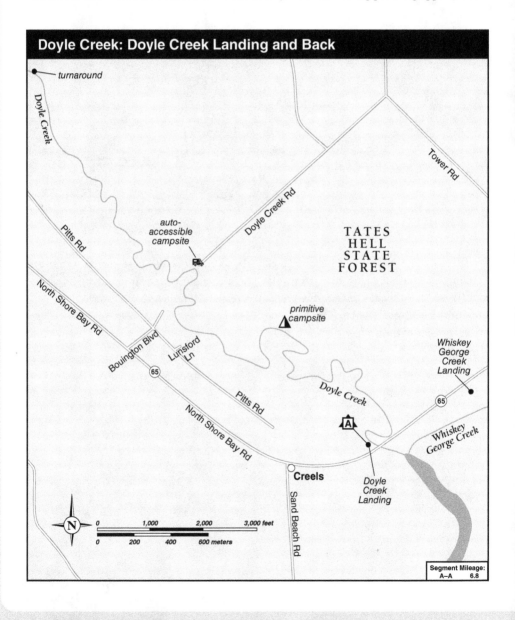

Doyle Creek: Doyle Creek Landing and Back

turnaround

Doyle Creek

Pitts Rd

Doyle Creek Rd

Tower Rd

auto-
accessible
campsite

TATES
HELL
STATE
FOREST

primitive
campsite

North Shore Bay Rd

Bouington Blvd

Lunsford
Ln

65

Whiskey
George
Creek
Landing

Pitts Rd

Doyle Creek

65

Whiskey
George Creek

North Shore Bay Rd

A

Creels

Sand Beach Rd

Doyle
Creek
Landing

N

0	1,000	2,000	3,000 feet

0	200	400	600 meters

Segment Mileage:	
A–A	6.8

galore. Doyle Creek presents a chance to paddle a tidal marsh stream to its headwaters where pines, oaks, and the vast forests of the Apalachicola River watershed close in on the paddler. Birdlife is abundant, from ospreys to red-winged blackbirds.

Doyle Creek is a good choice if you like smaller waterways, lesser tidal influence, and out-and-back paddling, eliminating the need for a shuttle. The tide here runs about 2 hours behind the given tide at the town of Apalachicola.

◇ MAPS APALACHICOLA WILDLIFE AND ENVIRONMENTAL AREA PADDLE TRAIL SYSTEM MAP; BEVERLY (USGS)

Doyle Creek Landing and Back

Class	I
Length	6.8 (out-and-back)
Time	4
Gauge	Visual
Level	Tidal
Gradient	N/A
Scenery	A

16 DESCRIPTION The staging area for Doyle Creek is a large, grassy flat bordered in trees. The ramp is partly washed away, leaving the launch for paddlers only. Head upstream from the FL 65 bridge, on a tidal waterway bordered in grasses. Forests rise on the edge of the estuary. The stream turns right toward FL 65 then heads north and begins its meandering, ever-narrowing route. After a mile, come along a low forest bluff cloaked in pine, oak, and palmetto, part of Tates Hell State Forest. At 1.3 miles, a camping flat, bordered in oaks, stands above the stream. Curve back into the marsh on a narrowing track. Pass a few cabins on the left bank, then swing back to pass an auto-accessible piney campsite at 2.2 miles. Doyle Creek narrows to less than 30 feet in places, and you may swing around fallen trees. At 3.4 miles, Doyle Creek splits. This is a good place to turn around, but if you want to explore further, head up the right channel. Expect tight turns from here on.

◇ DIRECTIONS To reach the put-in/take-out at Doyle Creek Landing from Eastpoint (intersection of US 98 and FL 300), head east on US 98 for 3.7 miles, turn left (north) on FL 65, and follow it 8.2 miles to the signed Doyle Creek Landing, on the right immediately after the bridge over Doyle Creek.

◇ GAUGE Visual. This tidal waterway holds adequate water year-round.

DOYLE CREEK IS BORDERED BY TIDAL GRASSES AND WOODLANDS.

17 OWL CREEK

⟡ **OVERVIEW** Draining Post Office Bay and other swamps of the southwestern Apalachicola National Forest, Owl Creek—a tributary of the Apalachicola River—has long been an intriguing paddling destination. Most paddlers start their trips at Hickory Landing, a national-forest recreation area with a boat ramp and campground. Paddlers can also start on Black Creek, a tributary of Owl Creek, and then paddle into Owl Creek, then down to Hickory Landing and beyond to the Apalachicola River. Furthermore, creekside cypress–tupelo swamps beg exploration, as does Devon Creek, another tributary of Owl Creek downstream from Hickory Landing. Devon Creek presents a narrow, winding paddling prospect, canopied in aquatic hardwoods. As you can see, there is many a method to exploring the Owl Creek drainage.

⟡ **MAPS** Apalachicola National Forest map; Beverly (USGS)

Ashley Landing to Hickory Landing

Class	I
Length	2.8
Time	2
Gauge	Visual
Level	N/A
Gradient	N/A
Scenery	A

17 DESCRIPTION This paddle can be done using a bike or foot shuttle—it's just a little more than 3.0 miles between landings. After leaving remote Ashley Landing, head left (westerly) on 60-foot-wide Black Creek. Multiple small sloughs break off, but keep west on the appropriately named coffee-colored stream, bordered in cypress and tupelo trees. In winter, their barren limbs form silvery clusters above darkened bases, while summer

An eerie canopy over Devon Creek

Owl Creek: Ashley Landing to Hickory Landing

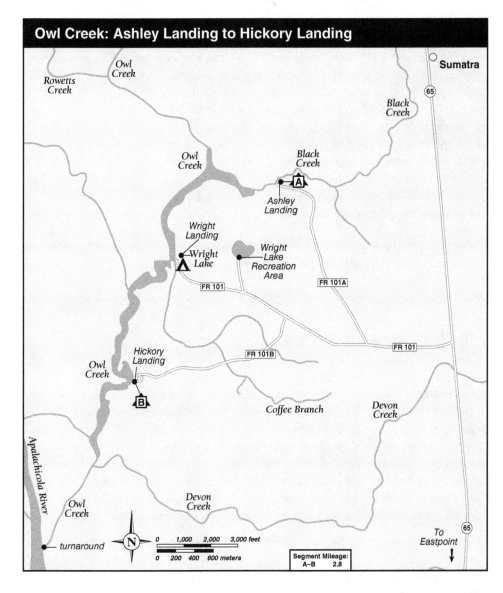

finds them deep green. Pines rise in the distance above the south bank. At 0.5 mile Black Creek meets Owl Creek. Head left, southerly, down much wider Owl Creek. The current is negligible, allowing a side foray up Owl Creek.

Southbound paddlers may see a floating house or two before passing Wright Landing, a national-forest ramp, on the left at 1.3 miles. Coffee Branch enters here and may be explored too. At this point, Owl Creek angles southwesterly and briefly narrows before widening. Look for sizable trees with gnarled, wide bases as you keep southerly. Curve around a line of trees, then reach Hickory Landing at 2.4 miles. Check out the sulphur spring near the ramp. Beyond here, there is no access on Owl Creek, but you can easily paddle to the Apalachicola River and back, or all the way back to Ashley Landing for that matter.

On the way down, pass Devon Creek at 3.2 miles. It isn't easy to find but may be marked with flagging tape; a GPS downloaded with topo maps will come in handy here. Devon Creek is worthy of exploration, but be prepared to work around fallen trees under a veil of swamp hardwoods. From Devon Creek, it is 0.8 mile to the fast-moving Apalachicola River. So if you're paddling from Ashley Landing down to the Apalachicola and back to Hickory Landing, you have a 5.6-mile trip, not including a side trip on Devon Creek.

✧ **SHUTTLE** To reach the take-out at Hickory Landing from Eastpoint (intersection of US 98 and FL 300), head east on US 98 for 3.7 miles, turn left (north) on FL 65, and follow it 22.8 miles to signed Wright Lake Road/Forest Road 101. Turn left on FR 101 and follow it 1.2 miles to Hickory Landing Road/FR 101B. Follow FR 101B for 1.2 miles to Hickory Landing.

To reach the put-in from the take-out, backtrack on FR 101B to FR 101. Turn right on FR 101 and follow it 0.6 mile to Ashley Landing Road/FR 101A. Follow FR 101A for 1.2 miles to the dead end at Ashley Landing.

✧ **GAUGE** Visual. Owl Creek has adequate water year-round.

18 RIVER STYX

✧ **OVERVIEW** Primeval in appearance—and reality—the River Styx presents an opportunity to paddle a wild waterway. I can only imagine what led to the naming of the River Styx, but I bet it had something to do with getting lost (no such concerns with today's GPS-armed paddler). The stream flows west from the Apalachicola National Forest into a network of channels linking swamps of the Apalachicola National Estuarine Reserve before meeting the Apalachicola River. The Styx presents many faces en route to its mother stream—first it is a wide, slow waterway, and then it gets some current and makes convolutions, finally narrowing to a fallen-tree-bordered channel. White Oak Landing, with its concrete ramp, makes a convenient starting point.

✧ **MAPS** APALACHICOLA NATIONAL FOREST MAP; WEWAHITCHKA, KENNEDY CREEK (USGS)

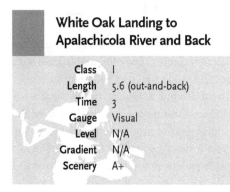

White Oak Landing to Apalachicola River and Back

Class	I
Length	5.6 (out-and-back)
Time	3
Gauge	Visual
Level	N/A
Gradient	N/A
Scenery	A+

18 **DESCRIPTION** You really are out in the sticks when you embark on the River Styx from White Oak Landing. From the boat ramp, head left, though you can go upstream too. The low piney bluff of White Oak Landing rises to your left, while a menagerie of willow, river birch, cypress, and oak finds its place. The current is imperceptible. Paddle beyond the national forest and into the estuarine reserve, though you won't know the difference.

River Styx: White Oak Landing to Apalachicola River and Back

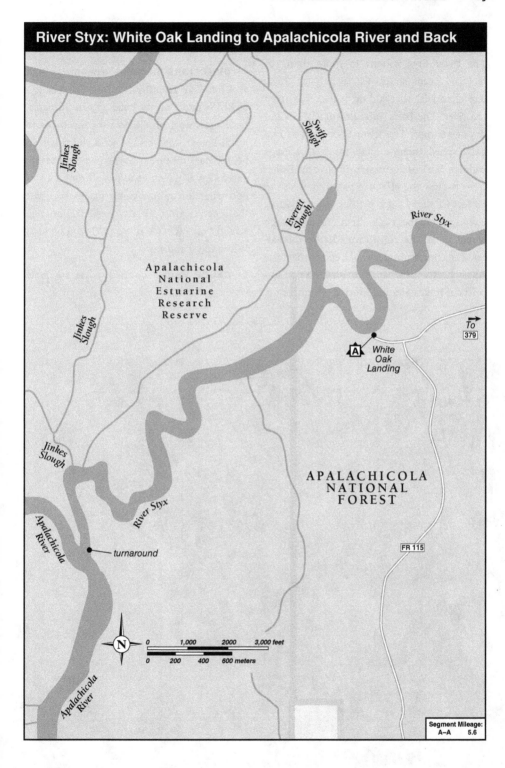

Swift Slough

Jinkes Slough

Everett Slough

River Styx

Apalachicola
National
Estuarine
Research
Reserve

Jinkes Slough

To
379

A White
Oak
Landing

Jinkes
Slough

River Styx

APALACHICOLA
NATIONAL
FOREST

Apalachicola
River

turnaround

FR 115

N

| 0 | 1,000 | 2000 | 3,000 feet |

| 0 | 200 | 400 | 600 meters |

Apalachicola
River

Segment Mileage:	
A–A	5.6

By 0.4 mile, Everett Slough enters on the right and adds its flow—and current. The River Styx widens to more than 150 feet and heads southwest. Watch for "mystery channels" that add or deduct flow from the river. The banks are alternately low but dry or swampy. The River Styx narrows and gains speed, though not so much an average paddler can't easily return upstream. Fallen trees narrow the effective paddling width to 30 feet in places. At 2.5 miles, a big channel comes in on the right, then Jinkes Slough comes in on the right immediately thereafter. Continue around a final bend to meet the Apalachicola River at 2.8 miles. Don't be surprised if Jinkes Slough, Everett Slough, or the "mystery channels" call you to explore them on your return trip.

✧ **DIRECTIONS** To reach the put-in/take-out at White Oak Landing from the intersection of FL 65 and County Road 379 in Sumatra, head northwest on CR 379 for 8.2 miles to reach Forest Road 115. Make a sharp left on FR 115, passing through a private hunt camp, and follow it 3.4 miles to pass through a second collection of hunt-camp shacks. Just past the second camp, FR 115 goes left, but keep straight on FR 115A and quickly dead-end at White Oak Landing.

✧ **GAUGE** Visual. River Styx has adequate water year-round.

A HERON TAKES FLIGHT OVER THE RIVER STYX.

19 NEW RIVER

✧ **OVERVIEW** The New River originates in the far north of the Apalachicola National Forest, draining a wide region of Liberty County bordered by the Apalachicola River on the west and the Wakulla River to the east. It can be paddled south of the FH 13 bridge, commonly known as Carr Bridge, along a corridor of the New River–Mud Swamp Wilderness. Many fallen logs and riverine obstructions make this a challenging paddle. The New River then breaks into impassable channels before becoming one main channel again in the southeast corner of the wilderness. Here, it leaves the national forest and enters Franklin County and Tate's Hell State Forest. By this point, the river has generally sufficient flow for year-round paddling and is more open. The dark, Gulf-bound waterway begins to widen and become tidally influenced before leaving the state forest, reaching Carrabelle, and opening into the Gulf at Dog Island. State Forest access points along River Road and River Road West, plus a bridge, ramp, and day-use area off Gully Branch Road, make trips of differing lengths very easy.

✧ **MAPS** Tate's Hell State Forest map; Owens Bridge, Tates Hell Swamp, Pickett Bay (USGS)

New River East Campsite 7 to Pope Place Camp

Class	I
Length	11
Time	6
Gauge	Phone, visual, web
Level	N/A
Gradient	0.8
Scenery	A

19 DESCRIPTION The river is about 30 feet wide as it enters Franklin County. The state forest has developed many access points–campsites along the upper river, which are visible as clearings from a boat. Each access point–campsite has a picnic table and fire ring. Although roads parallel much of the lower New River, the complete lack of development along its banks and anywhere in the vicinity creates a wilderness aura and natural soundscape. Oaks and cedars are common on the upper river. The New tortuously twists, forming sandbars on the insides of bends while higher sandbanks border the outside. Small branches feed the New. Occasionally, pine-studded bluffs reach directly to the river. Beyond the vision of a paddler, much of the state forest is pine plantation. It is 6.0 miles from New River East Campsite 7 to Gully Landing, with its picnic pavilion, well, and boat ramp.

As you continue downriver, the 50-foot-wide New offers occasionally straighter sections and more river accesses, mostly on the west bank. Sandbars end and the river becomes tidally influenced. The banks begin to lower, pines extend to the water, and the river widens to 80 feet. Pope Place access is on the right-hand (west) bank. Below Pope Place, access is difficult in the state forest due to grass banks. Tides begin to influence the paddle. Beyond the state forest, houses begin to appear and the river widens so that it opens itself to winds and becomes popular with motorboats, therefore losing its appeal to paddlers. It is 5.0 miles from Gully Landing to Pope Place.

New River: New River East Campsite 7 to Pope Place Camp

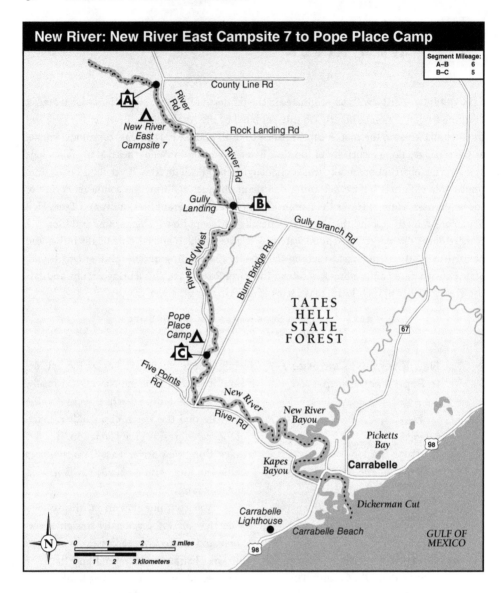

Segment Mileage:
A–B   6
B–C   5

County Line Rd

River Rd

A

New River
East
Campsite 7

Rock Landing Rd

River Rd

Gully
Landing

B

Gully Branch Rd

River Rd West

Burnt Bridge Rd

T A T E S
H E L L
S T A T E
F O R E S T

67

Pope
Place
Camp

C

Five Points
Rd

New River

River Rd

New River
Bayou

Picketts
Bay

98

Kapes
Bayou

Carrabelle

Dickerman Cut

Carrabelle
Lighthouse

Carrabelle Beach

GULF OF
MEXICO

N

0   1   2   3 miles
0   1   2   3 kilometers

98

⟡ **SHUTTLE** To reach the lowermost access from the southwest side of the US 98 bridge over the New River in Carrabelle, take River Road west and away from the Gulf. After 1.2 miles, veer left at the Y-intersection onto Mill Road. After 0.8 mile, bear right (northwest) at another Y to stay on Mill Road. After 3.0 miles, just past the bridge over Trout Creek, veer right (north) onto River Road West and follow it 1.4 miles to Pope Place Camp, on the west side of the river.

To reach the uppermost access, continue north on River Road West 5.3 miles to reach Gully Branch Road. Turn right (east) on Gully Branch Road, crossing the bridge over New River and a good access point. Turn left on River Road and follow it 2.5 miles up to Rock Landing Road. Turn left on Rock Landing

Road, then turn right on River Road and, in 1.8 miles, reach New River East Campsite 7. There is a landing and campsite here. New River East Campsite 7 is 0.6 mile south of County Line Road, on the east side of the river. High-clearance vehicles are recommended on the sandy state-forest roads.

Florida State Forests charge fees for day use, camping, and use of off-road vehicles, among other fees. Call the number below or visit tinyurl.com/floridastateforests for the latest information.

◆ **GAUGE** Phone, visual, web. Call Tate's Hell State Forest at 850-697-3734 for the latest river conditions. The best way to determine the water level is in person, but note that the New River is normally floatable year-round. A helpful gauge for determining average river levels is New River near Sumatra, Florida.

A SLOW-FLOWING BEND ON THE NEW RIVER

 LOST CREEK

◆ **OVERVIEW** Similar to its sister stream the Sopchoppy River in location, terrain, and color, Lost Creek is also located almost entirely within the Apalachicola National Forest, keeping its banks wild and open to the public. Formed from wetlands in the heart of the national forest, Lost Creek flows southeast 10 or so miles, winding through Cow Swamp and Mosquito Bay, and then disappears into a sink just west of Crawfordville, earning its name. The waterway twists every bit as much as the upper reaches of the Sopchoppy. The only bit of development on Lost Creek is on its south bank near Arran. Paddlers can enjoy seeing the biodiversity of Apalachicola National Forest from the seat of their boat. This waterway is highly dependent on local rainfall.

◆ **MAPS** APALACHICOLA NATIONAL FOREST MAP; CRAWFORDVILLE WEST (USGS)

Forest Road 350 to County Road 368

Class	I–I+
Length	8.5
Time	4
Gauge	Web
Level	4.5
Gradient	2
Scenery	A

20 **DESCRIPTION** Short boats manned by agile and crafty paddlers are recommended on this untamed, extremely narrow and twisting waterway. By the time Lost Creek has reached the put-in at the FR 350 bridge, it has gathered in a clearly defined channel (an excess of fallen trees, strainers, and clear channels keeps paddlers off Lost Creek upstream of the FR 350 bridge). The FR 350 bridge is the sane starting point.

Immediately the creek breaks off into islands, making choosing the correct channel a guessing game among the cypress and tupelo. The canopied waterway can extend 20 feet across, but growth leaves the effective paddling width barely a boat wide. Water flows into adjacent swamps where the banks are ill-defined. If you want a wilderness paddling experience, Lost Creek offers that; however, there will be challenges, such as fallen trees, strainers, cypress knees, and overhanging vegetation, as well as sharp bends. Wear long pants and shirts to avoid being scratched by the brush. Pine and holly rise on higher banks.

At 1.9 miles, paddle past rotting bridge pilings of a long-forgotten road. The banks rise a bit and Lost Creek continues its convolutions.

ABOUT TO SQUEEZE THROUGH A NARROW
SECTION OF UPPER LOST CREEK

Lost Creek: Forest Road 350 to County Road 368

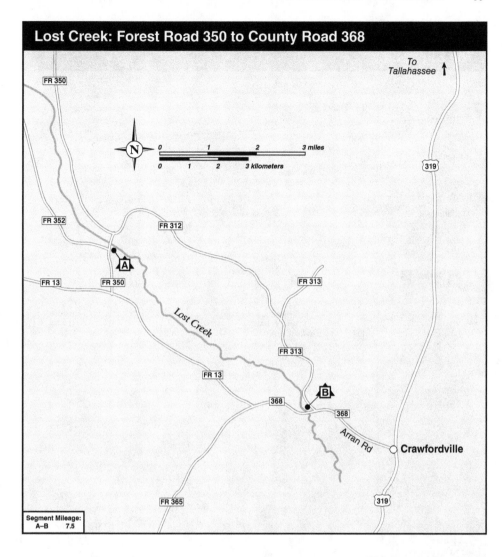

Segment Mileage:
A–B   7.5

In places, cypress trees grow midriver. After 4.5 miles, bluffs rise on bends. Pass under a power line at 5.5 miles. The river is now relatively wide and easy to float. The south bank becomes private property, while the north bank remains national forest until you reach the CR 368 bridge.

✧ **SHUTTLE** To reach the take-out from the intersection of US 319 and Arran Road/FL 368 in Crawfordville, drive west on FL 368 for 2.2 miles to the bridge over Lost Creek. Access is on the northeast side of the river.

To reach the put-in, continue west on FL 368 beyond the take-out—the road becomes FR 13, and the pavement gives way to sand. Follow FL 368/FR 13 a total of 5.0 miles to FR 350. Turn right (north) on FR 350 and follow it 1.0 mile to the bridge over Lost Creek. Access is on the southeast side of the bridge.

✧ **GAUGE** Web. The USGS gauge Lost Creek at Arran, Florida, should read at least 2.5 feet to be paddleable at all. Between 2.5 and 4.5 feet, paddlers will encounter logs. Above 4.5 feet is better paddling.

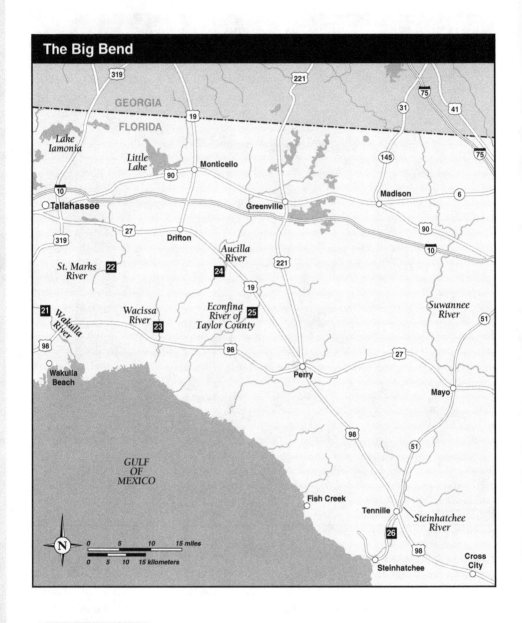

The Big Bend

21 WAKULLA RIVER

◇ **OVERVIEW** Here's your chance to paddle the waterway that emerges from the world's largest and deepest freshwater spring. That is saying a lot and is a point of pride for Florida paddlers. The Wakulla is a large river originating at Wakulla Springs, with Indian Springs, Sally Ward Spring, and McBride Slough also contributing their crystalline waters. The spring is now a first-rate Florida state park.

Aboriginal peoples have been coming to Wakulla Springs for thousands of years, and today visitors still come to see the massive upwelling and abundant wildlife along the river, as well as stay at a celebrated lodge near the spring. Manatees are spotted year-round. Once privately held, the clear-as-air springs and adjacent deep forests were the backdrop for many a movie. As such, the springs and the first 3 miles of the river were fenced in just above FL 365. This fence—kept in place by the state of Florida when the springs became a state park—prevents access to the first 3 miles of this navigable-to-boats stream. The old Tallahassee–St. Marks Rail-Trail runs parallel to the Wakulla and provides an alternative shuttle option for hikers and bikers.

◇ **MAPS** Crawfordville East, St. Marks (USGS)

FL 365 to Wakulla River City Park

Class	I
Length	6
Time	3
Gauge	Web, visual
Level	Spring-fed
Gradient	0.2
Scenery	B

21 DESCRIPTION Paddlers can put in and take out at the FL 365 bridge simply by paddling downstream and returning up the river, especially since the current tends to flow mildly. The clear water of the wide stream enhances your wildlife-viewing opportunities. The Wakulla flows around several islands, but the deep, broad nature of the river allows paddlers to choose which side of the islands to paddle on. It is 4.0 miles from FL 365 to US 98. A public access is located on the southeast side of the bridge, next to an outfitter. It is 2.0 miles farther to the take-out at Wakulla River City Park, on the east bank of the river.

Wakulla River: FL 365 to Wakulla River City Park

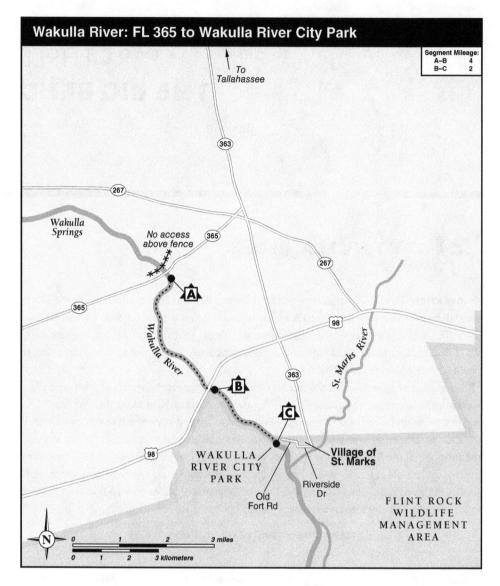

Segment Mileage:	
A–B	4
B–C	2

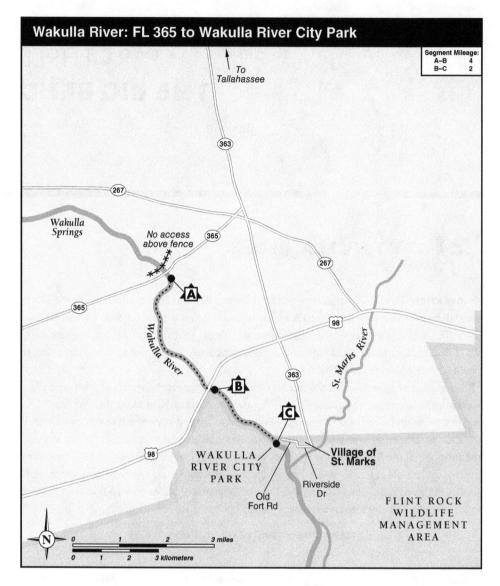

✧ **SHUTTLE** To reach the take-out from the intersection of US 319 and Woodville Highway/FL 363 in Tallahassee, drive south on FL 363 for 15.8 miles to reach a T-intersection in the village of St. Marks. Turn right on Riverside Drive and, in 0.2 mile, turn left on Old Fort Road. Follow the road west 0.4 mile—the name changes to Yacht Lane past the intersection with Fire Escape Road—and, just past the St. Marks Yacht Club on your left, make a quick jog right on City Park

Avenue to end at Wakulla River City Park and a boat ramp.

To reach the put-in from Tallahassee, take FL 363 South 10.2 miles. Turn right (west) on FL 267, then turn quickly left (south) on Shadeville Road/FL 365 and follow it 2.2 miles to the bridge over the Wakulla River.

✧ **GAUGE** Visual. The Wakulla River is spring-fed and remains paddleable year-round. However, a relevant gauge is Wakulla River near Crawfordville, Florida.

22 ST. MARKS RIVER

✧ **OVERVIEW** The St. Marks River flows through swampy terrain with a preponderance of cypress, magnolia, palm, and other lowland vegetation. The color of this clear, blue-green river results from its limestone bottom, and it has a variety of waterweeds above and below the surface. The current is mild, but it is possible to paddle upstream easily.

The uppermost reaches of the St. Marks River drain ponds north of US 90, but the river here is a minute stream, hardly deserving the river moniker. However, the St. Marks becomes truly riverine—and paddleable—when clear Horn Spring flows about 350 feet to feed the St. Marks River. And flowing freely and boldly for 2.5 miles, the St. Marks promptly exits to the underworld, flowing underground, below the renowned St. Marks Natural Bridge, a historical aboriginal river crossing and the site of an 1865 battle between the Confederates and the Yankees that kept Tallahassee as the only state capital east of the Mississippi that remained in Rebel hands. The St. Marks rises from the netherworld below the natural bridge, staying aboveground for its final 11 miles to merge with the Wakulla River and flow 3 miles on to the Gulf of Mexico.

Several springs in the area of the Natural Bridge are also additional reoccurrences of the St. Marks River. These include Natural Bridge Spring and at least four springs in the Rhodes Springs group. They rise in an area with a dense growth of vegetation, swamp, and karst features, such as sinkholes and solution tubes. The river does not rise as a well-defined riverbed until about 0.75 mile south of FL 260 at St. Marks Springs. This area is closed to public access.

✧ **MAPS** WOODVILLE, ST. MARKS (USGS)

A Natural Bridge to Horn Spring and Back

Class	I
Length	5 (out-and-back)
Time	3.5
Gauge	Visual
Level	Spring-fed
Gradient	0.5
Scenery	A

22A **DESCRIPTION** This segment actually starts with you paddling upstream from Natural Bridge to Horn Spring, then back downstream, since access roads to Horn Spring are posted. Despite this segment of the St. Marks River being short and it being necessary to paddle upstream, the lush riverside woodland—rife with impressive cypress trees amid deep swamps—offers paddlers an eyeful of gorgeous Big Bend beauty. The trip to Horn Spring and back totals 5.0 miles.

Two adjacent springs actually compose milky-blue Horn Spring. The main spring is larger, about 80 feet across and 30 feet deep beneath overhanging trees. The smaller spring is about 30 feet in diameter. Their combined flow puts the river into the St. Marks River.

In addition to the flow from Horn Spring, coffee-colored yet partly spring-fed Chicken Branch adds its flow, entering the west bank just below the horn Spring's inflow. Additional spring seeps and dark streamlets add volume to the river and riverside swamps.

St. Marks River A–B: Natural Bridge to St. Marks Spring

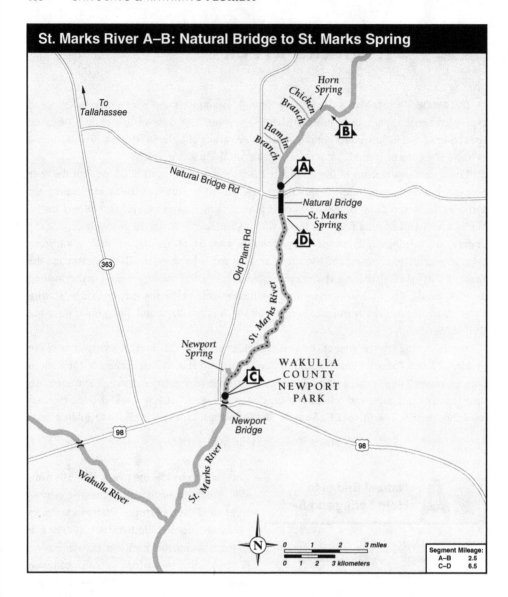

Keep your eyes open for magnificent wide-based cypresses towering over a wealth of trees, namely palms and magnolias.

◇ **DIRECTIONS** To reach the put-in/take-out from the intersection of US 319 and Woodville Highway/FL 363 in Tallahassee, drive south on FL 363 for 4.6 miles. Turn left (east) on Natural Bridge Road and drive 6.2 miles to Natural Bridge Battlefield Historic State Park. An entrance fee applies (see "Fees and Permits," page 6). The access is on the left, just before a bridge as the road turns to sand.

◇ **GAUGE** Visual. Horn Spring feeds this section, keeping it paddleable year-round.

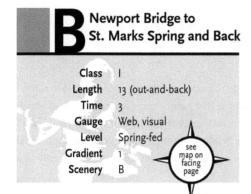

B Newport Bridge to St. Marks Spring and Back

Class	I
Length	13 (out-and-back)
Time	3
Gauge	Web, visual
Level	Spring-fed
Gradient	1
Scenery	B

see map on facing page

22B **DESCRIPTION** Due to lack of public access at St. Marks Spring, this paddle is also an out-and-back proposition. Paddlers can head upstream from the Newport Bridge, but it's a round-trip of about 13.0 miles. Allow ample time to paddle up and mostly float back down, and check the current flow rate against historical averages before engaging a trip here.

The clear and gorgeous river emerges wide and fairly fast from St. Marks Spring but then narrows and slows down a mile below the upwelling. High banks alternate with swampy shores. About a mile above Newport Bridge, watch on the west bank for the inflow of Newport Spring, once known as Brewer Sulphur Spring. Newport Spring is 0.3 mile up a run from the St. Marks River. The spring

was once the site of an 1800s spa. The remote resort advertised the spring's highly pungent sulfurous waters as a medical cure. A hotel, cabins, and a dance hall once graced the spring, now left to nature and occasional locals. Tides moderately influence current speed and water levels on this lower section of the St. Marks, sometimes exposing rocky shoals that can make paddling upstream a little more challenging.

It is 5.0 miles below the Newport Bridge to the confluence of the St. Marks and the Wakulla River. Motorboaters ply this stretch of waterway, making it less desirable for paddlers.

♦ DIRECTIONS To reach the put-in/take-out from the intersection of US 319 and Woodville Highway/FL 363 in Tallahassee, take FL 363 South 13.9 miles to US 98. Turn left on US 98 East and drive 2.5 miles, crossing the Newport Bridge over the Wakulla River; just past the bridge, turn left to access the boat launch at Newport Park.

♦ GAUGE Visual. This part of the St. Marks is fed by St. Marks Spring and is paddleable year-round. However, a relevant gauge is St. Marks River near Newport, Florida.

23   WACISSA RIVER

✧ **OVERVIEW** Modern-day paddlers in their plastic boats were long preceded by aboriginal Floridians plying dugout canoes in this waterway fed by a host of huge springs, most of which are accessible only by boat—the so-called land around these springs is more swamp than land. Most of the waterside terrain is part of the Aucilla Wildlife Management Area, hosting the real Florida where wildlife from bears to otters to wading birds thrives in deep remote forests in a wilderness where land and water are intertwined.

From Wacissa Springs, the Wacissa River flows wide for the first 5 miles then narrows. About 2 miles above Goose Pasture Recreation Area, the waterway becomes wide again and continues wide for another 0.5 mile. However, the river begins to flow off into swamps near Goose Pasture.

Beyond Goose Pasture, the Wacissa flows into the historic Slave Canal, built in the 1830s to link the Wacissa and Aucilla Rivers. This way, locals could ship cotton from the uplands to the Gulf of Mexico for trade. The two rivers merge just upstream of US 98. Here, the Aucilla River emerges from underground at Nutall Rise. From this point, the Aucilla continues its journey to the Gulf. The access at the US 98 bridge marks the end of the official state paddling trail and is also where most paddlers end their Wacissa adventure.

✧ **MAPS** Wacissa, Nutall Rise (USGS)

A   Wacissa Springs to Goose Pasture

Class	I
Length	10
Time	4
Gauge	Web, visual
Level	7.5
Gradient	2
Scenery	A

23A **DESCRIPTION** Wacissa Springs is a fun place to paddle, just exploring and not necessarily heading deep downriver beyond the 12 named springs scattered along the upper 3.0 miles of the river. Big Blue Spring, about a mile downriver flowing into the east bank, is of special note. The pool, popular with cave divers, stretches 120 feet across and is reputed to be nearly 50 feet deep.

Calico Landing is about 2.5 miles below the headspring on the west bank and makes for a good stopping spot; however, it is not recommended as an access, since it requires four-wheel drive. If you are on a there-and-back paddle from Wacissa Spring, Cedar Island—about 3.0 miles below the headspring—marks the end of the spring concentration and is a good place to turn around.

The current speeds as a chute near what is known as Wacissa Dam, where an old narrow-gauge railroad crossed the river. Downstream of the former rail line, low islands divide the river into multiple channels, not all of which are passable. If you get stopped, simply back up and choose another channel. Welaunee Landing, which also requires four-wheel drive vehicles, is about 8.0 miles downstream on the east bank via a side channel and could be a break spot.

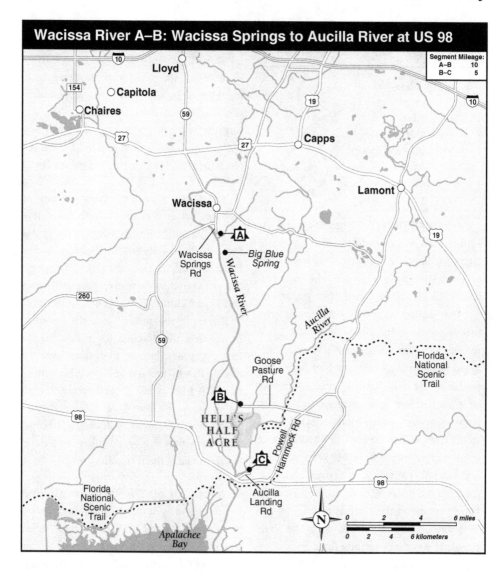

Wacissa River A–B: Wacissa Springs to Aucilla River at US 98

Segment Mileage:
A–B   10
B–C   5

Lloyd

Capitola

Chaires

Capps

Lamont

Wacissa

A

Wacissa Springs Rd

Big Blue Spring

Wacissa River

Aucilla River

Goose Pasture Rd

Florida National Scenic Trail

B

HELL'S HALF ACRE

Powell Hammock Rd

C

Florida National Scenic Trail

Aucilla Landing Rd

Apalachee Bay

0   2   4   6 miles
0   2   4   6 kilometers

◊ **SHUTTLE** To reach the take-out from the Newport Bridge over the Wakulla River, take US 98 East 15.7 miles, beyond the bridge over the Aucilla River. Turn left on Powell Hammock Road/County Road 680, heading northeast. After 4.3 miles, turn left (west) on Goose Pasture Road—watch for signs indicating GOOSE PASTURE RECREATION AREA—and follow it 2.8 miles to a dead end at the recreation area.

To reach the put-in from the Newport Bridge over the Wakulla River, take US 98 East 7.7 miles to the intersection with FL 59. Turn left (north) on FL 59 and follow it 13 miles to Wacissa Springs Road. Turn right (south) on Wacissa Springs Road and follow it about 0.5 mile until it dead-ends at a boat ramp.

◊ **GAUGE** Visual. The Wacissa is a spring-fed river and is floatable year-round.

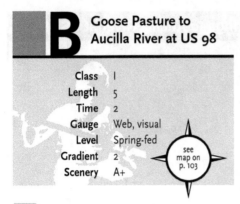

B Goose Pasture to
Aucilla River at US 98

Class	I
Length	5
Time	2
Gauge	Web, visual
Level	Spring-fed
Gradient	2
Scenery	A+

see
map on
p. 103

23B **DESCRIPTION** You might want to bring a GPS on this paddle, which has some tricky sections. On the upside, the important sections have been signed in the past and with any luck will be signed when you arrive.

After putting in at Goose Pasture, immediately paddle to the river's west side. Trace the current down a slender waterway bordered in swamps for about a half mile. The course opens to a channel about 25–30 feet wide for another mile. Begin watching for large cypresses spaced along the left bank as the river widens. There will be a couple of small sloughs on the right, but keep paddling and watch for signage such as paint blazes on the trees at the Slave Canal entrance. You will know you are on the correct track if you see limestone rocks along the banks of the Slave Canal. If you don't see any lined rock after a bit, turn around. Expect a few fallen trees and snags in the wildlife-rich area. Watch for overhead obstructions too. This route was purportedly found by aboriginals then dug out and widened by slaves.

Toward the end of the canal, the current slackens and the water deepens. Upon reaching the Aucilla, head upstream a few hundred yards to the boat landing on the river. The convergence of the Wacissa and Aucilla will be a welcome and easily recognized sight. But if you reach the US 98 bridge, you've gone too far.

SHUTTLE To reach the take-out from the Newport Bridge over the Wakulla River, take US 98 East 13.8 miles, just beyond the bridge over the Aucilla River. Turn left on Aucilla Landing Road, the first road east of the bridge, to reach a public boat ramp on your left, immediately past Hunter Haven Lane to your right.

To reach the put-in from the Newport Bridge over the Wakulla River, take US 98 East 15.7 miles, beyond the bridge over the Aucilla River. Turn left on Powell Hammock Road/CR 680, heading northeast. After 4.3 miles, turn left (west) on Goose Pasture Road—watch for signs indicating GOOSE PAS-TURE RECREATION AREA—and follow it 2.8 miles to a dead end at the recreation area.

GAUGE Visual. The Wacissa is a spring-fed river and is floatable year-round. A relevant gauge is Aucilla River near mouth near Nutall Rise, Florida (this gauge is at the confluence of the Aucilla and Wacissa). The gauge should average around 7.5 for the best paddling through the Slave Canal and the lower Wacissa.

OUTCROPS ARE COMMON ON THE WACISSA RIVER.

24   AUCILLA RIVER

◇ **OVERVIEW** The Aucilla originates just south of Boston, Georgia, and exhibits many characteristics as it heads south, sometimes posing as a lake, other times as a marsh, sometimes flowing aboveground, sometimes underground. Just north of US 27 in Florida, the Aucilla becomes what we paddlers imagine a river to be and proceeds about 30 miles until it goes underground again. The river ends its underground sojourn 5 miles south of its sink and quickly meets the waters of the Wacissa, flowing through a man-made canal on to the Gulf. Remains of two man-made dams on the upper section may provide a fine break-in whitewater paddle for novices. But where the Tallahassee Hills drop off the limestone karst, a stretch of real whitewater appears, dropping 8–10 feet over 30 yards: Big Rapid.

After a few more miles through jungle-esque hammock forest, the Aucilla goes underground. A majority of the riverside terrain is part of the Middle Aucilla Conservation Area, keeping the banks wild and natural. It is overseen by the Suwannee River Water Management District. The stretch of river described below is the official state paddling trail.

◇ **MAPS** LAMONT, LAMONT SOUTHEAST, NUTALL RISE (USGS)

Federal Road 1 to River Sink

Class	I
Length	24.5
Time	Varies
Gauge	Web
Level	45–51.9
Gradient	1.8
Scenery	A

24 DESCRIPTION The upper access off Federal Road 1, the preferred alternative to the US 19/US 27 access, adds 4.5 miles to the paddle. The stream is small and swift here. It is 4.5 miles from the put-in to the US 27 bridge. About 1 mile below US 27 are the remains of the first of two man-made dams. Constructed of native limestone, they have been washed away, resulting in fun shoals. Unlike most other dams, they were not excavated or reinforced in any way and are free of dangerous metal poking from concrete or hidden hazardous hydraulics. Novice paddlers usually navigate the shoals without difficulty, but if you're in doubt, they can easily be carried around.

This section of the river is primarily of the drop-and-pool nature, with stretches of slow water broken by rocky shoals and small drops. The high banks have typical hardwood forests; some swampy areas provide a contrast of cypress, magnolia, and titi. Camping areas are plentiful in the riverside woods. The Lanier Road access, also known as the Middle Aucilla access, is passed on the west bank 6.5 miles below US 27. You will reach an old railroad bridge and a rough access 1.5 miles before the County Road 257/CR 14 bridge. It is 12.5 miles from the US 27 bridge to the CR 257/CR 14 bridge.

Below CR 257/CR 14, high banks with copious limestone outcrops overlook a fairly swift current of coffee-colored water. Palms

Aucilla River: Federal Road 1 to River Sink

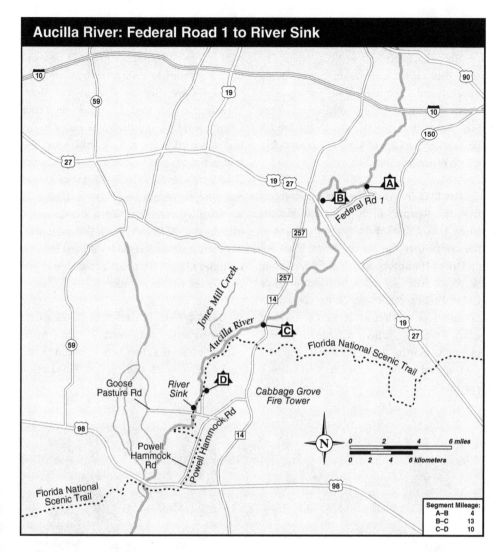

Segment Mileage:

A–B	4
B–C	13
C–D	10

and oaks stretch toward the stream. You will come to the initial rapid of this run about 2.0 miles downstream. Shoot a small, rocky shoal, then make a sharp right-hand bend as the current then speeds farther while curving sharply left. The twisting rapid runs for about 50 yards.

Ahead, Jones Mill Creek flows in from the west bank. This tributary tumbles down a limestone ledge upon meeting the Aucilla, creating a fine swimming locale. At 6.5 miles below CR 257/CR 14, you reach Big Rapid, which can be scouted by road access. The cataract drops 8 or so feet in a distance of 100 feet. Big Rapid is not something to take lightly. You will hear the roar of whitewater well upstream of Big Rapid, and if you didn't scout by vehicle, then pull over at the top of the rapid and scout from the left (east) bank where a path runs along the Aucilla. At normal flows, Big Rapid is run on the east side, whereas at higher water it can be run on the right or left. Smart paddlers will scout Big Rapid, considering the abundance of rocks along and in the cataract as well as the possibility of strainers getting stuck among the rocks. This makes it essential that the rapid be scouted prior to running.

More shoals occur below Big Rapid. The river continues downstream before going underground. The river emerges again at Nutall Rise and, with the confluence of the Slave Canal from the Wacissa just above US 98, flows to the Gulf of Mexico. Access below US 98 is limited.

✧ **SHUTTLE** To reach the lowermost access from the Newport Bridge over the Wakulla River, take US 98 East 15.7 miles, beyond the bridge over the Aucilla River. Turn left on Powell Hammock Road/CR 680, heading northeast. After 4.3 miles, turn left (west) on Goose Pasture Road—watch for signs indicating GOOSE PASTURE RECREATION AREA—and follow it west 0.9 mile to a graded road leading right (north). Turn right at the graded road, signed PUBLIC RIVER ACCESS, and follow it 1.0 mile to the river access on the left.

To reach the uppermost access, backtrack to Goose Pasture Road; then turn left (northeast) on Powell Hammock Road/CR 680 and drive 2.2 miles to a T-intersection, with the Cabbage Grove fire tower off to your right. Turn left (north) at this junction on Taylor County Road 14 and drive 4.6 miles to the first of two bridges over the Aucilla—past this bridge, the dirt road becomes Jefferson County Road 257. Keep forward on CR 257 and, after 7.9 miles, turn right (southeast) on US 19/US 27; drive 1.3 miles, crossing a second bridge over the Aucilla River to reach Federal Road 1. Turn left (east) on Federal Road 1 and follow it 2.3 miles to a left turn onto a graded road that reaches the river in 0.5 mile.

✧ **GAUGE** Web. The relevant USGS gauge is Aucilla River at Lamont. The minimum runnable level is 45 feet, with ideal conditions being between 48 and 50 feet. Flood stage is 54 feet.

THE SPRING-FED AUCILLA FLOWS CLEAR PAST GOOSE PASTURE.

25 ECONFINA RIVER OF TAYLOR COUNTY

✧ **OVERVIEW** The Econfina River of Taylor County, in the Big Bend, is not to be confused with Econfina Creek of Washington and Bay Counties (see page 48). This Econfina is lesser known as a paddling destination and is certainly underused as such. That may change, though, because the Econfina has been designated as a National Recreation Trail.

Born in the swamps of Pedro Bay east of Perry, the Econfina gathers water and becomes a stream in the far east of Taylor County. The official trail starts at the County Road 20 bridge, but fallen trees and submerged logs generally keep it impassable to all but the most strenuous paddlers until the US 98 bridge. Here, a boat ramp allows easy access to the beginning of a beautiful trip through the junglelike terrain of a swamp river. Part of the river is bordered by Suwannee River Water Management District lands, and downstream more river shore is state-park land, keeping the atmosphere remote.

✧ **MAPS** JOHNSON HAMMOCK, NUTALL RISE, SNIPE ISLAND (USGS)

US 98 to Econfina River State Park

Class	I
Length	6
Time	4
Gauge	Web
Level	140
Gradient	2
Scenery	A

25 DESCRIPTION This canopied black-water stream flows swiftly toward the Gulf at US 98. It is 20–30 feet wide here. Palms and oaks hang over the stream, while cypresses grow tall and stately along the river and in the swamps behind the banks. Palmetto covers the floor of the high ground beneath the trees. Lily pads thrive in still waters. Expect to pull over or around downed trees along the way. The banks are often low, and water drifts off into cypress sloughs. The main channel is easily discernible, though, and sometimes small, wooded islands force the stream to work around them.

Pass under a power line at 1 mile. Just downstream, look for an elevated logging tram crossing the swamp and the pilings of an old bridge on the river's edge. After many twists and turns, enter an area known as the Mill Pond. Here, the current slackens and waterweeds grow along the edge of a much wider stream. These waterweeds form the river channel. High ground here and there allows you to relax out of the boat.

Just below the Mill Pond, the Econfina narrows and resumes its fast-moving ways. Here are the concrete abutments of an old bridge that may be rebuilt. State-park property begins on river right. The swift water continues southwesterly and ends just beyond the Mossy Hammock Road bridge. Here, the Econfina broadens a bit and houses become more common, although public lands extend farther downstream. Tidal influences change the current's speed, but it is not long before you reach the state-park boat ramp on river right. It is a little more than 2.0 miles from here to the Gulf.

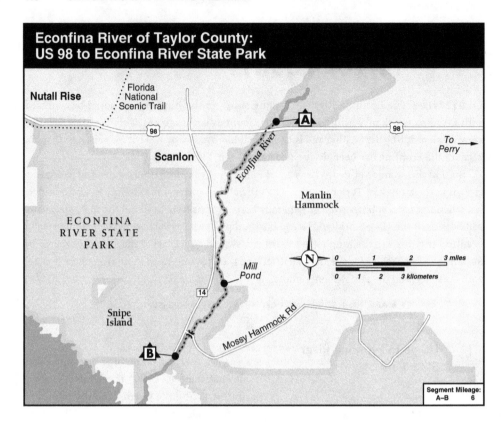

**Econfina River of Taylor County:
US 98 to Econfina River State Park**

Nutall Rise

Florida National Scenic Trail

Scanlon

Econfina River

Manlin Hammock

ECONFINA RIVER STATE PARK

Mill Pond

Snipe Island

Mossy Hammock Rd

To Perry

N

0   1   2   3 miles
0   1   2   3 kilometers

Segment Mileage:
A–B   6

◇ **SHUTTLE** To reach the take-out from the intersection of US 90 and US 19 in Perry, drive west on US 98 for 20.2 miles to Aucilla River Road/County Road 14. Turn left (south) on CR 14, which dead-ends at the Econfina River State Park boat launch, 6.1 miles ahead. A fee is required for this launch (see "Fees and Permits," page 6).

To access the put-in from the same intersection in Perry, take US 98 West 18.1 miles to the bridge over the Econfina River. A boat ramp is on the northeast side of the bridge.

◇ **GAUGE** Web. The USGS gauge is Econfina River near Perry, Florida. The minimum recommended runnable level is 140 cfs.

26 STEINHATCHEE RIVER

Once there was a legend that told of a river that went to hear a fountain sing. The song was so beautiful that the river decided to sing it to the ocean. All the way to the shores of the ocean the river sang. Soon, the mountains heard of the song that the river was singing and came from all over the land to listen. And because the song was so beautiful the mountains settled down and stayed to listen forever.

—ALGONQUIAN INDIAN LEGEND

⟡ OVERVIEW Often paddling enthusiasts will drive along, span a bridge over a waterway, and look down to see if the waterway has paddling potential. If you've traveled US 98 along the Big Bend, you've probably crossed the Steinhatchee River and wondered about its paddling potential. It is paddleable and is a state-designated paddling trail. Furthermore, it includes a "waterfall"—Steinhatchee Falls—over which you can paddle. But before you throw your boat onto your vehicle, be aware that the upper river, above US 98, flows into a sink and doesn't connect to the lower river. The upper river is scenic and is bordered by Suwannee River Water Management District (SRWMD) lands, as is much of the lower river, which becomes tidally influenced near the town of Steinhatchee.

⟡ MAPS CLARA, JENA, STEINHATCHEE (USGS)

Steinhatchee Falls to Mouth of Steinhatchee River

Class	I (II)
Length	7
Time	Varies
Gauge	Web
Level	Spring-fed
Gradient	1.2
Scenery	B–

26 DESCRIPTION The Steinhatchee River is fed by Steinhatchee Springs and drains Mallory Swamp. It flows south toward the Gulf before going underground just north of US 98, near the hamlet of Tennille, and reemerging 0.5 mile south. Here it stays aboveground the rest of the way to the salt water. Paddlers can put in at Steinhatchee Falls or at an access a mile or so above it. This way, you can run the falls or not. If you feel this limestone ledge that forms a 3-foot drop is too imposing, just start below it. This ledge was used by American Indians and early settlers as a river crossing—even Andrew Jackson used it during the Seminole Wars.

The first segment stays in SRWMD lands and offers a natural setting on either side of the blackwater. As you close in on the town of Steinhatchee, houses appear on the banks and the river becomes affected by the tides, which will affect the time it takes you to make it downriver.

There are many fish camps and landings in Steinhatchee. Intrepid paddlers will make it to the mouth of the river and a boat ramp, but the trip can be shortened by using an upstream fish camp or marina of your choosing as an ending point. An outfitter offering shuttles and boat rentals is located on the river at US 98, but you must reserve your rental or shuttle at least 24 hours in advance. It is 7.0 miles from the falls to the river mouth.

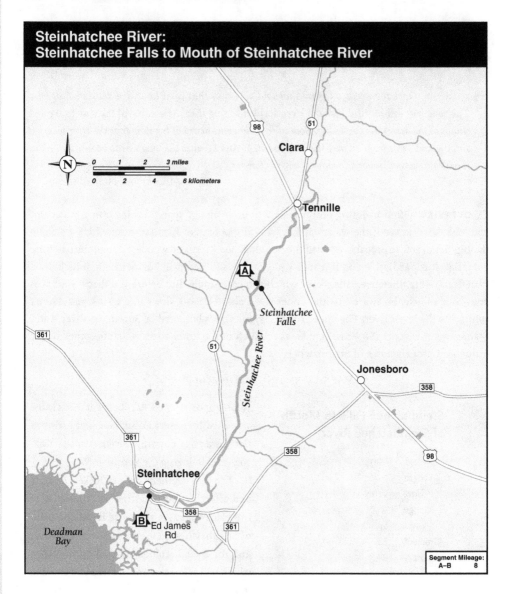

Steinhatchee River: Steinhatchee Falls to Mouth of Steinhatchee River

⟨⟩ SHUTTLE To reach the take-out from the intersection of US 90 and US 19 Perry, take US 19/US 98/US 27A South 28.3 miles to FL 51 in Tennille. Turn right (south) on FL 51 and drive 9.1 miles to the intersection of Riverside Drive/FL 51 and 10th Street East in Steinhatchee. Turn left (south) on 10th Street to cross the bridge over the Steinhatchee River. In 0.3 mile, take your first right onto County Road 358 to reach the take-out ramp at the mouth of the river, 0.7 mile ahead.

To reach the take-out from the same intersection in Perry, take US 19/US 98/US 27A South 28.3 miles to FL 51 in Tennille. Turn right (south) on FL 51 and, in 1.8 miles, look for a left turn and a sign indicating STEINHATCHEE FALLS. Follow this road and veer right as it splits to reach the falls in 1.1 miles (the left split leads to the access above the falls).

◇ **GAUGE** Web. The USGS gauge that is helpful for determining river levels for any given period of time is Steinhatchee near Cross City, Florida.

A CALM DAY ON THE STEINHATCHEE

The Northern Peninsula

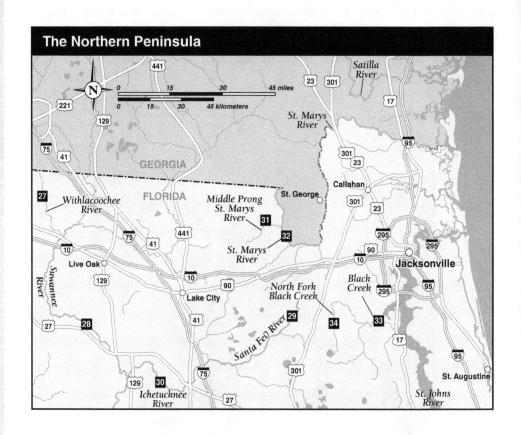

27 WITHLACOOCHEE RIVER (NORTH)

◆ **OVERVIEW** This is one of two rivers named Withlacoochee in Florida; they're commonly referred to using both their shared name and their locations. A large and significant tributary of the Suwannee, this northern Withlacoochee River is a state-designated paddling trail with Georgia beginnings. It drains lands northwest of Valdosta and meanders south for 70 miles to enter the Sunshine State.

Not surprisingly, the Withlacoochee resembles its mother stream, the Suwannee: limestone outcroppings border high banks where coffee-colored waters flow steadily past flanks of tupelo and cypress trees, broken by occasional shoals that can liven up a paddle. These rocky shoals leave the Withlacoochee to smaller boats. However, you may see local anglers vying for bass, bream, and catfish from johnboats.

The Withlacoochee also mimics the Suwannee with clear and alluring springs along its banks. Blue Springs is a good example. Located near FL 6, this spring served aboriginal Floridians as well as early Florida settlers as a source of drinking water. It is now the main attraction of Madison Blue Springs State Park. The preserve protects the spring and has a paddler launch. Yet another spring called Suwannacoochee—appropriately melding the names of the Suwannee and the Withlacoochee—is located on the west side of the "With" just above its confluence with the Suwannee. A public swimming pool was once fed by this spring. You can even see what's left of the pool by the river.

The Withlacoochee does not enjoy the wealth of sandbars found on the upper Suwannee; therefore, paddling campers have to look harder for campsites—that is, get out of the boat and physically look—and that includes along the high riverbanks where live oaks, pines, magnolia, and birches are found.

A significant yet noncontiguous portion of the banks lies within Twin Rivers State Forest. Look for boundary markers and camp within these public lands.

◆ **MAPS** Suwannee River WMD Ramps and Launches map; Clayattville (Georgia), Pinetta, Octahatchee, Ellaville (Florida) (USGS)

Georgia State Line to Suwannee River State Park

Class	I–I+
Length	28
Time	Varies
Gauge	Web
Level	N/A
Gradient	1.5
Scenery	B

27 **DESCRIPTION** There happens to be a boat ramp nearly exactly on the Florida–Georgia line, and this County Road 145 boat launch marks the beginning of the designated Florida state paddling trail. That being said, the Withlacoochee is paddleable in the Peach State from its confluence with the Little River down to the Florida border. Paddlers who like smaller waterways could start even farther up at the GA 37 bridge—if the rain has been falling.

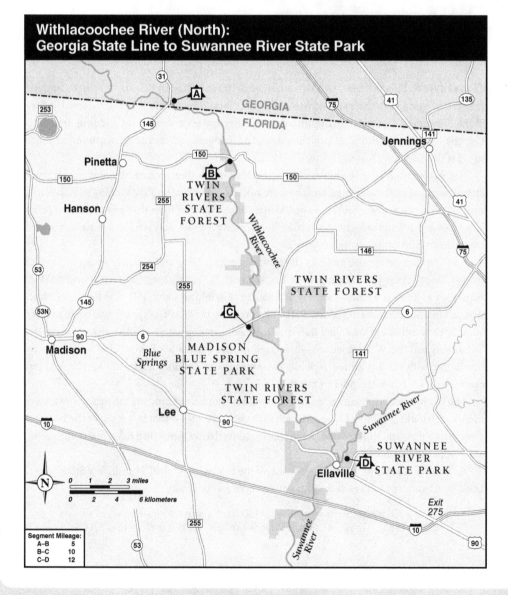

Withlacoochee River (North): Georgia State Line to Suwannee River State Park

At the state line, the Withlacoochee stretches about 100 feet across and flows steadily. It soon shows off a few small shoals that break in the boater. It is 5.0 miles from the state line put-in to CR 150. Portions of the state forest stretch above and below CR 150. Where Twin Rivers State Forest lands are absent, you will see occasional houses and camps along the riverbanks below CR 150. Around 7.0 miles downstream of CR 150, watch for a 10- to 12-foot opening where water goes rushing out of the river into the high banks on the Withlacoochee's east side, flows for 80 yards, and then disappears—yet one more piece of evidence of the intricate plumbing system that lies underneath the limestone strata of Florida. It is 11.0 miles from CR 150 to FL 6 and Madison Blue Springs State Park.

Just below FL 6, reach Blue Springs and Madison Blue Springs State Park. The upwelling spans 25 feet in diameter and 25 feet in depth over a limestone-and-sand bottom. A limestone bank rises on the spring's south side. Blue Springs has a canoe/kayak launch, but neither overnight parking nor camping is allowed. Below FL 6, shoals are fewer and the current slackens, yet the riverside banks rise, exposing fascinating limestone strata in a multiplicity of forms. Paddlers working close to the banks will spot several unnamed springs adding their flow to the Withlacoochee, especially at lower flows.

Pass under the CR 141 bridge about a mile before meeting the Suwannee River (no access). Watch the right bank for concrete-enclosed Suwannacoochee Spring, stretching 20 feet across. After making the confluence with the Suwannee River, paddlers must muster their energy, then turn north up the Suwannee to paddle upstream a little ways to the Suwannee River State Park boat ramp. It is 12.0 miles from FL 6 to the state park.

◇ **SHUTTLE** To reach the lowest take-out from the intersection of FL 53 and US 90 in Madison, travel 16.0 miles east on US 90 to the bridge across the Suwannee River. Cross the river and continue 0.8 mile to the first road to the left. This is the entrance to Suwannee River State Park. An entrance fee applies (see "Fees and Permits," page 6).

To reach the uppermost put-in from the same intersection in Madison, drive four blocks north on Duval Street/FL 53 to Livingston Street/FL 145, and turn right. Travel northeast on FL 145 for 13.6 miles to the bridge across the Withlacoochee, just over the state line in Georgia. A boat ramp is on the northwest side of the bridge.

◇ **GAUGE** Web. The USGS gauge is Withlacoochee River near Pinetta, Florida. The gauge should read at least 54 feet for best paddling conditions.

28   SUWANNEE RIVER

◆ **OVERVIEW** The Suwannee River is Florida's most notable paddling waterway. Neither grandiose in size, nor in length, nor in riverside towns, it is the epitome of a true Southern waterway. Spelled a variety of ways, the name *Suwannee* is common throughout the southeastern United States, but Florida's Suwannee is synonymous with Dixie and the Old South.

This Sunshine State waterway is inarguably Florida's most famed and popular paddling destination, despite its Georgia origins. Even the most casual paddler knows about the Suwannee River. Made famous in folklore by Stephen Foster's classic song "Old Folks at Home" ("Way down upon the Swanee River . . ."), it flows some 235 miles—206 of those in the Sunshine State—before emptying into the Gulf of Mexico at the town of Suwannee.

The Suwannee is one of the finest touring rivers around and a first-rate adventure when paddled in its entirety. Mostly flatwater, it has one recommended portage at Big Shoals via a marked portage trail. None of the other shoals are sufficiently challenging to cause a problem. Boat ramps and paddler launches are frequent along the river, allowing trips of varied lengths. Limited supply runs can be made at White Springs, Branford, and Fanning Springs—all river towns—and private and public campgrounds.

The Suwannee originates in the also-renowned Okefenokee Swamp. The winding watercourse emerges from the Okefenokee just above Fargo, Georgia, then loops and curves across the Florida peninsula before discharging into the Gulf of Mexico. The uppermost river corridor contains sandy banks, rocky shoals, and a wealth of singing waterfalls created where tributaries drop into the Suwannee. Elsewhere, wooded shoreline swamps provide overflow basins when the waters get high. Regal cypress and squat trunked tupelo trees rise in the river and along the banks, many of which are protected as public lands: state parks, water-conservation lands, easements, and other public entities. Access is as plentiful as the wildlife.

The upper river has fewer feeders, namely the Withlacoochee River (North), the Alapaha River, and a few creeks, resulting in a slow and lazy current except where shoals are found along white limestone banks and Spanish moss–draped trees. About 6.0 miles above White Springs, paddlers will encounter Big Shoals, the biggest rapid in Florida, and it is big—dropping 8–10 feet! Paddlers will then find the first jewels in the dazzling crown of the Suwannee River: the fantastic array of springs that stretches down the waterway nearly to the Gulf. These springs vary in size and volume. Many are first-magnitude, and the collective flow of these upwellings adds greatly to the size and volume of the river.

The mighty Suwannee, with a personality all its own, a personality that draws in paddlers from first-timers to those who visit no other river, changes faces as water levels change. At high water, fast current and lively shoals make river runs fun but turn Big Shoals into a honeycolored foaming, frothing, brawling roar of whitewater. However, low water exposes another face where white sandbars and beige dripping limestone walls reflect in still water, a river where springs, caves, and cities of cypress knees line rising banks.

Annual patterns find the Suwannee high during the late winter and spring then lowering during the summer and fall. Many paddlers consider fall to be the Suwannee's finest hour: low water exposing sandbars, pleasant warm days and cool nights, fewer bugs, and fall's cornucopia reflecting on the still waters.

The often-protected shoreline harbors the wealth of flora and fauna indigenous to North Florida. You will see cypress and gum trees by the thousands, big loblolly pines, fragrant Southern magnolias, colorful red maples, prickly American hollies, straight tulip trees, brushy willows, and swaying river birches. Paddlers will spot deer and alligators, maybe an otter, as well as beavers, raccoons, and perhaps an armadillo on higher ground. Songbirds, raptors, and waterfowl each find their niche on the wild corridor that is the Suwannee River.

Downstream from Suwannee River State Park, the river broadens and becomes more appealing to motorboats; the bigger the Suwannee gets downstream, the larger and more powerful the boats you may encounter. Intermittent enclaves of river houses along the waterway have docks and boats, adding to the traffic. However, a wealth of public lands, including state forests, state parks, Lower Suwannee National Wildlife Refuge, along with the myriad tracts acquired by the Suwannee River Water Management District (SRWMD) throughout the Suwannee River Valley, keep the river wild in appearance if not in fact. The SRWMD, which covers 15 counties, has acquired more than 50,000 acres on the Suwannee, including 70% of the river frontage in the upper river basin, and has developed the Suwannee River Wilderness Trail, which has become a series of river camps—cabins, chickees, and campsites along the river. For specifics on campsites and reservations, call 800-868-9914 or visit suwanneeriver.com.

LUXURIANT SANDBARS OFTEN BORDER THE SUWANNEE RIVER.

Camping is allowed on SRWMD lands but is strictly prohibited within the wildlife refuge, making campsites scarce on the lowermost river near the town of Suwannee. SRWMD has an excellent handout, obtainable online, that lists all the boat ramps and canoe launches on the Suwannee that paddlers will find very helpful. Even better is the *Suwannee River Wilderness Trail Paddling Guide,* which has mile-by-mile river details and shows public lands for canoe and kayak campers.

Among other adventures on the Suwannee, I have paddled this river from top to bottom in one trip, and I proclaim it as the finest touring river in the state and a first-rate adventure when floated in its entirety. Moreover, the Suwannee River is easy, leisurely paddling for even a novice paddler. Big Shoals can be easily scouted and portaged if necessary, and none of the other shoals are sufficiently challenging to cause a problem. Boat ramps and paddler launches are frequent along the river, allowing trips of varied lengths.

There—now it's up to you to create your own Suwannee River adventure.

⟡ **MAPS** SUWANNEE RIVER WMD RAMPS AND LAUNCHES MAP; FARGO, NEEDMORE (GEORGIA), FARGO SOUTHWEST, BENTON, WHITE SPRINGS EAST, LIVE OAK EAST, HILLCOAT, FORT UNION, ELLAVILLE, FALMOUTH, MADISON SOUTHEAST, DOWLING PARK, DAY, MAYO, MAYO SOUTHEAST, O'BRIEN, BRANFORD, HATCHBEND, WANNEE, FANNING SPRINGS, MANATEE SPRINGS, VISTA, EAST PASS, SUWANNEE (FLORIDA) (USGS)

A Fargo, GA, to County Road 6

Class	I (II)
Length	22
Time	Varies
Gauge	Web
Level	Spring-fed
Gradient	1.2
Scenery	B–

28A **DESCRIPTION** At Fargo, the Suwannee River has flowed 17.0 miles from Billy's Lake in the Okefenokee Swamp and stretches 60–70 feet wide at low water. The state of Georgia has an interpretive center with a boat ramp at the bridge crossing in Fargo. This makes a first-rate access, but determined paddlers can start in the Okefenokee or just outside its border at a private landing off GA 177. The banks are 2–5 feet high, sandy, and interspersed with large, swampy overflow areas. Campers have to look hard for a campsite, usually in woods above the river as opposed to sandbars, which are small and limited in these parts. Don't expect much in the way of current, but Cypress Creek enters from the east and Suwannacoochee Creek from the west a few miles below Fargo, adding volume.

Enter Florida at 12.0 miles. The boundary is roughly marked by Toms Creek. SRWMD lands border much of the river once you're in Florida. Pass primitive Roline Launch a couple of miles into Florida and Turner Bridge ramp about 4.0 miles downstream. Both are on the west bank. Run a small shoal just above the CR 6 bridge.

⟡ **SHUTTLE** To reach the take-out from the intersection of US 441 and US 90 in Lake City, Florida, drive north 23.4 miles on US 441/FL 47 to Northwest Bay Creek Street/CR 6. Turn left on CR 6 and follow it 2.8 miles to the bridge over the Suwannee River.

To reach the uppermost put-in, head to Fargo, Georgia, 38.0 miles north of Lake City and 9.1 miles north of the Florida–Georgia state line, at the intersection of US 441 and GA 94. The access is at the Suwannee River Visitor Center, which has a boat ramp.

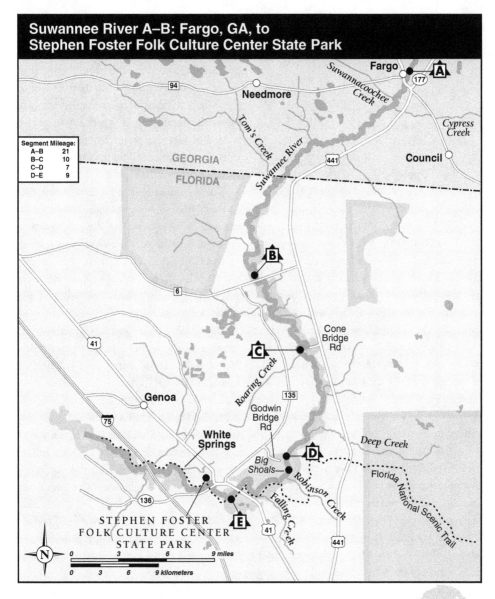

Suwannee River A–B: Fargo, GA, to Stephen Foster Folk Culture Center State Park

Fargo

Needmore

94

Suwannacoochee Creek

Tom's Creek

Suwannee River

Cypress Creek

Council

441

177

A

Segment Mileage:	
A–B	21
B–C	10
C–D	7
D–E	9

GEORGIA

FLORIDA

B

6

Cone Bridge Rd

41

C

Roaring Creek

Genoa

75

135

Godwin Bridge Rd

White Springs

Deep Creek

Big Shoals

D

Robinson Creek

Florida National Scenic Trail

136

STEPHEN FOSTER FOLK CULTURE CENTER STATE PARK

Falling Creek

E

41

441

N

| 0 | 3 | 6 | 9 miles |
| 0 | 3 | 6 | 9 kilometers |

◇ **GAUGE** Web. The USGS gauge is Suwannee River at White Springs, Florida. It should read between 51.6 and 65 feet for the best paddling.

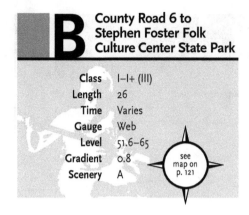

B County Road 6 to Stephen Foster Folk Culture Center State Park

Class	I–I+ (III)
Length	26
Time	Varies
Gauge	Web
Level	51.6–65
Gradient	0.8
Scenery	A

see map on p. 121

28B **DESCRIPTION** You will see a few houses near CR 6, but much of the right bank is SRWMD lands, where steep banks make finding campsites more challenging. Limestone outcrops can be found in the steep segments while tupelo and cypress line the river elsewhere. As the banks rise, vegetation changes to live oaks and pines, creating a scenic effect, accentuated by the dark tannic waters of the Suwannee, rendered black in the Okefenokee Swamp. It is 10.0 miles from CR 6 to Cone Bridge Road.

High banks and lazy current continue below the Cone Bridge Road access, yet the relaxed pace allows you to soak in the natural beauty of the river corridor. Roaring Creek enters the river from the west just below Cone Bridge Road. Deep Creek, a paddleable stream, flows in from the east about 3.0 miles above Big Shoals. This clean, wild tributary drains a significant portion of the Osceola National Forest.

Warning signs about Big Shoals are found well above the rapids. The roar is unmistakable. Scout Big Shoals from the left bank, the same side of the river as the portage trail. At low to normal water levels, run Big Shoals against the west bank. At higher levels, the rapids become stronger and will have standing waves 2–3 feet high when really rocking.

The rapid consists of a double drop, with the upper drop having a curl coming in from each side so that it has to be run exactly in the middle to keep the boat dry. Thirty yards below the upper drop is another drop of 4 feet with a standing wave at the bottom. Just below the final drop is a rock, strategically located at just the point that paddlers have started congratulating themselves on having successfully run the rapids.

The strenuousness of Big Shoals depends on water volume. Scout it before you run it. If in doubt about your skill or the turbulence of the water, use the portage. Wise campers will unload their gear and tote their stuff around Big Shoals. Wear your personal flotation device. Large, sharp limestone boulders are hidden in this rapid.

Big Shoals Public Land has a canoe/kayak access, picnic area, and hiking and mountain-biking trails. Those wishing to paddle Big Shoals use the old Godwin Bridge access, then head down to the US 41 bridge access. Interestingly, the Florida Trail saddles alongside the Suwannee at Big Shoals and traces the waterway downstream for almost 60 river miles. View an alluring waterfall on the east bank where Robinson Creek enters the Suwannee just below Big Shoals. Robinson Creek also flows forth from the Osceola National Forest. Also, look for Bell Springs just downstream from Robinson Creek. It is the most-northern named spring on the Suwannee.

Downriver from Big Shoals, the river slows again. However, Little Shoals, a series of rocky ledges, rises a mile or so upstream from White Springs and noisily speeds you downstream. Falling Creek enters from the east at Little Shoals. It is 14.0 miles from Cone Bridge Road to the US 41 bridge.

At US 41, the river reaches the town of White Springs and the official beginning of the Suwannee River Wilderness Trail, along with a boat ramp. Just below the FL 136 bridge, you will find the spring-house for what used to be called White Sulphur Springs, around which a series of spas and sanatoriums had their heyday until a 1911 fire. From there on, the spas and the town declined until outdoor-related tourism uplifted the community. The spring is enclosed by the concrete foundations of the former bathhouse.

Less than a mile downstream, paddlers reach Stephen Foster Folk Culture Center State Park—a mouthful of a name. Nevertheless, its facilities are many: a museum, a carillon tower, picnic tables, restrooms, walking trails, and camping facilities. It is a little more than 2.0 miles from the US 41 bridge down to the boat launch at Stephen Foster Folk Culture Center State Park.

◇ **SHUTTLE** The lowermost take-out is just west of White Springs, off US 41, at Stephen Foster Folk Culture Center State Park.

From Exit 439 off I-75, take FL 136 east for 3.1 miles; turn left at Spring Street/US 41 and keep straight (west) at the next intersection to enter the park. An entrance fee applies (see "Fees and Permits," page 6). The boat launch is about a mile west of the park entrance, just south of the camper-cabin loop.

To reach the put-in from White Springs, follow the directions above to Spring Street/US 41, but turn right instead of left. Head east five blocks (0.5 mile) on US 41 and turn left (north) on Suwanee Street/CR 135. Go two blocks and bear right to stay on CR 135, heading east, then north. After 14.6 miles, turn right on Northwest Bay Creek Street/CR 6 and follow it 1.1 miles east to the bridge over the Suwannee River.

◇ **GAUGE** Web. The USGS gauge is Suwannee River at White Springs, Florida. It should read between 51.6 and 65 feet for the best paddling.

C Stephen Foster Folk Culture Center State Park to Suwannee River State Park

Class	I
Length	40
Time	Varies
Gauge	Web
Level	51.6–65
Gradient	0.7
Scenery	A

28C **DESCRIPTION** Varied access points make this section either a great overnight-camping endeavor or good for several day paddles. At White Springs, the river turns and flows to the west. The Florida Trail begins to follow the north bank of the Suwannee from White Springs and will continue to do so to

Suwannee River State Park, adding the possibility of a self-shuttle. Below White Springs, the high limestone banks continue with only an occasional small sandbar.

Five miles downriver and within sight of I-75, Swift Creek enters from the north. It is well named, rushing through a rocky canyon into the river. I-75, 8.0 miles downriver, offers no access to the river. It marks the beginning of an area of lower banks and beautiful sandbars. It is less than 2.0 miles from I-75 to Woods Ferry River Camp, one of the Suwannee River Wilderness Trail camps.

SRWMD public lands continue on much of the river between US 41 and US 129. Limestone walls are still found along the river, but if one side of the river is high, the other side will be low. Occasionally, vertical limestone banks on both sides create a castlelike corridor

Suwannee River C–E:
Stephen Foster Folk Culture Center State Park to Branford

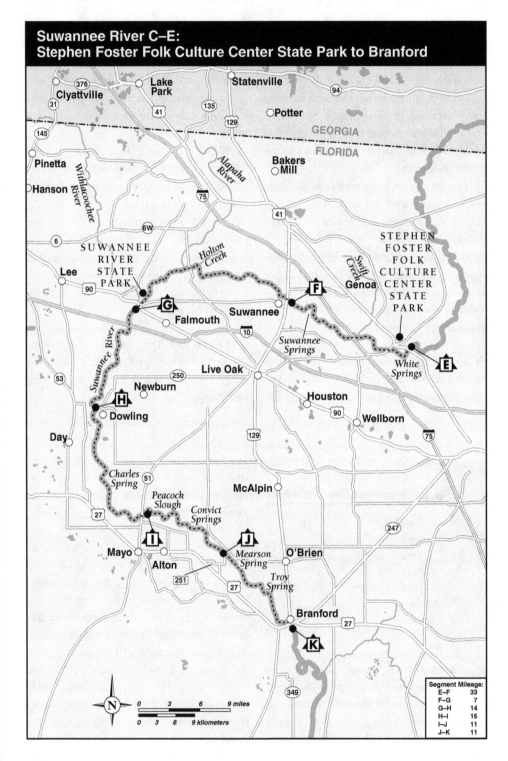

Segment Mileage:

E–F	33
F–G	7
G–H	14
H–I	15
I–J	11
J–K	11

of beauty. Upon closer examination, paddlers will find small caves and grottoes worn into the limestone. Aquatic sounds echo from these walls as you paddle along. Other times you may hear dripping water deep in the caves.

As you float within 3.0 miles of Suwannee Springs, look for a small waterfall amid a residential community on the north bank. The scenery is classic Suwannee River, with its sandbars, sweeping limestone-walled bends, and live oaks draped in Spanish moss, all through which flows the coffee-colored waters of the Suwannee.

It is 18.0 miles from Stephen Foster Folk Culture Center State Park to Suwannee Springs and the US 129 bridge. Suwannee Springs exudes Old Florida. It came to be in the 1830s, and by the 1850s a fancy resort hotel was built around the springs. Owners even peddled bottled water from this upwelling. All we see today are the rock retaining wall separating Suwannee Springs from the Suwannee River, a few houses, and the abandoned (and current) US 129 bridge. At least six individual springs comprise the Suwannee Springs, four of them outside the wall that contains the main spring. Swimmers, sunbathers, and paddlers flock here during the summertime to enjoy the beach at a nearby bend.

The Spirit of the Suwannee campground and music venue occupies the south bank below US 129; then you pass abandoned

PHOTOGRAPHING SUWANNEE SPRINGS

railroad bridge pilings. Mill Creek flows in the north bank 3.5 miles downstream from the current US 129 bridge. Admire the high limestone banks, as they are progressively lessening. The Suwannee has more straight sections, steep banks, and fewer sandbars. Campers should scout public lands for campsites up high banks in the woods.

Holton Creek River Camp is 9.0 miles below the US 129 Bridge, about 1.5 miles upstream of Holton Creek's north bank entrance to the Suwannee River. In turn, Holton Creek is about 4.0 miles upstream from the Suwannee's confluence with the Alapaha River. Holton Creek emerges from Holton Spring, a first-magnitude upwelling 1 mile up the spring run from the Suwannee River. Just before the CR 249 bridge, reach Alapaha Rise, the dark-colored true emergence of the Alapaha River. Even though the riverbed mouth of the Alapaha is a half mile downstream, this riverbed is often dry, since the Alapaha's flow has disappeared in numerous holes in the riverbed upstream.

Underground plumbing aside, you pass under the CR 249 bridge, then reach Gibson Park, a Hamilton County recreation area with a boat ramp, picnic site, and campground. It is 15.0 miles from US 129 to the Alapaha. Despite the irregular inflow contributions of the Alapaha River, the Suwannee widens even more. The boundaries of Suwannee River State Park begin on the west side of the river 2.0 miles downstream of the Alapaha River mouth. Pass

the CR 141 boat ramp 2.5 miles downstream and the main state park area 2.5 miles down from the CR 141 boat ramp. The state park offers a boat ramp, hiking trails, campsites, cabins, water, and electricity. The confluence with the Withlacoochee River is just downstream from the state park. It is 8.0 miles from the Alapaha to Suwannee River State Park.

◇ **SHUTTLE** To reach the lowermost takeout in this section from the intersection of US 129 and US 90 in Live Oak, head west on US 90 for 12.2 miles; then turn right (north) on Stagecoach Road to enter Suwannee River State Park. An entrance fee applies (see "Fees and Permits," page 6). In 0.6 mile, the main park road curves right, then left, past the campground on your right, to dead-end at the boat launch.

The uppermost put-in is just west of White Springs, off US 41, at Stephen Foster Folk Culture Center State Park. From Exit 439 off I-75, take FL 136 east for 3.1 miles; turn left at Spring Street/US 41 and keep straight (west) at the next intersection to enter the park. An entrance fee applies (see "Fees and Permits," page 6). The boat launch is about a mile west of the park entrance, just south of the camper-cabin loop.

◇ **GAUGE** Web. The USGS gauge is Suwannee River at White Springs, Florida. It should read between 51.6 and 65 feet for the best paddling.

D Suwannee River SP to FL 51

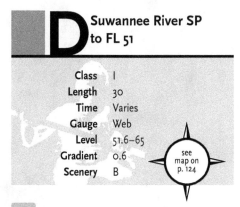

Class	I
Length	30
Time	Varies
Gauge	Web
Level	51.6–65
Gradient	0.6
Scenery	B

see map on p. 124

28D DESCRIPTION Downstream from its confluence with the Withlacoochee, the Suwannee widens to 150 feet before narrowing again. Occasional shoals cross the river, depending on water levels. Twin Rivers State Forest occupies the northwest bank. Pass under US 90 just downstream of the state park, then I-10 at 3.0 miles. Anderson Spring, just below I-10 on the east bank of the river, is a shallow pool about 50 feet in diameter with an often-dry 150-foot run to the Suwannee. Live oaks line the Suwannee's sandy banks, occasionally broken by limestone walls where nameless springs boil up. Cypress trees decline in number and sandbars are fewer, often covered with grasses. Reach the town of Dowling Park after 14.0 miles. Dowling Park River Camp is across the river from the Advent Christian Village in the town of Dowling Park. The Dowling Park boat ramp is at the CR 250 bridge just below the river camp.

Houses border the river, save for occasional SRWMD lands, which are marked. Pass the Sims ramp a little less than 2.0 miles downstream on the west bank, then the Christian Tract launch about a mile farther down. Reach Charles Spring about 6.0 miles below the CR 250 bridge. Here, translucent, sky-blue pools are divided by a small limestone bridge.

Charles Spring flows down a short run into the Suwannee River. A pair of boat ramps are located nearby on either side of the river. Allen Mill Pond Spring Run enters a mile farther on the west bank. Multiple spring vents emerge then flow about a half mile to the river. This is part of Lafayette Blue Springs State Park.

Reach Blue Springs of Lafayette Blue Springs State Park at 25.0 miles. It offers a boat ramp, cabins, and a walk-in tent campground accessible from the water. Perry Spring emerges from the south bank 3.0 miles below Lafayette Blue Springs State Park. A small spring pool makes a short run before emptying into the Suwannee.

Take out at the public boat ramp about 2.0 miles farther on the right, just after the Hal W. Adams (FL 51) Bridge.

⟡ SHUTTLE To reach the take-out from the intersection of US 129 and US 90 in Live Oak, head south on Ohio Avenue/US 129 and, in 0.5 mile, turn right (west) on 11th Street Southwest/FL 51. Drive six blocks and bear left around the traffic circle; then turn left at the SOUTH SR 51 sign, heading southwest. After 17.5 miles, reach the Hal W. Adams Bridge over the Suwannee River; cross the bridge and take the first left to reach the Hal Adams Bridge public boat ramp, on the south bank.

To reach the put-in from the same intersection in Live Oak, head west on US 90 for 12.2 miles; then turn right (north) on Stagecoach Road to enter Suwannee River State Park. An entrance fee applies (see "Fees and Permits," page 6). In 0.6 mile, the main park road curves right, then left, past the campground on your right, to dead-end at the boat launch.

⟡ GAUGE Web. The USGS gauge is Suwannee River at White Springs, Florida. It should read between 51.6 and 65 feet for the best paddling.

A TRIBUTARY CREATES A SMALL WATERFALL ON THE SUWANNEE.

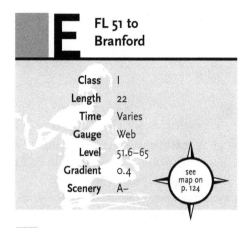

E

FL 51 to Branford

Class	I
Length	22
Time	Varies
Gauge	Web
Level	51.6–65
Gradient	0.4
Scenery	A–

see map on p. 124

28E **DESCRIPTION** The land is lower here, resulting in more pressure on the underlying limestone, making the aquifer more likely to break through, creating springs. Pass Telford Spring, less than 1 mile east of FL 51 on the east bank. Look for a small, clear pool with a run of 100 feet to the Suwannee. Houses stand directly across the river, and a boat ramp is just downstream. Peacock Slough River Camp stands on the north bank 2.5 miles down from FL 51.

Running Springs, 4.0 miles downstream of FL 51, is privately owned and fenced. An old iron bridge appears just below Running Springs. This former railroad bridge has a large cylindrical pylon in the center. Between the pylon and the metal span are wheels. Back when the bridge was functional, these wheels would allow the entire span to pivot from its usual location crossing the river to run parallel with the watercourse, allowing paddle wheelers with tall smokestacks to pass.

Pass the Hardenbergh ramp on river right at 5.0 miles. Convict Springs, at 6.0 miles, has a privately owned campground nearby. The spring vent, enclosed with a concrete wall, is in the northern end of a 20-by-50-foot teardrop-shaped pool.

Navigate between a few narrow wooded islands abutted by mild but perceptible shoals that save a few strokes of the paddle. Royal

Spring is 2.0 miles below Convict Springs. Royal Spring has a 100- by 200-foot-wide pool that is now a Suwannee County park with a boat ramp. Pass the lesser-used Fort Macomb boat ramp on river right at 11.0 miles.

Mearson Spring, at 12.0 miles, discharges about 80 feet into the Suwannee from a 25-by-50-foot pool bordered by high banks. SRWMD lands are more common on the last half of this section. Adams Tract River Camp stands at 13.0 miles. Troy Spring, now protected as a state park, enters at 17.0 miles. This first-magnitude spring emits 66 million gallons of water daily. Visible in its depths is the *Madison,* a Confederate supply ship that was intentionally run aground to keep it from falling into Union hands. The hull of this steamboat points toward the head of the spring. A boat dock makes stopping easy.

Little River Springs, at 19.0 miles, makes a 150-foot spring run, and its mouth is bordered by beaches. The vent is the entrance to a cave system of which more than 6,000 feet of underwater passages have been mapped. A boat ramp enters the river here. Branford Springs is southeast of the junction of US 27 and US 129 at the town of Branford. Part of Ivey Memorial Park, Branford Springs pumps 6.8 million gallons daily into the Suwannee.

✧ SHUTTLE To reach the take-out from the intersection of US 129 and US 90 in Live Oak, drive south on US 129 for 24.7 miles to Branford and US 27. Turn right on US 27 and, after one block, turn left into Ivey Memorial Park, on the east side of the river. The boat launch is on your right, just before the parking lot.

To reach the put-in from the intersection of US 129 and US 27 in Branford, head west across the river on US 27. After 17.5 miles, turn right (north) on FL 51 in Mayo. Drive 3.1 miles farther and, just before the Hal W. Adams Bridge, turn right to reach the Hal

Adams Bridge public boat ramp, on the south bank of the Suwannee. Note that the ramp is quite steep, so you'll have to carry, cart, or trailer your craft to put in.

⟡ **GAUGE** Web. The USGS gauge is Suwannee River at White Springs, Florida. It should read between 51.6 and 65 feet for the best paddling.

≈≈

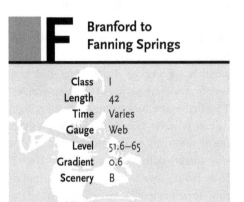

F Branford to Fanning Springs

Class	I
Length	42
Time	Varies
Gauge	Web
Level	51.6–65
Gradient	0.6
Scenery	B

28F **DESCRIPTION** Branford Springs is a popular cave-diving area. Below Branford Springs, pass along some SRWMD lands, where there are campsites aplenty, interspersed with houses. Limestone banks become still more sporadic below Branford. On higher ground are live oaks and pine. Low-slung humps of willow, river birch, and cypress line the river. Behind many of these humps are extensive swamps that fill when summer's thunderstorms drift over the Suwannee River valley.

PHOTOGRAPHING AN ALLIGATOR NEAR THE SUWANNEE'S CONFLUENCE WITH THE SANTA FE RIVER

Suwannee River F–G: Branford to Gulf of Mexico

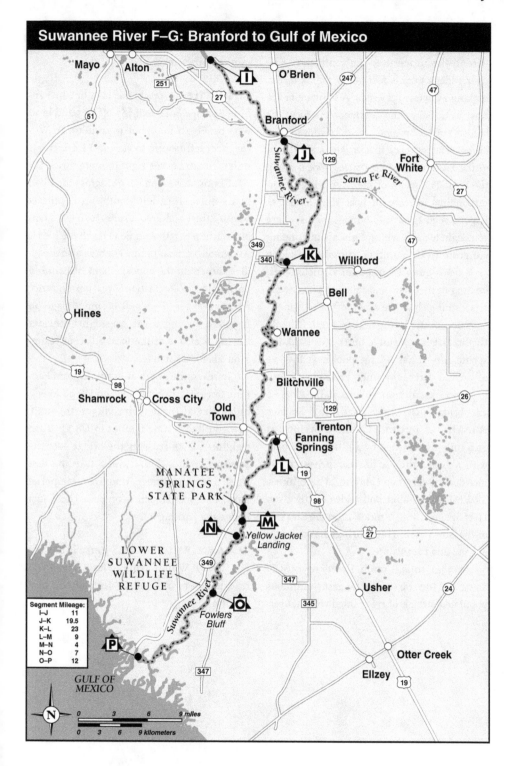

Mayo
Alton
251
27
O'Brien
247
47

51

Branford

Suwannee River

J
129
Fort White

Santa Fe River

349
340
K
Williford
47

Bell

Hines

Wannee

19
98
Blitchville
129
26

Shamrock   Cross City
Old Town
Trenton
Fanning Springs

MANATEE SPRINGS STATE PARK

L
19

98

N
M
Yellow Jacket Landing

AU 27

LOWER SUWANNEE WILDLIFE REFUGE

349
347
345
Usher
24

Suwannee River

O
Fowlers Bluff

P

Otter Creek

347
Ellzey
19

GULF OF MEXICO

Segment Mileage:	
I–J	11
J–K	19.5
K–L	23
L–M	9
M–N	4
N–O	7
O–P	12

N

0   3   6   9 miles
0   3   6   9 kilometers

Come to the confluence of the Santa Fe River at 10.0 miles. A Spanish mission stood here in the 1600s near the confluence. The river widens to 200 feet below the Santa Fe, making a fairway for winds. A segment of the west bank below the confluence is SRWMD lands. Turtle Springs, at 12.0 miles, is a keyhole-shaped pool that makes a short run to the Suwannee. More houses appear along the river. The width of the river brings a corresponding increase in boat size. Manatees may be seen here. In addition, this is where you begin to see warning signs about jumping sturgeon. In the summer, sturgeon—as long as 6 feet—jump in response to motorboats, landing in the boats and injuring passengers. It is a strange but true aspect of the Suwanee.

Rock Bluff Springs is on the left bank. Cypress trees with huge buttresses flank the spring run. It has a large pool near the site of an old ferry crossing. Privately owned, it pumps 27 million gallons daily. The FL 340 bridge just below Rock Bluff Springs is reached at 19.5 miles. Gornto Springs, at 21.0 miles, is abutted by a little county park with a boat ramp, a few campsites, and a nice dock. Below Log Landing, at 24.0 miles, SRWMD lands abut both sides of the river. Hart Springs, at 33.0 miles, is on the east side of the Suwannee. Hart Springs has a campground and camp store.

At 38.0 miles, reach the town of Old Town and the start of the longest continuous populated stretch of river, lined with houses. The banks remain populated until Fanning Springs and the US 98 bridge, the last span over the Suwannee.

◇ **SHUTTLE** To reach the take-out in Fanning Springs, take Exit 387 off I-75 and head west on FL 26 for about 30.0 miles. In Wilcox, bear left (south) to stay on FL 26. In 1.4 miles, FL 26 curves right to merge with US 98. Continue west on US 98, across the river; in 1.1 miles, turn left (south) on Southeast 989th Street and, in 0.2 mile, turn left again on Southeast 155th Avenue to reach the Joe H. Anderson Sr. boat ramp. There is also a paddler launch on the opposite bank at Fanning Springs State Recreation Area (an entrance fee applies; see "Fees and Permits," page 6). If you're leaving a car overnight, consider leaving it at one of the local adjacent campgrounds for a small fee.

To reach the put-in at Branford from Fanning Springs, continue west on US 98 for 3.2 miles. In Old Town, turn right (north) on FL 349 and follow it 24.3 miles to US 27. Turn right on US 27, crossing the bridge over the Suwannee, and, in 2.4 miles, take the first right after the bridge into Ivey Memorial Park. The boat launch is on your right, just before the parking lot.

◇ **GAUGE** Web. The USGS gauge is Suwannee River at White Springs, Florida. It should read between 51.6 and 65 feet for the best paddling.

G Fanning Springs to Gulf of Mexico

Class	I
Length	34
Time	Varies
Gauge	Web
Level	51.6–65
Gradient	0.6
Scenery	B

see map on p. 131

28G **DESCRIPTION** The US 98 bridge at Fanning Springs is the lowermost bridge over the river. The town of Fanning Springs is a product of the Seminole Wars, having started out as Fort Fanning in 1836. The fort was later occupied by Confederate troops during the Civil War. From here, they successfully sank a 90-foot Union gunboat with cannon fire near the mouth of the springs. Divers can still see the gunboat.

The springs are protected as a state park. Beyond Fanning Springs, on the east bank, is Andrews Wildlife Management Area. This 4,000-acre parcel, home to the largest remaining tract of hardwood forest in the Suwannee Valley, was acquired in 1985 through the Save Our Rivers program. Four Florida State Champion trees grow here: Florida maple, persimmon, river birch, and bluff oak. Cattails and sawgrass appear occasionally on the banks.

Manatee Springs State Park is reached after 9.0 miles. Paddlers access the park by heading directly up the gorgeous spring run alongside a boardwalk. It boils up more than 80,000 gallons of clear water per

CAMPSITE ON THE LOWER SUWANNEE

minute, where lots of fish, turtles, and other aquatic life thrive.

The river remains very wide from here on out. Paddlers should pick a bank to hang alongside for wind protection and better scenery. Yellow Jacket Landing, at 12.0 miles, is the last landing on the west bank. From here on down, the land is mostly part of the Lower Suwannee Wildlife Refuge with no camping allowed. This refuge protects most of the lower Suwannee River basin and also fronts 26.0 miles of the Gulf Coast, making this one of the largest undeveloped river deltas in the United States. A few houses will indicate Fowlers Bluff, on the east bank at 18.0 miles.

Tidal influence becomes significant below Fowlers Bluff, with small tidal creeks spurring off the Suwannee. As you near the town of Suwannee, hug the west bank. When you see houses, look for the sign for Suwannee Marina, up Demory Creek. This access is actually 4.0 miles above the mouth of the Suwannee River, which becomes even wider with salt marsh grasses and palm islands.

✧ SHUTTLE To reach the lowermost takeout from the intersection of US 98 and FL 349 in Old Town, head south-southwest on FL 349 to the town of Suwannee. After 23.1 miles, turn left on East Canal Street, then make a quick right on Southeast 228th Street and follow it 0.4 mile south to the Suwannee Marina (352-542-9159, suwanneemarina inc.150m.com). Let the staff know if you wish to leave a car overnight, and leave them your name and tag number. Offer to pay a parking fee when you arrive.

To reach the put-in, backtrack to Old Town on FL 349 and turn right on US 98, heading southeast. In 3.2 miles, turn right (south) on Southeast 989th Street and, in 0.2 mile, turn left on Southeast 155th Avenue to reach the Joe H. Anderson Sr. boat ramp. There is also a paddler launch on the opposite bank at Fanning Springs State Recreation Area (an entrance fee applies; see "Fees and Permits," page 6). If you're leaving a car overnight, consider doing so at one of the nearby campgrounds for a small fee.

✧ GAUGE Web. The USGS gauge is Suwannee River at White Springs, Florida. To ensure the best paddling, check for a reading of between 51.6 and 65 feet.

PADDLERS LET DOWN THEIR CANOE AT THE LOWER END OF THE BIG SHOALS PORTAGE (SEE PAGE 122).

29   SANTA FE RIVER

◇ **OVERVIEW** The Santa Fe has many characteristics that make it not only a historical river but also a river of fine natural beauty. Santa Fe is Spanish for "Holy Faith." Its headwaters, in the Santa Fe Lakes of Alachua County, merge and flow through the Santa Fe Swamp, then flow northwest for nearly 20 miles as a small, nonnavigable stream until it reaches Worthington Springs, where determined paddlers can fight their way downstream.

By the time the Santa Fe reaches the FL 241 bridge above O'Leno State Park, it becomes an easy and fun float, but the river goes promptly underground at O'Leno, traversing the underworld for 3 miles to reemerge at River Rise State Preserve. The natural bridge was used by aboriginal Floridians, early settlers, and other Florida wayfarers who traced historical roads crossing the natural bridge.

Upon its reemergence, the Santa Fe flows solidly, stretching about 100 feet across. From the River Rise to the confluence with the Suwannee, the Santa Fe boasts dozens of significant springs, including the celebrated springs of the paddleable Santa Fe tributary the Ichetucknee River.

In addition to its wealth of springs, the Santa Fe flows through a cross-representation of north-central Florida's biodiversity, from pine flatwoods to rolling sand hills to jungle-esque hardwood hammocks to gloomy swamps. The variety of habitats is reflected in the variety of birds and mammals that call the Santa Fe home. Limited conservation lands and parks protect some banks.

◇ **MAPS** SUWANNEE RIVER WMD RAMPS AND LAUNCHES MAP; WORTHINGTON SPRINGS, MIKESVILLE, HIGH SPRINGS, HIGH SPRINGS SOUTHWEST, FORT WHITE, HILDRETH (USGS)

A   Worthington Springs to O'Leno State Park

Class	I
Length	11
Time	7
Gauge	Visual, web
Level	N/A
Gradient	1
Scenery	B

29A **DESCRIPTION** The land around Worthington Springs once contained a resort of sorts—including a hotel, swimming pool, bathhouse, and recreation hall. The only remnant of this past is the concrete pool housing Worthington Springs. You will find the springs on the north bank of the Santa Fe, now part of Chastain-Seay Park, which has nature trails, picnic areas, and a boat launch.

At the put-in, the Santa Fe extends around 60 feet wide and steadily flows without obstructions. But don't be misled by this mild appearance. Shortly above County Road 241, willow trees crowd the waterway, allowing limited passage through which the agile paddler must use his skills. After banging around in the willows, get ready for Confusion Willow Swamp. Multiple channels split and narrow through a mile-long tangle of willow trees. This very challenging section of the Santa Fe should be paddled only in normal to high water and during winter, when the willows are leafless. Additionally expect fallen trees to add to the challenge.

Santa Fe River A–C: Worthington Springs to Suwannee River

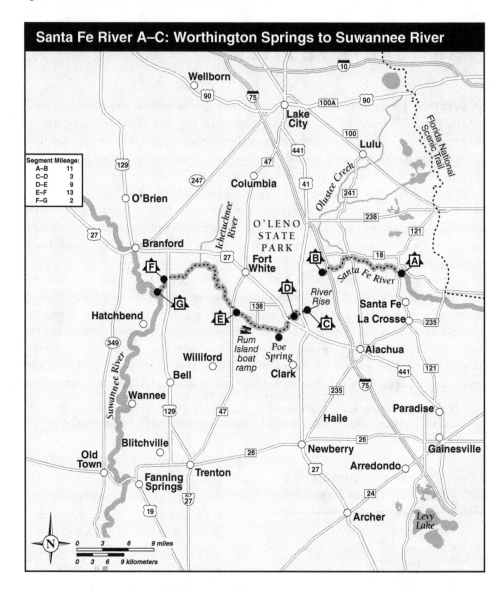

Segment Mileage:
A–B	11
C–D	3
D–E	9
E–F	13
F–G	2

It is 6 tough miles from Worthington Springs to CR 241. There is no official launch at CR 241. Paddlers who put in at CR 241 can enjoy the upper river without the tangles of Confusion Willow Swamp. Beyond the hellish willow swamp above CR 241, the coffee-colored river feels surprisingly wide and flows deep and slow. The riverbanks rise, interposed with swamps. Rare, small sandbars form on some curves and make for stopping spots. Pastures and houses can be found on the higher banks.

Olustee Creek is a major tributary. Here, the river deepens and widens more. Even at that, paddlers regularly travel up Olustee Creek from the Santa Fe for a wild, natural experience. From the confluence with Olustee Creek to I-75 (no access) it is about a mile. There is a public ramp just below I-75 off Bible Camp Road.

Below I-75, the Santa Fe River tapers, then flows into O'Leno State Park. Enjoy the rocky shoal just above the state-park take-out, just upstream of the river sink. The section between the O'Leno take-out and the river sink is off-limits to paddlers due to River Sink's environmental sensitivity. It is 2.0 miles from the Bible Camp Road landing to the state-park take-out.

⟨⟩ SHUTTLE To reach the take-out from High Springs, drive north on US 41/US 441. A little more than 4 miles from the bridge over the Santa Fe, bear right on Southeast Sprite Loop and take it 0.2 mile to the entrance of O'Leno State Park. An entrance fee applies (see "Fees and Permits," page 6).

Turn right on the main park road and follow it 1.8 miles to the parking area, which is adjacent to the boat launch.

To reach the put-in from the intersection of US 441 and FL 121 in Gainesville, drive north on FL 121 for 16.5 miles and, after crossing the bridge over the Santa Fe, turn left on Southwest 118th Road into to Chastain-Seay Park, on the northwest side of the river. The park has a boat ramp under the FL 121 bridge.

⟨⟩ GAUGE Visual, web. This run is recommended only in winter after heavy rains. The USGS gauge helpful in determining flow rates for any given time period is the Santa Fe River at Worthington Springs, Florida.

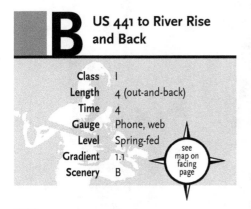

B US 441 to River Rise and Back

Class	I
Length	4 (out-and-back)
Time	4
Gauge	Phone, web
Level	Spring-fed
Gradient	1.1
Scenery	B

see map on facing page

29B DESCRIPTION The state paddling trail begins here. It is a 4.0-mile round-trip from the US 41/US 441 access to River Rise, through preserved banks owned by the state, making for a scenic and rewarding adventure. You will be paddling upstream against the current at first, but at least you will be fresh. It is about an hour upstream if you steadily paddle, then you can enjoy the upwelling to ultimately let the current return you to the put-in, soaking in the riverside scenery.

The upwelling is in the midst of River Rise Preserve State Park, where the Santa Fe

emerges as a swift river flowing under 5-foot-high, deeply forested banks. As you paddle downstream, the banks alternate between swampy sections and high and dry shores. Hornsby Spring lies between the put-in and the River Rise. The main spring flows from the boundaries of Camp Kulaqua Christian Retreat. This spring run is extremely scenic. Look for other, smaller spring boils along the run. A little upstream of and within sight of the US 41/US 441 bridge, look on the south bank for the inflow of Darby Spring and Hornsby Spring.

⟨⟩ DIRECTIONS This out-and-back paddle has just one access point. From the intersection of Main Street/US 41 and Santa Fe Boulevard/US 441 in High Springs, travel northwest on US 41/US 441 for 1.6 miles. Turn left (northwest) onto Boat Ramp Road and take it 0.6 mile to the High Springs boat ramp, on the southwest side of the bridge over the Santa Fe River. Santa Fe Canoe Outpost, just off US 441 before the bridge, offers canoe and kayak rentals, shuttle service, and launching for a fee.

 GAUGE Phone, web. Call Santa Fe Canoe Outpost for the latest river conditions. From here down, the Santa Fe is normally paddle-able year-round as it is spring-fed. However, the USGS gauge helpful in determining flow rates for any given time period is Santa Fe River near Fort White, Florida.

A PADDLER FISHES FOR DINNER ON THE SANTA FE RIVER.

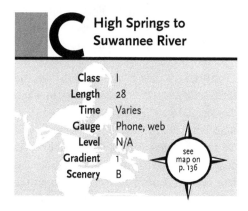

C High Springs to Suwannee River

Class	I
Length	28
Time	Varies
Gauge	Phone, web
Level	N/A
Gradient	1
Scenery	B

see map on p. 136

29C **DESCRIPTION** This section can be broken into varied segments, allowing paddlers to tailor their distance and desires for day or overnight trips. Accesses can be found at bridges over the river at US 27, FL 47, and US 129. At the US 441 access, the slow-flowing Santa Fe stretches about 120 feet across, with undulating banks minus sandbars. The right-hand bank from US 441 to US 27 is part of the River Rise State Preserve. Float over several shallow shoals. The underground plumbing plays havoc with the river. At low water levels, you will see a spot where the river divides; part of it enters a sink near the north bank, then emerges again as a midriver boil just upstream of the US 27 bridge. It is 3.0 miles from the US 441 access to the US 27 bridge.

A plenitude of incredible springs attracts both paddlers and cave divers to the 10-mile section from US 27 to FL 47. Additionally, the shallow nature of the river, combined with rocky shoals, dissuades most motorboaters from plying this part of the Santa Fe. Finally, low swampy banks discourage development, preserving its natural aura.

The higher banks just below US 27 harbor a few houses. About 1.5 miles downstream from US 27, you will find Allen Spring on the right bank. At lower flows, discover several small, unnamed springs welling up from the banks. Poe Spring, a quarter mile below

Allen Spring, is the centerpiece of a popular county park and linked to the Santa Fe by a 60-yard run. It emerges from a horizontal cavern bordered by other spring boils. Downstream from Poe Spring, paddlers will find low banks and shoreline swamps with still more small springs.

Watch on the left bank for Lilly Spring, a mile downstream from Poe Spring. This is the home of Ed the Hermit, also known as Naked Ed. . . . Next, gaze for Jonathan Spring on the right bank, just before you reach a river island. Rum Island Spring is on the right bank, near the lower end of the island. This body of water is part of Rum Island Spring County Park, which has a boat launch and is 7.0 miles downstream from US 441.

Your Santa Fe spring search continues. Find the 500-foot run of Blue Spring entering the river's left bank. Little Blue Spring, Johnson Spring, and Naked Spring upwell from the swamps near Blue Spring. It is hard to miss the Ginnie Spring run and its origin, a large, 50-foot-deep oval pool. An extensive cave system with some thousands of feet of passages attracts cave divers by the score, with a whole private campground and development centered on the springs. July Spring on the right bank and Devil's Eye and Devil's Ear springs on the left are just below Ginnie Springs. These are also popular cave-diving sites.

The first of four rocky yet easily navigable rapids is encountered about a mile below Ginnie Spring. The addition of the upstream springs has increased river volume and current. Campsites are limited because of both the posted property and the swampy terrain. But there are Suwannee River Water Management District lands (SRWMD) on the south bank before FL 47.

From FL 47 to US 129 (13.0 miles), civilization has encroached on the river's right bank. These banks rise, climaxing with the tall narrows of Hollingsworth Bluff. Enjoy the three rocky rapids before the Ichetucknee confluence. After the Ichetucknee meets the Santa Fe, the lack of rocky shoals and increased water volume make the Santa Fe ripe for motorboaters, from ski boats to pontoon barges.

Watch for Northbank Spring on the right-hand bank about a half mile below FL 47. Wilson Spring is 1.5 miles downstream. You will find a boat ramp at Wilson Spring Road. Part of the south bank is Fort White Mitigation Park, and just above the Ichetucknee are SRWMD lands. After the confluence with the Ichetucknee, the Santa Fe, not surprisingly, widens and deepens further.

It is 2 more miles from US 129 to the confluence with the Suwannee River. This final portion is for those who want to say that they did the whole thing. This is a wide, windy stretch of river that is crowded with every kind of motorized watercraft. There are some interesting springs, however, including Pleasant Grove Springs, on the left bank just above the confluence with the Suwannee.

◇ **SHUTTLE** To reach the take-out from the intersection of US 27 and US 41 in High Springs, take US 27 northwest to US 129 in Branford. After 19.4 miles, turn left (south) on US 129 and follow it 2.9 miles over the bridge over the Santa Fe, where there's a potential take-out at Lemmon Memorial Park, on the right. Keep traveling south on US 129 beyond the bridge; in 1.7 miles, just past CR 138, turn right (west) on Northwest 102nd Place and follow it to Northwest 38th Court. In 1.1 miles, turn right on Northwest 38th Court and follow it to the dead end at the G. C. Butler boat landing (a.k.a. the Wanamake boat ramp) just above where the Santa Fe meets the Suwannee. Ellie Ray's RV Resort, off US 129 about a mile north of this boat ramp, offers its own launch and safer parking for a fee.

THE TERRAIN BORDERING THE SANTA FE HARBORS A WEALTH OF FLORIDA PLANT COMMUNITIES.

To reach the put-in from the intersection of Main Street/US 41 and Santa Fe Boulevard/US 441 in High Springs, travel northwest on US 41/US 441 for 1.6 miles. Turn left (northwest) onto Boat Ramp Road and take it 0.6 mile to the High Springs boat ramp, on the southwest side of the bridge over the Santa Fe River. Santa Fe Canoe Outpost, just off US 441 before the bridge, offers canoe and kayak rentals, shuttle service, and launching for a fee.

◊ **GAUGE** Phone, web. Call Santa Fe Canoe Outpost at 386-454-2050 for the latest river conditions. From here down, the Santa Fe is normally paddleable year-round, as it is spring-fed. However, the USGS gauge helpful in determining flow rates for any given time period is Santa Fe River near Fort White, Florida.

30 ICHETUCKNEE RIVER

◊ **OVERVIEW** The Ichetucknee River proves that even though a river can originate as a spring, it can still be a river upon its emergence from the netherworld. Though such waterways are often referred to as spring runs or creeks, the 6-mile journey of the "Itch" from its headwaters at Ichetucknee Springs to its end at the confluence with the Santa Fe is officially classified as a river. No matter the classification—river, spring run, creek—the spring-rich Ichetucknee is a delight for the Florida paddler. River trippers, pushed by a gentle current, float over sand-bottomed, crystalline waters, passing a host of upwellings during the scenic run. Furthermore, the upper banks are protected as Ichetucknee Springs State Park.

◊ **MAPS** HILDRETH (USGS)

Ichetucknee Springs to US 27

Class	I
Length	3.5
Time	2
Gauge	Phone, web
Level	Spring-fed
Gradient	1.1
Scenery	A

30 DESCRIPTION The state paddling trail originates at Ichetucknee Springs State Park. The paddle begins about 50 yards below the Ichetucknee Head Spring. The 72°F water is subsequently fed by Cedar Head, Blue Hole,

Roaring, Singing, Boiling, Grassy Hole, Mill Pond, and Coffee Springs. Scan the translucent waters for other unnamed springs. The banks are completely natural, lying with the state park, which charges an entrance fee.

Tubers flock to the Ichetucknee during the summer months, and park rangers heavily regulate the traffic. However, tubes, inflatable canoes, kayaks, and rafts are not permitted to launch from the state park from the day after Labor Day through the Friday before Memorial Day, unless they are Coast Guard–certified as a vessel. Furthermore, all food and drink must be in nondisposable containers, though tubers cannot take any food or drink items.

Ichetucknee River: Ichetucknee Springs to US 27

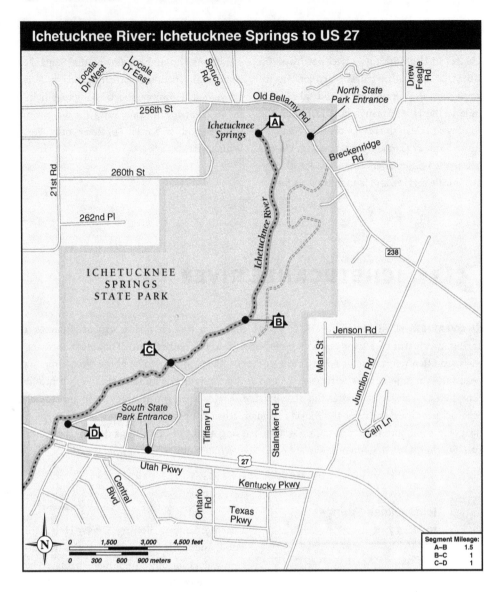

It is a 3.5-mile trip to the park's south take-out near US 27 and the end of the state paddling trail. If you choose to make the remaining 2.0 miles below US 27 to meet the Santa Fe, you must then paddle an additional 4.0 miles on that river to reach the next access. The house-laden scenery of that stretch of the Santa Fe doesn't compare with that of the Ichetucknee in the state park. From October through March or April, canoeists and kayakers usually have the Ichetucknee to themselves. Try for this time slot if at all possible, and leave summertime to the tubers.

◇ **SHUTTLE** To reach the take-out from the intersection of US 27 and US 41 in High Springs, take US 27 North 14.3 miles to the southern entrance of Ichetucknee Springs State Park, just before the US 27 bridge over the Ichetucknee River.

An entrance fee applies (see "Fees and Permits," page 6). The southmost take-out is just above the western end of the tram route that services the southern end of the park.

To reach the put-in at the northern entrance to the state park, backtrack 1.4 miles on US 27, turn left (north) on Junction Road, and follow it 1.6 miles to CR 238. Turn left on CR 238 and follow it an additional 1.6 miles to the state-park entrance, on your left.

✧ **GAUGE** Phone. Call Ichetucknee River State Park at 386-497-2511 for the latest water conditions. Note, however, that the river is spring-fed and offers a reliable flow. A gauge of interest is Ichetucknee River at US 27 near Hildreth, Florida.

31 MIDDLE PRONG ST. MARYS RIVER

✧ **OVERVIEW** The Middle Prong is a wild and swift stream, making a twisting, slender course through a corridor of stalwart cypress and tupelo trees, which forms midstream obstacles that the paddler must negotiate. The Middle Prong recalls its sister the North Prong of the St. Marys River. However, instead of draining Georgia's Okefenokee Swamp as the North Prong does, the Middle Prong drains Florida's Big Gum Swamp and Buckhead Swamp of the Osceola National Forest. Because the river flows through the national forest, the remote banks of the Middle Prong are home to deer, bears, and lesser mammals and birds, including the red-cockaded woodpecker.

✧ **MAPS** Osceola National Forest map; Macclenny Northwest, Taylor (USGS)

East Tower to County Road 127

Class	I+
Length	10
Time	6
Gauge	Web
Level	220
Gradient	3.3
Scenery	A

31 DESCRIPTION The river comes to be after it exits the northeast side of a pond near Osceola National Forest's East Tower Hunt Camp. Despite traversing a swamp, Middle Prong's current makes the waterway's channel clear. But just because the river course is easy to follow doesn't mean that the river is easy to paddle—expect fallen trees and overhanging vegetation that make this more suited to the wilderness paddler who likes a challenge.

A rough access to the stream can be found among the willows on the northwest side of the CR 125 bridge. The Little River, which drains the Pinhook Swamp, flows in below the CR 125 bridge. Just a mile farther down, at CR 122, is a better access.

As you progress downstream, the terrain changes from lowlands and swampy areas to higher banks and upland pine forests. Paddlers can continue downstream 2.0 miles to the confluence with the North Prong St. Marys River, a beautiful setting. However, there is no access until 9.0 miles down the main St. Marys, at the FL 121 bridge.

⟡ **SHUTTLE** To reach the take-out from Exit 333 off I-10, take CR 125 north 10.7 miles; at the Y, bear right (north) on CR 127 and follow it 3.9 miles to the bridge over the Middle Prong.

To reach the put-in, continue north 0.5 mile on CR 127 and turn left (west) on CR 122. In 3.5 miles, turn right (north) on CR 125 and, in 0.4 mile, turn left (south) on CR 250. Follow it 4.8 miles toward East Tower and the bridge over the Middle Prong. The access is on the southeast side of the bridge.

⟡ **GAUGE** Web. The USGS gauge is St. Marys River near Macclenny, Florida. The minimum reading should be 220 cfs. Be apprised that this gauge is below the confluence of the North and Middle Prongs; therefore, a thunderstorm could theoretically hit one prong more than the other and give a bad reading for the prong you choose to paddle.

32   ST. MARYS RIVER

⟡ **OVERVIEW** The St. Marys River is one of Florida's finest touring streams. Originating in Georgia's Okefenokee Swamp as the North Prong of the St. Marys, the river soon forms the Florida–Georgia boundary. Downstream, the Middle Prong St. Marys adds its flow from the east side of Buckhead Swamp in the Big Gum Swamp of Florida's Osceola National Forest. After the two prongs merge, onward the St. Marys River flows in a giant horseshoe to end its run at the Atlantic Ocean near Fernandina Beach.

Despite its 130-mile length and its status as a state-designated paddling trail, the St. Marys is one of Florida's lesser-known waterways. Get to know it. The big horseshoe pattern of the St. Marys heads south for about 10 miles, then easterly for 12 miles, then back north again. During this giant curve, the St. Marys flows under FL 2 twice. After passing under FL 2 the second time, the St. Marys continues in its northbound ways for more than 30 miles before turning east to empty into the Atlantic. The river's numerous long bends, combined with this giant horseshoe, can disorient directionally challenged paddlers.

Paddlers plying the uppermost part of this riverway will be navigating the slender, snaking, and swift North Prong under a canopy of bald cypress and tupelo. With the inflow of the Middle Prong St. Marys, the official St. Marys comes to be and widens, and snow-white sandbars appear inside bends while bluffs rise elsewhere and swamps find their place on lower banks. Development is limited along these banks, while campsites are plentiful, making it a fine overnighting adventure. The best river section to tour is the 77 miles from Moniac to US 1 near Folkston.

The St. Marys has been considered for Wild and Scenic status, and concern for the river has evolved into an organization known as the St. Marys River Management Committee, which seeks to meld the interests of concerned citizens and adjoining government entities. They produce a good-quality river map. For the map and more information about the river basin, visit stmarysriver.org.

⟡ **MAPS** St. Marys River Guide map; Moniac, Macclenny Northwest, Macclenny West, Macclenny East, Macclenny Northeast, St. George, Toledo, Folkston, Boulogne (USGS)

A Moniac to FL 121

Class	I–I+
Length	17
Time	Varies
Gauge	Web
Level	180
Gradient	2.6
Scenery	A

32A **DESCRIPTION** High banks crowd the narrow, swift upper section of the North Prong, while tupelo and cypress rise along and in the waterway, forcing paddlers to finesse their way through the living obstacles. Riverbank trees shade the 15- to 20-foot-wide North Prong, its dark tannin coloration flowing over a white-sand bottom that is revealed in shallow waters.

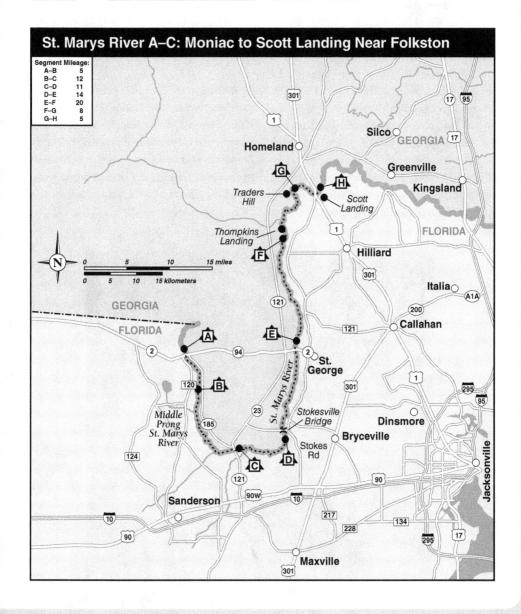

St. Marys River A–C: Moniac to Scott Landing Near Folkston

Segment Mileage:

A–B	5
B–C	12
C–D	11
D–E	14
E–F	20
F–G	8
G–H	5

Just after putting in, paddlers must navigate a troublesome section beneath a railroad bridge, with old cut pilings interspersed with the current pilings. After the first 2.0 miles, the banks rise sheer, making the land challenging to access. Small islands appear in the river just above the CR 120 bridge. It is 5.0 miles from the GA 94/FL 2 bridge to the CR 120 bridge. This difficult access requires carrying boats and gear for about 50 yards from the northwest side of the bridge.

Below CR 120, high banks, small islands, and a speedy current characterize the North Prong. Meet the Middle Prong 3.0 miles south of the CR 120 bridge. The Middle Prong enters swiftly. Here, the official St. Marys River is born, subsequently widening as well as shallowing. Sizable sandbars will be found inside curves, despite continued high banks where pines and palmettos reign. The St. Marys maintains its southbound ways on this leg one of the great horseshoe, then turns east a few miles above FL 121.

✧ **SHUTTLE** To reach the take-out from Exit 335 off I-10, take FL 121 North 7.1 miles through Macclenny to the bridge over the St. Marys River, which straddles the Florida–Georgia line. A paddler launch is on the southwest side of the bridge, on the Florida side.

To reach the put-in, continue north on the bridge into Georgia, where FL 121 becomes GA 23, and in a quick 0.4 mile veer left onto GA 185, heading northwest. After 13.0 miles, turn left on GA 94 and follow it 0.3 mile to the bridge over the St. Marys. Access is on the southeast side of the bridge before GA 94 crosses the river back into Florida as FL 2.

✧ **GAUGE** Web. The USGS gauge is St. Marys River near Macclenny, Florida. The minimum reading should be 180 cfs. Be apprised that this gauge is below the confluence of the North Prong and Middle Prong; therefore, a thunderstorm could theoretically hit one prong more than the other and give a bad reading for the prong you choose to paddle.

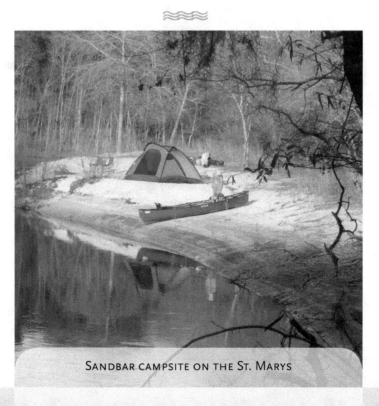

SANDBAR CAMPSITE ON THE ST. MARYS

B   FL 121 to GA 94/FL 2
Near St. George

Class	I
Length	25
Time	Varies
Gauge	Web
Level	180
Gradient	1
Scenery	B

see map on p. 145

32B DESCRIPTION At the FL 121 bridge, where the official Florida state paddling trail begins, the now-slower-flowing St. Marys stretches 50–75 feet wide below 15-foot-high banks. Despite an overall easterly course, the first 3.0 miles of the waterway below FL 121 seem in a continual turn of some sort or another. Nevertheless, the St. Marys straightens out after the South Prong St. Marys adds its flow to the main stem.

High and steep banks flank this straight stretch. After passing the straight area, reach St. Marys Cove Landing, a Baker County public park, on river right. Beyond here, houses line the Florida side of the once again twisting river. About 2.0 miles below the houses, the St. Marys flows under the Stokesville Bridge. It is 11.0 miles from FL 121 to the Stokesville Bridge.

An agglomeration of big sandbars near the Stokesville Bridge makes it a popular place. After a mile or so of continual turns above high banks, the St. Marys straightens yet again. Alternating curving sections and straight sections continue in superlatively scenic fashion almost to the GA 94/FL 2 bridge. Houses appear on the Georgia side above the GA 94/FL 2 bridge. It is 14.0 miles from the Stokesville Bridge to the GA 94/FL 2 bridge.

✧ **SHUTTLE** To reach the take-out from Exit 335 off I-10, take FL 121 North through Macclenny 7.1 miles and cross the bridge over the St. Marys into Georgia, where FL 121 becomes GA 23. In a quick 0.4 mile, veer left onto GA 185; after 13.0 miles, turn left on GA 94 and follow it 0.3 mile to the bridge over the St. Marys. Access is on the southeast side of the bridge before GA 94 crosses the river back into Florida as FL 2.

To reach the put-in, backtrack to the GA 23/FL 121 bridge. A paddler launch is on the southwest side of the bridge, just over the state line in Florida.

✧ **GAUGE** Web. The USGS gauge is St. Marys River near Macclenny, Florida. The minimum reading should be 180 cfs.

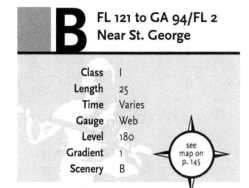

SWIFT, NARROW CHANNELS CHARACTERIZE THE UPPER ST. MARYS RIVER.

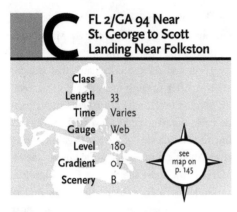

C FL 2/GA 94 Near St. George to Scott Landing Near Folkston

Class	I
Length	33
Time	Varies
Gauge	Web
Level	180
Gradient	0.7
Scenery	B

see map on p. 145

32C **DESCRIPTION** From FL 2/GA 94, this remote stretch of river twists and turns to the extreme, with many fallen trees, before straightening out. The pattern continues with high-banked straight segments between sandbar-bordered bends. This is a remote section with few river accesses. Look for the remains of an old bridge just above Thompkins Landing. It is 20.0 miles from the FL 2/GA 94 bridge to Thompkins Landing.

Most paddlers consider the section from Thompkins Landing to Scott Landing the final desirable stretch for paddlers. The alternating straight and curving stretches continue below 10-foot-high, sometimes-piney banks alternating with sporadic swampy shores, including still sloughs where grasses and lily pads find a home.

Reach historic Traders Hill, on the Georgia side, after 8.0 miles. The park features a boat ramp, picnic tables, restrooms, and campsites. Amazingly, this spot was once the seat of Charlton County, Georgia, when the St. Marys was the primary avenue of transportation in these parts. Traders Hill was as far up the St. Marys as riverboats could float goods to the locale. Scan the spot for old dock pilings from those bygone days.

Below Traders Hill, the St. Marys really starts to widen. Though all freshwater, the river shows saltwater influence by being pushed up and down with the tides and a changing of current speed. Pass under a busy railroad bridge about a mile before the US 1 road bridge. Look for a house built on the abutment of an old bridge just below the railroad trestle. Below US 1, houses appear, but it is less than a mile farther to Scott Landing public boat ramp on the Florida side. It is 5.0 miles from Traders Hill to Scott Landing. Ralph E. Simmons Memorial State Forest keeps the Florida bank wild below Scott Landing.

Another 50.0 miles of waterway await the paddler between Scott Landing and the Atlantic Ocean. However, they should expect larger and larger motorboats to accompany them downriver. That being said, determined paddlers do ply the entire river to the town of St. Marys, Georgia, and even farther to Fort Clinch State Park in Florida.

SHUTTLE To reach the take-out from Exit 28A/28B (New Kings Road) off I-295 near Jacksonville, take US 1/US 23/US 301 North 29.2 miles to Lake Hampton Road, just before the bridge over the St. Marys. Turn right (east) on Lake Hampton Road and, in 1.7 miles, turn left (north) on Scott Landing Road and follow it to the ramp and St. Marys River Fish Camp at the river.

To reach the put-in, backtrack to Lake Hampton Road and head west across US 1/US 23/US 301; after the intersection, Lake Hampton Road becomes County Road 121. Follow CR 121 south 19.1 miles to Crawford Kent Road/FL 2. Turn right (west) on FL 2 and, in 1.5 miles, cross the St. Marys River into Georgia, where the road becomes GA 94. A boat ramp is located on the southwest (Georgia) side of the bridge.

GAUGE Web. The USGS gauge is St. Marys River near Macclenny, Florida. The minimum reading should be 180 cfs.

33 BLACK CREEK

✧ **OVERVIEW** Overshadowed by the motorboat-heavy and less-paddler-friendly St. Johns River, Black Creek is a favorite of greater Jacksonville kayakers and canoeists. A tributary of the St. Johns, Black Creek flows through a moist, tree-canopied ravine cutting beneath sandy pine and scrub-oak forests punctuated with plenty of houses. Far from being the only Black Creek in Florida, it gets its moniker from coffee-colored tannic waters colored that way by decaying vegetation.

Originating near the community of Penney Farms, Black Creek snakes its way some 20 miles from FL 16 to empty into the St. Johns River. Paddlers primarily ply the first 14 miles, as the lowermost 6 miles are extremely broad, tidal, and used extensively by large motorized craft.

✧ **MAPS** BLACK CREEK RAVINES MAP; PENNEY FARMS, MIDDLEBURG, MIDDLEBURG SOUTHWEST (USGS)

FL 16 to Old Ferry Road Boat Landing

Class	I
Length	14
Time	Varies
Gauge	Web
Level	2–4
Gradient	1.1
Scenery	C

33 **DESCRIPTION** Wise paddlers will check the USGS gauge, stationed at the FL 16 bridge, as Black Creek rises and falls rapidly with local rainfall. The ideal level is 2–4 feet. If the water is lower than 2 feet, paddlers will be pulling their craft over fallen trees, but if the water is above 4 feet, paddlers will be floating through standing and overhanging trees.

At FL 16, Black Creek flows solidly and stretches 20 feet across, with white sandbanks rising 10 feet from the black water. Trees grow along and over the sand-bottomed watercourse as it continually twists. Watch for submerged logs and stumps while negotiating the tirade of turns below intermittent tall sand bluffs. A noisy rock ledge rapid adds excitement about a mile downstream. Black Creek alternately turns along high curving banks and plows straight ahead under tree canopy. Houses become commonplace.

About 2.0 miles above the County Road 218 bridge, the banks are fully developed, with docks and boathouses along the water with homes on higher ground. Here, Black Creek widens, slows, and develops lily pad–laden sloughs. It is 7.0 miles from the FL 16 bridge to the CR 218 bridge. There is no parking at the CR 218 bridge. However, paddlers could park their vehicles at nearby businesses with permission after quickly loading and unloading their boats at the bridge.

Reach the Black Creek Ravines Conservation Area on the south bank, 2.0 miles below the CR 218 bridge. This 965-acre area protects seepage slopes and steep ravines that harbor a variety of flora and fauna along a 2.7-mile segment of the south shore. There is a designated primitive campsite for overnight paddlers. Hiking can be added to the mix, as a trail leaves the campsite; for a camping permit, call the St. Johns Water Management District office at 386-329-4404.

At 2.5 miles below the CR 218 bridge, North Fork Black Creek adds its flow. Here, paddlers can head upstream a half mile on North Fork

Black Creek: FL 16 to Old Ferry Road Boat Landing

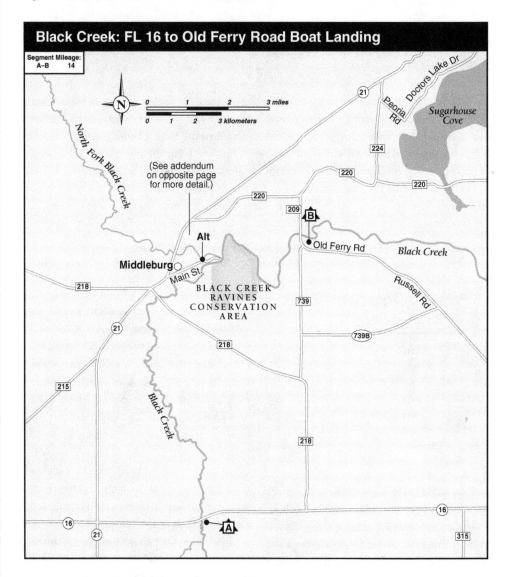

Segment Mileage:
A–B   14

(See addendum on opposite page for more detail.)

North Fork Black Creek

Sugarhouse Cove

Doctors Lake Dr

Peoria Rd

21

224

220

220

220

209

B

Alt

Middleburg

Old Ferry Rd

Black Creek

Main St.

BLACK CREEK RAVINES CONSERVATION AREA

Russell Rd

218

739

21

739B

215

218

Black Creek

218

16

16

21

A

315

Black Creek to use the North Fork ramp off Main Street in Middleburg, a much-preferred take-out than the CR 218 bridge on Black Creek proper. However, this section of Black Creek is tidal and wide, with some motorboaters. Beyond the conservation area, Black Creek's banks are fully civilized. At the CR 209 bridge, big boats will be found on the ever-widening waterway. It is 6.0 miles from the CR 218 bridge to the Old Ferry Road boat landing.

◊ **SHUTTLE** To reach the lowermost take-out from Exit 12 off I-295 near Jacksonville, take Blanding Boulevard/FL 21 South 7.8 miles, crossing the bridge over Black Creek. Turn left (south) on Henley Road/CR 739 and, in 2.7 miles, turn left (west) on Russell Road/CR 209. In 0.9 mile, turn left on Old Ferry Road and follow it 0.4 mile north to a public boat ramp on Black Creek.

Black Creek Addendum

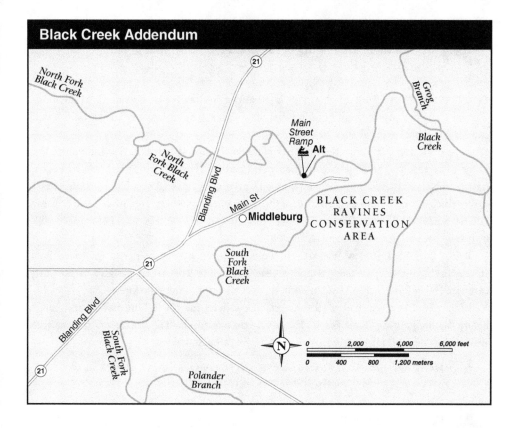

To reach the uppermost put-in from the take-out, backtrack to Russell Road/CR 209 and turn left (south) on Henley Road/CR 739. In 3.3 miles, turn left (east, then south) on CR 218. In 3.4 miles, turn right (west) on FL 16 and follow it 1.5 miles to the bridge over Black Creek. Access is on the southeast side of the bridge.

◇ **GAUGE** Web. The USGS gauge is South Fork Black Creek near Penney Farms, Florida. It should read between 2 and 4 feet for the best paddling on Black Creek. Below 2 feet will result in many pull-overs, and above 4 feet will be overly swift and put you in the trees in the upper sections.

34 NORTH FORK BLACK CREEK

◆ **OVERVIEW** North Fork Black Creek is a gem of a stream just outside of Middleburg. Blessed to be flowing through big Jennings State Forest, the intimate creek provides a wild paddling experience for greater Jacksonville.

Born on Camp Blanding, North Fork quickly picks up other tributaries and enters Jennings State Forest. The state-forest canoe trail begins at Powell Ford, where North Fork is narrow, relatively swift, and embedded in steep banks. Only intrepid paddlers with four-wheel-drive vehicles, ample time, and a desire for the challenge of paddling over, under, and between fallen trees will tackle this first 2.5 miles to Ellis Ford, the next access. Ellis Ford is accessible by two-wheel vehicles with decent clearance.

Below Ellis Ford, Yellow Water Creek enters. Obstacles diminish with increased flow. Interestingly, you will pass a few simple yet exciting rapids. The stream passes a backcountry campground before reaching Indian Ford, the last take-out in the state forest.

Indian Ford is accessible by all vehicles. Below here, the North Fork flows a mile or so before leaving Jennings State Forest. Houses become common. The North Fork merges with Black Creek near Middleburg, where there is a boat ramp downtown.

◆ **MAPS** JENNINGS STATE FOREST MAP; NORTH FORK BLACK CREEK CANOE TRAIL MAP; FIFTONE, MIDDLEBURG SOUTHWEST (USGS)

Powell Ford Landing to Indian Ford Landing

Class	I
Length	8
Time	Varies
Gauge	Web
Level	60
Gradient	1.5
Scenery	A+

34 DESCRIPTION The inflow of Long Branch near Powell Ford makes North Fork runnable. Uppermost North Fork Black Creek is tight, sometimes swift, and potentially jammed with logs. The stream gurgles southeasterly under a gorgeous canopy of cypress, gum, and overhanging live oak, with more vegetation thickening the steep banks.

Paddlers will be glad to see Ellis Ford, which is merely an easily missed primitive sand landing on a right-hand curve. Carefully scout the landing beforehand if you plan to end at Ellis Ford. The far better run is 5.0 miles from Ellis Landing to Indian Ford—easier access, fewer blowdowns. The wilderness feel is palpable—and surprising—considering the proximity to Jacksonville. The "real Florida" banks complement the tea-colored stream as it swiftly bends around innumerable curves bordered by high banks. Plan to dodge fallen trees and slide over burgundy shallows, though paddlers seem to keep this segment regularly cut.

Gullied tributaries feed the North Fork. The stream divides into occasional channels, further narrowing from its 20-foot width. Flow over a simple rapid 0.8 mile below Ellis Ford. Yellow Water Creek enters 2.0 miles downstream from Ellis Ford. North Fork widens and becomes much less clogged yet still presents superlative scenery. It is 3.0 miles from Ellis Ford to Knights Landing, on the

North Fork Black Creek:
Powell Ford Landing to Indian Ford Landing

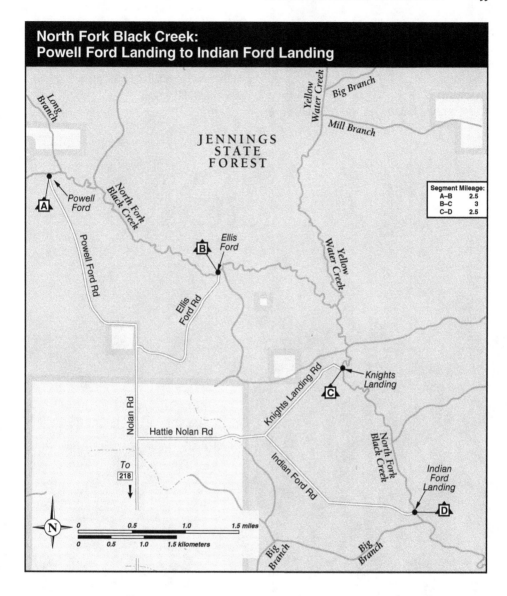

right. Look for a fenced parking area above the river. Pass another couple of noisy yet simple rapids a mile below Knights Landing. The water remains quick. Look for rock outcrops in the water here. The Indian Ford take-out is on the right at 5.0 miles.

⟡ SHUTTLE To reach the lowermost take-out, Indian Ford, from the intersection of County Road 218 and Blanding Boulevard/FL

21 in Middleburg, turn left (west) on CR 218 and, in 5.3 miles, turn right (north) on Nolan Road. Drive 1.9 miles, then turn right (west) on Hattie Nolan Road. At 1 mile, enter Jennings State Forest. At 2.3 miles, Hattie Nolan Road becomes Indian Ford Road. Follow it to the dead end at the landing. There is a parking fee (see "Fees and Permits," page 6).

To reach Ellis Ford—the recommended upstream landing—backtrack to turn right (north) on Nolan Road. Reenter the state forest in 0.5 mile, then, in another 0.5 mile, veer right on Ellis Ford Road to reach Ellis Ford Landing.

◇ **GAUGE** Web, visual. The USGS gauge is North Fork Black Creek near Middleburg, Florida. The discharge should be a minimum of 60 cfs. It is advisable to call Jennings State Forest at 904-291-5530 for the latest paddling conditions, especially if you plan to paddle upstream of Ellis Ford.

THE UPPER STREAM IS NARROW, SWIFT, AND EMBEDDED IN STEEP BANKS.

MUCH OF NORTH FORK BLACK CREEK FLOWS
THROUGH JENNINGS STATE FOREST.

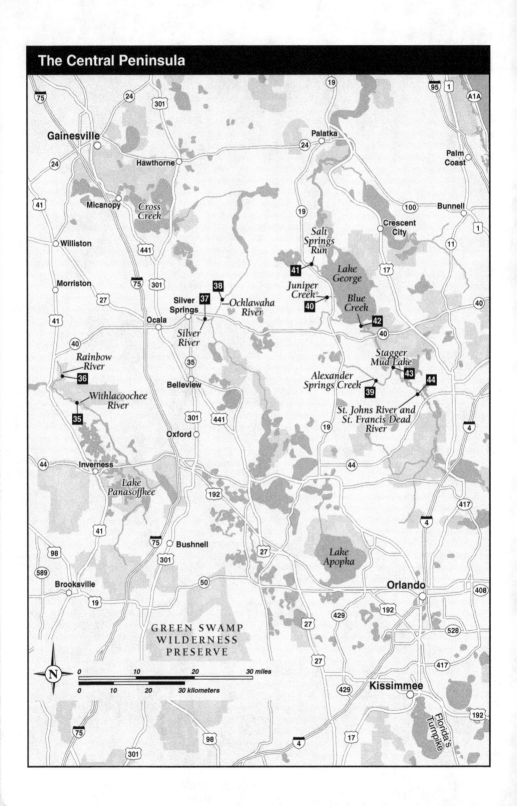

The Central Peninsula

35 WITHLACOOCHEE RIVER (SOUTH)

◇ **OVERVIEW** You just have to wonder how two rivers in Florida ended up with the unlikely name of Withlacoochee, but such is the case. This Withlacoochee River, commonly referred to as the Withlacoochee River South, is a river with many faces, from high-banked, narrow stream to wider, slower waterway bordered by remote swamps to swift and winding wilderness waterway to remote natural lakes where birdlife is abundant. Some sections are lined with houses, while others are as far from civilization as you can get in 21st-century Central Florida.

The Withlacoochee South can be floated in its entirety with good planning, or it can be divided into sections. Much of the river is bordered by the Withlacoochee State Forest, conservation easements or watershed-recharge lands, or wildlife preserves. The Withlacoochee, whose lowermost reaches near the Gulf fell victim to the properly abandoned Cross Florida Barge Canal, extends 100 miles long, with 84 miles of quality paddling, almost all of which is a state-designated paddling trail. I have done the entire river in one trip and found it a rewarding adventure.

The headwaters of the Withlacoochee emerge from the aptly named Withlacoochee River Swamp, then flow west and north before becoming paddleable near the community of Lacoochee. From here, the waterway reveals changing faces as it heads north—yes, north—to Dunnellon, the end of the line for most paddlers. Below Dunnellon, the Withlacoochee has been permanently altered in its final miles to the Gulf at Yankeetown.

From Lacoochee to Dunnellon, not only does the actual waterway change but the shores and banks alter as well, morphing from wooded swamps to high-banked hardwoods and pines, along grassy lakes, sloughs, and ponds of cypress ponds, to live oak–clad bluffs. In populated areas, you will observe in repair and disrepair arrays of docks behind which stand dwellings of comparable status.

The Withlacoochee's most remote reaches border the wildlife-rich Tsala Apopka Lakes, connected to the Withlacoochee by channels and waterweed-rimmed ponds. Usage along the Withlacoochee also varies greatly, from populous parcels where outfitters run kayaks, canoes, and tubes during the warm months to shallow, weedy lakes left only to paddlers and the occasional airboat.

The river below Dunnellon enters a man-made lake, Lake Rousseau, then leaves the lake as a straight-line channel, a legacy of the abandoned Cross Florida Barge Canal.

◇ **MAPS** WITHLACOOCHEE STATE FOREST MAP; LACOOCHEE, ST. CATHERINE, WAHOO, NOBLETON, RUTLAND, LAKE PANASOFFKEE NORTHWEST, STOKES FERRY, DUNNELLON SOUTHEAST, DUNNELLON (USGS)

A Lacoochee Park to Nobleton

Class	I
Length	25
Time	Varies
Gauge	Phone, web
Level	N/A
Gradient	0.7
Scenery	B

35A **DESCRIPTION** The uppermost put-in is located in the Richloam Tract of the Withlacoochee State Forest, leaving you 2.0 miles of wilderness floating before emerging at the County Road 575 bridge. However, the uppermost put-in is questionable for leaving your car for an extended period. At CR 575, a paddle livery offers better parking and can shuttle you to the top if you want to go the whole way.

A moderate current pushes the 35-foot-wide waterway over rocky shoals under banks of live oak, pine, and palmetto around 10 feet high. Cypress borders the stream much of the way. Below CR 575, 2.0 miles from Lacoochee Park, houses mostly border the river until the

FL 50 bridge, 9.0 miles downstream. Shortly below FL 50, state-forest land along the left-hand bank makes camping possible but is far from a wilderness experience. It is 2.0 miles from CR 575 to US 301 and 2.0 miles from US 301 to US 98. Watch for a sulphur spring on river left about a mile below the US 98 bridge. It is 6.0 miles from US 98 to the FL 50 bridge. The FL 50 bridge has a primitive access on the northeast side of the bridge, near a fence, but it should be used only as a drop-off point due to a lack of parking.

It is 7.5 miles from FL 50 to Silver Lake. The river has widened to 50 feet, with lower banks, some swamp sloughs, and more sandbars. However, limestone rock continues to present itself, and cypress trees and their strange knees continue to display amazing shapes. You will pass several state-forest recreation areas ahead.

Reach Crooked River Campground 5.0 miles below the FL 50 bridge, River Junction Recreation Area 1.5 miles farther. The Little Withlacoochee enters on river right here, and you can actually paddle up the Little Withlacoochee to the camping area. Beyond River Junction, the main Withlacoochee widens, then flows into Silver Lake, a scenic body of

Withlacoochee River (South) A–C: Lacoochee Park to Dunnellon

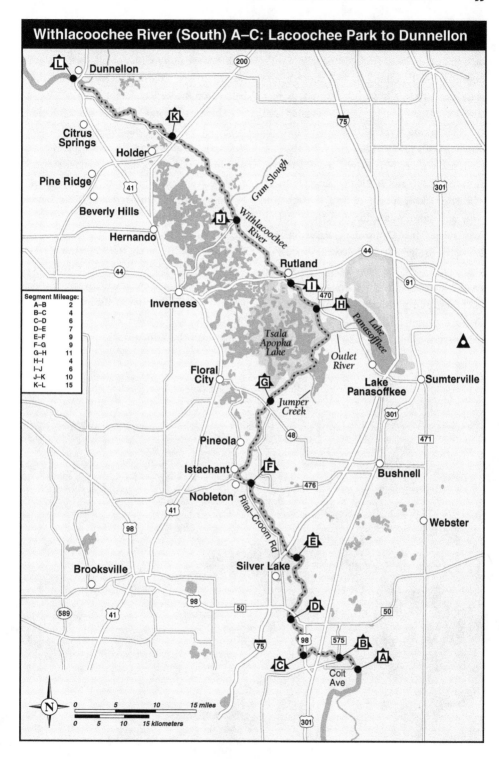

Segment Mileage:

A–B	2
B–C	4
C–D	6
D–E	7
E–F	9
F–G	9
G–H	11
H–I	4
I–J	6
J–K	10
K–L	15

water marred by the overhead crossing of I-75. Silver Lake Recreation Area is situated on a hill on the west shore of the lake, a mile beyond River Junction. As with much of the state forest in this area, hiking trails border the river. Download a state-forest map and consider taking some of these paths in combination with your paddle.

It is 8.0 miles from Silver Lake Recreation Area to CR 476 and Nobleton Canoe Outpost. The river closes north of I-75 but remains wide and slow. Watch for the official primitive Croom Canoe Camp on the left-hand bank below the bridge. A mile below Silver Lake on your right, pass the Iron Bridge Recreation Area, with picnic tables and a boat launch, near old bridge pilings. Ahead, pass under a power line, then enter a swampy section, where the river narrows and becomes swift and canopied.

Watch for the river split and signed channel leading right to Hog Island Recreation Area, with a fine campground, potable water, a boat ramp, and a picnic area, which you reach a mile below Iron Bridge Recreation Area.

The two channels merge quickly below Hog Island, and paddlers swiftly flow through winding cypress swamp. Houses become evident and the river widens at CR 476, especially on the right-hand bank. Nobleton Canoe Outpost operates just below the CR 476 Bridge.

✧ **SHUTTLE** To reach the lowermost take-out in Nobleton from the intersection of FL 44 and US 41 in downtown Inverness, take US 41 South 15.6 miles to CR 476. Turn left on CR 476, and follow it east 5.3 miles to the bridge over the Withlacoochee and the canoe

STOPPING AT A SANDBAR NEAR RIVER JUNCTION CAMPGROUND

rental on the left, just before the bridge. There is also a public park on the river, west of the canoe rental at the CR 476 bridge.

To reach the uppermost put-in from the take-out, continue east on CR 476. After 9.3 miles, turn right on US 301 and head south 10.9 miles to FL 50. Turn left on FL 50 and head east 1.0 mile to CR 575. Turn right, go south on CR 575, and follow it beyond the bridge over the Withlacoochee River to 2.9 miles to Durden Road. Turn left (south) on Durden Road and, after 0.4 mile, turn left on Coit Road and follow it east to Lacoochee Park. Enter Lacoochee Park and, after 0.5 mile, turn right (south) at the first sand road and follow it a little more than a mile to a high bluff bordered in concrete posts, over-looking the river.

✧ **GAUGE** Phone, web. Call Withlacoochee River RV Park and Canoe Rental at 352-583-4778 for river information. The USGS gauge helpful in determining flow rates for any given day is Withlacoochee River at Trilby, Florida.

≋

B Nobleton to Rutland

Class	I
Length	20.5
Time	Varies
Gauge	Phone, web
Level	N/A
Gradient	0.2
Scenery	B+

see map on p. 159

35B **DESCRIPTION** The Withlacoochee divides a half mile below CR 476, swiftly flowing amid swamp woods. Stay with the left channel, shortly passing Nobleton Wayside Park. The channels soon unite. Continuing north, the river displays a new face, widening to enter and exit several shallow and waterweed-bordered lakes, where alligators, wading birds, and raptors can be found among the cypresses that ring the still waters.

Enter Lake Townsen, part of a regional park, a mile beyond Nobleton Wayside Park. Skirt around small islands on the north end of Lake Townsen. The river narrows and houses resume in places, yet pasturelands rise on the right bank. Watch for the remains of an old bridge ahead. Open onto Lake Anne 4.0 miles below Lake Townsen. Swampy banks line the shore and the river beyond. Open onto cypress-bordered Lake Nelson 2.0 miles downstream of Lake Anne. The river narrows a bit, and you reach the Wynnhaven boat ramp on the east side of the FL 48 bridge 7.0 miles below Nobleton and CR 476.

Below FL 48, swampy shores continue to keep back riverside development and the Withlacoochee enters the Tsala Apopka Lake region, a series of lakes and swamps with little current except where the river splits into small channels among islands. The locale exudes old, wild Florida—the *real* Florida, where birds are as populous as people in cities. Trippers will find campsites very few, corresponding to the lack of high ground.

Enter mile-long Bonnet Lake about a mile downstream of FL 48. Pass one landing on the west bank, and then the river narrows again. The banks are now the public lands of Flying Eagle Preserve and Withlacoochee State Forest. It is 13.5 miles from FL 48 to FL 44.

You can find some dry land near Board Island, a half mile beyond the north end of Bonnet Lake. Here, a smaller channel splits left as the main river keeps straight. Follow the smaller channel a short distance to high ground cloaked in live oak and palm on the left bank. This high ground is actually on the mainland just west of Board Island. Here are the GPS coordinates for Board Island: **N28° 44.933' W82° 12.833'**. Airboats become more common in this stretch of shallow waters. Pass around a second island below Board Island, then open onto a small lake with an arm reaching to the south.

Four miles downstream from the FL 48 bridge, grassy Jumper Creek feeds the Withlacoochee. At this point, the Withlacoochee turns north and remains lakelike, yet often breaks into waterweed-bordered channels. Look for the downstream current if you are unsure as to which way to go.

Pass a small bit of high ground on river right before reaching Otter Slough, 7.0 miles below the FL 48 bridge. About a half mile ahead, enter Princess Lake, where the Outlet River enters from the east, draining Lake Panasoffkee. Marsh Bend County Park has a boat launch about a mile east up the Outlet River, at the CR 407 bridge. North of Princess Lake, the river divides into channels, with houses on the right bank. There is a small lock and dam at the Carlson area, 1.5 miles north of Princess Lake and 11.0 miles below FL 48, but don't expect it to be manned. You can portage on either side of the drop. A public boat ramp here enables entry both above and below the small lock.

From the dam, the Withlacoochee becomes shallow, with underwater weeds discouraging motorboats and sometimes frustrating paddlers in the slowest, shallowest sections. Try to stay in the current with the moving channels. The FL 44 access, Rutland Park, is reached via a short canal on the

BIRDLIFE IS ABUNDANT ON THE LAKES OF THE MIDDLE WITHLACOOCHEE RIVER (SOUTH).

southeast bank of the river 2.5 miles from Carlson. From the Carlson Dam downstream, you will see mile markers on the river.

⟡ **SHUTTLE** To reach the lowermost take-out from the intersection of FL 44 and US 41 in downtown Inverness, head east on FL 44; at the second intersection, south of Cooter Lake, bear left to continue east on FL 44, and take it 7.1 miles to the bridge over the Withlacoochee River. The Rutland Park public boat ramp is located on the southeast side of the bridge, and the river is accessed via a short canal.

To reach the uppermost put-in in Nobleton from the same intersection, take US 41 South 15.6 miles to CR 476. Turn left on CR 476, and follow it east 5.3 miles to the bridge over the Withlacoochee and the canoe rental on the left, just before the bridge. There is also a public park on the river, west of the canoe rental at the CR 476 bridge.

⟡ **GAUGE** Phone, web. Call Nobleton Outpost for river information at 352-796-4343. The USGS gauge helpful in determining flow rates for any given day is Withlacoochee River at Nobleton, Florida.

≋

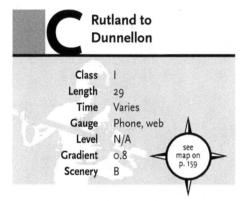

C Rutland to Dunnellon

Class	I
Length	29
Time	Varies
Gauge	Phone, web
Level	N/A
Gradient	0.8
Scenery	B

see map on p. 159

35C **DESCRIPTION** North of FL 44, the river widens, the shallows cease, the current flows past hardwood swamps. Moccasin Slough enters on river left a mile downstream. The right bank harbors the public lands of Half Moon Wildlife Management Area, while the higher left bank has houses. A public boat ramp is found at CR 581, a housing enclave where the now-burned Turner Fish Camp once stood. It is 6.0 miles from FL 44 to CR 581. Beyond CR 581, the west bank becomes part of Potts Preserve, more wildland. A half mile below CR 581, on the east bank, spring-fed Gum Slough enters on river right. It can be paddled but has snags aplenty that hopefully will be cleared if you choose to explore

it. A good launch point is from Potts Preserve, where there is also a camping area across from Gum Slough.

Gum Slough's inflow increases the current before the river begins dividing around numerous low, swampy, and weed-bordered isles teeming with wildlife. Watch on river left, 5.0 miles below the Gun Slough entrance, for a spring. Dubbed Citrus Blue Spring, it is in a little cove on river left and has a dike that cuts the 120-foot-diameter spring off from its natural inflow into the Withlacoochee. Below Citrus Blue Spring, houses are found on the west bank, while the right bank is mostly Gum Slough Conservation Easement. Reach FL 200 3.0 miles below Citrus Blue Springs. FL 200 has an access at Grey Eagle Park. It is off East Spruce Drive a half mile downriver from the FL 200 bridge. It is 9.5 river miles from CR 581 to FL 200.

Beyond FL 200, the right bank is part of the Halpata Tastanaki Preserve, while the left banks have houses. The banks overall are rising, with high, dry land in many spots as opposed to the nearly endless cypress shores of the lakes region. The river has narrowed and has good current. Pass the three spots that make up the Two Mile Prairie Canoe Camp, 4.0 miles downstream of FL 200. They are part of a small parcel of the Withlacoochee State Forest on the west bank. This is the last public-lands campsite before Dunnellon. Do not pass it up unless you plan to paddle all the way to Dunnellon. Beyond here, the Withlacoochee opens into a large swamp, changing faces yet again. It divides into channels around islands with a solid current.

At the northeast end of the swamp, 4.5 miles below Two Mile Prairie Canoe Camp, the river breaks up into hill-bordered lakes with houses on the high ground. Two miles downstream, after passing under the Withlacoochee State Trail, a rail-trail, the crystalline Rainbow River enters on the right. From here, paddlers are 1 mile from Dunnellon and the take-out. It is 13.0 miles from FL 200 to Dunnellon.

✧ **SHUTTLE** To reach the take-out from the intersection of FL 44 and US 41 in downtown Inverness, take US 41 North 17.0 miles to the bridge over the Withlacoochee River in Dunnellon. Just after you cross the bridge, take the first left to the boat ramp at City Hall, just north of the bridge.

To reach the uppermost put-in from the take-out, backtrack on US 41 South to FL 44 and turn left (east). At the second intersection, south of Cooter Lake, bear left to continue east on FL 44, and take it 7.1 miles to the bridge over the Withlacoochee River. The Rutland Park public boat ramp is located on the southeast side of the bridge, and the river is accessed via a short canal.

✧ **GAUGE** Phone, web. Call Nobleton Canoe and Boat Rental for river information at 352-796-4343. The USGS gauge helpful in determining flow rates for any given day is Withlacoochee River near Holder, Florida.

PADDLERS HAVE TO PORTAGE AROUND THIS DAM AT CARLSON.

36   RAINBOW RIVER

◇ **OVERVIEW** The Rainbow River is a short tributary of the Withlacoochee River, near the town of Dunnellon. It has historically been a tourist attraction and has been heavily developed. Houses line much of the riverbank between Rainbow Springs and the Rainbow River's confluence with the Withlacoochee. Rainbow Springs is protected as a Florida state park, but it can be extremely crowded, especially during the summer months. There is a kayak/canoe launch in the park, but you have to carry your craft more than a quarter mile from the parking area. However, kayaks and canoes can be rented from a waterside concessionaire. Downstream, Marion County runs a park where paddlers can launch their boats and enjoy the unspoiled, ultraclear waters, where fish, turtles, and other underwater life are easily visible in both the depths and shallows of the river.

This run can be quite busy on weekends with tubers, canoeists, kayakers, and motorboaters all vying for a spot on the water.

◇ **MAPS** DUNNELLON (USGS)

K. P. Hole Park to County Road 484

Class	I
Length	3.6
Time	2
Gauge	Visual, web
Level	N/A
Gradient	0.4
Scenery	B

36 **DESCRIPTION** Paddlers who want to get on the water but don't feel like paddling hard should make this easy run from K. P. Hole Park to CR 484. If you feel like getting a workout, you can paddle upstream from K. P. Hole to the state park, then drift back down past K. P. Hole and on to the take-out. The water and aquatic life here are fascinating. A snorkel is in order for those inclined. Swaying grasses and boulders contrast with sandy sections of the river bottom. Some parts of the river are surprisingly deep. The wild underwater nature of the run contrasts mightily with the house-lined banks. Birdlife is abundant despite the development. Some

sections of the river have wooded banks of moss-draped cypress, providing relief from the house parade, especially beyond the 2.0-mile mark. The county ban on alcohol and disposable food containers is strictly enforced on the river. Tubes and canoes are available for rent at K. P. Hole Park.

◇ **SHUTTLE** To reach the take-out from the intersection of US 41 and CR 484/Pennsylvania Avenue in Dunnellon, head east 0.8 mile on CR 484 to the bridge over the Rainbow River and a canoe/kayak/tube exit on the southeast side of the bridge.

To reach the put-in from the same intersection, continue north on US 41 for 2.4 miles. Turn right (east) on Southwest 99th Place and cross the railroad tracks. In 1.1 miles, just after the railroad tracks, turn left (north) on Southwest 190th Avenue and follow it 0.6 mile to K. P. Hole Park, on your right.

◇ **GAUGE** Visual, web. The Rainbow River is spring-fed and is runnable year-round. However, the USGS gauge helpful to determine flow rates for any given day is Rainbow Springs near Dunnellon, Florida.

Rainbow River: K. P. Hole Park to County Road 484

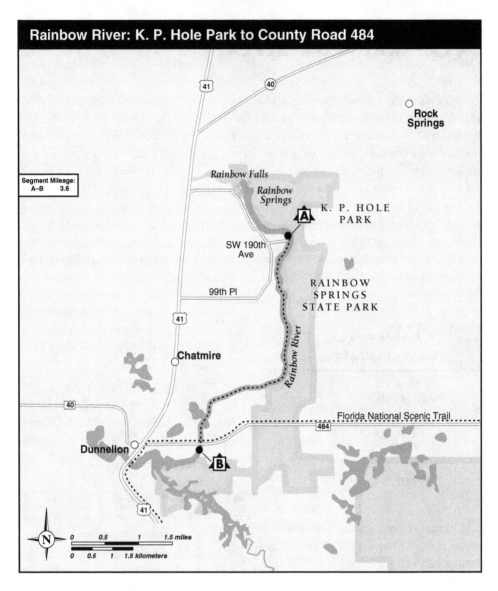

37 SILVER RIVER

◇ **OVERVIEW** Silver Spring, which feeds the Silver River, has long been a Central Florida tourist attraction. Located east of Ocala, the beautiful Silver River corridor below the springs is part of Silver Springs State Park. River access has been improved with the establishment of the park. Now you can follow the current downstream from the headspring to the Silver River's confluence with the Ocklawaha, rather than beating your way upstream from the Ocklawaha all the way to the headspring.

◇ **MAPS** SILVER SPRINGS STATE PARK MAP; OCALA EAST, LYNNE (USGS)

Silver Springs State Park to Ray Wayside Access

Class	I
Length	5
Time	Varies
Gauge	Phone, web
Level	Spring-fed
Gradient	1
Scenery	A

37 **DESCRIPTION** The Silver River is where the first glass-bottomed boats were used. And they are still in use today, to see the array of aquatic life below the water's surface. I can still remember touring Silver Springs as a kid, looking down on another world. Nowadays, the headspring area and downstream to the Ocklawaha River are a Florida state park. There is a fee canoe-and-kayak launch at the park's main entrance at the headspring, and a free second launch (still requiring a park entrance fee) that requires a half-mile carry to the put-in. I have done both—pay the launch fee, it is worth it. Canoes and kayaks can be rented at the headspring.

Once on the river, you can enjoy spring water measured at 550 million gallons of water flowing per day. It is 2.0 miles from the springhead launch to the carry launch. It is 3 more miles downstream to the Ocklawaha River through junglelike banks with waterweeds bordering the steady current. The take-out is downstream on the west bank of the Silver River, at Ray Wayside Park, which is reached via a short canal.

◇ **SHUTTLE** From Exit 352 off I-75 in Ocala, drive east on FL 40. After 11.9 miles, bear right on Northeast 28th Lane and, in 0.5 mile, reach the take-out at Ray Wayside Park, before you reach the bridge over the Ocklawaha River.

To reach the put-in, backtrack 3.9 miles west on FL 40 to the main entrance to Silver Springs State Park, on your left. An entrance fee applies (see "Fees and Permits," page 6).

◇ **GAUGE** Phone, web. Call Silver Springs State Park at 352-261-5840 for the latest river conditions. The USGS gauge helpful in determining flow rates for any given day is Silver River near Ocala, Florida.

Silver River: Silver Springs State Park to Ray Wayside Access

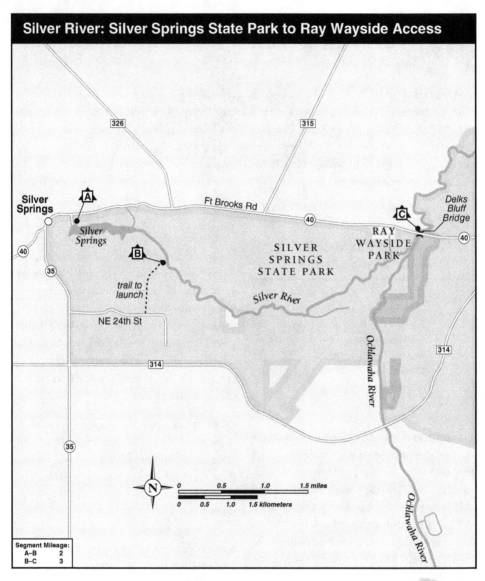

326

315

Ft Brooks Rd

Silver Springs

A

Silver Springs

40

35

B

trail to launch

NE 24th St

40

SILVER
SPRINGS
STATE PARK

Silver River

Ochlawaha River

C

Delks Bluff Bridge

RAY
WAYSIDE
PARK

40

314

35

314

Ochlawaha River

N

0	0.5	1.0	1.5 miles

| 0 | 0.5 | 1.0 | 1.5 kilometers |

Segment Mileage:	
A–B	2
B–C	3

38 OCKLAWAHA RIVER

✧ **OVERVIEW** The Ocklawaha is a fabulous paddling river. However, it was forever altered when it was to be a primary waterway for the Florida Cross State Canal. Before the peninsula-dividing canal was permanently halted, parts of Ocklawaha were extensively channelized and developed, yet most of the Ocklawaha flows in its natural wild cast. Ironically, condemnation of the river's borderlands has now resulted in protected banks on the Ocklawaha and a pre-served corridor that is the Cross Florida Greenway.

Some sections of the river have been rendered less than desirable for paddling. The stretch of river from Moss Bluff to County Road 314 was channelized to allow muck farming. Down-stream, Rodman Dam, part of the ill-fated canal, alters the river, but it's a decent lake paddle for those inclined and must be paddled to link disparate wild segments of river.

That being said, the recommended sections are among the best in the state. Wildlife-management areas border most of the river, making for a wild setting and overnight-camping opportunities. The geologically ancient Ocklawaha has carved a mile-wide valley. The low-sediment waterway coloration varies with proximity to tannin-filled swamps but maintains a blackish hue throughout. Cypress and tupelo border much of the river, while sweet bay and maple occupy slightly drier margins. Higher ground holds live oak, magnolia, and beech trees. Avian life is thick on the river corridor, with songbirds, raptors, and wading birds. I have found the fishing to be productive, especially for red-breasted bream and shellcrackers. Deer and bears find a home in the seemingly impenetrable backwoods, where the river flows through the Ocala National Forest and other public lands bordering the Ocklawaha.

✧ **MAPS** OCALA NATIONAL FOREST MAP; LYNNE, FORT MCCOY (USGS)

FL 40 to County Road 316

Class	I
Length	20
Time	Varies
Gauge	Phone, web
Level	N/A
Gradient	1.4
Scenery	A

38 DESCRIPTION This run can be broken into two segments: FL 40 to Gores Landing and Gores Landing to Eureka West. The put-in starts on a canal that leads to the lower-most part of the spring-fed Silver River and shortly meets up with the Ocklawaha; then the river begins winding north through hardwood forests and swamps with sporadic bluffs rising about 15 feet from the water's edge. About 4.0 miles downstream of the FL 40 bridge, tributaries join the dark river as it courses through lush forests that scream "wild Florida." Spring and fall are excellent times to see this swamp hardwood forest of cypress and gum color out. The river current is moderate. Lilies border the inside of river bends where the current slackens.

Wildlife-management areas on both banks keep the river wild in appearance. A public campground and boat ramp will be found at Gores Landing, 10.0 miles downstream from

Ocklawaha River: FL 40 to County Road 316

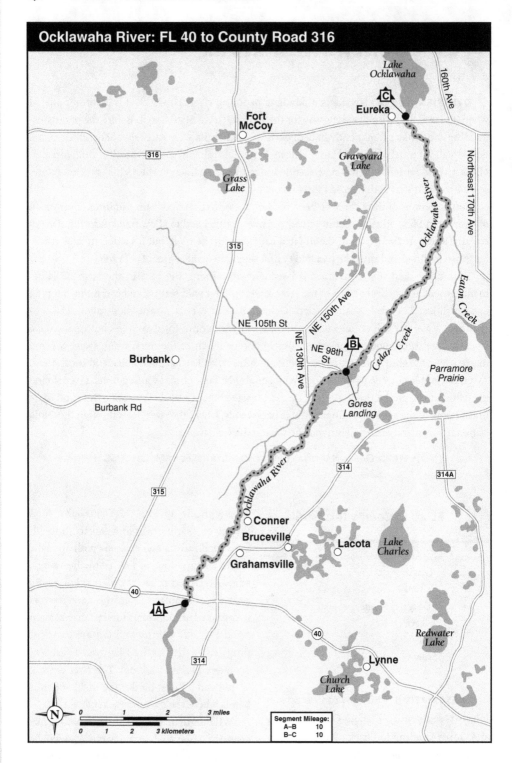

Segment Mileage:
A–B   10
B–C   10

FL 40. Paddlers with an explorative bent will make short forays into Dead River and Cedar Creek. Eaton Creek flows in from the east bank after journeying from Eaton Lake in the Ocala National Forest. Below this confluence, a very high bluff with some houses rises.

It is only 2.0 miles from Eaton Creek to a boat landing on the east bank just before going under the CR 316 bridge. Just beyond the bridge, paddlers will pass an old circular concrete bridge abutment. This is a remnant of the days when steamboats plied the Ocklawaha. Their high smokestacks couldn't pass under bridges of that time, so the bridges were built so they could pivot and allow passage of the steamboats. The Eureka West boat

landing, one of the Cross Florida Greenway recreation areas, is just beyond the abutment on river left.

Ambitious paddlers can continue beyond Eureka West into Rodman Reservoir. Below CR 316, the river enters the reservoir. Paddlers traversing the impoundment will spyglass plentiful wading birds. The current is negligible here, and the open waters are subject to winds. An access can be found near Orange Springs and another access near Kenwood. Paddlers can curve east with the lake and head onward to Rodman Dam, where the low earthen structure allows easy paddler access. Paddlers continuing on can portage over the dam with minimal

ALLIGATOR-EYE VIEW OF THE OCKLAWAHA RIVER

difficulty. I've done it numerous times. Land toward the middle of the dam, then scout your route.

Below Rodman Dam, it's an additional 5.0 miles to the ramp at FL 19. The old river channel comes in on the right, below the dam run. Then the river breaks into numerous channels and exudes a gorgeous, remote aura with wild, protected banks. Stay right at the first split, beyond the old river channel, and look for flagging tape and/or sawn limbs. From here it is 4 more miles to meet the St. Johns River at Little Lake George. The river splits many times on the way, so be aware and generally stay with the southernmost channels. The last big bluff is near an old American Indian mound. It was once Davenport Landing, a river stopping point for the old steamboats. The US Forest Service has erected an interpretive display here.

Additionally, paddlers can put in 3.0 miles above FL 40 at CR 314, or even farther up at Moss Bluff and the CR 464 bridge. However, the Ocklawaha is channelized in a 40-foot-wide canal most of the way. Beyond the channelized portion, the river is about 50 feet wide, and beautiful hardwood forests begin. The spring-fed Silver River enters from the west shortly before FL 40.

◇ **SHUTTLE** To reach the lowermost take-out from Exit 352 off I-75 in Ocala, take FL 40 East 10.9 miles to CR 315. Turn right (north) on CR 315 and, in 10.8 miles, turn right on CR 316. After 3.8 miles, turn left (northeast) on Northeast 152nd Place, left again on Northeast 152nd Court Road, right on Northeast 154th Street, and then left again to reach the Eureka West Boat ramp.

To reach Gores Landing from Ocala, follow the directions above to CR 315. Turn right (north) on CR 315 and, in 6.4 miles, turn right (east) on Northeast 105th Street. In 2.1 miles, turn right (south) on Gores Landing Park Road; in 0.8 mile, turn left (south) on Northeast 98th Street and follow it to end at Gores Landing. There is a launch fee at this park, which has a resident on-site.

To reach the uppermost put-in from the accesses above, backtrack on CR 315 to FL 40 and turn left, heading east. In 1.0 mile, bear right on Northeast 28th Lane and, in another 0.5 mile, reach the put-in at Ray Wayside Park, before you reach the bridge over the Ocklawaha River.

◇ **GAUGE** Phone, web. Call Ocklawaha Canoe Outpost at 352-236-4606 for the latest river conditions. The USGS gauge helpful in determining flow rates for any given day is Ocklawaha River at Moss Bluff, Florida.

LOOKING FOR WILDLIFE ALONG THE OCKLAWAHA

39 ALEXANDER SPRINGS AND ALEXANDER SPRINGS CREEK

✧ **OVERVIEW** Alexander Springs runs through the heart of the Ocala National Forest and is the centerpiece of a popular recreation area. Alexander Springs Creek emerges from a first-magnitude spring emitting 76 million gallons of water a day, creating a springhead pool spanning 200 feet across. Swimmers, divers, and paddlers can be found enjoying the waters. Beyond the springhead, the creek runs down a wide channel bordered by palm, maple, pine, and live oak draped in Spanish moss. Water lilies, cattails, and other vegetation thrive atop the water, channeling the stream flow.

Paddlers will choose their route among braided channels created by the watery vegetation. Downstream, islands create channels of their own. There is an entrance fee at Alexander Springs. If you want to avoid the fee, you can start at County Road 445, but you will miss the uppermost part of the run. Be aware that Alexander Springs Recreation Area also has a good-quality campground. The lowermost part of the run, from 52 Landing to the St. Johns River, is a seldom-paddled, first-rate adventure in the federally designated Alexander Springs Wilderness.

✧ **MAPS** OCALA NATIONAL FOREST MAP; ALEXANDER SPRINGS, LAKE WOODRUFF (USGS)

A Alexander Springs to 52 Landing

Class	I
Length	7
Time	3
Gauge	Visual
Level	Spring-fed
Gradient	0.7
Scenery	A

39A DESCRIPTION The run begins just below the roped-off swim area at the 72°F springhead. The clear water is immediately evident. Keep an eye out for wildlife above and below the surface. Pass under the CR 445 bridge at 1 mile. Alexander Springs Creek flows wide for the first 5.0 miles but is broken into channels created by aquatic vegetation at the surface. Underwater vegetation sways in the current of this crystalline spring run.

Downstream, a few houses are located along Ellis Landing, on the south bank. The waterway tapers and curves, sometimes flowing around palmy islands. The 52 Landing is on the left bank. The concessionaire at Alexander Springs Recreation Area does rent canoes but no longer provides shuttles.

✧ **SHUTTLE** To reach the take-out from Exit 352 off I-75 in Ocala, take FL 40 East into Ocala National Forest. After 40.7 miles, turn right (southwest) on CR 445A, In 0.6 mile, bear left at the intersection to continue south on CR 445. In 4.7 miles, turn left (east) on Forest Road 18; then, in 1.8 miles, veer right and follow FR 18 for 2.9 more miles to its end, at a landing on lower Alexander Springs Creek. Note that FR 18 can be soupy after prolonged rains.

To reach the put-in from the take-out, backtrack on FR 18 to CR 445. Turn left (west) on CR 445, crossing the bridge over Alexander Springs Creek, and in 1.1 miles reach the

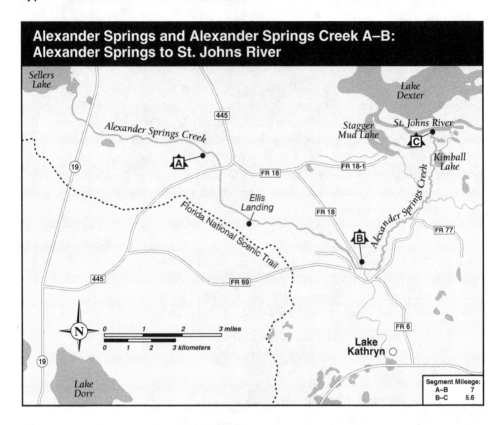

Alexander Springs and Alexander Springs Creek A–B: Alexander Springs to St. Johns River

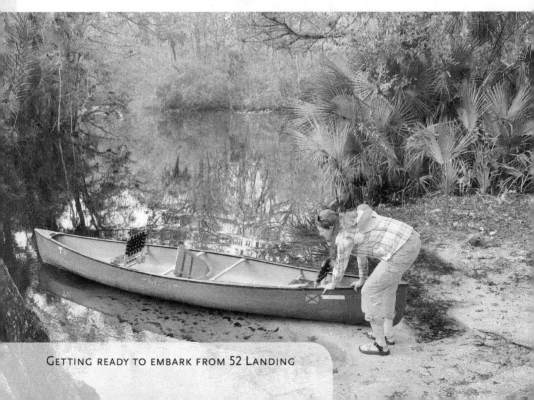

entrance to Alexander Springs Recreation Area, on your right. Follow the entrance road north 0.2 mile; the boat launch is a short distance to your right, past the parking area.

You must pay a day-use fee to enter Alexander Springs Recreation Area; for the latest information, call 352-669-3522 or visit www.fs.usda.gov/ocala (click "Recreation" and then "Alexander Springs").

✧ **GAUGE** Visual. This spring averages more than 70 million gallons per day and should always be runnable.

LONE PADDLER ON
ALEXANDER SPRINGS CREEK

B 52 Landing to St. Johns River

Class	I
Length	11.2 (out-and-back)
Time	6
Gauge	Visual
Level	N/A
Gradient	0.3
Scenery	A

39A DESCRIPTION This run along lower Alexander Springs Creek takes place almost entirely within Alexander Springs Wilderness of the Ocala National Forest. The scenery is inspiring and the run is challenging—you make the 5.6-mile paddle down to the St. Johns River, then paddle back upstream, since there are no public landings on the St. Johns for miles. The uppermost part of this run is swift, with many turns. The stream then widens and slows its last 2.0 miles. It is a trip you will be willing to make twice, to appreciate the rugged scenery.

Leave the 52 Landing amid close-knit banks of cypress, gum, palm, and oaks. The winding current takes you by a water gauge and then a bluff on your left. The stream flows by a small enclave of dwellings on river right for about a quarter mile. One mile into the run and you are back in wilderness again. The dark water twists and curls on sharp bends, sometimes around tree clusters posing as islands. Fallen trees are cut out by other boaters.

Come near sporadic bluffs. At 2.8 miles, pass a dug channel leading right to a former boat ramp near Forest Road 77, closed since the area's wilderness designation. The bluffs cease. At 3.4 miles, remote and rugged Get Out Creek enters on your right. Dare yourself to explore it.

By 3.6 miles, Alexander Springs Creek has widened, the current slows, and you might see a motorboat angler or two. Waterweeds adorn the streamside here. At 4.5 miles, reach a short channel leading right to Kimball Lake. By now, the banks are swampy, with no dry ground.

At 5.0 miles, pass another channel leading to Kimball Lake. From here the stream takes you to the wide St. Johns at 5.6 miles. Note the manatee warning signs. There is nowhere to stop in this vicinity. Also, allow yourself ample time to paddle back upstream to 52 Landing—it takes longer to go upstream than it will downstream.

◇ **DIRECTIONS** The put-in/take-out for lower Alexander Springs Creek is the same as the take-out described in the previous segment.

◇ **GAUGE** Visual. This spring averages more than 70 million gallons per day and should always be runnable.

LOWER ALEXANDER SPRINGS CREEK LIES ALMOST ENTIRELY WITHIN FEDERALLY DESIGNATED WILDERNESS.

40   JUNIPER SPRINGS AND JUNIPER CREEK

◆ **OVERVIEW** Juniper Springs flows almost as clear as air. Back in the 1930s, when the Ocala National Forest recreation area was developed, the spring upwelling was enclosed in a rock-and-concrete wall, creating an alluring swimming pool. You will see an old waterwheel that was once used to make electricity for the site using the spring's outflow.

The put-in is a short distance below the waterwheel. Juniper Creek starts barely wide enough for a kayak or canoe below rich, canopied woodland. It then enters the gorgeous Juniper Prairie Wilderness, through which it flows until just above the FL 19 bridge. Paddlers will use all their skills navigating the sharp turns, cypress stumps, and overhanging palms and other trees. Kayaks in excess of 14 feet are not recommended. After rains, the crystalline waters can become stained, and the resulting higher water can make the run even more challenging. Be apprised that this run can be very busy on nice weekends, and inexperienced paddlers can turn the run into a nightmarish game of "bumper boats." Go during the week if possible.

◆ **MAPS** OCALA NATIONAL FOREST MAP; JUNIPER SPRINGS (USGS)

Juniper Springs to FL 19

Class	I+
Length	7
Time	4
Gauge	Visual
Level	Spring-fed
Gradient	3.7
Scenery	A+

40 **DESCRIPTION** Your adventure starts when you carry your boat through beautiful palm-topped woods on a paved trail to Juniper Creek. Most of the stream is very narrow and constricted with palm trees, cypress trees, live oaks, and dense vegetation. Be prepared to duck under and work around numerous overhanging trees. The water is so clear that its depths are deceptive. Fern Hammock Springs adds to the flow.

A sign indicates your entry into Juniper Prairie Wilderness. Halfway Landing is a designated stopping spot in the wilderness. Not surprisingly, it is about halfway through the run and offers no put-in or take-out access. The next public access from the put-in is at FL 19, so you must do the entire run, though the challenges of the ultranarrow waterway have caused enough fights that argumentative couples have desired an early egress.

Downstream of Halfway Landing, Juniper Creek occasionally widens over grassy underwater vegetation and splits around cigar-shaped palm islands. Watch for alligators sunning hereabouts. Sweetwater Springs comes in from the left-hand bank but is not open to the public. Old bridge pilings running across the stream indicate you are close to FL 19.

Juniper Springs remains open and relatively wide until you pass under the FL 19 bridge to find the official access on the right bank. Adventurous paddlers can continue their trip 3.0 miles to big Lake George, but the next access is a few miles east at Volusia Bar Wharf, the Lake George boat ramp that is also the launch point for Blue Creek, profiled

Juniper Springs and Juniper Creek: Juniper Springs to FL 19

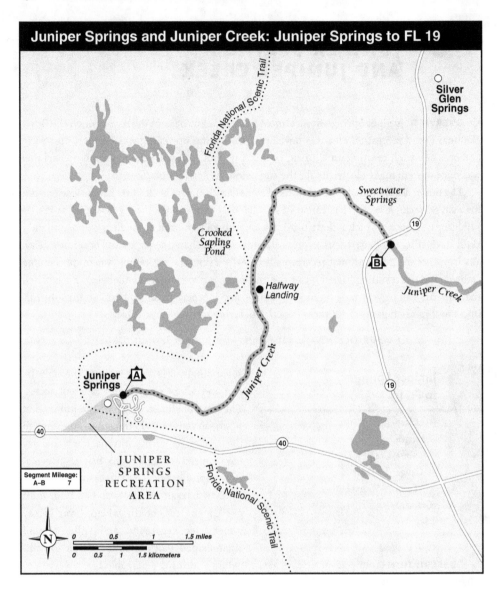

a bit later (see page 181). If you try this, prepare for potential wind and waves, especially if the winds are out of the north. The Juniper Springs Recreation Area rents canoes and kayaks and provides shuttle service for their boats as well as private craft.

SHUTTLE To reach the take-out from Exit 352 off I-75 in Ocala, head east on FL 40 into Ocala National Forest. After 35.1 miles, turn left (north) on FL 19 and follow it 3.4 miles to reach Juniper Wayside Park. The parking area and take-out are on the southeast side of the bridge over Juniper Creek.

To reach the put-in from the take-out, backtrack on FL 19 to FL 40. Turn right (west) on FL 40 and drive 4.4 miles to the entrance to Juniper Springs Recreation Area, on your right. A day-use fee applies; call 352-625-2808 or visit juniper-springs.com for the latest information. Follow the entrance road north 0.2 mile, then bear left to follow the road another 0.3 mile to the parking area. The canoe launch is a few yards to the right via a paved trail.

 GAUGE Visual. Juniper Creek is spring-fed and has a nearly constant flow.

PARTS OF JUNIPER CREEK ARE JUNGLE-ESQUE, LIKE THIS ONE.

41 SALT SPRINGS AND SALT SPRINGS RUN

◇ **OVERVIEW** Salt Springs, so named for the minerals in its waters, pours forth more than 60 million gallons of water per day. A vast recreation area has been developed around these springs, including a campground, swimming area, day-use area, and marina downstream from the springs.

Despite the overwhelming presence of humans on its upper stretches, the setting becomes wild once downstream. Salt Springs Run is known for its wildlife. However, this scenery comes with a price as the 4-mile trip ends at Lake George, where there is no take-out, forcing paddlers to paddle upstream against the current. Paddlers can scout part of their run via the Salt Springs Trail, which leads to the south bank of the run below the springs.

◇ **MAPS** Ocala National Forest map; Salt Springs (USGS)

Salt Springs to Lake George and Back

Class	I
Length	8 (out-and-back)
Time	5.5
Gauge	Visual
Level	Spring-fed
Gradient	1.0
Scenery	B+

41 DESCRIPTION This can be a very crowded and busy run during the summer and on nice winter weekends. The run starts at the Salt Springs marina. You can paddle upstream a short distance to the springs. Fish are normally seen finning around the spring boils. From the springs, the clear, wide channel of Salt Springs Run heads east for Lake George. Marsh borders the river. There is high ground on river left near the site of the Indian Mounds.

Once at Lake George, 4.0 miles below Salt Springs, paddlers can relax at Salt Springs Bar and look over one of Florida's most picturesque lakes. If you want to explore the lake, Salt Springs Cove, to the left of Lake George after you leave Salt Springs Run, is one of the most gorgeous shorelines in the state.

With the bountiful wildlife and historical value of this run, paddlers continue to hope that the US Forest Service will one day install a ramp at the lower end of the run, eliminating the out-and-back nature of the run as it currently exists.

◇ **DIRECTIONS** To reach Salt Springs Marina from Exit 352 off I-75 in Ocala, head east on FL 40 into Ocala National Forest. After 35.1 miles, turn left (north) on FL 19 and follow it 15.6 miles. Turn right and follow the marina entrance road about 0.4 mile to the launch.

◇ **GAUGE** Visual. Salt Springs Run is a spring-fed waterway, floatable year-round.

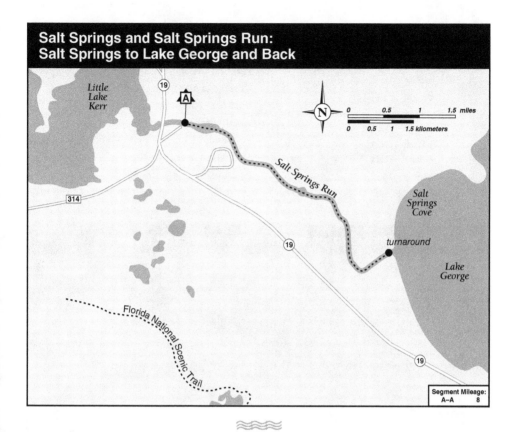

**Salt Springs and Salt Springs Run:
Salt Springs to Lake George and Back**

Little Lake Kerr

Salt Springs Run

Salt Springs Cove

turnaround

Lake George

Florida National Scenic Trail

Segment Mileage:
A–A   8

42   BLUE CREEK

✧ **OVERVIEW** Blue Creek is essentially a channel of the St. Johns River, running through the Ocala National Forest before rejoining the St. Johns just before the St. Johns enters massive Lake George, one of my favorite stillwater paddling places in the Sunshine State. Blue Creek is known for alligators and manatees in the summertime. However, any time of year will treat the paddler, though Blue Creek is run by motorboats. So if you are looking for solitude, paddle this stream when you think the boaters will be home.

The trip starts on Lake George. Get a taste of the apparently boundless lake before turning up the St. Johns, then spurring into Blue Creek, bordered on both sides by national forest. The winding run leads through a natural setting until reaching the community of Astor and the St. Johns River. Your best bet here is to turn down the St. Johns, enjoying the current, since the initial paddle on Blue Creek is upstream. This loop circles Blue Island. *Note:* There is a public ramp on Blue Creek in Astor, if you wish to avoid backtracking.

✧ **MAPS** OCALA NATIONAL FOREST MAP; ASTOR (USGS)

Lake George to St. Johns River and Back

Class	I
Length	7.5 (out-and-back)
Time	4
Gauge	Visual
Level	N/A
Gradient	N/A
Scenery	A

42 **DESCRIPTION** The Lake George boat ramp may be muddy. After launching, head right on the shore of massive Lake George. If the lake is glassy, sky and water meld into the distance. A boating channel is visible in the weed-bordered lake.

Paddle by a few private lake homes and then you are astride the Ocala National Forest, with its moss-draped, wooded shores of cypress. After a quarter mile, leave the lake

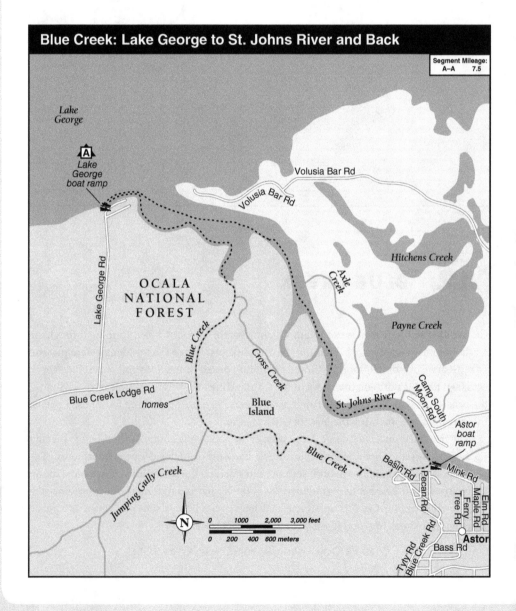

Blue Creek: Lake George to St. Johns River and Back

Segment Mileage:
A–A   7.5

and turn into the St. Johns River. The current is against you. Stay on the right shore, noting the boating channel markers in the river.

At 1 mile, enter a cove on the right bank. It leads up Blue Creek. Begin the circumnavigation of Blue Island, entering Blue Creek proper. The current will be against you. The stream is about 80 feet wide, with weedy banks from which rises dense forest. Blue Creek is a no-wake zone, protecting the manatees that ply its waters.

At 1.4 miles, Cross Creek leaves left. At 2.0 miles, pass a private inholding then Jumping Gully Creek, both on river right. Open to the community of Astor and its boat ramp at 4.0 miles. The public ramp has a roofed picnic area for stopping. Dry ground is scarce in these parts.

Just ahead, you can turn into the St. Johns, enjoying its current. The banks remain wild, save for a fish camp on river right. Navigational markers and motorboats are common. Paddle by a little dry ground in a palm hammock before leaving Blue Island. From there, open onto big Lake George and hope the winds aren't from the north.

✧ **DIRECTIONS** From the intersection of County Road 445 and FL 40 in the hamlet of Astor Park, head west on FL 40 for 1.5 miles, then turn right (north) on Blue Creek Lodge Road/CR 9883. Follow it 2.5 miles, then turn left on Lake George Road. Dead-end at the boat ramp after 1 mile.

✧ **GAUGE** This paddle is always runnable, but a gauge of interest is St. Johns River at Astor, Florida.

THE FIRST PART OF THIS PADDLE TAKES PLACE ON HUGE LAKE GEORGE.

43   STAGGER MUD LAKE

◇ **OVERVIEW** More and more paddlers are looking for paddling circuits—loops—that cover new and wild water while avoiding shuttles. This paddling trip is a response to that and is an official blueway under the banner of Lake County. It starts at a rustic fish camp on Lake Dexter, part of the greater St. Johns River, then explores part of Lake Dexter to find an ancient Indian mound at Bowers Bluff. Next, reach island-studded Stagger Mud Lake, one of the all-time great Florida lake names. The wild shores are part of the Ocala National Forest and are a fine place to spot waterfowl, songbirds, and raptors. Add to your adventure by paddling up Stagger Creek until it closes in. After you've circled Stagger Mud Lake, it's a simple backtrack to the landing on Lake Dexter.

◇ **MAPS** OCALA NATIONAL FOREST MAP; ASTOR, LAKE WOODRUFF (USGS)

Lake Dexter to Stagger Creek and Back

Class	I
Length	7.5 (out-and-back)
Time	4
Gauge	Visual
Level	N/A
Gradient	N/A
Scenery	A

43 **DESCRIPTION** Leave the fish-camp boat ramp and head south on Lake Dexter, plying the lily pad–laden shore. Shortly border the Ocala National Forest, enjoying the expanse of Lake Dexter to your left and the untamed shoreline to your right. Curve into a richly wooded cove, returning to the main lake at 2.0 miles. Continue hugging the right-hand shore. Pass near channel marker 15 to your left, then turn right into the current-filled St. Johns River at Idlewilde Point. Keep a close eye on the shore here.

At 2.7 miles, you will come to the Bowers Bluff shell midden, on the right bank. This snail shell mound is estimated to be more than 3,000 years old and is now covered in

VULTURES GATHER ABOVE STAGGER MUD LAKE.

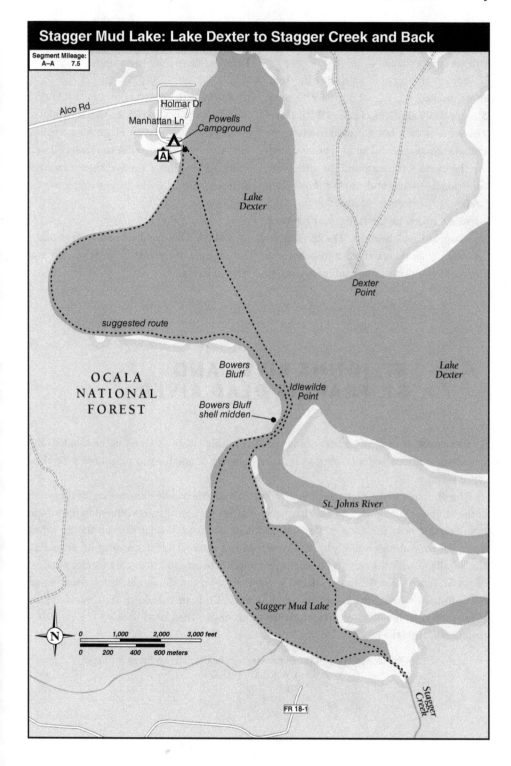

Stagger Mud Lake: Lake Dexter to Stagger Creek and Back

Segment Mileage:
A–A   7.5

Alco Rd

Holmar Dr

Manhattan Ln

Powells
Campground

A

Lake
Dexter

Dexter
Point

suggested route

OCALA
NATIONAL
FOREST

Bowers
Bluff

Lake
Dexter

Idlewilde
Point

Bowers Bluff
shell midden

St. Johns River

Stagger Mud Lake

N

0   1,000   2,000   3,000 feet

0   200   400   600 meters

FR 18-1

Stagger
Creek

trees. However, shells are visible along the bank, and it's about the only dry ground you will see on the paddle.

Beyond the mound, stay with the right shore, leaving the St. Johns River to enter Stagger Mud Lake. What a name! What a lake! The water is dark but not muddy. However, the lake bottom is soft mud, perhaps lending the name. Cruise around the still water, admiring its islands and ample wildlife from bald eagles to egrets to woodpeckers.

At 4.5 miles, in the lake's southeast corner, Stagger Creek beckons. The creek is 60 feet wide, then tapers about a mile beyond. Explore if you please, but it adds distance to the paddle. From here, paddle north up Stagger Mud Lake, returning to the river and then Lake Dexter and the boat ramp.

✧ **DIRECTIONS** From the intersection of County Road 445 and FL 40 in the hamlet of Astor Park, head east on FL 40 for 2.2 miles, then turn right on paved Alco Road. Follow it south and east for 4.1 miles, then turn right to reach Powells Campground and a private fee ramp.

✧ **GAUGE** This paddle is always runnable, but a gauge of interest is St. Johns River at Astor, Florida.

44   ST. JOHNS RIVER AND ST. FRANCIS DEAD RIVER

✧ **OVERVIEW** It used to be that paddlers looked at big rivers as places to be avoided. But nowadays, if there's water flowing—no matter how big or small—you might see a kayak or canoe plying it.

The St. Johns River is one such body of water, and this paddle explores an ideal portion of the St. Johns, along with an old channel that offers historical enhancement to the adventure. Starting near the town of DeLand, paddlers can head downstream on the St. Johns River, bordered almost entirely by wildlife refuge and national forest, creating eye-appealing scenery. Bend with the waterway, scoping for wildlife before you turn up a former channel of the St. Johns—the St. Francis Dead River. Paddle up the slender channel, reaching an old tram track where you can get out and link to the St. Francis Hiking Trail, exploring an abandoned river town. After that, circle the embayment, then head back up the St. Johns, this time against the current.

✧ **MAPS** OCALA NATIONAL FOREST MAP; ST. FRANCIS DEAD RIVER RUN MAP; LAKE WOODRUFF (USGS)

Ed Stone Park to St. Francis Dead River and Back

Class	I
Length	10.5 (out-and-back)
Time	5.5
Gauge	Visual
Level	N/A
Gradient	N/A
Scenery	A

DESCRIPTION This adventure starts at Ed Stone Park. Leave north into the St. Johns River. It isn't long before you're paddling along an almost entirely wild and natural shoreline with the Ocala National Forest on one side and Lake Woodruff National Wildlife Refuge on the other. Channel markers are placed for motor boaters.

Pass River Forest Group Camp; then, at 1 mile, near marker 39, curve left around

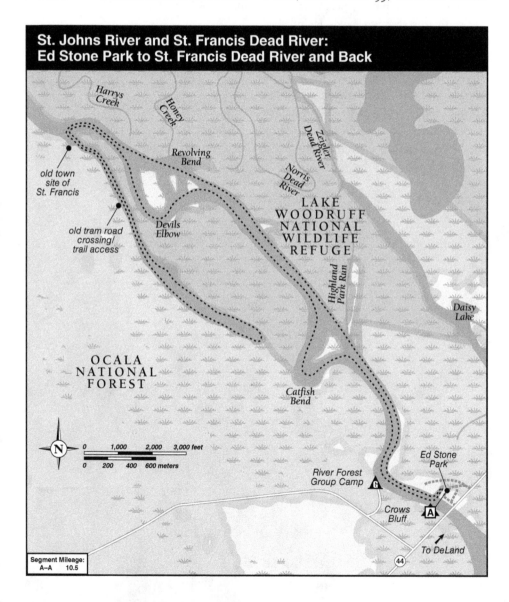

St. Johns River and St. Francis Dead River:
Ed Stone Park to St. Francis Dead River and Back

Harrys Creek
Honey Creek
Revolving Bend
Zeigler Dead River
Norris Dead River
old town site of St. Francis
old tram road crossing/ trail access
Devils Elbow
LAKE WOODRUFF NATIONAL WILDLIFE REFUGE
Highland Park Run
Daisy Lake
OCALA NATIONAL FOREST
Catfish Bend
N
0   1,000   2,000   3,000 feet
0   200   400   600 meters
Ed Stone Park
River Forest Group Camp
Crows Bluff
To DeLand
44
Segment Mileage:
A–A   10.5

Catfish Bend, only to reenter the main channel of the St. Johns. The banks are swampy. At marker 32, again curve left on the Devils Elbow, around a few islands. At 3.7 miles and channel marker 26, cut acutely left up the St. Francis Dead River, a narrow, weed-bordered channel, formerly the primary channel of the St. Johns.

Once a thriving river town connected to the outside world by steamboat traffic, St. Francis was a trading post where timber and citrus swapped hands for finished goods used by area settlements. When the railroads laid tracks through nearby DeLand, steamboat shipping died off. By 1935, St. Francis was abandoned. Although the forests have reclaimed the area, you can still see evidence of the old settlements via a hiking trail accessed on the paddle, including an old spring and dock site.

Come to a raised tram road and bridge site at 4.3 miles—this is a good place to land your craft and explore. On your right (west), follow the tram road to the St. Francis Trail, then turn right (north) on the blazed hiking trail to visit the old town site.

The paddle continues up the St. Francis and the old river channel's end, then turns back at 5.5 miles. From here, backtrack down the St. Francis then up the St. Johns, exploring alternate routes if desired.

◇ **DIRECTIONS** From the intersection of US 17/US 92 and FL 44 in DeLand, take FL 44 West 5.2 miles to Ed Stone Park, on your right just before the bridge over the St. Johns River. The put-in and take-out are the same.

◇ **GAUGE** This paddle is always runnable, but a gauge of interest is St. Johns River near DeLand, Florida.

PADDLING ALONG THE ST. JOHNS

The St. Francis Dead River is an old channel of the St. Johns River.

The Central Highlands

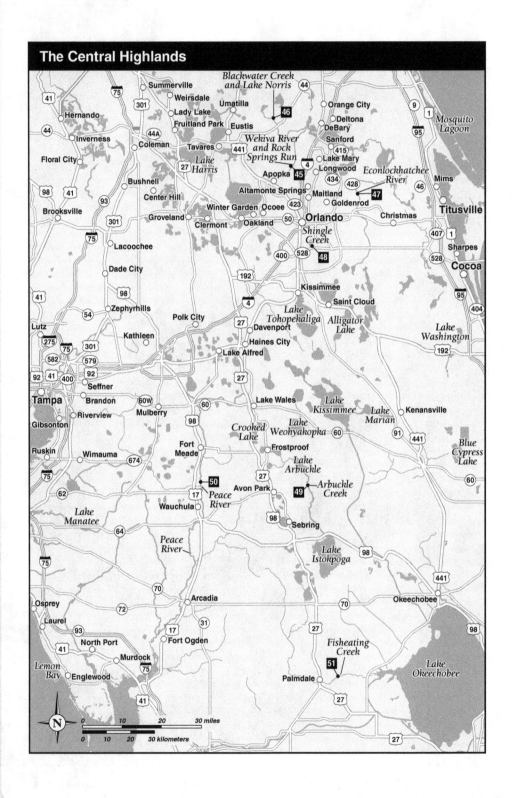

45 WEKIVA RIVER AND ROCK SPRINGS RUN

◇ **OVERVIEW** Rock Springs Run and the entire Wekiva River are state-designated paddling trails. These surprisingly untamed waterways draw in paddlers from the Orlando area and beyond; thus, they can be crowded during the warm months and on weekends. Protected park lands and preserves keep the banks of the crystal-clear streams astonishingly wild and natural. Semitropical Florida wetlands are highlighted by palm, cypress, and live oak, draped in resurrection ferns and Spanish moss. It is truly an oasis amid ever-expanding greater Orlando.

The lowermost portion of the Wekiva River, below FL 46, is bordered by the Lower Wekiva River Preserve State Park, but to run this segment you must paddle 2 miles on to the St. Johns River, which is very broad and developed.

◇ **MAPS** SORRENTO, SANFORD SOUTHWEST, FOREST CITY (USGS)

A

Kings Landing to Wekiva Island

Class	I
Length	8
Time	4
Gauge	Visual
Level	Spring-fed
Gradient	1.2
Scenery	A

45A **DESCRIPTION** From Kings Landing, paddlers must first navigate a small canal to reach Rock Springs Run. From the canal, join the deeply channeled 40-foot-wide Rock Springs Run, bordered by lily pads and waterweeds. These weeds clog the shores, creating an effective channel 10–15 feet wide. Bring your short kayak or a canoe to negotiate the twists and turns on Rock Springs Run. Also, try to avoid this run on summer weekends, or you will be negotiating among other paddlers and tubers.

The first 4.0 miles of the run are archetypal Florida waterway, protected as Wekiwa Springs State Park and Rock Springs Run State Preserve. Few will course through this stream disappointed: a wealth of native vegetation rises along the shores, complete with a tree canopy. Designated backcountry campsites add to this designated state waterway.

Following these first 4.0 miles, Rock Springs Run widens up to 100 feet and shallows. Here, you can spot the sand bottom between flowing waterweeds. The river eventually narrows again and subsequently deepens under tree canopy.

TALL TREES FORM A CANOPY OVER THE RIVER IN MANY PLACES.

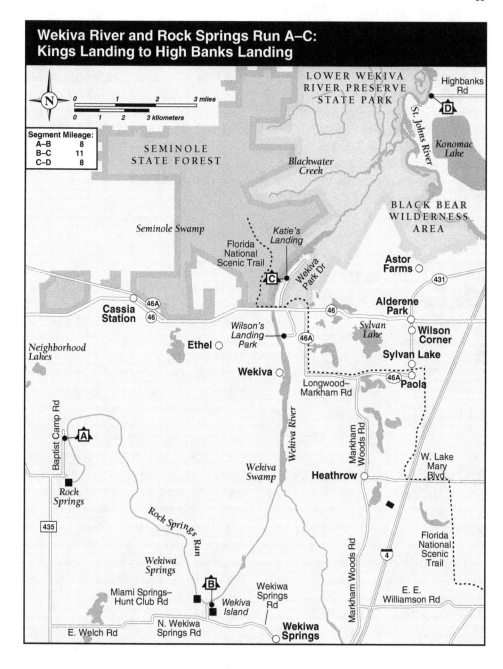

Wekiva River and Rock Springs Run A–C: Kings Landing to High Banks Landing

Segment Mileage:	
A–B	8
B–C	11
C–D	8

Paddlers may turn right and paddle up to the entrance to Wekiwa Spring upon reaching the confluence with the Wekiva River. This is the location of Wekiwa Springs State Park, which has camping as well as canoe and kayak launching facilities.

Despite the current, the half-mile paddle up to Wekiwa Spring is well worth the energy you'll expend.

Shortly below the confluence of the Wekiva River and Rock Springs Run is Wekiva Island. This is a privately owned public-access facility with kayak and canoe rentals, a restaurant, a store, and a dock.

✧ **SHUTTLE** To reach the take-out from the intersection of US 441 and Park Avenue/FL 435 in Apopka, drive north 2.3 miles on FL 435 to East Welch Road. Turn right on East Welch Road and, in 2.8 miles, turn left (north) on Wekiwa Springs Road. In 3.2 miles, turn left (north) on Miami Springs Drive to reach Wekiva Island, 0.5 mile farther.

To reach the put-in, backtrack on East Welch Road to FL 435. Turn right (north) on FL 435 and, in 3.5 miles, turn right (east) on East Kelly Park Road; continue 0.3 mile and turn left on Baptist Camp Road. Continue north 0.8 mile to King's Landing. There is a small fee for launching.

✧ **GAUGE** Visual. Rock Springs Run is spring-fed and runnable year-round.

B Wekiva Marina to Katie's Landing Below FL 46

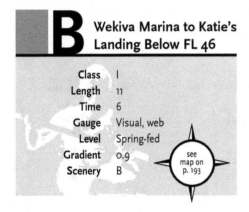

Class	I
Length	11
Time	6
Gauge	Visual, web
Level	Spring-fed
Gradient	0.9
Scenery	B

see map on p. 193

45B **DESCRIPTION** After you leave the marina, the Wekiva River turns north. River width varies from 50 to 150 feet, occasionally splitting around midriver islands. Watch for the Buffalo Trace designated campsite on river left. The right bank is protected as Wekiva River Buffer Conservation Area, while the left bank is within the confines of Rock Springs Run State Preserve.

Three miles downriver, the Little Wekiva River enters from the right. The Wekiva expands to more than 300 feet, seemingly a lakelike grassy swamp. Watch the left bank for a canal linking the river to Wekiva Falls, a private tourist attraction that offers canoe and kayak rentals and camping, as well as a fee-based take-out service. This shallow, grassy area continues to FL 46.

Wilson's Landing Park is on the right about a mile beyond Wekiva Falls. It has a take-out, restrooms, and water. The FL 46 bridge is not far downstream. A free take-out, Katie's Landing, part of Lower Wekiva River State Park, is on the right-hand bank about a mile below FL 46 and is the best place to end this segment of the Wekiva.

✧ **SHUTTLE** To reach the take-out from Exit 94 off I-4, take FL 434 West 0.2 mile to Markham Woods Road and turn right (north). Drive 7.4 miles and turn left (west) on Markham Road. In 1.3 miles, turn right (north) on Longwood–Markham Road and follow it 1.5 miles to FL 46. Turn left (west) on FL 46 and follow it 0.6 mile to Wekiva Park Drive. Turn right on Wekiva Park Drive and follow it north about a mile to Katie's Landing, on the left.

To reach the put-in from the take-out, backtrack to FL 434 on Markham Woods Road. Turn right (west) on FL 434 and, in 0.7 mile, turn right (north) on Wekiva Springs Road. Follow Wekiva Springs Road 3.2 miles to a stoplight at Miami Springs Drive/Hunt Club Boulevard. Turn right (north) on Miami Springs Drive to reach Wekiva Island, 0.5 mile farther.

✧ **GAUGE** Visual, web. Wekiva River is spring-fed and runnable year-round. The USGS gauge helpful in determining flow rates for any given day is Wekiva River near Sanford, Florida.

≈≈≈

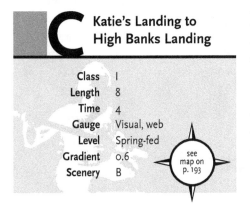

C Katie's Landing to High Banks Landing

Class	I
Length	8
Time	4
Gauge	Visual, web
Level	Spring-fed
Gradient	0.6
Scenery	B

see map on p. 193

45C DESCRIPTION This trip encompasses both the lowermost Wekiva River and a portion of the St. Johns. Heading north from Katie's Landing, the river is bounded by waterweeds on the insides of bends and marshy yet wooded banks on the other. The river is soon bordered by Lower Wekiva River Preserve State Park on both banks, lending a surprisingly wild atmosphere considering the proximity to urban areas. Occasional snags rise up from dusky waters. Dry land is limited—pull over when you have an opportunity. Expect to share the river with anglers in johnboats.

Reach the St. Johns River after 6.0 miles. Motorboats become common. Channel markers are situated in the river. The waterway is wider here. Continue north with the preserve still on the left (west) bank, while houses are on the right bank. At 8.0 miles, reach High Banks Landing, on your right.

THIS WATERWAY MAINTAINS A SURPRISING DEGREE OF REMOTENESS.

◇ **SHUTTLE** To reach the take-out from Exit 108 off I-4, go west on Dirksen Drive 2.0 miles to US 17/US 92 North (Charles Richard Beale Boulevard). Turn right on US 17/US 92 and, in 1.8 miles, turn left (west) onto Highbanks Road. Follow Highbanks Road 3.0 miles to the dead end at High Banks Landing.

To reach the put-in from the take-out, backtrack to I-4 and take it 5 miles toward Orlando. Take Exit 101C onto FL 46, heading west. In 4.6 miles, turn right (north) on Wekiva Park Drive just before bridging the Wekiva River, and follow it about a mile to Katie's Landing, on the left.

◇ **GAUGE** Visual, web. The Wekiva River is spring-fed and runnable year-round. The USGS gauge helpful in determining flow rates for any given day is Wekiva River near Sanford, Florida.

46 BLACKWATER CREEK AND LAKE NORRIS

◇ **OVERVIEW** Blackwater Creek—tight and hauntingly beautiful as it snakes through an ancient, maybe prehistoric, cypress swamp—is thought by many locals to be the "impassable waterway." Born on the waters of Lake Norris, it stretches for more than 20 miles, mostly through the Seminole Forest, eventually emerging onto the Wekiva River just upstream from the St. Johns River.

Many hardy souls have tried to traverse the entire waterway and have met with difficulties—extreme difficulties. The middle section is mined with dead snags hiding in tea-stained low water, and nature has barricaded the lower reaches with countless deadfalls. Past the confluence with Seminole Creek and Sulphur Run, the waterway makes for a lesser-done trip to the Wekiva. That said, there is a paddle access in the Seminole State Forest a little upstream of Sulphur Run from which you can paddle 4.6 miles down to the Wekiva. *Note:* To access this launch, call the state forest at 352-360-6677 to obtain a permit and gate code. Once you're at the Wekiva, you can paddle about 3 miles downstream to High Banks Landing (see previous page) or backtrack up Blackwater Creek.

Most folks paddle upstream on the Blackwater to Lake Norris, then tool around on the lake. Intrepid paddlers will try the 4 miles downstream from Lake Norris Road to the County Road 44A bridge. Below that, you are on your own. The primeval cypress forest is sometimes hypnotizing, and the mood may be broken only by the passing of an animal resident.

Lake Norris, part of the St. Johns River Water Management District Lands, is the jewel of the trip. The 2,352-acre preserve protects an extensive hardwood swamp forest on the west bank. There are purportedly upward of 100 osprey nests on the lake. The cypress woodlands extend into the lake, creating a 150-foot-wide buffer in many places—an intriguing area to explore—that plays host to wildlife aplenty. The adventuresome boater can spend hours investigating the lakeshore, weaving a kayak through the maze of cypress. And, except for one Boy Scout camp and a few rustic home sites, the surrounding area is a de facto wilderness sanctuary.

◇ **MAPS** PAISLEY, PINE LAKES (USGS)

A Blackwater Creek Bridge to Lake Norris and Back

Class	I
Length	2–7 (out-and-back)
Time	Varies
Gauge	Visual, web
Level	N/A
Gradient	0.5
Scenery	A

46A **DESCRIPTION** From the bridge, turn left and paddle upstream toward Lake Norris. At moderate to high water conditions, you will encounter very few obstructions, while at lower water you must negotiate some deadfalls and bottom snags. There is a very slight current, and the meandering streambed creates a lively, challenging slalom course. Watch for two sets of ancient wood pilings crossing the creek. They were set years ago for bridge construction. The first is about 0.5 mile from the

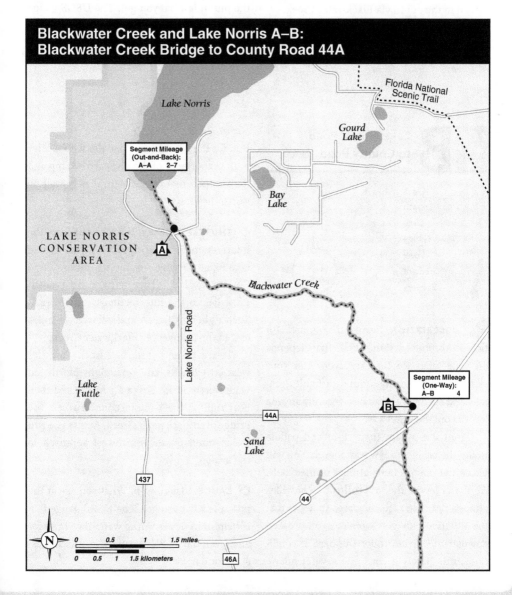

Blackwater Creek and Lake Norris A–B: Blackwater Creek Bridge to County Road 44A

Lake Norris

Florida National Scenic Trail

Gourd Lake

Segment Mileage (Out-and-Back):
A–A   2–7

Bay Lake

LAKE NORRIS CONSERVATION AREA

Ⓐ

Blackwater Creek

Lake Norris Road

Lake Tuttle

Segment Mileage (One-Way):
A–B   4

Ⓑ

44A

Sand Lake

437

44

N

0   0.5   1   1.5 miles

0   0.5   1   1.5 kilometers

46A

put-in, and the second spans the mouth of the stream that meets Lake Norris at 1 mile.

Lake Norris is a large body of water, and wind conditions can kick up sizable waves, so it's best to paddle around the periphery of the lake. Besides, that's where the gnarled cypress forest grows out of the water, so the scenery is much more tantalizing. For the best trip into this forest, paddle along the west side of the lake. Turn around at your discretion or paddle the entire lakeshore. Then return to the put-in via Blackwater Creek.

 DIRECTIONS From the intersection of FL 19 and FL 44 in Eustis, take FL 44/Orange Avenue 8.6 miles east to County Road 437. Turn left and drive north 1.8 miles to the intersection with CR 44A. Turn right and travel 0.5 mile east to Lake Norris Road. Turn left (north) on Lake Norris Road, drive 2.5 miles, and then bear right at the Y-intersection to access the bridge over Blackwater Creek. Access is down a dirt ramp on the northwest approach to the bridge.

 GAUGE Visual, web. What you see at the put-in is what you get. The USGS gauge helpful in determining flow rates for any given day is Blackwater Creek near Cassia, Florida.

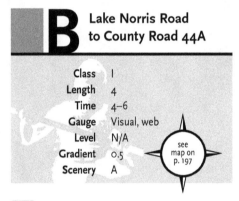

B Lake Norris Road to County Road 44A

Class	I
Length	4
Time	4–6
Gauge	Visual, web
Level	N/A
Gradient	0.5
Scenery	A

see map on p. 197

46B **DESCRIPTION** Beautiful? You bet! Difficult? Absolutely! Fun? Well, that depends on your tolerance for carryovers and your skills at maneuvering around difficult deadfalls and such, as well as how recently anyone has cut out the waterway.

From the put-in, turn right and paddle under the bridge. At low water levels, you will encounter obstructions almost immediately. At higher levels, the first mile or so provides almost clear passage. Beware, though, that the situation only gets worse as you proceed downstream. Even under the best of conditions, this trip will consume several hours.

But, for the adventurous paddler who tackles it, the experience of the enclosed swamp and the solitude that comes with it may well be worth the effort.

 SHUTTLE To reach the take-out from the intersection of FL 19 and FL 44 in Eustis, take FL 44/Orange Avenue 8.6 miles east to County Road 437. Turn left and drive north 1.8 miles to the intersection with CR 44A. Turn right on CR 44A and follow it 3.7 miles east to the bridge over Blackwater Creek.

To reach the put-in, backtrack 3.2 miles west on CR 44A and turn right (north) on Lake Norris Road. Drive 2.5 miles, and then bear right at the Y-intersection to access the bridge over Blackwater Creek. Access is down a dirt ramp on the northwest approach to the bridge.

 GAUGE Visual, web. What you see at the put-in is what you get. The USGS gauge that is helpful in determining water-flow rates for any given day is Blackwater Creek near Cassia, Florida.

47 ECONLOCKHATCHEE RIVER

◇ **OVERVIEW** The Econlockhatchee River, known to locals as the "Econ," is a jewel in the midst of fast-developing eastern Orange and Seminole Counties. This beautiful stream has mostly escaped the rampant growth that has consumed many of the area's natural attributes. The upper river challenges your paddling skills as it winds through the dim light of a mysterious cypress forest. Not far below the CR 419 bridge, the river reacquires a wild aura as it passes through the Little Big Econ State Forest. Things are slow and easy on the lower river as the Econ enters the open expanse of the St. Johns valley.

Those with a bent for the supernatural may be interested in the glowing Oviedo Lights. Many people claim to have seen them at night above the water while standing on the CR 419 bridge. This strange luminescent phenomenon has long been part of the local lore of the Econ.

◇ **MAPS** OVIEDO SOUTHWEST, OVIEDO, GENEVA (USGS)

A FL 50 to County Road 419

Class	I
Length	15
Time	8
Gauge	Web
Level	N/A
Gradient	1
Scenery	A

47A DESCRIPTION This section of the Econ will bring your paddling skills to the fore— sharp turns, cypress knees, deadfalls, and moderately swift current all present a challenge. (Check stream conditions beforehand.) During low water, the number of carryovers becomes intolerable, and the river can be dangerous after major rainstorms. The towering cypresses keep the stream in perpetual shade, which makes this stretch attractive for summer paddling. The beauty of the cypress forest and wild nature of the streamside setting provide a memorable trip.

Fifteen miles can be an excessive run on such a twisty stream. Start early and plan for a long day. Keep an eye out for submerged concrete obstacles under the CR 420 bridge 2.0 miles into the run. Three power lines will be encountered beyond the bridge. The Econ's banks are not very accessible during the early going, but sandy banks appear beyond the 6.0-mile point. A major milestone occurs at the confluence with the Little Econlockhatchee River. From this point, it is just a short distance to the bridge at CR 419.

◇ **SHUTTLE** To reach the take-out from Exit 215 off I-95, drive 17.5 miles west on FL 50 and turn right (north) on Chuluota Road, which becomes CR 419 in Seminole County. Keep north and west on CR 419 for 8.3 miles. Turn right on Willingham Road just before the CR 419 bridge over the Econlockhatchee; the parking area for the take-out will be immediately to your left. The launch requires a carry to the river.

Note: At press time, the recommended put-in, off FL 50 near Bithlo, was in flux while new eastbound and westbound bridges over the Econ were being completed. Check the author's website, johnnymolloy.com, for updates as they become available.

Econlockhatchee River A–B: FL 50 to FL 46

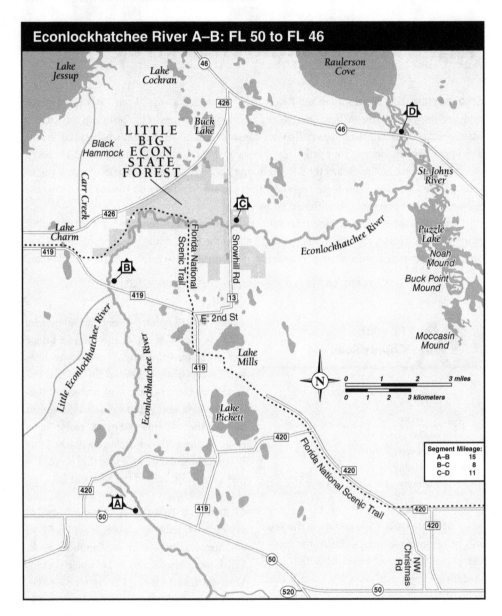

Segment Mileage:	
A–B	15
B–C	8
C–D	11

◇ GAUGE Web. The Econlockhatchee River is normally paddleable year-round. The USGS gauge helpful in determining flow rates for any given day is Econlockhatchee River near Oviedo, Florida. Below 11 feet, the river may have many exposed snags. Flood stage is 18 feet—stay off.

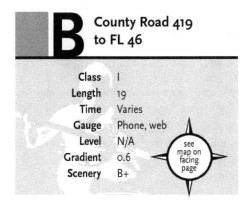

B County Road 419 to FL 46

Class	I
Length	19
Time	Varies
Gauge	Phone, web
Level	N/A
Gradient	0.6
Scenery	B+

see map on facing page

47B **DESCRIPTION** This segment encompasses the official state-designated paddling trail. It can be broken into two portions and is also suitable for camping since much of the sand-bottomed river travels through the Little Big Econ State Forest, ending at the Snowhill Road bridge. There is a designated camping zone along the river in the forest. It is 8.0 miles from CR 419 to Snowhill Road bridge.

The character of this section of the Econ is markedly different from that of the previous section. However, the state forest setting maintains a wild aura. The cypress trees give way to hardwoods on high, sandy banks. The river bottom stays sandy. Fallen trees still pose occasional obstacles. Seasonal wildflowers add color and interest. Cedars are abundant in places.

After the first 2.0 miles the Econ widens, the current eases a bit, and deadfalls cease to be a problem. However, before reaching an abandoned railroad trestle spanning the river 2.0 miles from Snowhill Road, the river narrows and twists again. The trestle now supports a footbridge over which travel the Florida Trail and the Flagler Trail. The Snowhill Road access is located behind the state forest office and a fee is required.

The paddling is easy below the Snowhill Road bridge. The river is moderately wide, the current is slow, and deadfalls are not a problem. The riverbanks are high, sandy, and shaded by oaks during the first 8.0 miles. The banks become lower as the 8.0-mile point is passed; the oaks are replaced first by cabbage palms and then by grassy prairie as the St. Johns valley is entered.

The Econ merges into the St. Johns River above the FL 46 bridge. Turn north and paddle toward the FL 46 bridge, visible in the distance. The St. Johns is wide at this point and can be rough on windy days, so stick to the left bank. There is considerable powerboat and airboat traffic on the St. Johns, so use caution.

◇ **SHUTTLE** To reach the lowermost take-out from the intersection of FL 434 and CR 419 in Oviedo, head east a short distance on CR 419 and bear left (northeast) on CR 426. In 7.8 miles, turn right (southeast) on FL 46 and, after 5.6 miles, bear left into C. S. Lee Park, on the northwest side of the bridge over the St. Johns River.

To reach the put-in from the take-out, backtrack on FL 46 to CR 426. Turn left (southeast) on CR 426 and, after 5.3 miles, turn left (south) on Lockwood Boulevard. In 1.8 miles, turn left (east) on CR 419 and drive 0.7 mile. Just past the bridge over the Econ, turn left onto Willingham Road; immediately on your left is the parking area for a paddler launch that requires a carry to the river.

◇ **GAUGE** Phone, web. Call Seminole Paddle Adventures at 407-925-7896, located near the put-in, for river conditions. The Econ is normally paddleable year-round. The USGS gauge helpful in determining flow rates for any given day is Econlockhatchee River near Oviedo, Florida.

48   SHINGLE CREEK

◇ **OVERVIEW** Often described as the headwaters of the Everglades, Shingle Creek drains the lakes and hills of southern Orange County, then flows south near Kissimmee into Lake Tohopekaliga. Though civilization has caught up to the area, paddling Shingle Creek is a unique experience and certainly one of the best paddling trails in Florida. The adventure of paddling the creek through a cypress forest becomes an instantaneous trip into a wild segment of the Sunshine State unimaginably situated in greater Orlando.

Your starting point is the concessionaire situated at Shingle Creek Regional Park, off busy Vine Street/US 192. Paddling here is evolving, but efforts are under way to expand the accessible Shingle Creek mileage. For now, paddlers can head upstream a mile or so, but the downstream trip is a real treat. Here, you pass the historic Shingle Creek community, then enter a cypress forest, where a marked trail—and the current—take you amidst a wild, wet, and wonderful swamp—yet development is just beyond sight. You'll twist and turn among the big trees then emerge on an open yet winding, still-untamed waterway.

The paddle then passes houses yet remains worthwhile all the way to Lake Tohopekaliga, where you can take out at the ramp in downtown Kissimmee. Other possibilities are in the works, including paddles to publicly owned Makinson Island, with campsites and trails.

◇ **MAPS** KISSIMMEE (USGS)

Steffee Landing to Lakefront Park in Downtown Kissimmee

Class	I
Length	9.5
Time	Varies
Gauge	Web
Level	N/A
Gradient	1.3
Scenery	B+

48 DESCRIPTION The uppermost point, Babb Landing, is merely a stopping point, not a launch. The actual launch is Steffee Landing, a mile downstream, where The Paddling Center at Shingle Creek is located. Paddlers heading upstream will sneak under the low Vine Street Bridge and then enter a natural corridor bordered in cypress–live oak–red maple woods, part of Shingle Creek Conservation Area.

The channel alternately narrows then widens, with a mild current. After a mile, an access trail from the Babb Homestead, part of Shingle Creek Regional Park and Babb Landing, is reached on your left. This is a good place to turn around. We hope additional upstream mileage will become available in the future.

More-adventurous paddlers will choose to head downstream from Steffee Landing. First enter a narrow wooded blackwater stream, quickly passing a historic structure. After a few bends, Shingle Creek widens. Reach a landing on the left, part of the park. It has a covered picnic area. Pass a couple of houses on river left, then enter the cypress swamp and the marked paddling trail. Trace the signs as you wend your way through a

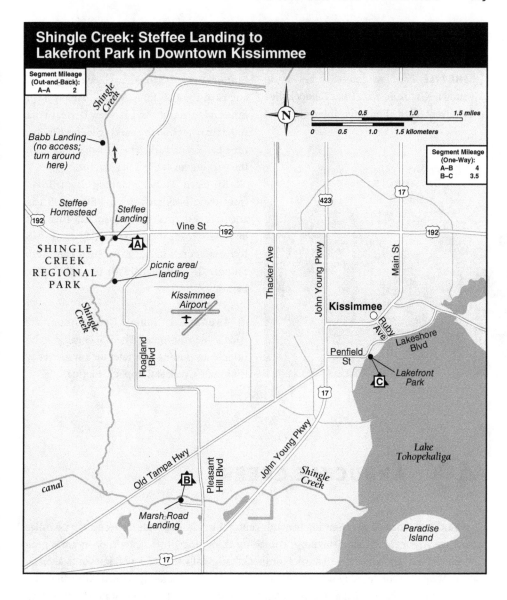

Shingle Creek: Steffee Landing to Lakefront Park in Downtown Kissimmee

Segment Mileage (Out-and-Back):
A–A   2

Segment Mileage (One-Way):
A–B   4
B–C   3.5

Shingle Creek

Babb Landing (no access; turn around here)

Steffee Homestead

Steffee Landing

192

SHINGLE CREEK REGIONAL PARK

Vine St   192

picnic area/ landing

Shingle Creek

Kissimmee Airport

Hoagland Blvd

Thacker Ave

John Young Pkwy

423

17

192

Main St

Kissimmee

Ruby Ave

Lakeshore Blvd

Penfield St

Lakefront Park

17

Lake Tohopekaliga

canal

Old Tampa Hwy

Pleasant Hill Blvd

John Young Pkwy

Shingle Creek

Marsh Road Landing

17

Paradise Island

0   0.5   1.0   1.5 miles
0   0.5   1.0   1.5 kilometers

---

primeval, canopied cypress swamp, as wild in appearance as the heart of a jungle. There may be fallen trees to work around. A good mile of this opens to a curving, sandbar-bordered, still-scenic stream.

Then, 3.0 miles from Steffee Landing, Shingle Creek turns left (east) as a canal enters on the right. Shingle Creek widens, then nears a few houses and goes under Old Tampa Highway at 3.5 miles. From here, watch right as you pass the Marsh Road Landing at 4.0 miles. Beyond Marsh Road Landing, float beneath Pleasant Hill Road, then under John Young Parkway at 5.0 miles.

The last part of Shingle Creek before entering Lake Tohopekaliga remains natural. Watch for winds on Lake Toho. Makinson Island is southeast, but to reach the Lakefront

Park take-out at Big Toho Marina, head left (north) on the shore of Lake Toho for 1.5 miles.

✧ **SHUTTLE** The lowermost access is in downtown Kissimmee, on Lake Tohopekaliga at Lakefront Park. From the intersection of John Young Parkway/US 17/US 92 and Vine Street/US 192 in Kissimmee, take US 17/US 92 South 0.9 mile and turn left on West Emmett Street, then go five blocks (0.5 mile) and turn right on Ruby Avenue. Follow it 0.1 mile and turn right on Lakeview Drive. In 0.2 mile, turn left into the parking lot for Kissimmee Lakefront Park. The launch is just past the parking lot at Big Toho Marina.

To reach Steffee Landing from Lakefront Park, backtrack to Vine Street/US 192 and follow it west for 2.9 miles. Turn left on Yates Road, then turn left again on US 192 eastbound; in 0.2 mile, turn right into Shingle Creek Regional Park to reach Steffee Landing.

✧ **GAUGE** Web. Shingle Creek is normally paddleable year-round. The USGS gauge helpful in determining flow rates for any given day is Shingle Creek at Campbell, Florida.

ENTERING CYPRESS WOODS
ON SHINGLE CREEK
Photo: John Jacobs

49 ARBUCKLE CREEK

✧ **OVERVIEW** Located near Sebring in south-central Florida, Arbuckle Creek flows 23.0 miles from Lake Arbuckle to Lake Istokpoga, stretching through cypress strands, open grass prairies, ranch land, and an occasional oak hammock. Originally the creek was known to aboriginals as *Weokufka,* or "muddy water," although later it was apparently named Arbuckle after a family of local settlers. Lake Istokpoga (an Indian word for "dangerous waters"), at 27,692 acres, is one of the five largest lakes in the state, and in early spring it is drawn down, causing low water levels in Arbuckle Creek.

For the first 10.0 miles, the creek runs along the western border of Avon Park Bombing Range. A portion of this range is a wildlife-management area and becomes very active with hunters during the winter hunting season. Fishing is very productive in the creek, with fine concentrations of bass, bluegill, and shellcracker; wild turkeys are frequently seen along the banks. Paddlers will likely encounter some boaters and anglers along the waterway and, in general, will find them quite friendly.

✧ **MAPS** LAKE ARBUCKLE, LAKE ARBUCKLE NORTHEAST,
LAKE ARBUCKLE SOUTHEAST, LORIDA (USGS)

A

Lake Arbuckle to Arbuckle Creek Road

Class	I
Length	12
Time	6
Gauge	Web
Level	N/A
Gradient	0.3
Scenery	B+

49A **DESCRIPTION** These first 2.0 miles constitute the most scenic section along the entire creek. Most paddlers do this as an out-and-back endeavor, often exploring Lake Arbuckle a bit. It snakes through a dense cypress swamp and is lined with tall trees shading a large percentage of the waterway. The channel is only about 30 feet wide, and the current is swift as indicated by the bottom vegetation bending to follow the flow.

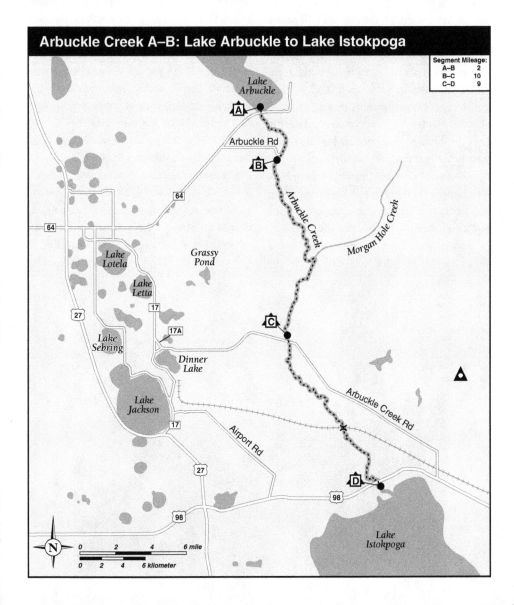

Arbuckle Creek A–B: Lake Arbuckle to Lake Istokpoga

Segment Mileage:	
A–B	2
B–C	10
C–D	9

Numerous overhangs, deadfalls, and submerged logs obstruct the creek, requiring careful maneuvering to negotiate. Wildlife is abundant, and it is not uncommon to see turtles, barred owls, and red-tailed hawks.

The boat ramp is on the south shore of Lake Arbuckle. After launching, the paddler should border the shore to the east, then pass under the County Road 64 bridge and enter the creek. The pilings from an old railroad trestle will be encountered 2.1 miles from the put-in. After 0.2 mile, the paddler will pass a short, dredged canal on river right that leads to a boat ramp on Arbuckle Road. Beyond the boat ramp canal off Arbuckle Road, the right shoreline opens up into ranch land, while a dense cypress swamp remains on the other shore. Pass a few houses on your right shortly into the paddle. Be apprised that you may have to battle through hyacinth jams.

About 4.0 miles into the trip, Morgan Hole Creek enters on the left, and the surrounding vegetation opens up. Marsh grass on the east and a high dike on the west line the creek.

Eight miles from the put-in, the creek separates into two channels. The one to the right follows the dike past a rancher's culvert and pumping station, while the left passage flows through a cypress stand. Both lead into the lakelike area described earlier. The Arbuckle Creek Road bridge is about a mile downstream of this point. The take-out is at a ramp on the right, immediately upstream of the bridge.

⟡ SHUTTLE To reach the take-out from the intersection of Memorial Drive and Cornell Street/FL 17 in the town of Avon Park, proceed east and then south on FL 17 for 6.8 miles, past Lakes Lotela and Letta, to the intersection with CR 17A/Arbuckle Creek Road, just north of Dinner Lake. Turn left (east) on Arbuckle Creek Road and follow it 6.2 miles; just before the bridge over Arbuckle Creek, bear left into the parking area for the boat ramp, on the northwest side of the bridge.

To reach the put-in from the same intersection in Avon Park, drive north on Memorial Drive 0.5 mile and turn right (east) on East Main Street/CR 64. In 2.1 miles, bear left (northeast) to stay on CR 64, and follow it 6.8 miles to the south end of Lake Arbuckle.

GENTLE ARBUCKLE CREEK

Camp Arbuckle is on the left (north) side of the road, just west of the bridge over Arbuckle Creek. The access is down a concrete ramp; a nominal fee is charged (call 813-986-2951 for more information).

⬦ **GAUGE** Web. Arbuckle Creek is normally paddleable year-round. The USGS gauge helpful in determining flow rates for any given day is Arbuckle Creek near De Soto City, Florida.

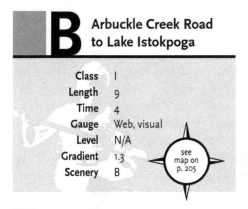

B Arbuckle Creek Road to Lake Istokpoga

Class	I
Length	9
Time	4
Gauge	Web, visual
Level	N/A
Gradient	1.3
Scenery	B

see map on p. 205

49B **DESCRIPTION** For the first 4.5 miles of this section, the creek traverses open ranch land. Although there are numerous pockets of cypress and oak, they are too widely scattered to provide shade. The next 1.5 miles pass through a dense oak forest. Paddle under a railroad bridge 5.5 miles from the put-in, a little after a small rapid formed by a series of limestone rocks and a drop in the creek bed. The rapids should be run over two small standing waves just to the left of an islet on the right side of the channel. At low water, exposed rocks in midcreek and a limestone ledge along the left make it very difficult to negotiate this area.

One-half mile past the rapids, the main creek channel enters a man-made canal. Tall spoil banks are partially vegetated, interrupted only by cuts where the original creek bed, now overgrown with aquatic plants, meanders across the canal. About 1 mile from the take-out, the canal begins to follow the original channel as it snakes gently past a cypress swamp on the left.

Immediately after the creek passes under the US 98 bridge, you will encounter a fish camp on the right. The take-out is up a concrete boat ramp into the camp, where there will be a nominal ramp-users' charge.

⬦ **SHUTTLE** To reach the take-out from the intersection of US 27 and CR 700/US 98 in Sebring, head east on CR 700/US 98 and follow it 9.4 miles. Just before the bridge over Arbuckle Creek, a boat ramp is located on the southwest side of the bridge, at Neiberts' Fishing Resort. Call 863-655-1416 for information on fees.

To reach the put-in from the take-out, continue east 2.8 miles on CR 700/US 98. Turn left on Arbuckle Creek Road and travel north for 1.2 miles, then bear left (northwest) at the intersection to stay on Arbuckle Creek Road, and drive 8.0 miles farther. Just past the bridge over Arbuckle Creek, turn right (north) into the parking lot for the boat launch.

⬦ **GAUGE** Web, visual. Arbuckle Creek is normally paddleable year-round. The USGS gauge helpful in determining flow rates for any given day is Arbuckle Creek near De Soto City, Florida.

50 PEACE RIVER

◇ **OVERVIEW** The Green Swamp, northeast of Tampa, is the headwaters for four of the finest rivers in the state: the Ocklawaha, Withlacoochee, Hillsborough, and Peace. The Peace River flows for approximately 133 miles from Lake Hancock near Bartow in Polk County to Charlotte Harbor near Punta Gorda. The river basin encompasses 2,400 square miles of primarily agricultural and ranch land, and numerous creeks and streams empty into the river along its entire length.

The Peace is considered to be 1 of the 13 major coastal rivers in Florida, which means it has an average discharge at its mouth of 1,000 cfs or more. As might be expected, almost 70% of the annual flow in the river (on average) occurs from June through October, after the onset of wet summer weather. Despite the high nutrient levels caused by the discharge from phosphate mines and agriculture, the river retains a fair water quality and indeed supports a fine population of fish.

The Peace River is steeped in a rich natural and cultural history. In 1842, by virtue of an agreement between General William Jenkins Worth and the infamous Native American chief Billy Bowlegs, the Peace was established as the boundary between native territory to the east and land for the white man to the west. During the Seminole Wars, numerous battles occurred along the banks of the Peace. At the confluence of the Peace and Payne Creeks, south of Bowling Green, the Seminoles attacked a trading post at the start of the Third Seminole War, and one of the last battles of that war was fought near Fort Meade.

The Peace River can be paddled for 70 miles from Bartow to Arcadia. Below Arcadia, the Peace becomes wide and is frequented by motorboats and personal watercraft, losing its appeal to paddlers.

Narrow, deep channels with high banks alternate with broad sections and quiet pools as the river passes through dense woodlands. Sand bluffs give way to shoreline flats, thickly carpeted with grasses and enclosed by the surrounding woods, making ideal campsites. The nearby forest abounds with deer and other wildlife, and the observant paddler will see numerous bird species, including herons, egrets, and kingfishers.

◇ **MAPS** HOMELAND, BOWLING GREEN, WAUCHULA, ZOLFO SPRINGS, GARDNER, LIMESTONE, NOCATEE (USGS)

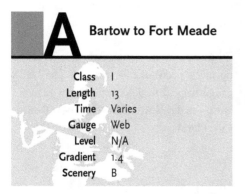

A Bartow to Fort Meade

Class	I
Length	13
Time	Varies
Gauge	Web
Level	N/A
Gradient	1.4
Scenery	B

50A DESCRIPTION The upper Peace flows out of Lake Hancock in central Polk County before becoming paddleable near Bartow. The official start of the state canoe trail is at the FL 60 bridge in Bartow. This uppermost section of the Peace will be impassable at low water. The river is narrow and swift at times, with moss-draped trees shading the waterway. Expect to encounter riffles and even mild

Peace River A: Bartow to Fort Meade

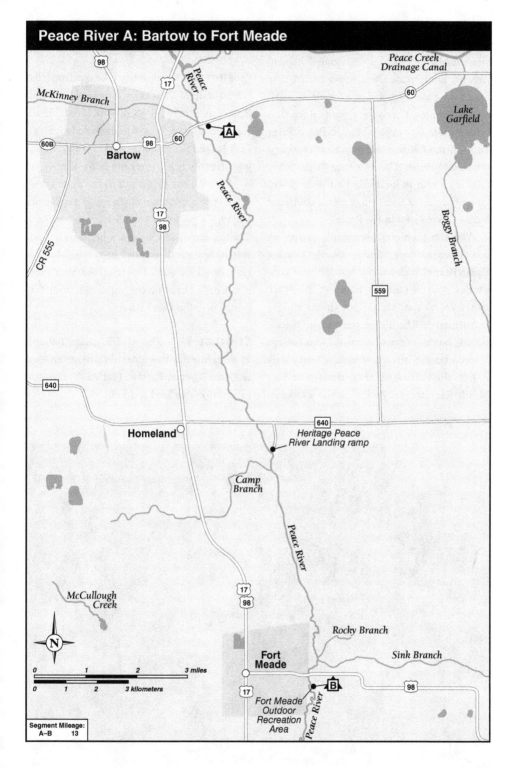

Segment Mileage:
A–B   13

shoals, as well as some wider, slower sections. Prepare to pull over a fallen log or two. The shoreline is protected as integrated habitat-network lands along these upper banks, save for a few spots. Pass under a couple of small private bridges. Reach the County Road 640 bridge after 6.0 miles. Mosaic Peace River Park, in the CR 640 vicinity, is a reclaimed phosphate mine. The Heritage Peace River Landing ramp is located a half mile downstream of the CR 640 bridge on the southeast side, at a wide spot in the Peace.

You can then continue south downriver 6.0 miles to Fort Meade, shortly passing Camp Branch on your right. Additional tributaries pour in tannins, painting the Peace its tea coloration. More light shoals will be encountered. The Peace widens in places, yet the banks remain forested. Waterweeds thicken on the insides of bends. Low bluffs rise on the outside of other bends. The Fort Meade Recreational Park is on the southeast

side of the 0.3-mile downstream of the US 98 bridge.

◇ **SHUTTLE** To reach the take-out from the intersection of Charleston Avenue/US 17 and Broadway Street/US 98 in Fort Meade, head 1.4 miles east on US 98 to the boat launch at Fort Meade Recreational Park, on your right just after the bridge over the Peace River.

To reach the FL 60 put-in from the same intersection, continue north for 10.7 miles on US 17/US 98 to Bartow. Turn right on East Church Street and, in 0.4 mile, turn left on North Restwood Avenue. In 0.1 mile, turn right on FL 60 East. The ramp entrance road is 0.3 mile ahead on the right, just after the bridge over the Peace River.

◇ **GAUGE** Web. The USGS gauge helpful in determining flow rates for any given day is Peace River at Bartow, Florida. The minimum runnable level is 40 cfs.

THE AUTHOR PADDLES THE PEACE RIVER.

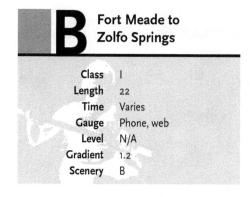

B Fort Meade to Zolfo Springs

Class	I
Length	22
Time	Varies
Gauge	Phone, web
Level	N/A
Gradient	1.2
Scenery	B

50B **DESCRIPTION** By the time the Peace reaches Fort Meade, the river is around 25 feet wide and meanders south. Many access points allow for trips of varied distances. It is 3.0 miles from Fort Meade to the CR 657 bridge access and another 7.0 miles to the FL 664 bridge access, where it enters Hardee County and reaches the CR 664A bridge and Paynes Creek State Historic Site after 13.0 miles. The state park has a canoe and kayak launch.

Little Charlie Creek enters the river 4.0 miles farther, just below the lower CR 664A bridge. Gentle riffles sliding over a rock bottom occasionally speed up the moderate current. Pass Hardee County Conservation Easement lands on the east bank. It is 4.0 miles from the state park to the lower CR 664A Bridge access and 2.5 miles farther to the Crews Park access in Wauchula. From Wauchula to Pioneer Park, it is another 5.0 miles. Thompson Branch comes in from the west between the two accesses.

⟡ SHUTTLE To reach the take-out from the intersection of Charleston Avenue/US 17 and Broadway Street/US 98 in Fort Meade, head south on US 17 for 17.9 miles. After crossing the bridge over the Peace River, take the first right, Wilbur C. King Boulevard, into Pioneer Park, and drive 0.5 mile west to reach the public boat launch.

To reach the put-in from the same intersection, head 1.4 miles east on US 98 to the boat launch at Fort Meade Recreational Park, on your right just after the bridge over the Peace River.

⟡ GAUGE Phone, web. Call Canoe Outpost at 863-494-1215 for the latest river conditions. The Peace is normally paddleable year-round. The USGS gauge helpful in determining flow rates for any given day is Peace River at Fort Meade, Florida.

Peace River B–D: Fort Meade to Arcadia

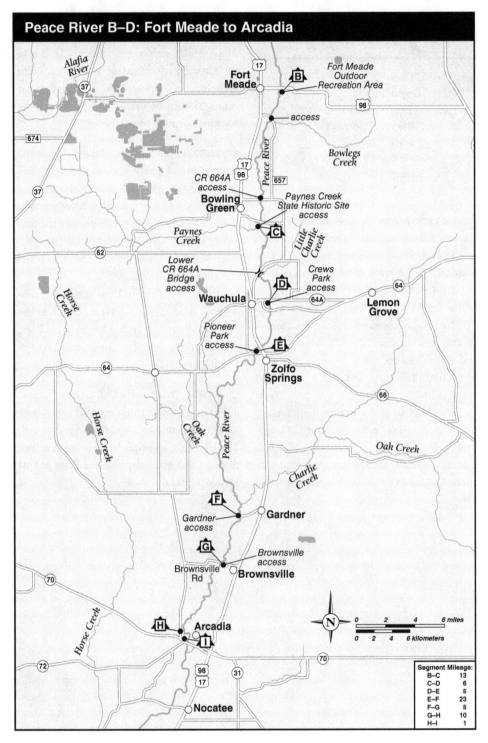

Alafia River

37

17

Fort Meade

B

Fort Meade Outdoor Recreation Area

98

access

674

Peace River

Bowlegs Creek

37

17
98

657

CR 664A access

Bowling Green

Paynes Creek State Historic Site access

C

Paynes Creek

Little Charlie Creek

62

Lower CR 664A Bridge access

Crews Park access

D

64

Horse Creek

Wauchula

64A

Lemon Grove

Pioneer Park access

E

Zolfo Springs

64

66

Horse Creek

Oak Creek

Peace River

Oak Creek

Charlie Creek

F

Gardner access

Gardner

G

Brownsville access

Brownsville Rd

Brownsville

70

N

0   2   4   6 miles

0   2   4   6 kilometers

Horse Creek

H

Arcadia

I

72

98
17

31

70

Nocatee

Segment Mileage:	
B–C	13
C–D	6
D–E	5
E–F	23
F–G	5
G–H	10
H–I	1

C Zolfo Springs to Gardner

Class	I
Length	23
Time	Varies
Gauge	Phone, web
Level	N/A
Gradient	1.1
Scenery	A

50C **DESCRIPTION** Although this long section can be paddled in a single day, that would do it an injustice—it is ideal for camping. Despite the large number of groups using this river on busy weekends during spring and fall, fine campsites are so numerous that you can be virtually certain of finding one. A word of warning, though: the majority of the land along this section is private property, owned by the Ben Hill Griffin Peace River Ranch, and they have a policy against campers using the eastern shore of the river. Heed the NO TRESPASSING signs stationed along the left bank. The western shore, except for a few posted areas, is open for camping.

The launch area at Pioneer Park is down a concrete ramp. Below the ramp on the river, a V-formation of rocks creates a small shoal. Half a mile from the put-in, the river passes beneath the FL 64 bridge, the last such structure you'll encounter until a wooden bridge at 13.0 miles. Tall bluffs support a forest of palm, oak, and cypress. Small streams flow noisily into the river at intervals.

In the cool, dry winter season—which is also the prime time for paddler camping—the river will run nominally low. This will expose numerous sandbars and create shallow pools. In addition, deadfalls and normally submerged logs will surface. Although minor obstacles for the canoeist and kayaker, these features prove to be major obstructions for powerboaters and may restrict their access to this section of the Peace, a blessing for all paddlers.

Several bigger tributaries intersect the river along this section. Troublesome, Hickory, Oak, and Limestone Creeks enter from the west, and Charlie Creek, the largest contributor, comes in from the east. Limestone Creek is a very descriptive name. It flows into the Peace about 16.0 miles from Pioneer Park, and its presence is announced far in advance by the appearance of limestone rock formations along the banks. The banks of Limestone Creek are also lined with rock; at low water, the undercutting due to erosion is clearly visible.

Charlie Creek, also called Charlie Apopka Creek, is a corruption of a Native American name that literally translates as "trout-eating place." This is a popular area for hunting fossils, most notably shark's teeth. This significant feeder stream, just above Gardner, adds considerable flow to the Peace.

SHUTTLE To reach the take-out from the intersection of US 17 and FL 64 in Zolfo Springs, travel south on US 17 for 10.2 miles to the town of Gardner. Turn right (west) onto River Road Southwest, at the PEACE RIVER PUBLIC BOAT LANDING sign. Continue on this road for 1.5 miles until it dead-ends at the boat ramp. There is ample parking in the area.

To reach the put-in from the same intersection, head 0.1 mile north on US 17, turn left (west) onto Wilbur C. King Boulevard into Pioneer Park, and follow it 0.5 mile west to the public boat launch.

GAUGE Phone, web. Call Canoe Outpost at 863-494-1215 for the latest river conditions. Peace River is normally paddleable year-round. The USGS gauge helpful in determining flow rates for any given day is Peace River at Zolfo Springs, Florida.

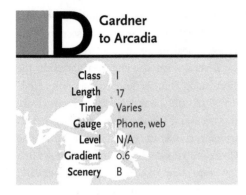

D
Gardner to Arcadia

Class	I
Length	17
Time	Varies
Gauge	Phone, web
Level	N/A
Gradient	0.6
Scenery	B

50D **DESCRIPTION** With the addition of Charlie Creek, the river widens to 80 or more feet. The river, however, is less winding. The few bends do create larger sandbars. The current moderates, but fallen trees are common in the river. The banks remain high, with occasional low swampy areas, where willows are abundant. Both sides of the creek are posted with very few places to camp, other than the Brownsville boat ramp, which has a fine campground, and Oak Hill, owned by Canoe Outpost. The Brownsville boat ramp is reached after 5.0 miles and is on the east bank.

Houses become common for a while after Brownsville. The most popular day trip on the Peace extends from the Brownsville boat ramp to Arcadia, a distance of 10.0 miles. After Walker Branch enters the river from the west, bends resume for a couple of miles, then the river straightens again. The river passes under a wooden railroad trestle a mile above Arcadia. The Canoe Outpost access is on the right, shortly beyond the trestle.

◇ **SHUTTLE** To reach the take-out from the intersection of River Road and US 17 in Gardner, head south on US 17 for 10.0 miles. In Arcadia, turn right (west) on Hickory Street/FL 70 and follow it 1.5 miles. After crossing the Peace River, turn right (north) on American Legion Drive to reach the boat launch.

To reach the put-in from the same intersection, turn left (west) onto River Road Southwest, at the PEACE RIVER PUBLIC BOAT LANDING sign, and follow it 1.5 miles until it dead-ends at the boat ramp. There is ample parking in the area.

◇ **GAUGE** Phone, web. Call Canoe Outpost at 863-494-1215 for the latest river conditions. Peace River is normally paddleable year-round. The USGS gauge helpful in determining flow rates for any given day is Peace River at Arcadia, Florida.

LATE FALL THROUGH EARLY SPRING IS THE BEST TIME FOR A PADDLE-CAMPING TRIP ON THE PEACE RIVER.

51   FISHEATING CREEK

◇ **OVERVIEW** Fisheating Creek is undoubtedly one of the prettiest streams in Florida. Tea-colored water journeys swiftly through thick cypress swamps and beside hardwood hammocks only to open into small lakes where wildlife abounds. This area, especially the upper creek, is in an area little disturbed by humans.

Now managed by the state of Florida, Fisheating Creek had been in the hands of ranchers who left the river as it was, and no development occurred. The high-water mark of the stream-shed is now the boundary of a wildlife-management area. Wildlife does abound here—turkeys, deer, hogs, alligators aplenty, and more birds than I can identify. Special rules apply to the upper watershed, as you have to pass through private land to reach the put-ins; therefore, only the state-sanctioned concessionaire operating the waterside campground and livery near Palmdale is allowed to take paddlers upstream. You must contact the outfitter to reach the upper Fisheating Creek access, upstream of US 27.

You can paddle upstream directly from US 27, but it is a tough paddle, practically speaking, because of swift currents. Downstream from US 27, paddlers can put in and head down or put in at the public ramp on FL 78 near Lake Okeechobee and head upstream. It pays to contact the concessionaire before attempting a trip downstream of US 27.

Originating in Highlands County from a swamp near Hen Scratch, Fisheating Creek flows south down a channel before resuming its original banks and becoming paddleable near the town of Venus. It is here that the wildlife-management area and attendant restrictions ensue. Starting at Ingrams Crossing, the river makes a tortuous yet beautiful course for US 27, in a Florida reminiscent of a century ago. Below US 27, the creek continues for another 20 miles. However, waterweeds have blocked boat progression in places. I continually hope the weeds will be cleared, allowing a trip all the way to the "Big O" from upper Fisheating Creek. Furthermore, drawdowns on Okeechobee and the annual dry season occasionally render the creek too shallow in winter. Spring and fall are popular times to paddle. Longer kayaks may have trouble negotiating sections of the river.

◇ **MAPS** FISHEATING CREEK CANOE TRAIL MAP;
LA BELLE NORTHWEST, PALMDALE, LAKEPORT (USGS)

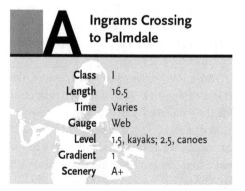

A   Ingrams Crossing to Palmdale

Class	I
Length	16.5
Time	Varies
Gauge	Web
Level	1.5, kayaks; 2.5, canoes
Gradient	1
Scenery	A+

51A **DESCRIPTION** This section, simply one of the most scenic in the state, can be halved for a day trip of 8.0 miles. The full 16.5 miles is best done as an overnight trip. The entire segment passes through the Fisheating Creek Wildlife Management Area and lives up to its name.

The paddle itself begins at Ingrams Crossing. Here, the southbound creek is 30–40 feet wide and is bordered by cypress and

Fisheating Creek A–B: Ingrams Crossing to Okeechobee

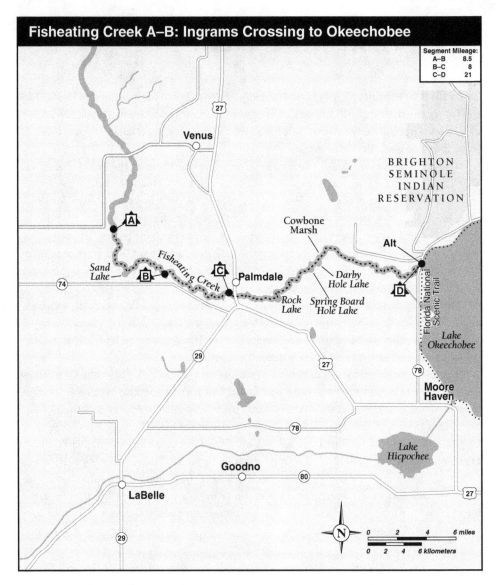

Segment Mileage:
A–B   8.5
B–C   8
C–D   21

live oak hammocks. Air plants and Spanish moss fight for space on the streamside trees. The creek soon narrows and reveals its winding nature. The serpentine stream opens into lakes, where the current slackens and the scenery varies. Campsites are more abundant up here.

The creek turns east at Sand Lake, a shallow body of water bordered by marsh. Below the lake begin miles of traveling through glorious cypress swamp, which is often only 10 feet wide or narrower. The current speeds up in these swamps, keeping paddlers on their toes. In other places Fisheating Creek widens and narrows at a whim.

After 8.0 miles, the creek enters the Burnt Bridge area. This is the starting point for the wonderful day trip leading down to Palmdale and US 27. The pattern of lakes and narrow streams continues. Sandbars become more frequent as Fisheating Creek nears US 27. The take-out is located at Picnic Lake.

✧ **SHUTTLE** The shuttle on this upper section must be handled by Fisheating Creek Outpost, located at 7555 US 27 North, about 125 miles due south of Exit 55 off I-4 in Orlando. From the intersection of Broadway Street and US 27 in Palmdale, drive south 0.6 mile and turn right (west). For information on shuttle rates, call 863-675-5999 or visit fisheatingcreekoutpost.com.

✧ **GAUGE** Web. The USGS gauge is Fisheating Creek at Palmdale, Florida. The minimum recommended runnable level is 2.5 for canoes and 1.5 for kayaks.

B Palmdale to Okeechobee

Class	I
Length	21
Time	Varies
Gauge	Web
Level	1.5, kayaks; 2.5, canoes
Gradient	0.8
Scenery	A

51B DESCRIPTION This section is wild and beautiful as well but more open. Fisheating Creek continues east under US 27, twisting and winding its way toward Lake Okeechobee. The cypress swamps continue east of Palmdale, alternating with a series of lakes. Rock Lake is reached after 5.0 miles; Spring Board Hole Lake comes next. Darby Hole Lake is the last in the series.

At 8.0 miles, the stream enters Cowbone Marsh, an open area that has been choked by weeds in the past and is impassable in that state. It seems no one has made it through the marsh in some time. Apparently the state

FISHEATING CREEK'S SWIFT CHANNELS RUN AMONG CYPRESS TREES.

agreed to maintain a water route through the entirety of Fisheating Creek, but that hasn't happened due to lawsuits between the state and environmentalists, an ongoing controversy. Check on the status before attempting a trip through the area. However, if you start at either end, normal water levels are adequate. Paddlers often start on FL 78 near Okeechobee and paddle upstream to the blocked point, or downstream from US 27 and return.

Cowbone Marsh continues for 3.0 miles and then comes to one last lake area, known as Double Lakes. The last 8.0 miles are stream paddling, often through open ranch lands broken by occasional oak hammocks.

◇ **SHUTTLE** To reach the take-out from the intersection of US 27 and FL 80 West in Clewiston, take US 27 North 9.7 miles to Moore Haven, then take FL 78 North 8.8 miles to the boat ramp at Fisheating Creek.

To reach the put-in from Moore Haven, backtrack on FL 78 to US 27. Turn right on US 27, heading west, then north. After 15.3 miles, turn left to reach Fisheating Creek Outpost, off US 27 just north of the bridge over Fisheating Creek.

◇ **GAUGE** Web. The USGS gauge is Fisheating Creek at Palmdale, Florida. The minimum recommended runnable level is 2.5 for canoes and 1.5 for kayaks.

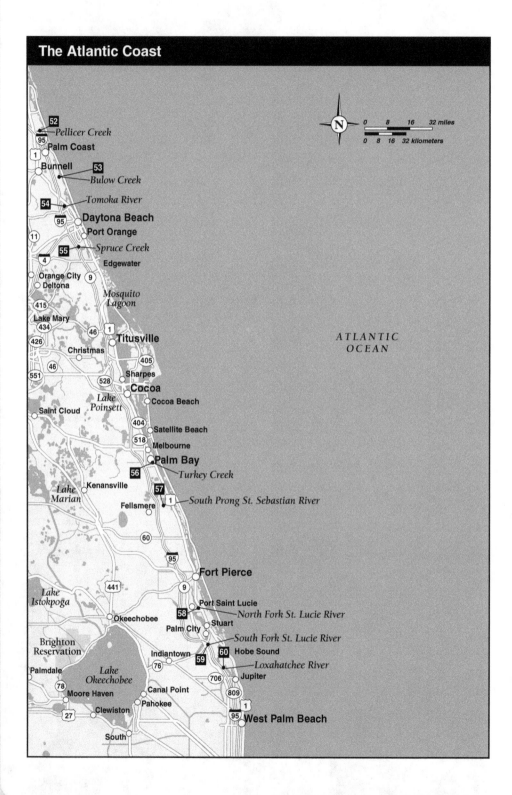

The Atlantic Coast

PART SEVEN
THE ATLANTIC COAST

52 PELLICER CREEK

◇ **OVERVIEW** The powers that be in Florida realized ahead of the curve what a treasure they have in Pellicer Creek. Before the lands along this coastal waterway could be developed, the St. Johns River Water Management District bought them, and today 8 miles of shoreline on the south bank, from the upper river section down to the creek mouth at the Matanzas River, are preserved.

The official state paddling trail runs from just above the confluence of Pellicer Creek and Cracker Creek, just west of US 1, to Princess Place Preserve. Much of the north bank east of I-95 was already part of Faver-Dykes State Park. The newer lands were once part of Princess Estate, a lodge built of coquina blocks.

The paddling here covers the transition from freshwater to tidal stream. If you paddle the lower creek, consider the tides and wind, which can push unabated across the open marsh flats. It is 2 miles from the Faver-Dykes State Park launch to the Princess Place Preserve launch.

◇ **MAPS** FAVER-DYKES STATE PARK MAP; DINNER ISLAND NORTHEAST (USGS)

Cracker Creek to Princess Place Preserve

Class	I
Length	5.5
Time	2.5
Gauge	Visual
Level	Tidal
Gradient	Tidal
Scenery	A

52 DESCRIPTION Bring your camera on this photogenic waterway, a state-designated paddling trail. Paddlers can start their trip on Cracker Creek, accessed at Pellicer Creek Campground off US 1. This lovely creek, draped in hardwoods hanging over the water, is a warm-up before you enter Pellicer Creek (you can also paddle Cracker Creek upstream). If the winds are howling, you can head upstream on Pellicer; downstream you will pass under the US 1 bridge. Below the US 1 bridge, the right bank houses the Florida Agricultural Museum.

After passing under the noisy I-95 bridge, the lands become protected on both banks. The right bank is part of the 3,900-acre Princess Place Preserve, with trails and a boat ramp of its own, should you decide to continue east 1.5 miles beyond the Faver-Dykes boat ramp. Marsh grass is present, and tidal influence is felt on the lower creek. Often one bank will have pines, palms, and cedars, while the other side will have marsh grass. Most paddlers start at the Faver-Dykes boat ramp and execute

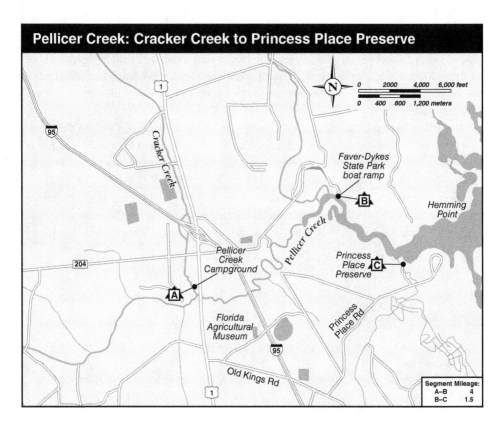

Pellicer Creek: Cracker Creek to Princess Place Preserve

Segment Mileage:
A–B   4
B–C   1.5

an out-and-back endeavor, either upstream or down to Princess Place Preserve and back. Boats can be rented both at Princess Place Preserve and Faver-Dykes State Park.

✧ **SHUTTLE** To reach the Princess Place Preserve take-out from Exit 298 off I-95, head south 1.4 miles on US 1 to Old Kings Road. Turn left on Old Kings, passing back under the interstate, and watch for the left turn into Princess Place Preserve in 1.6 miles. Once inside the preserve, follow the signs for 2.5 miles to the boat ramp.

To reach the Faver-Dykes boat launch from Exit 298 off I-95, take US 1 North about 0.1 mile, then turn right on Faver-Dykes Road to reach Faver-Dykes State Park. An entrance fee applies (see "Fees and Permits," page 6). Once inside the state park, follow the signs about 2.8 miles to the boat launch.

To reach the upper access from Exit 298 off I-95, head south on US 1 and, after 0.6 mile, turn right into Pellicer Creek Campground, a private enterprise, just before the bridge over Pellicer Creek. Note that you must enter a security code at the gate; for more information, call 904-458-7275.

✧ **GAUGE** Visual. This tidal creek is floatable year-round.

---

53 BULOW CREEK

✧ **OVERVIEW** Bulow Creek is a trip back into Florida history as well as an opportunity to explore a coastal marsh. The put-in is near Ormond Beach at the Bulow Plantation Ruins Historic State Park. This site is a relic of the early 1800s, when a number of sugar plantations dotted the Florida Atlantic coast. These plantations were burned and abandoned during the Second Seminole War. Paddlers should take the opportunity to visit the old sugar mill and other ruins. There are also nature trails that are worth exploring. Bulow Plantation and the adjacent Bulow Creek State Park form a substantial portion of the west bank of upper Bulow Creek. The park is noteworthy for its rich stand of hardwood hammock.

Bulow Creek originates in Graham Swamp, approximately 3.5 miles upstream from Bulow Plantation. The creek is an easy 13-mile day trip starting out at the plantation, going upstream to the origin, and then paddling down to the terminus at the Intracoastal Waterway at High Bridge Park. This covers the entirety of the state-designated paddling trail. An alternate take-out on Walter Boardman Lane reduces the trip length to 10.5 miles. If you don't want to paddle upstream or backtrack, the trip from the plantation put-in to the take-out at High Bridge Park is 5.5 miles.

✧ **MAPS** FLAGLER BEACH EAST, FLAGLER BEACH WEST (USGS)

Bulow Plantation to High Bridge Park

Class	I
Length	5.5
Time	3
Gauge	Visual
Level	Tidal
Gradient	Tidal
Scenery	B–

53 DESCRIPTION Bulow Creek flows lazily in a generally north–south direction. Bulow Plantation is located at the transition between the cabbage palm hammock that lines upper Bulow Creek and the grassy coastal marsh of lower Bulow Creek. As you paddle upstream from the plantation, the grassy marsh is gradually succeeded by a narrower stream with margins overhung with palms and swamp hardwoods. A fair number of osprey

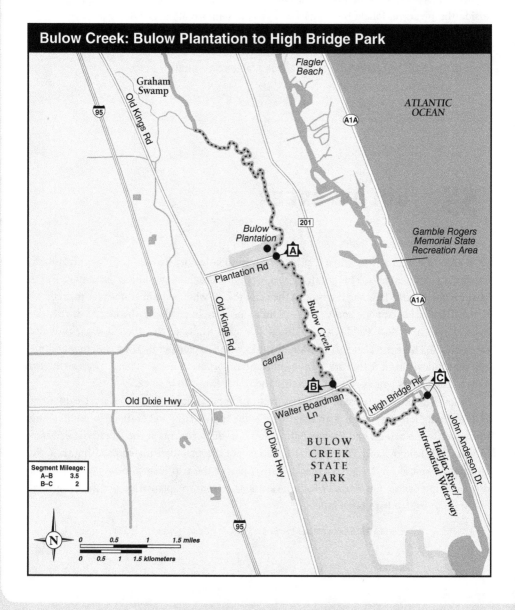

Bulow Creek: Bulow Plantation to High Bridge Park

Segment Mileage:
A–B   3.5
B–C   2

nests can be seen along this stretch of Bulow Creek, making paddling especially rewarding during spring, when the ospreys are building nests and feeding their young.

At 3.5 miles upstream from the plantation, the snags and deadfalls of Graham Swamp make further progress difficult, and most paddlers will head back downstream. Going south from Bulow Plantation, the creek flows through a broad, grassy coastal marsh. A stream enters from the right at 0.8 mile, as does a canal at 1.5 miles. You reach a large, grassy island at 1.8 miles, with the main channel going to the right.

The alternate take-out on Walter Boardman Lane is located at 3.5 miles. After another mile of paddling, a channel branches off to the right. This is the natural Bulow channel. The straight-ahead channel is a man-made shortcut to the Intracoastal Waterway. The natural channel meanders almost 2.0 miles to reach the Waterway, whereas the man-made channel is less than 1.5 miles to the same point. Paddlers taking the natural channel should turn right where the stream

again intersects the man-made channel at 0.2 mile from the take-out.

◇ **SHUTTLE** To reach the lowermost access from Exit 278 off I-95, take Old Dixie Highway east, noting Old Kings Road as you pass. In 0.8 mile, bear left at the intersection on Walter Boardman Lane, crossing Bulow Creek at an access before reaching High Bridge Road in 1.2 miles. Make a right onto High Bridge Road, crossing the bridge over the Halifax River, and in 1.8 miles reach High Bridge Park on your right. There is a boat ramp on the southeast side of the bridge.

To reach the uppermost access, backtrack to Old Dixie Highway and turn right (north) on Old Kings Road. In 1.9 miles, turn right on rough Plantation Road—look for a sign for BULOW PLANTATION RUINS HISTORIC STATE PARK on your left—and follow it to enter the state park and reach the boat launch. An entrance fee applies (see "Fees and Permits," page 6).

◇ **GAUGE** Visual. Bulow Creek is a tidal stream that can be paddled year-round.

LOOKING OUT OVER BULOW CREEK

54   TOMOKA RIVER

◆ **OVERVIEW** The north-flowing Tomoka River drains a narrow coastal region between the Halifax River lagoon and the St. Johns River valley. The Tomoka provides a diverse paddling experience. The upper (southern) river is narrow and flows between tall cypresses; in contrast, the lower (northern) river is broad and flows through the open expanses of a coastal marsh. A substantial portion of the lower Tomoka lies within Tomoka State Park and presents a natural shoreline.

The Timucuan Indian town at the site of the park prompted early Spanish explorers to name the stream Río de Timucas (River of the Timucuans). Later settlers corrupted *Timucas* to *Tomoka*.

Because Ormond Beach and Daytona Beach have grown so much, upper river accesses have been cut off. The most popular launch is at the state park, where paddlers are welcome and boats are for rent. There is also a public launch at Sanchez Park, across the river from the state park, just north of US 1. Strickland Creek and Thompson Creek, branches of the Tomoka River, are within the state park and provide excellent paddling opportunities of their own.

◆ **MAPS** TOMOKA STATE PARK MAP; DAYTONA BEACH, ORMOND BEACH (USGS)

Tomoka State Park to FL 40 Bridge and Back

Class	I
Length	16 (out-and-back)
Time	Varies
Gauge	Visual
Level	Tidal
Gradient	Tidal
Scenery	C

54 **DESCRIPTION** With the closings of many former landings on the Tomoka River, a paddle here is likely to be an out-and-back proposition. Most paddlers start and end their trips at Tomoka State Park because of this. From the park launch, you can head north beyond the landing into the wide-open Tomoka Basin and the Halifax River.

Most paddlers, however, head south, or upstream, toward the North Beach Street Bridge, then return. Paddlers first pass Strickland Creek, then Thompson Creek on river left. Ahead, on the right, is the access at the

Tomoka Estates subdivision, which you reach 2.7 miles from the state-park launch. Parking is limited to five or so cars here, though.

Ahead, parts of the left bank are beautifully forested with palm, cedar, and pine. Streamflow ceases around the US 1 bridge, and the river is tidally influenced. It is 4.0 miles from the Tomoka State Park boat launch to US 1 (no access), making an 8-mile out-and-back trip. Considerable residential development is apparent on the right bank, while the left bank is all marsh, but the natural character of the marsh has been altered by a large number of mosquito-control canals cut back into the marsh. Launching is not permitted at Riverbend Nature Park, about a mile upstream of the US 1 bridge.

It is 4.0 miles from the US 1 bridge to the FL 40 bridge (no access). Below (north of) I-95, the river is broad; above (south of) I-95, Groover Branch enters on the right. The banks are lined predominantly with tall palm trees. A large number of these palms have

Tomoka River: Tomoka State Park to FL 40 Bridge and Back

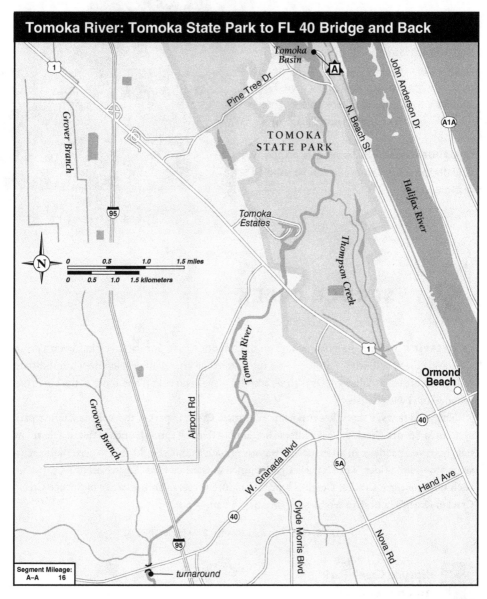

toppled into the water, and many are submerged just a few inches below the surface. Self-propelled craft can easily clear most of these trees, but powerboats must stay farther out in the channel—a welcome benefit for paddlers. Numerous osprey nests are located along the Tomoka, and these birds may be seen per¬forming their household chores.

Above the FL 40 bridge, it is possible to paddle upstream for 1.5 more miles to Priest Branch and beyond, but fallen trees will likely become problematic beyond here. Just remember that you're going to have to paddle back to either the Tomoka River Estates launch or the state park—and that it's 16 miles from the state-park launch to the FL 40 bridge and back.

✧ **DIRECTIONS** To reach the Tomoka State Park access from Exit 268 off I-95, take FL 40

East 4.3 miles to North Beach Street in the town of Ormond Beach. Turn left (north) on North Beach Street and, in 4.1 miles, turn right at the KAYAK AND CANOE RENTALS sign to reach the boat launch at Tomoka State Park, another 0.8 mile ahead. There is a fee to enter the park (see "Fees and Permits," page 6).

✧ **GAUGE** Visual. The Tomoka is primarily a tidally influenced river and can be paddled year-round.

≈≈≈

PADDLING A SIT-ON-TOP KAYAK
OVER THE TOMOKA

55 SPRUCE CREEK

✧ **OVERVIEW** As with many waterways on the Atlantic Coast, Spruce Creek has been a desirable target for people who want to live on the water. The attendant development around such residential areas has followed. Over time, accesses have been cut off and more of the creek has become lined with houses.

The good news is that a lower portion of Spruce Creek is part of the Volusia County park system, in Spruce Creek Park. Paddlers should note that the canoe launch is not usable at low tide; however, paddlers in an estuarine waterway such as this should always plan their excursions around the tides. The Cracker Creek launch at Gamble Place, upstream of I-95, has no such tidal concern. Cracker Creek is a private nature preserve on the banks of Spruce Creek. Cracker Creek's hours are Wednesday–Sunday, 9 a.m.–5 p.m.

✧ **MAPS** NEW SMYRNA BEACH, SAMSULA (USGS)

Spruce Creek Park to Cracker Creek

Class	I
Length	7
Time	Varies
Gauge	Visual
Level	Tidal
Gradient	Tidal
Scenery	C

55 **DESCRIPTION** The paddle leaves Spruce Creek Park in a canal through marsh grass. Keep along the north shore of Strickland Bay to enter Spruce Creek. Paddlers in fragile boats should avoid the razor-sharp shells in the bay. Pass under the Florida East Coast Railroad bridge after 1 mile and enter Spruce Creek. Ahead is a very pronounced horseshoe

Spruce Creek: Spruce Creek Park to Cracker Creek

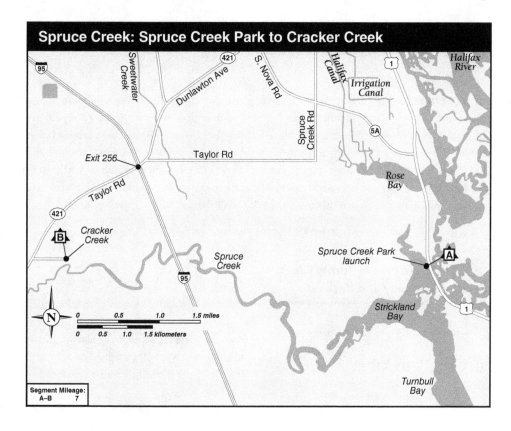

Segment Mileage:
A–B   7

bend. A narrow channel to the right offers a shortcut that eliminates more than 0.5 mile of the trip. Those taking the long way around the bend will pass the imposing bluffs for which Spruce Creek is known. The creek continues to wind its way generally northwest until reaching the I-95 bridge.

Above I-95, you will run into some development. En route to Cracker Creek preserve, you will pass under the Williamson Street Bridge. It is about 2.0 miles from I-95 to Cracker Creek. Spruce Creek is a designated Outstanding Florida Water.

 SHUTTLE To reach the Cracker Creek access from Exit 256 off I-95, head east on Taylor Road/FL 421 and, after 1.5 miles, turn left at the CRACKER CREEK CANOEING sign. Follow the signs to the Cracker Creek office.

To reach Spruce Creek Park from Exit 256 off I-95, take FL 421/Dunlawton Avenue east 2.1 miles to Nova Road/FL 5A. Turn right (south) on FL 5A and follow it 2.5 miles to US 1. Turn right (south) on US 1 and follow it 0.9 to Spruce Creek Park, on your right.

 GAUGE Visual. Spruce Creek is heavily influenced by tides. Paddlers should avoid the Spruce Creek Park canoe launch at low tide and plan their paddle around the tidal fluctuation, or simply start at Cracker Creek if the tides are unfavorable.

56 TURKEY CREEK

◇ **OVERVIEW** Turkey Creek provides a pleasant half day of paddling that includes an opportunity to explore a nature sanctuary run by the Audubon Society. Lower Turkey Creek flows through a hardwood swamp that puts on a fall display of reds, yellows, and oranges but is bordered by houses on its outermost edges. The upper portion of the creek winds through the hardwood hammocks and high, sandy bluffs of Turkey Creek Sanctuary and is worth every stroke to get there. A paddler landing at the sanctuary enjoys access to a network of interpretive nature trails. Be apprised that this out-and-back paddle can get busy on weekends.

◇ **MAPS** MELBOURNE EAST (USGS)

Goode Park to Turkey Creek Sanctuary and Back

Class	I
Length	4 (out-and-back)
Time	2
Gauge	Visual
Level	Tidal
Gradient	Tidal
Scenery	B

56 **DESCRIPTION** The trip upstream commences in the estuarine mouth of Turkey Creek at the Indian River lagoon and proceeds through a broad region of braided channels that can be confusing. The outermost channels are bordered by houses. Hopefully, the best way will be signed on your trip. Waterfowl are plentiful, and manatees are occasionally seen.

The main drainage of Turkey Creek trends southwest and passes under Port Malabar Boulevard 1.25 miles from Goode Park. This is where the paddling gets really good. Enter Turkey Creek Sanctuary, and the character of the stream changes dramatically, leaving the

PADDLING INSIDE TURKEY CREEK SANCTUARY

Turkey Creek: Goode Park to Turkey Creek Sanctuary and Back

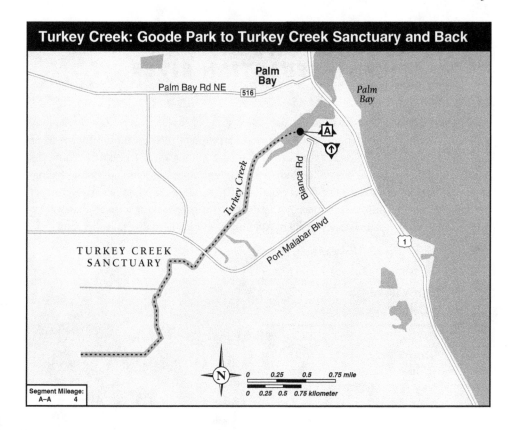

residential development behind. The channel narrows and the current quickens as the stream flows through a rich, dimly lit forest of palms and live oaks broken by sand bluffs where pines grow. Paddlers should be alert for numerous deadfalls where turtles are often seen.

Reach the sanctuary's canoe/kayak landing at 1.75 miles. Here, paddlers can park their boats and explore the boardwalks of the sanctuary, or they can continue 0.25 mile above the landing to a water-control structure and the turnaround point of the paddle.

⟡ SHUTTLE To reach the put-in/take-out of this out-and-back paddle from Exit 173 off I-95, take Malabar Road Southeast/FL 514 East 4.1 miles to US 1 in Malabar. Turn left on US 1 and follow it north 1.6 miles to Port Malabar Boulevard. Turn left on Port Malabar Boulevard and follow it 0.4 mile to Bianca Drive Northeast. Turn right on Bianca Drive and follow it 0.6 mile to a dead end and a boat ramp at Goode Park.

⟡ GAUGE Visual. Turkey Creek is tidally influenced and is paddleable year-round.

57   SOUTH PRONG OF THE ST. SEBASTIAN RIVER

◇ **OVERVIEW** The St. Sebastian River, also called simply Sebastian Creek, is a three-prong system. The North Prong and South Prong share a common mouth into the Indian River lagoon with a man-made flood-control canal. The South Prong meanders north behind the coastal ridge that separates it from the Indian River. Sluggish streamflow and a wide channel on the lower river provide an easy day of paddling after winding through the narrower upper section. Large oaks hang out from steep but accessible banks overlooking ultraclear tan waters. Donald McDonald Park makes an excellent paddling base and alternative take-out point.

◇ **MAPS** Fellsmere, Sebastian (USGS)

County Road 512 to Dale Wimbrow Park

Class	I
Length	5
Time	2.5
Gauge	Visual, web
Level	N/A
Gradient	Partly tidal
Scenery	B

57 **DESCRIPTION** The South Prong starts out narrow, 20 feet or so, and sections of the channel have tree cover. Other sections are open and shrouded by vines. Paddlers should be alert to submerged deadfalls during the first 1.5 miles—especially while negotiating the switchbacks in the moderate current. There is some residential development downstream.

The South Prong opens up below the 2.0-mile point. The meanders become tortuous, and in some places the stream nearly doubles back on itself. Banks are mostly low, with occasional sand bluffs. Cabbage palms, ferns, and oaks lean out to provide roosts for anhingas and herons. Gators and turtles also call this stream home. The South Prong

THE CALM WATERS OF THE SOUTH PRONG

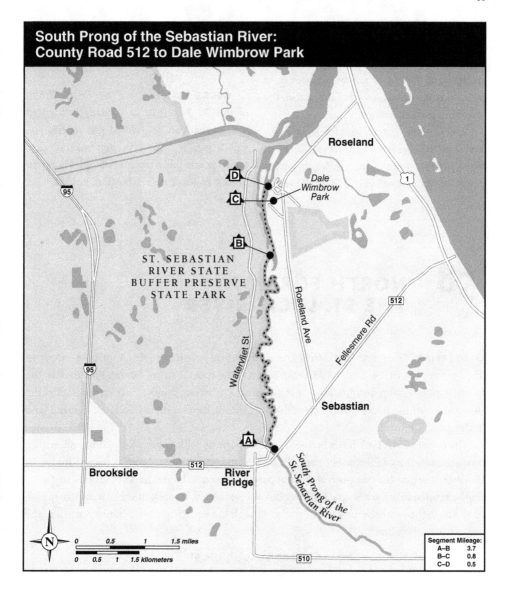

South Prong of the Sebastian River:
County Road 512 to Dale Wimbrow Park

Roseland

Dale Wimbrow Park

ST. SEBASTIAN
RIVER STATE
BUFFER PRESERVE
STATE PARK

Roseland Ave

Fellesmere Rd

512

Watervliet St

Sebastian

Brookside

River Bridge

512

South Prong of the
St. Sebastian River

510

Segment Mileage:	
A–B	3.7
B–C	0.8
C–D	0.5

0   0.5   1   1.5 miles

0   0.5   1   1.5 kilometers

has numerous dead-end false channels and sloughs awaiting the unwary paddler.

Downstream, the west bank becomes part of the St. Sebastian River State Buffer Preserve, where the banks remain wild. The preserve has a boat landing near the old John Carleton home site. The preserve also has hiking trails aplenty, so you can double your fun.

The South Prong, now devoid of current, has widened to nearly 200 feet as it nears Dale Wimbrow Park, 0.8 mile below the preserve boat landing. The channel into the Dale Wimbrow boat ramp soon appears on the right. Campers at Donald McDonald Park can continue 0.5 mile downstream to a slough on river right and use the campground landing.

◇ **SHUTTLE** To reach the take-out from Exit 156 off I-95, take CR 512/Fellsmere Road east 3.7 miles to Roseland Road. Turn left (north) on Roseland Road and follow it 2.1 miles to Dale Wimbrow Park, on your left across the road from the Sebastian Airport.

To reach the put-in, backtrack on Roseland Road to Fellsmere Road/CR 512. Turn left (west) on Fellsmere and, in 1.3 miles, turn right (north) on Watervliet Street. Follow Watervliet 0.3 mile to Canoe Launch Road and turn right to reach a small park and launch just for hand-propelled craft, about 0.2 mile ahead.

◇ **GAUGE** Visual, web. The South Prong of the St. Sebastian is a tidally influenced stream that can be paddled year-round. The USGS gauge helpful in determining flow rates for any given period is South Prong St. Sebastian River near Sebastian, Florida.

58 NORTH FORK OF THE ST. LUCIE RIVER

◇ **OVERVIEW** The North and South Forks of the St. Lucie River join to form an extensive drainage system that enters the Atlantic Ocean at the coastal city of Stuart. Fortunately, the North Fork has been designated as a state aquatic preserve, a move that has protected the river and its immediate environs from the burgeoning development that is consuming land in this part of Florida.

The upper North Fork flows between banks overhung with large oaks, palms, and maples with an understory of ferns. Numerous side streams enter the St. Lucie at regular intervals. However, topographic maps reveal these apparent streams to be remnants of oxbows that were short-circuited many years ago. The river below Prima Vista Boulevard is not attractive to paddlers due to the extensive powerboat traffic, though the aquatic preserve borders much of the downstream shoreline.

◇ **MAPS** ST. LUCIE (USGS)

White City Park to River Park Marina

Class	I
Length	4
Time	2
Gauge	Visual
Level	Tidal
Gradient	Tidal
Scenery	B

58 DESCRIPTION The St. Lucie flows south from White City Park through a corridor of high banks with some houses but is mostly bordered by the richly wooded aquatic preserve. Paddler-only canoe docks provide stopping and picnicking spots to enhance the experience. These are not launch points but merely welcome waysides. The main channel averages 80–100 feet wide, so deadfalls are

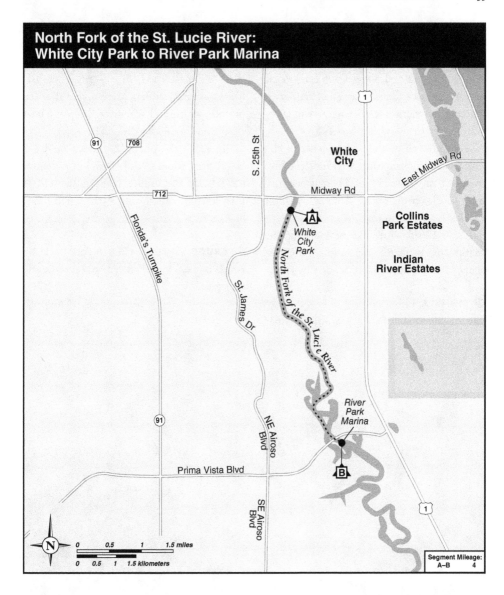

North Fork of the St. Lucie River: White City Park to River Park Marina

not a problem, but obstacles will be encountered on some of the old oxbows.

A set of power lines crosses the river 1.5 miles downstream. Paddlers with plenty of time on their hands will want to explore some of the oxbows. Most of these oxbows return to the main channel, but a few are dead ends.

At 3.0 miles, the river passes through a wide spot that has the appearance of a small lake. Channel markers indicate the way on the lower river. Begin to look for mangroves here, and expect tidal influences to increase. An intersection of five channels with a small island in the center indicates that Prima Vista Boulevard is just 0.1 mile away. After passing under Prima Vista Boulevard, paddlers must circle around a large peninsula to the right to reach the River Park Marina boat ramp.

Paddlers can also stroke the North Fork upstream from White City Park, passing other protected shores, including Platts Creek Mitigation Park and Sweetwater Hammock, which also has a canoe dock. The river here is twisting and more creeklike, narrow and preferable when the winds are howling.

Paddlers will reach the confluence of Five Mile Creek and paddleable Ten Mile Creek just past the 25th Street Bridge. There is one final canoe dock up the south shore of Ten Mile Creek at George Lestrange Preserve. A spillway near the Florida Turnpike prohibits farther continuous upstream travel on Ten Mile Creek, about 5.0 miles upstream of White City Park.

✧ **SHUTTLE** To reach the take-out from Exit 126 off I-95, take CR 712/Midway Road 4.9 miles east to US 1. Turn right on US 1, heading south 3.3 miles to Prima Vista Boulevard. Turn right to head west on East Prima Vista Boulevard and, in 0.9 mile, take the first left into River Park Marina, just after the bridge over the St. Lucie River. There is a boat ramp and canoe/kayak rental here.

To reach the put-in, backtrack on US 1 to CR 712/Midway Road. Turn left (west) on CR 712 and, in 1.1 miles, just over the bridge, turn left into White City Park, which has a boat launch.

✧ **GAUGE** Visual. The North Fork St. Lucie River is tidally influenced and paddleable year-round.

THE CURRENT ON THE NORTH FORK ST. LUCIE CAN BE NONEXISTENT IN PLACES.

59 SOUTH FORK OF THE ST. LUCIE RIVER

◇ OVERVIEW Though dominated by the St. Lucie Canal coming out of Lake Okeechobee on its lowermost reaches, the St. Lucie River has a surprisingly wild and preserved segment of its upper South Fork that makes for a scenic paddling escape. Furthermore, most of its banks are protected as part of Halpatiokee Regional Park. The tidally influenced brackish water twists as an ever-narrowing serpentine stream bordered in a riot of vegetation, morphing from salty mangroves to canopies of epiphyte-covered live oaks. Small islands and dead-end oxbows provide additional exploration opportunities.

This stream is a no-wake zone for motorboaters. Crowded vegetation leaves its upper stretches to paddlers only. Halpatiokee Regional Park has a strategically located concessionaire that offers a launch and kayak/canoe rentals at the paddle's beginning. Be apprised that this is an out-and-back endeavor, with no upper take-out; thus, it's a 6.4-mile round-trip.

◇ MAPS HALPATIOKEE REGIONAL PARK MAP; INDIANTOWN SOUTHEAST, GOMEZ (USGS)

Near FL 76 to Upper Halpatiokee Regional Park Landing and Back

Class	I
Length	6.4 (out-and back)
Time	2
Gauge	Visual
Level	Tidal
Gradient	Tidal
Scenery	B

59 DESCRIPTION This paddle deserves two scenery ratings; the first mile is lesser, as houses detract, but the upper stretch is superlative: a visual slice of wild Florida.

Leaving from the concessionaire, you will head upstream, away from the low Gaines Avenue Bridge, which deters most motorboat traffic (additionally, the entire paddle is in a no-wake zone). Mangroves border much of the waterway at first. The right-hand bank heading upstream is wild parkland, while the first mile on the left-hand bank is bordered in houses cut with occasional canals. To stay on track, hang with the right, natural bank until you pass the houses; then join the left bank, as most of the river oxbows and island loops leave right. If you stay with the left bank, you will be lost in the surprisingly wild scenery, yet not lost in actuality. South Fork St. Lucie narrows from 80 to 30 feet in width as you head upstream, tracing its ceaseless meanders. Birds and alligators, even an occasional manatee, may be sighted.

At 1.2 miles, reach a three-way channel. Stay left here to continue upriver; otherwise, you can paddle around Treasure Island. Vegetation becomes more tropical, yet pine flatwoods rise above the lush, ferny banks. Sharp turns are the norm. The South Fork continues to narrow, and you may squeeze between low overhanging or inundated limbs.

Reach the upper park landing at 3.2 miles (no vehicle access). Here, a short, man-made cut slopes up the right shore, making a boat ramp of sorts. The oak-shaded clearing has picnic tables. You can also access Halpatiokee

South Fork of the St. Lucie River: Near FL 76 to Upper Halpatiokee Regional Park Landing and Back

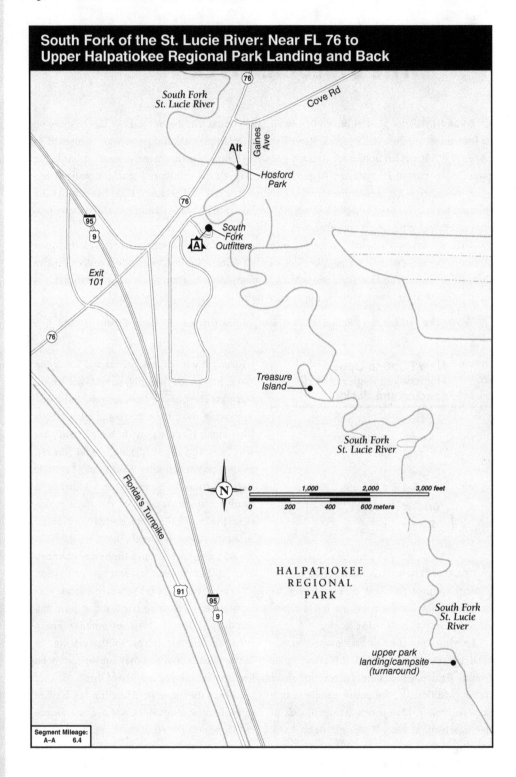

Segment Mileage:
A–A   6.4

Regional Park's trail system from this locale, should you want to stretch your legs. Finally, with prior reservations, paddlers can camp here. You can venture upstream about 10 more minutes before a pair of culverts prevents further progress and signals your turn-around point.

Note: Hosford Park, just a short piece downstream of the concessionaire put-in, offers an alternate launching point—a boat ramp with floating dock—in case the opening/closing hours of the concessionaire are incompatible with your paddling schedule.

◇ DIRECTIONS To reach the put-in/take-out from Exit 101 off I-95 near Stuart, take FL 76 East 0.2 mile to a traffic light at Southwest Lost River Road. Turn right here into Halpatiokee Regional Park; then, with the Sunoco gas station on your right, take a quick left into the signed entrance for South Fork Outfitters, the park concessionaire.

◇ GAUGE Visual. The South Fork St. Lucie River is tidally influenced and paddleable year-round.

THE SOUTH FORK OF THE ST. LUCIE IS AN EVER-NARROWING SERPENTINE STREAM BORDERED IN A RIOT OF VEGETATION.

60   LOXAHATCHEE RIVER

✧ **OVERVIEW** The Loxahatchee is the only stream in Florida to be designated a National Wild and Scenic River, and just a few minutes on the stream will convince you that this designation is richly deserved. The upper river is a delight to kayakers and canoeists as it zigzags through a stunningly beautiful cypress swamp. Shortly after entering Jonathan Dickinson State Park, the Loxahatchee changes abruptly as it takes on the sedate character of an estuarine mangrove swamp.

It is customary for paddlers to take a lunch break at the Trapper Nelson Interpretive Site. Trapper Nelson, "the wild man of the Loxahatchee," was a locally famous eccentric who developed a unique homestead, zoo, and gardens decades ago along the Loxahatchee. Canoe docks, picnic facilities, and drinking water are available at Trapper Nelson's. Park rangers give daily presentations on the lore, vegetation, and wildlife of the site. (*Loxahatchee* translates from Seminole as "Turtle River.")

During low water, common in winter, paddlers will have to pull their boats, and longer kayaks will have difficulty maneuvering the sharp bends and fallen trees of the upper Loxahatchee.

Jonathan Dickinson State Park rents boats for there-and-back trips on the river, and a private outfitter rents boats and provides shuttles at the put-in. Paddlers can paddle up- or downstream at their leisure from these locales, eliminating the need for a shuttle.

✧ **MAPS** Rood (USGS)

River Bend Park to Jonathan Dickinson State Park

Class	I
Length	6.5
Time	2–4
Gauge	Phone, web
Level	N/A
Gradient	2
Scenery	A+

60 **DESCRIPTION** Soon after you leave River Bend Park, moderately fast water will sweep you into a cypress forest. Adept maneuvering is required to dodge cypress knees and negotiate the sharp turns. Ahead, a carryover ramp traverses an old dam. Dappled sunlight filters through the canopy of tall cypresses that line the Loxahatchee.

Strangler figs entwine many of the cypresses, and pond apple trees are seen. Since this section of river has no true banks (unless the water is low), there are few opportunities to go ashore before you reach Trapper Nelson's.

An Indian mound lies back from the east bank at 1.2 miles. A low concrete dam at 1.3 miles provides a carryover ramp. This dam has a drop of about 2 feet, and during normal water conditions most people paddle straight over the top. The Florida Turnpike and I-95 bridges are encountered at 1.5 miles.

Trapper Nelson's dock is a welcome sight at the halfway point and provides a pleasant spot to stop for lunch. Soon after you leave Trapper Nelson's, there is an abrupt transition from cypress forest to mangrove swamp.

Loxahatchee River: River Bend Park to Jonathan Dickinson State Park

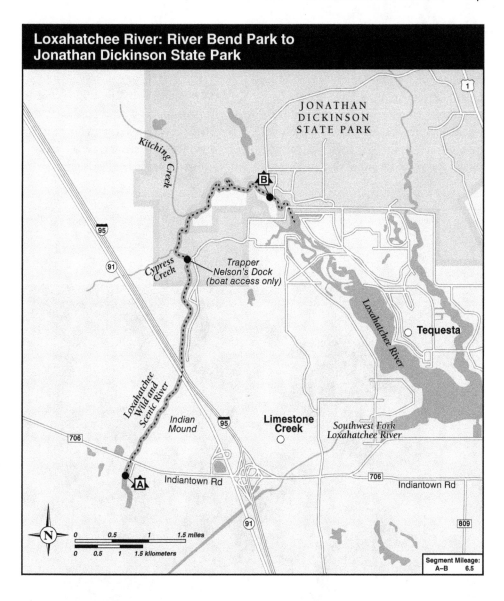

The Loxahatchee broadens and the current becomes imperceptible as the river comes under tidal influence. High wind sometimes presents a challenge on this stretch. Cypress Creek enters from the left at 3.3 miles, as does Kitching Creek at 3.6 miles. Before reaching the boat ramp at Jonathan Dickinson State Park, the river passes the park's canoe-rental area. Do not take out here—continue to the

park's public boat ramp, visible up a short channel to the left.

◇ **SHUTTLE** To reach the take-out from Exit 87A/87B off I-95, take FL 706/Indiantown Road 4.0 miles east to US 1. Turn left on US 1 North and follow it 5.0 miles to Jonathan Dickinson State Park, on your left. An entrance fee applies (see "Fees and Permits," page 6). Follow the signs 4.1 miles east and then south to the park boat ramp.

To reach the put-in, backtrack to I-95 and continue west on Indiantown Road 1.3 miles to Riverbend Park. Use the main park entrance, not the east or west entrance. Parking is in front of the outfitters, and you'll have to carry your boat from the parking area to the river. Be aware that on Tuesday and Wednesday, the Riverbend gates close at 3:30 p.m. Park outside the gates during this time.

GAUGE Phone, web. The Loxahatchee is runnable year-round, but call Jonathan Dickinson State Park at 772-546-2771 for the latest river conditions. A relevant gauge is Loxahatchee River near Jupiter, Florida.

TRAPPER NELSON'S PLACE ON THE LOXAHATCHEE

The Southwest Gulf Coast

GULF
OF
MEXICO

Weeki Wachee River — 61
Brooksville
Bushnell
Center Hill
441 434
Orlando
Groveland
Clemont
Spring Hill
41B
Lacoochee
429 91
Hudson
Dade City
435
Port Richey
471
417
Elfers
Holiday
Hillsborough River
Polk City
192 4
Davenport
19A
62 Kathleen
98
570
27
Palm Harbor
589 275
579 580
542
Winter Haven
19
41B
Tampa
Waverly
Belleair Beach
60
Indian Rocks Beach Largo
Riverview
Mulberry
Lake Wales
Seminole
Gibsonton
Alafia River
Bay Pines
Saint Petersburg
Fort Meade
Ruskin
63
Frostproof
Sun City Center 64 — Little Manatee River
37
Avon Park
679
62
Wauchula
Sebring
275
Manatee River
Holmes Beach Bradenton
65
64
17
66
Cortez
70
Longboat Key
789 Sarasota
Arcadia
70
758
Osprey 66 — Myakka River
Prairie Creek
Laurel
41
67 31
North Port 771 75
68
17
Shell Creek
Englewood
Punta Gorda
Caloosahatchee River and Hickeys Creek
Charlotte Harbor
78
Boca Grande
69
80
Pine Island Sound
Fort Myers
29
Cape Coral
82
J. N. "Ding" Darling — 70 Sanibel Fort Myers Beach
National Wildlife Refuge
71
Estero River
75 Immokalee
Bonita Springs
41
Marco Island
41

N

0   8   16   24 miles
0   8   16   24 kilometers

61 WEEKI WACHEE RIVER

◇ **OVERVIEW** Florida has approximately 320 springs that discharge an estimated 8 billion gallons of water a day. Seventy-seven of these are first-magnitude springs, meaning they discharge 64.6 million gallons per day or more. Of these, many have been left natural and incorporated into state parks or major recreation areas, while others, such as Weeki Wachee, were once developed commercially.

Weeki Wachee Springs is now a Florida state park, and its longtime status as an attraction continues. The natural aspects of the spring are protected, especially with the purchase of adjacent river lands by the Southwest Florida Water Management District. However, many riverside houses have been built, and others have been here for some time.

Weeki Wachee Springs is located west of Brooksville and north of Tampa. It is the source of a river of the same name, which flows for about 8 miles through coastal swamp until it empties into the Gulf of Mexico near the small town of Bayport. Bayport was once a major trade center, and the Weeki Wachee River was used as a transportation route for barges hauling goods to nearby Brooksville. This ended when the railroad was built through Brooksville.

The name *Weeki Wachee* comes from the Creek Indian language and literally means "little spring" (*Wekiwa-chee*). Contrary to its Native American name, Weeki Wachee is a major spring and does create a very swift current in the upper 6 miles of the river. Downstream of Rogers Park, the river broadens and slows as it begins to meander through a coastal tidal marsh. As the river approaches the Gulf of Mexico, its current becomes dominated by tidal action and the influence of the spring discharge diminishes.

A good run with little tidal influence extends from the livery at Weeki Wachee Springs to Rogers Park, 6 miles downstream. A concessionaire at the state park offers rentals and shuttles for this very run. Although several miles of this river are highly developed, especially the last two before Rogers Park, the upper river retains a wild character and is quite a beautiful place to paddle. But its high concentration of powerboat traffic on the weekends—especially in summer—makes me recommend it for weekday paddling only. If you must go on a weekend, do so in the early morning.

✧ **MAPS** BAYPORT (USGS)

Weeki Wachee Springs to the Gulf of Mexico

Class	I
Length	8
Time	4
Gauge	Visual, web
Level	N/A
Gradient	2.5
Scenery	B

61 **DESCRIPTION** The first section of the run is the best. The river is about 40 feet wide at the put-in and soon narrows to less than 20 feet. Both banks of the river are undeveloped, and the spring flows crystalline and colorful since few motorboats make it up this far. Wildlife is easily spotted below and above the water surface. Paddlers will have to keep their eyes downstream, too, as the river flows surprisingly swiftly. Water oaks and some palm trees are intermingled with the cypress in the adjacent woodland swamp that canopies the river. Other areas are open with grassy shoreline.

The first sign of civilization is a private campground at 2.0 miles, on river right. After 3.0 miles, the right bank is part of the

THE CLEAR WATERS OF THE WEEKI WACHEE ARE FUN TO PADDLE.

Weeki Wachee River: Weeki Wachee Springs to the Gulf of Mexico

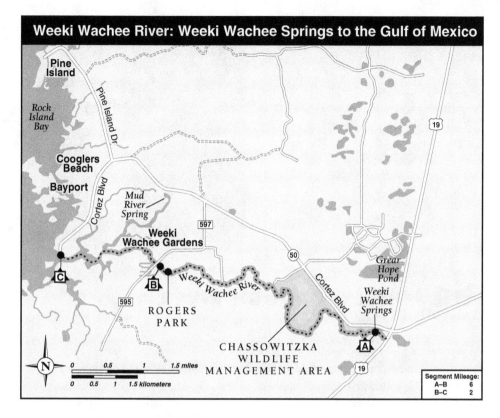

Chassowitzka Wildlife Management Area. Two developed beach and picnic areas make convenient points for paddlers to stop.

The development increases downstream, and if the motorboats are running, the river will cloud somewhat. Houses occupy one bank or another. Canals spurring off the Weeki Wachee will sometimes cause paddlers to stop briefly, but the proper course is either signed or very evident.

Reach Rogers Park and a boat launch after 6.0 miles. This park also has a swim area, restrooms, and boat launch. Below FL 595, you will travel through more dense development, past continuous seawalls and countless boat docks. After leaving the residential area, the river passes channel markers and side streams. Expansive tidal marsh grass borders the Weeki Wachee. The channel is about 200 yards wide here. The fishing is excellent, and manatees are frequently seen.

The Mud River comes in from the north 0.75 mile below the residential area, originating at Mud River Spring, and makes a very nice trip in its own right. The numerous side creeks and bays are interesting to explore in this lower tidal zone if you haven't had enough paddling yet.

✧ **SHUTTLE** To reach the lowermost access from the intersection of US 19 and FL 50/ Cortez Boulevard, west of Brooksville, travel west on FL 50 until the road dead-ends 6.6 miles ahead at a small park and the Gulf. There is a fishing pier at the end of the road and a boat launch up a short canal just before you reach the pier.

To reach the uppermost access from the same intersection, head south 0.2 mile on Commercial Way/US 19 to the parking area at the Weeki Wachee Springs attraction, and look for the road leading into the private

livery. For information on rental and launching rates, call 352-597-8484 or visit paddling adventures.com.

✧ **GAUGE** Visual, web. The Weeki Wachee is spring-fed and runnable year-round. The USGS gauge to help determine flow rates for any given time period is Weeki Wachee River near Weeki Wachee Springs, Florida.

62 HILLSBOROUGH RIVER

✧ **OVERVIEW** The Hillsborough is a long and diverse river, flowing for nearly 54 miles from the Green Swamp north of Lakeland to Hillsborough Bay in Tampa. The state-designated paddling trail is rich with history. Thousands of years ago, the Timucuan and Calusa tribes inhabited the surrounding land, and remnants of their burial mounds can still be found not far from the river. The Seminoles, a mixture of northern Creeks and the surviving Calusas, later emerged along the Hillsborough.

As American pioneers hungered for Florida land, they came in contact with these tribes, and the Seminole Wars were inevitably ignited. Fort Alabama, now called Fort Foster, was built along the river and remains as a reminder of that bloody conflict. The river was originally named *Lochcha-popha-chiska* ("river where one crosses to eat acorns") by the Seminoles, an obvious reference to their love of the large oak trees that line the shores. The British named it after the Earl of Hillsborough, a colonial secretary in the 1700s.

The river is fed by 690 square miles of natural drainage, most of which results from five main tributaries, including Flint and Blackwater Creeks. During the wet summer season, rain runoff swells the river, while during the dry winter and spring months, the water level is low and maintained primarily by base flow from Crystal Springs near the Green Swamp headwaters.

As the Hillsborough proceeds southwest toward Tampa Bay, it traverses a variety of terrain, predominantly a mixture of cypress and hardwood forests, much of which is protected by 16,000-acre Wilderness Park, part of Southwest Florida Water Management District Lands and managed by Hillsborough County. A series of riverside parks, part of the greater Wilderness Park, provides boat launching and places to relax. The well-known Seventeen Runs area is a mixed hardwood swamp, which contains southern red cedar, cabbage palmetto, and cypress.

Although the underlying surface in the area is sand and clay, numerous limestone formations in the upper river create frequent mild rapids. About 10 miles downstream of the Green Swamp, the river enters another protected area, Hillsborough River State Park, one of the oldest and largest parks in the state. Virtually all the riverfront from the Green Swamp head-waters to the I-75 overpass is protected by these preserves. The paddling is still pleasant until reaching Fowler Avenue, when greater Tampa overwhelms the river and it becomes a watery avenue between riverside homes.

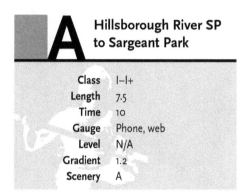

◇ MAPS ZEPHYRHILLS, WESLEY CHAPEL, THONOTOSASSA (USGS)

A   Hillsborough River SP to Sargeant Park

Class	I–I+
Length	7.5
Time	10
Gauge	Phone, web
Level	N/A
Gradient	1.2
Scenery	A

62A DESCRIPTION The uppermost public access is now at Hillsborough River State Park, since Crystal Springs was purchased by a bottled-water manufacturer. This upper section of the Hillsborough contains the well-known Seventeen Runs, an area of cypress swamp where the river branches into numer-ous swift, shallow creeks. The entrance to the Runs is about 3.0 miles downstream of the put-in. Before that point, the river chan-nel is broad and the current slow as it tra-verses a forest thick with oak, cypress, pine, and cedar. The water is darkly stained by the tannin seeping from the surrounding land, and it obscures the occasional limestone rock embedded in the sand bottom.

Just before the beginning of Seventeen Runs, pass Dead River Park on the left shore. This park offers river access but is open to vehicles only from Friday through Sunday. Kayaks are not advised to tackle Seventeen Runs, due to too much getting in and out of the boat to pull over logs and such.

Over the next several miles, you will encounter numerous deadfalls, and carry-overs are a certainty, depending on the water level. The river continues to separate into multiple branches, most being impassable due to shallow bottoms, or what appears to be an endless series of major obstructions. Good luck choosing the right channel. For the most part, the terrain in this area is thick with tree roots, leaf litter, deadfall, and some poi-son ivy. Very few places are clear enough for going ashore. In the last mile of this section, the river gradually broadens and the current slows. Allow a minimum of 6 hours between Dead River Park and John B. Sargeant Park.

The end of the section is marked by the appearance of a wooden boardwalk from Sargeant Park. At this point, Flint Creek enters from the left and the Hillsborough continues on to the right. The take-out is reached by paddling straight ahead past the boardwalk and into a narrow canal leading into John B. Sargeant Park. Canoe Escape, an outfitter, operates at Sargeant Park.

◇ SHUTTLE To reach the take-out from Exit 265 off I-75, take FL 582 1.0 mile east to US 301. Turn left on US 301 North and follow it 4.4 miles to John B. Sargeant Park, on your left. A parking fee applies; for more informa-tion, call 813-987-6208 or visit tinyurl.com /sargeantpark. A launching fee also applies; for more information, call 813-986-2067 or visit canoeescape.com.

To reach the put-in, continue north on US 301 for 7.5 miles to reach Hillsborough River State Park and its boat launch. An entrance fee applies (see "Fees and Permits," page 6).

◇ GAUGE Phone, web. Call Canoe Escape at 813-986-2067 for the latest river conditions.

Hillsborough River A–C:
Hillsborough River State Park to Rotary Park

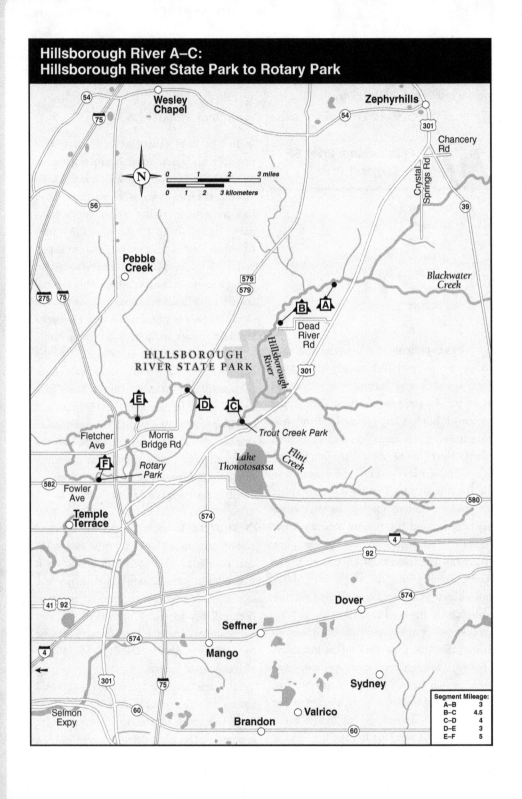

The Hillsborough River is normally paddleable year-round. The USGS gauge helpful in determining flow rates for any given time period is Hillsborough River at Morris Bridge near Thonotosassa, Florida.

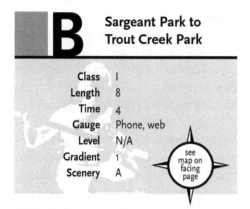

B Sargeant Park to Trout Creek Park

Class	I
Length	8
Time	4
Gauge	Phone, web
Level	N/A
Gradient	1
Scenery	A

see map on facing page

62B **DESCRIPTION** Part of the preserved Lower Hillsborough Flood Detention Area, this section of the Hillsborough is a popular winter paddle run that offers opportunities for observing wildlife. Access at this point is down a gentle slope into a small basin. From here, proceed north down a short, narrow canal and past a boardwalk on the right. The canal ends at the confluence of Flint Creek and the Hillsborough River.

At this point, you should turn left and proceed downstream. For the next several miles, the journey is quite pleasant. An occasional deadfall will be encountered, and although these may require a carryover, they may also block powerboats from using this section of river. The channel is broad and the water slow-moving as it passes through a protected tropical landscape of cypresses, oaks, and palms. At any given time, hundreds of white ibises might inhabit this area and treat you to a special show as they swoop through the trees en masse, filling the air with the sporadic sound of drumming wing beats.

At about 2.0 miles, the river turns north and continues in that general direction to Morris Bridge Park. As the sunlight filters through the dense forest foliage, it creates a patchwork of bright-green hues contrasted with deep shadows.

After 4.0 miles, the river passes beneath Morris Bridge. A boat launch is at the county park on the left, just past the bridge.

The tea-colored river meanders southwest from Morris Bridge, still in the protection of greater Wilderness Park. The canopied river keeps its sense of isolation amid many twists and turns. The Trout Creek Park boat launch is on river left.

SHUTTLE To reach the take-out from Exit 266 off I-75, take Morris Bridge Road 0.5 mile east to the entrance of Trout Creek Park. Turn left into the park and follow the road 1.3 miles north to the boat launch. A parking fee applies; for more information, call 813-987-6200 or visit tinyurl.com/troutcreekpark.

To reach the put-in, return to I-75 and head south to Exit 265. Head east on FL 582 for 1.0 mile; then turn left on US 301 North and follow it 4.4 miles to John B. Sargeant Park, on your left. A parking fee applies; for more information, call 813-987-6208 or visit tinyurl.com/sargeantpark. A launching fee also applies; for more information, call 813-986-2067 or visit canoeescape.com.

GAUGE Phone, web. Call Canoe Escape at 813-986-2067 for the latest river conditions. The Hillsborough River is normally paddleable year-round. The USGS gauge helpful in determining flow rates for any given time period is Hillsborough River at Morris Bridge near Thonotosassa, Florida.

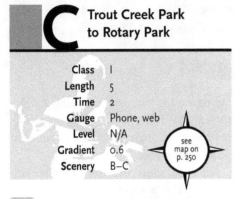

Trout Creek Park to Rotary Park

Class	I
Length	5
Time	2
Gauge	Phone, web
Level	N/A
Gradient	0.6
Scenery	B–C

see map on p. 250

62C DESCRIPTION The Hillsborough begins to open below Trout Creek Park, though it still retains its wild aura until the I-75 overpass. The river continues to meander below I-75 and then turns south at Lettuce Lake. Below Lettuce Lake, houses begin to appear along the banks with regularity.

Pass under the Fletcher Avenue Bridge at 3.0 miles. The city of Temple Terrace lies along the Hillsborough. The river jogs to the east before reaching Rotary Park, on busy Fowler Avenue. Below here, houses line the river and it loses any feel of remoteness, so this section will be a disappointment after you've experienced the tranquility of the upper river, despite the official Florida paddling trail extending to Rowlett Park, 10.0 miles below Rotary Park, with an intermediate access at Riverhills Park.

◇ SHUTTLE To reach the take-out from Exit 265 off I-75, take FL 582 West 0.3 mile and turn right on Morris Bridge Road; then, just before the entrance to the Fisherman's Landing apartment complex, turn left into Rotary Riverfront Park to reach its boat launch, at the west end of the road that circles the park.

To reach the put-in, return to I-75 and head north to Exit 266. Take Morris Bridge Road 0.5 mile east to the entrance of Trout Creek Park. Turn left into the park and follow the road 1.3 miles north to the boat launch. A parking fee applies; for more information, call 813-987-6200 or visit tinyurl.com/troutcreekpark.

◇ GAUGE Phone, web. Call Canoe Escape at 813-986-2067 for the latest river conditions. The Hillsborough River is normally paddleable year-round. The USGS gauge helpful in determining flow rates for any given time period is Hillsborough River at Morris Bridge near Thonotosassa, Florida.

63 ALAFIA RIVER

◇ OVERVIEW The Alafia (AL-uh-FYE) River extends about 45 miles from meager beginnings near the town of Mulberry until it widens into a substantial waterway and empties into Hillsborough Bay near Riverview. The North Prong flows east to west through the gently rolling hills of the Polk uplands and the flatwood forests of the Gulf coastal lowlands. In its upper reaches, the river meanders through cattle land and near phosphate mines; though these contribute to high nutrient concentrations and low dissolved oxygen levels, the Alafia retains a fair water quality.

The section of the Alafia covered in this guide extends 26 miles, from the Keysville Bridge in east Hillsborough County to the Alafia boat ramp in a residential area of the town of Riverview. Below the boat ramp, the river widens substantially; although it can be paddled, this is not recommended because of a large volume of powerboat traffic.

Between these points, the Alafia is moderately swift and, at numerous places, small formations of riverbed limestone have created short whitewater rapids. The river meanders through beautiful oak canopies and past areas heavily vegetated with cypress trees, cabbage palms, and palmettos. Though wildlife is not abundant on this river, you may see numerous bird species, opossums, raccoons, cattle, and possibly an alligator lazing on the riverside.

The Alafia passes through two county parks—Alderman's Ford and Lithia Springs, as well as Alderman's Ford Preserve. Lithia Springs has swimming, restrooms, shower facilities, and a developed camping area. Alderman's Ford has restrooms, a very nice nature walk along boardwalks and dirt trails, and a primitive-camping area.

The South Prong Alafia River offers limited paddling at the boat launch for Alafia River State Park, located south of Alderman's Ford County Park on County Road 39. Here, you can paddle upstream about a half mile, then open into Lake Hurrah, which offers good bass fishing. Paddlers can travel a half mile on the lake before the South Prong becomes choked with logs and debris.

Heading north, downstream, from the state-park put-in, the narrow, canopied stream is navigable for about a mile before it too becomes blocked by fallen trees. At this time, it is not possible to take the South Prong downstream to Alderman Ford County Park. Rangers strongly urge paddlers not to even try it.

✧ **MAPS** NICHOLS, KEYSVILLE, LITHIA, DOVER, RIVERVIEW, BRANDON (USGS)

A Keysville Bridge to Alderman's Ford Park

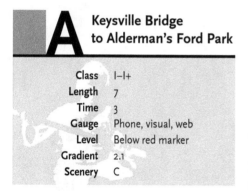

Class	I–I+
Length	7
Time	3
Gauge	Phone, visual, web
Level	Below red marker
Gradient	2.1
Scenery	C

63A **DESCRIPTION** The first 6.0 miles of this run are on the North Prong of the Alafia. For the first few miles, the river meanders through heavily vegetated landscape. In this section, the Alafia flows past nearby strip mines and cattle land, but these are not readily observable since the banks are high on both sides. Eventually, the right bank reaches a height of 30–40 feet, giving the river landscape a mountainlike quality.

Two and a half miles downstream from the put-in point, the river flows beneath a railroad trestle, turns to the right, and carries over a 30-yard stretch of very mild rapids. The Alafia enters the Alderman's Ford County Park boundary 1.5 miles later. In this area, cypress trees abound and the sides of the river are heavily vegetated.

About 1.5 miles past the boundary of Alderman's Ford, the river narrows to 10 or 15 feet, and the South Prong enters from the left. Approximately 0.5 mile later, the river flows beneath a footbridge, widens again, and passes under CR 39. Just before another footbridge crosses the river, a channel flows in sharply from the left. This channel leads to the take-out point, a nice wooden dock 100 yards upstream on the right.

This section of the Alafia is quite secluded—you will likely not see another person until Alderman's Ford. However, there are signs of civilization, and the beautiful scenery does not occur until the last couple of miles of the run. The primitive parking near the Keysville Bridge contrasts mightily with the well-developed Alderman's Ford area.

Alafia River A–C: Keysville Bridge to Alafia Boat Ramp

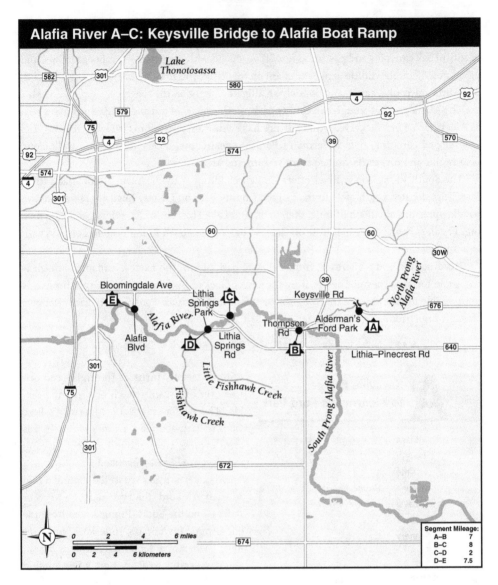

Segment Mileage:	
A–B	7
B–C	8
C–D	2
D–E	7.5

✧ **SHUTTLE** To reach the take-out from Exit 254 off I-75, take US 301 South 2.6 miles; then turn left (east) and follow Bloomingdale Avenue 5.7 miles to Lithia–Pinecrest Road/CR 640. Turn right, heading southeast on Lithia–Pinecrest Road, and follow it 7.1 miles to CR 39, passing the bridge over the Alafia River. Turn left on CR 39 and follow it north 1.0 mile, then turn left on Thompson Road and follow it 0.1 mile to Alderman's Ford Park, on the right.

An entrance fee applies; for more information, call 813-757-3801 or visit tinyurl.com/aldermansford.

To reach the put-in, backtrack on Thompson Road to CR 39 and turn left (north), passing the bridge over the Alafia River and continuing north 2.0 miles to Keysville Road. Turn right on Keysville Road and follow it east 1.8 miles to cross the bridge over the Alafia River. A rough access is on the southeast side of the bridge.

◇ **GAUGE** Phone, visual, web. Call Alafia River Canoe Rentals at 813-689-8645 for the latest river conditions. Also, at the Alderman's Ford Launch there's a pole at the launch—if the river level is at the red mark on the pole, do not undertake the trip unless you are a proficient paddler. The USGS gauge helpful in determining flow rates for any given time period is North Prong Alafia River at Keysville, Florida.

〜〜〜

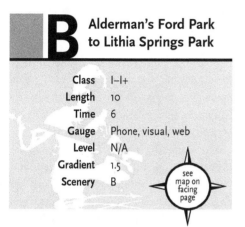

B Alderman's Ford Park to Lithia Springs Park

Class	I–I+
Length	10
Time	6
Gauge	Phone, visual, web
Level	N/A
Gradient	1.5
Scenery	B

see map on facing page

63B **DESCRIPTION** While the section of the Alafia from Keysville Bridge to Alderman's Ford is generally secluded, the section described here tends to be quite crowded and is the only part of the Alafia that is a state-designated paddling trail. On weekends it's a very popular area, but on weekdays it's quiet and you may be alone on the river. The popularity of this section is also evident in the moderate amount of trash littering the river and its banks. This offsets the otherwise-scenic beauty of the landscape.

The Alderman's Ford canoe-launch area is on a side channel off the main river. Proceed to the left from the wooden dock, and about 100 yards downstream make a gradual left turn onto the Alafia. At this point, the river passes beneath a footbridge, part of the county-park boardwalk system. In the next

THE AUTHOR TACKLES A MILD RAPID ON THE ALAFIA.

quarter mile, the river turns from due north to west to east and then begins a general westerly direction of flow.

This section of the Alafia meanders through beautiful oak and cypress woodlands, part of hiking trail–laced Alderman's Ford Preserve. The banks are occasionally 4–5 feet high. In most places, though, the shoreline is shallow and sandy. There is private property along the lower stretch of this run, so be sure to respect the property rights of others.

Between Alderman's Ford and Lithia Springs lie at least six sets of mild whitewater rapids. At low-water levels, some of these become impassable because of exposed rocks and require a portage or carryover. The first of these occurs approximately 1.5 miles downstream from Alderman's Ford, and the rest are spaced at irregular intervals.

At 5.0 miles, the river flows past a gouged-out area of forest. There is a sloped bank of white sand and a rickety-looking brick structure on each side. These are the remnants of an old railroad trestle that was disassembled years ago; this is not a safe place to stop for picnicking or camping.

At 8.0 miles, the Alafia passes beneath CR 640. One-quarter mile farther downstream, on the right, are the docks for Alafia Canoe Rental. It offers a good access point for a fee. The take-out at Lithia Springs Regional Park is 2.0 miles past the CR 640 bridge and is the end of the state-designated paddling trail. At this point, the river is flowing southwest and turning to the northwest.

SHUTTLE To reach the take-out from Exit 254 off I-75, take US 301 South 2.6 miles; then turn left (east) and follow Bloomingdale Avenue 5.7 miles to Lithia–Pinecrest Road/CR 640. Turn right, heading southeast on Lithia–Pinecrest Road, and follow it beyond the bridge over the Alafia River. After 3.1 miles, turn right (west) on Lithia Springs Road and follow it 1.9 miles to reach Lithia Springs Regional Park and a pay paddler launch. For information on fees, call 813-744-5572 or visit tinyurl.com/lithiaspringspark.

To reach the put-in, return to Lithia–Pinecrest Road, turn right (southeast), and follow the road 4.0 miles to CR 39. Turn left on CR 39 and follow it north 1.0 mile, then turn left on Thompson Road and follow it 0.1 mile to Alderman's Ford Park, on the right. An entrance fee applies; for more information, call 813-757-3801 or visit tinyurl.com/aldermansford.

GAUGE Phone, visual, web. Call Alafia River Canoe Rentals at 813-689-8645 for the latest river conditions. Also, at the Alderman's Ford Launch there's a red pole at the launch. If the river level is at the red mark on the pole, do not undertake the trip unless you are a proficient paddler. The USGS gauge helpful in determining flow rates for any given time period is Alafia River at Lithia, Florida.

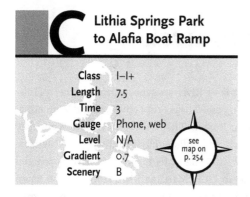

C Lithia Springs Park
to Alafia Boat Ramp

Class	I–I+
Length	7.5
Time	3
Gauge	Phone, web
Level	N/A
Gradient	0.7
Scenery	B

see map on p. 254

63C **DESCRIPTION** The first 3.0 miles of this section contains some of the most scenic landscapes on the entire Alafia. Huge oaks line high banks, and the tree canopy shades up to 75% of the river area. The shore is heavily vegetated with palmettos and numerous varieties of ferns and vines. The current is moderately swift and creates several sets of whitewater rapids as it flows over limestone rock formations. Countless overhanging trees and branches can snag the unwary paddler, especially when you're negotiating a tight turn.

From the put-in, you will pass under a large overhead pipe and swing around Lithia Springs County Park on the left. At 0.4 mile, the Lithia Springs basin, which is the park's swimming area, empties into the Alafia. The tannin-stained water is mixed with silt and dirt, and when it meets the crystal-clear discharge from the spring, it creates a noticeable contrast line.

Just past Lithia Springs, Little Fishhawk Creek enters the river from the south, and 1 mile later Fishhawk Creek enters, also from the south. Except at low-water levels, both can be paddled, although Little Fishhawk Creek is extremely narrow.

Four miles downstream of the put-in, the Alafia passes beneath Bell Shoals Bridge (no access), and from this point on the shoreline becomes highly developed. The river broadens and becomes quite sluggish. For the next 3.5 miles to the take-out, you will likely encounter much powerboat traffic. The take-out is on the right (east) side of the river, at a concrete boat ramp lined with high retaining walls.

⟡ **SHUTTLE** To reach the take-out from Exit 254 off I-75, take US 301 South 2.6 miles; then turn left (east) on Bloomingdale Avenue and follow it 2.6 miles to Kings Avenue. Turn right (south) on Kings Avenue and follow it 0.8 mile, then turn right on Ethyl Street and follow it 0.3 mile. Veer right on Ruth Avenue, then left on Alafia Boulevard at the fork; follow Alafia Boulevard 0.2 mile to the Alafia boat ramp, on your left.

To reach the put-in, backtrack on Kings Avenue to Bloomingdale Avenue and turn right (east). In 3.1 miles, turn right on Lithia–Pinecrest Road, heading southeast, and follow it beyond the bridge over the Alafia River. After 3.1 miles, turn right (west) on Lithia Springs Road and follow it 1.9 miles to reach Lithia Springs Regional Park and a pay paddler launch. For information on fees, call 813-744-5572 or visit tinyurl.com/lithiaspringspark.

⟡ **GAUGE** Phone, web. Call Alafia River Canoe Rentals at 813-689-8645 for the latest river conditions. The USGS gauge helpful in determining flow rates for any given time period is Alafia River at Lithia, Florida.

64 LITTLE MANATEE RIVER

✧ **OVERVIEW** For about 40 miles, the Little Manatee River stretches across southern Hillsborough County from its origin as a tightly twisting creek near Fort Lonesome and Wimauma, until it broadens and empties into Tampa Bay near Ruskin. The Little Manatee is now a mostly protected watershed, thanks to the state of Florida and Hillsborough County. Little Manatee River State Park has existed for some time now, and the state and county have purchased additional parcels. This protection is partly due to Little Manatee River's designation as an Outstanding Florida Water. Now, in ever-expanding coastal Florida, this river will remain an enchanting place to wet your boat.

If you paddle the Little Manatee River in the dry winter months, you will encounter a shallow, narrow waterway enclosed by steep banks, heavily vegetated with oaks, pines, willows, and an occasional cedar. High above, the trees form a thick canopy that shades most of the river and, below, numerous small beaches will invite you to stop and enjoy a refreshing swim.

If you paddle this river in the wet summer season, though, its character will be remarkably different. High water will cover a large number of the swimming beaches and, during periods of recent heavy rainfall, the swift current will race you through the branches of the overhead tree canopy. During times of especially high precipitation, it is best to avoid the section of the river upstream (east) of US 301 and remain in the downstream area, where the riverbed broadens and is not subject to rapid water-level fluctuations.

Distancewise, the paddling options on this river are numerous, with five good access points stretched along its 17-mile distance. Below US 301, the river can be paddled as an out-and-back if you don't want to use the outfitter conveniently located at US 301 or you simply don't have two cars for a shuttle. The busy period on this river is March–August.

✧ **MAPS** WIMAUMA, RUSKIN (USGS)

Little Manatee River Nature Preserve to 24th Street Access

Class	I
Length	17
Time	Varies
Gauge	Phone, web
Level	N/A
Gradient	1.5
Scenery	B

DESCRIPTION The uppermost section of the Little Manatee is also the wildest. Part of the Little Manatee River Nature Preserve, it's the most difficult to paddle at high water.

The narrow channel causes rapid water-level fluctuations after heavy rainfall, and the gradient of the riverbed produces a swift current that can propel the paddler through snags and overhanging tree branches. This section is also the site of a drop in the riverbed that, though unnoticeable at high water, creates a small waterfall at low water during the dry season.

The remainder of these first 3.5 miles snakes through tall, wooded banks and past a few small, sandy beaches until it flows beneath the bridge and a potential put-in/take-out at County Road 579.

The first 3.5 miles below CR 579 are much like the previous section. The narrow river

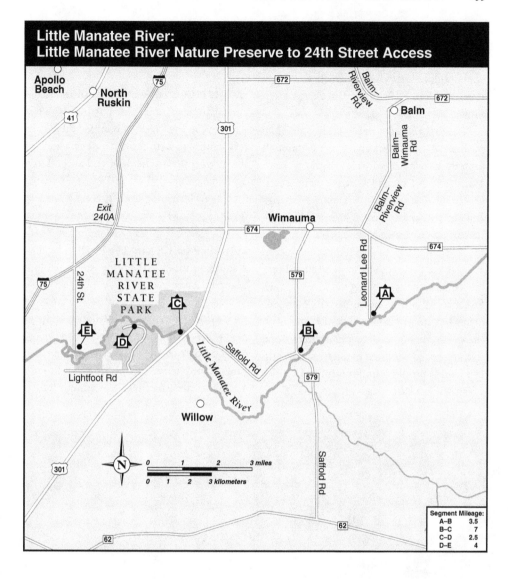

Little Manatee River:
Little Manatee River Nature Preserve to 24th Street Access

snakes its way through tall, wooded banks, and the swift current can race to high-water levels when rainfall has been heavy. Oaks and willows line the shore, creating a canopy that occasionally opens up as the river widens.

The observable riverside is totally undeveloped except for two major structures. The first, a water-intake gate for a local Florida Power Corporation plant, is located just past 6.0 miles. It appears quite suddenly through the trees and disappears just as quickly as the river turns sharply to the north and back into the surrounding woods. Less than 2.0 miles from here is an old, long-abandoned railroad trestle. This massive brick structure with overhead steel supports was built in 1913 and used by the famous *Orange Blossom Special.*

At low water, sandy beaches are exposed nearby, providing lovely places to stop for a rest. Below the trestle, the river broadens gradually and the tree canopy gives way to more open areas. There are fewer deadfalls and obstructions to negotiate, and the channel does not wind as much as it does upstream. Reach US 301 and an adjacent outfitter at 10.5 miles.

The first 3.0 miles below US 301 are quite pleasant as the river meanders gently through a pretty wooded area, which includes Little Manatee State Park and its access on the south shore. The first mile has numerous overhangs and obstructions that must be carefully negotiated, but it clears up beyond that.

Past 3.0 miles, the river broadens to about 150 feet and becomes shallow and slow. Enter "civilization" before ending the trip. The 24th Street access on the north bank is 6.5 miles below the US 301 bridge. The take-out is on the north shore, up an asphalt street ramp that appears to dead-end in the river. The official Florida paddling trail continues 3.5 miles to the Wildcat Park access off Stephens Road,

passing under I-75 en route. Part of the shore is protected as the Little Manatee Conservation Area.

◆ **SHUTTLE** To reach the lowermost access from Exit 240A/240B off I-75, take College Avenue/FL 674 West 0.8 mile, then turn left (south) on 24th Street Southeast and follow it 3.3 miles to the dead end at the Little Manatee River.

To reach the uppermost access from Exit 240A/240B off I-75, take College Avenue/FL 674 East 6.8 miles to Leonard Lee Road. Turn right on Leonard Lee Road and follow it south 2.3 miles to the bridge over the Little Manatee River.

◆ **GAUGE** Phone, web. Call Canoe Outpost at 813-634-2228 for the latest river conditions. The USGS gauge helpful in determining flow rates for any given time period is South Fork Little Manatee River near Wimauma, Florida.

IN PLACES, THE LITTLE MANATEE IS A SHALLOW AND NARROW WATERWAY.

65 MANATEE RIVER

◇ **OVERVIEW** The Manatee River flows into the Gulf of Mexico and Tampa Bay west of the city of Bradenton after extending for nearly 40 miles through central Manatee County. It is supplied principally from 150 square miles of watershed, and along its entire length countless creeks drain their contents into it. The river traverses the Gulf Coastal lowlands, and the surrounding area is marked by pine flatwoods, sand hills, and hammock communities.

Historically, the land was used for cattle grazing, farming, and harvesting timber, and many of the local coniferous trees were also used for turpentine production. Later, east of what is now the city of Bradenton, numerous small communities were quickly developed and almost as quickly disappeared. Rye was at the eastern end of a commercial boat traffic route that originated in Bradenton. Today, the area is growing much like all southwest Florida, but the riverbanks are still largely natural, especially near Rye Wilderness Park and the adjacent Boy Scout camp.

In the 1960s, a dam was constructed on the river and Lake Manatee was formed. This 2,400-acre reservoir provides potable water for Sarasota and Manatee Counties and is also part of Lake Manatee State Park, which offers boating, swimming, and camping. The dam gates are opened at irregular intervals to release overflow into the river, especially after heavy rains. In the narrow river channel near the dam, the discharge from the lake can raise the water level several feet in an hour. The opening of the gates is announced well in advance by a series of siren blasts from the dam structure.

◇ **MAPS** Parrish, Rye, Verna (USGS)

Rye Wilderness Park to Fort Hamer

Class	I
Length	7
Time	Varies
Gauge	Phone
Level	Tidal
Gradient	1.1
Scenery	B

65 **DESCRIPTION** This entire section encompasses the Upper Manatee state paddling trail. The lower you are on this river, the more tidally influenced it becomes. Because of this, many paddlers go one way and return to the same access point. Use the tides to your advantage!

The Lake Manatee Dam can be reached most easily by paddling upstream from Rye Wilderness Park. The dam is 3.0 miles upstream of Rye Wilderness Park. If the dam gates have been opened, the current will be swift, especially near the dam. In spite of these conditions, round-trips, even from Fort Hamer, are possible and done as much or more than one-way trips. Call Ray's Canoe Hideaway or the dam phone number (see "Gauge") for the latest information if you think a water release is likely.

March through early summer is the busy season on the Manatee. Two side streams on the lower river are worth taking for short trips. Mill Creek enters the Manatee from the south a mile east of Fort Hamer, and Gamble Creek enters from the north just downstream from there. Gamble Creek meanders for several miles through tall grasses typical of coastal marshes and is composed of numerous mazelike braided channels.

Manatee River: Rye Wilderness Park to Fort Hamer

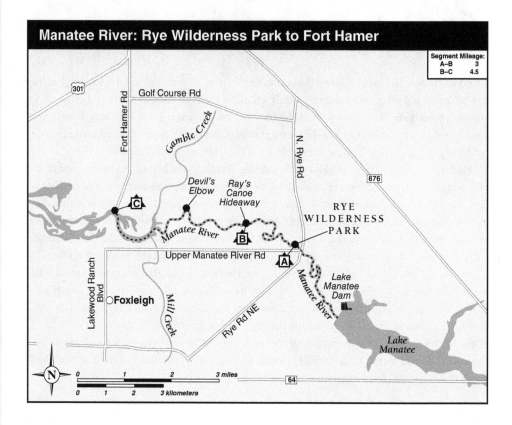

Segment Mileage:	
A–B	3
B–C	4.5

The river widens considerably below the confluence with Mill Creek. Powerboat traffic increases in the last section to Fort Hamer, making this part of the paddle less desirable. Below Fort Hamer, the river braids into wide channels before becoming so wide as to make winds and powerboats a factor.

East of Ray's Canoe Hideaway, the riverbed begins to narrow and bluffs gradually appear on the sides. Some of these are bare sand bluffs that drop into pleasant beaches ideal for rest stops. East of the Rye Road bridge, the bluffs are higher, with tall sand pines growing on them. Only an occasional building or trailer can be seen through the thick vegetation to mar the fine scenery in this area. If the dam gates are open, the roar of the rushing water can be heard at least a mile away.

As the dam is approached, you might encounter patches of discolored foam. This is formed as the water bubbles over the spillway at the foot of the dam. Due to swift current and possible obstructions, you should not approach the dam too closely.

⟨⟩ SHUTTLE To reach the take-out from Exit 224 off I-75, take US 301 North (you're actually heading east) toward Parrish. In 5.5 miles, as US 301 veers left (north), make an acute right turn onto Fort Hamer Road. Follow Fort Hamer Road south 3.1 miles to the dead end at a boat ramp on the Manatee River.

To reach the uppermost put-in, backtrack 2.3 miles on Fort Hamer Road; then turn right (east) on Golf Course Road and follow it 3.5 miles to North Rye Road. Turn right (south) on North Rye Road, and follow it 2.6 miles to Rye Wilderness Park and a canoe and skiff launch on the southwest side of the bridge over the Manatee River.

◆ **GAUGE** Phone. Call Ray's Canoe Hide-away for the latest river conditions at 941-747-3909. You can also call the Lake Manatee Dam office at 941-746-3020 for dam-release information.

66 MYAKKA RIVER

◆ **OVERVIEW** One of Florida's designated state scenic rivers, the Myakka originates in east central Manatee County, in cattle country. From there it winds southwesterly, enters Sarasota County, and becomes a central feature of Myakka River State Park, a 58-square-mile park. While in the park, the river merges with Clay Gully and opens into Upper Myakka Lake, a beautiful expanse of water known for its alligators. Upper Myakka Lake is the beginning for paddlers, and the river is generally paddleable year-round from this point.

Upper Myakka Lake empties into a river channel bordered by open grasses and some hardwood hammocks. The river then passes below the new, high FL 72 bridge and becomes much less traveled by boaters as it enters the state-park wilderness preserve. Entrance into the preserve is limited to 30 people per day, and a permit is required. The Myakka flows riverine for another 1.5 miles before opening into Lower Myakka Lake, which narrows and then opens again into the Deep Hole, which has been certified to be at least 142 feet deep.

Below Deep Hole, the river resumes its riverine characteristics and leaves Myakka River State Park. It then makes a winding, southerly course for Charlotte Harbor, where it empties into the Gulf. The section below the park is little paddled, due to a long run of 13.5 miles combined with a long shuttle. The river down here is quite scenic, and part of the riverbank is protected by the Carlton Tract, land owned by Sarasota County.

After passing below the I-75 overpass, the Myakka reaches Snook Haven County Park and a good place to take out. Below this point, the river quickly widens and becomes the domain of the powerboat set.

◆ **MAPS** MYAKKA RIVER STATE PARK MAP; MYAKKA CITY, OLD MYAKKA, MYAKKA RIVER (USGS)

A Upper Myakka Lake to Bridge at State Park

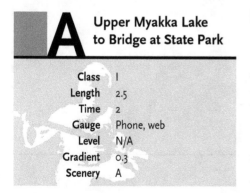

Class	I
Length	2.5
Time	2
Gauge	Phone, web
Level	N/A
Gradient	0.3
Scenery	A

66A **DESCRIPTION** This section is often paddled as an out-and-back. The boat ramp is at the south end of Upper Myakka Lake. During periods of low water, paddlers may have to portage around the weir at the south end of the lake. Nevertheless, paddlers have the option of extending their trip from the south end of Upper Myakka Lake to the north end of the lake, then paddling down to the river channel, winding among the grasses before coming to

Myakka River A–B: Upper Myakka Lake to Snook Haven

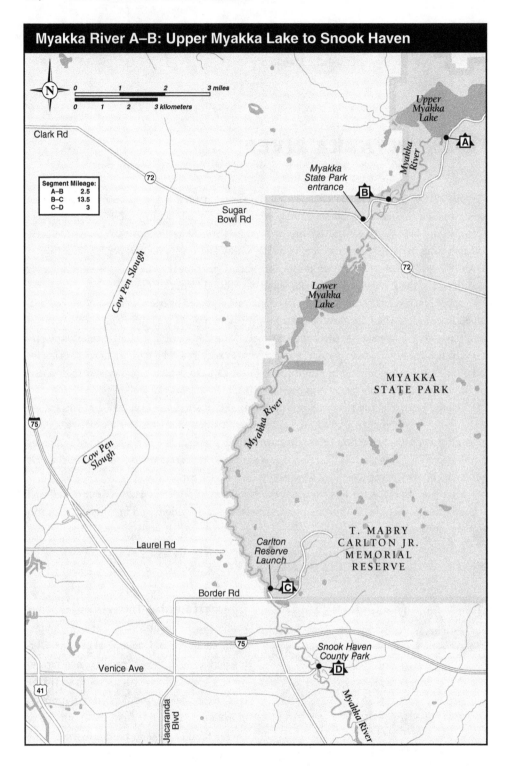

0   1   2   3 miles
0   1   2   3 kilometers

Clark Rd

72

Segment Mileage:
A–B   2.5
B–C   13.5
C–D   3

Myakka
State Park
entrance

B

Sugar
Bowl Rd

72

Upper
Myakka
Lake

A

Myakka
River

Cow Pen Slough

Lower
Myakka
Lake

MYAKKA
STATE PARK

75

Cow Pen
Slough

Myakka River

Laurel Rd

Carlton
Reserve
Launch

T. MABRY
CARLTON JR.
MEMORIAL
RESERVE

C

Border Rd

75

Snook Haven
County Park

D

Venice Ave

41

Jacaranda
Blvd

Myakka River

a Park Drive bridge over the river. This bridge is a popular alligator-viewing spot, and onlookers will be atop the bridge gator spotting.

Below the bridge, you may glimpse an old palm cabin built by the Civilian Conservation Corps back in the 1930s. There is a small picnic area nearby. Paddlers may want to take out just downstream of here, at the south picnic and parking area. Be apprised that much of this paddle is on open water and is extremely subject to winds, especially during winter, which is also when many tourists are on the river. There is no launching or parking at the high FL 72 span.

◇ **SHUTTLE** To reach the take-out from Exit 205 off I-75, take Clark Road/FL 72 East 8.6 miles to Myakka River State Park. Turn left

to enter the park and head north up the park road 0.1 mile, then turn right to reach a picnic area. An entrance fee applies (see "Fees and Permits," page 6).

To reach the put-in, continue north past the entrance station on the main park road, bridging the Myakka, and in 2.7 miles bear left at the fork to reach the concession area, 0.3 mile farther. The boat ramp is just past Myakka Outpost, on the edge of Upper Myakka Lake. Canoes and kayaks are available for rent here; for information on rates, call 941-923-1120 or visit myakkaoutpost.com.

◇ **GAUGE** Phone, web. Call Myakka River State Park at 941-361-6511 for the latest river conditions. The USGS gauge to help determine flow rates for any given time period is Myakka River at Myakka City, Florida.

B Myakka River State Park to Snook Haven

Class	I
Length	16.5
Time	9
Gauge	Phone, web
Level	N/A
Gradient	0.5
Scenery	A

see map on facing page

66B **DESCRIPTION** The addition of the launch area at the Canton Reserve shortens a long paddle to 13.5 miles. When planning this endeavor, make sure to build the time for a long shuttle into your day.

After leaving the state park, pass under the high FL 72 bridge. The river twists and turns before opening into Lower Myakka Lake. Most paddlers enjoy the river and Lower Myakka Lake, then backtrack upstream.

A PALM TREE BENDS OVER THE RIVER IN MYAKKA RIVER STATE PARK.

Below Lower Myakka Lake, the river narrows and is bordered by high sandy banks, grown up with laurel oaks, live oaks, and palms. Expect occasional blowdowns to stretch across the river; boats can generally pass, however. The limestone river bottom creates occasional shoals, especially when the river pinches in. The current is generally mild to nonexistent, except where the river narrows.

Paddlers will have to portage around a dam on the river below the wilderness area. Portage on river left, in the Carlton Tract, as river right is posted. Be very careful around posted land down here—some landowners will exercise their rights.

You will come to the Carlton Reserve Launch 12.5 miles below the FL 72 bridge. After you pass under the I-75 bridge, motorboats will become more common. The Snook Haven boat ramp is now a county park.

⟡ SHUTTLE To reach the take-out from Exit 191 off I-75, take River Road south to East Venice Avenue. Turn left (east) on Venice Road and follow it 0.7 mile to Snook Haven County Park.

To reach the put-in from Exit 205 off I-75, take Clark Road/FL 72 East 8.6 miles to Myakka River State Park. An entrance fee applies (see "Fees and Permits," page 6). Turn left (north) to enter the park and head up the main park road 2.8 miles. Bear left at the fork to reach the concession area, 0.3 mile farther. The boat ramp is just past Myakka Outpost, on the edge of Upper Myakka Lake. Canoes and kayaks are available for rent here; for information on rates, call 941-923-1120 or visit myakkaoutpost.com.

⟡ GAUGE Phone, web. Call Myakka River State Park at 941-361-6511 for the latest river conditions. The USGS gauge to help determine flow rates for any given time period is Myakka River near Sarasota, Florida.

THE SCENIC MYAKKA RIVER

67 PRAIRIE CREEK

✧ **OVERVIEW** Flowing into the northeast corner of Charlotte Harbor, Prairie Creek provides a glimpse into Old Florida, of the landscape that cracker cowboys roamed before housing retirees became more profitable. Prairie Creek flows from eastern Charlotte and DeSoto County ranchlands before widening, breaking into numerous channels and old oxbows. It then merges into Shell Creek at a water-supply dam.

An accessible upper stretch of Prairie Creek provides a quality freshwater paddling experience. Here, you can head up the dam-slowed stream that incessantly twists and narrows, eventually to become canopied and increasingly swift. This upper stretch can be paddled nearly 5 miles before fallen trees and creek size prohibit further travel, depending on whether other paddlers have kept this uppermost of the uppermost stretch open.

Part of the waterway passes through Prairie Creek Preserve, a 1,600-acre wildland delivering wilder banks. The lower stretch can be done as a 6-mile end-to-end paddle, combined with the lower part of Shell Creek. However, you must carry around the dam that holds back water—a 150-acre lake—for Punta Gorda's aqua supply.

✧ **MAPS** Prairie Creek Preserve, Cleveland, Fort Ogden (USGS)

Upper Prairie Creek to Riverside Boat Ramp on Shell Creek

Class	I
Length	11
Time	Varies
Gauge	Web
Level	N/A
Gradient	1.2
Scenery	B+

67 **DESCRIPTION** The best trip on Prairie Creek is upstream from the Washington Loop Road bridge. The stream is about 60 feet wide here. After passing a few houses near the road, the stream becomes more wild than not. Alternating swampy and high banks deter development more than high-banked Shell Creek to the south.

Regal cypresses border the shore, as do sturdy oaks and placid palms. The current is slow due to the downstream dam that houses Punta Gorda's drinking water. Occasional islands and small sloughs may temporarily confuse the paddler, but the primary stream will reveal itself. In narrow spots, look for cut limbs and logs. Wildlife is abundant, from birds to alligators.

You will enter Shell Creek Preserve after 2.0 miles, enhancing the adventure. Your return trip will be with the current.

Downstream of Washington Loop Road provides a wider, looping waterway with oxbows aplenty and alternate channels. The current will stop altogether as you reach the watershed lake. After carrying around the dam, you are on Shell Creek. Convolutions continue, alternate channels exist, and the waterway is tidally influenced.

To reach the Riverside Drive ramp, stay with the main (south) channel. The ramp is tucked between houses, so stay alert.

✧ **SHUTTLE** To reach the lower Riverside boat ramp from Exit 164 off I-75 near Punta Gorda, take US 17 East 4.3 miles to Riverside

Prairie Creek and Shell Creek

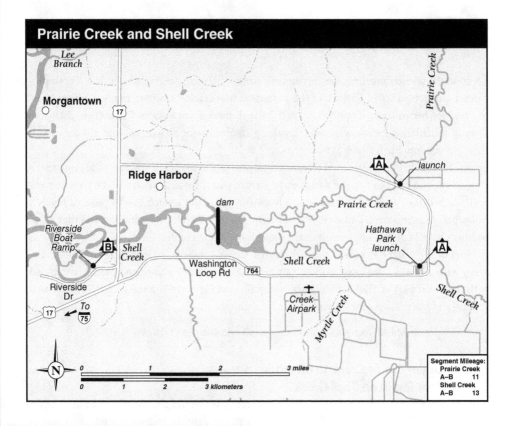

Lee Branch

Morgantown

17

Ridge Harbor

dam

Prairie Creek

launch

A

Riverside Boat Ramp

B   *Shell Creek*

Hathaway Park launch

A

Washington Loop Rd   764

Shell Creek

Riverside Dr

Shell Creek

17   To 75

Creek Airpark

Myrtle Creek

N

0   1   2   3 miles
0   1   2   3 kilometers

Segment Mileage:
Prairie Creek
A–B   11
Shell Creek
A–B   13

Drive, on your left just before the bridge over Shell Creek. Follow Riverside Drive 0.4 mile and look for the brown RIVERSIDE BOAT RAMP sign on your right; the ramp is a short distance ahead, tucked between two houses.

To reach the Washington Loop Road bridge access from Riverside Drive, continue north on US 17 over the Shell Creek Bridge 1.4 miles, then turn right on Washington Loop Road/County Road 764. Follow it 4.0 miles to the small two-lane bridge over Prairie Creek. The primitive launch, with limited parking, is on your left after the bridge crossing.

◇ **GAUGE** Prairie Creek is paddleable year-round, but a gauge of interest is Prairie Creek on CR 764 near Punta Gorda, Florida.

SWAMP LILY ON THE BANK OF PRAIRIE CREEK

68 SHELL CREEK

◇ **OVERVIEW** A tributary of the Peace River (page 208), Shell Creek flows into the northeast corner of Charlotte Harbor. Its headwaters drain the ranchlands of eastern Charlotte County, and the stream is a designated Charlotte County Blueway. Named for embedded crustaceans in its upper banks, Shell Creek can be paddled to its uppermost narrow reaches east of Hathaway Park—the primary paddler access—and west to the Riverside boat ramp in Charlotte Harbor.

Downstream from Hathaway Park, Shell Creek passes many houses while making a serpentine course to be dammed at Punta Gorda's water-supply impoundment. This is also where Prairie Creek adds its flow. Below the dam, Shell Creek splits into channels, passes under the US 17 bridge, and then both comes under increasing tidal influence and experiences significant motorboat traffic.

A paddler's best bet is to head upstream from Hathaway Park, into ranch country and Shell Creek Preserve. Though houses are present at first, natural banks are common too. The creek continues to narrow and the current swiften, but the scenery is rewarding.

◇ **MAPS** CLEVELAND, BERMONT (USGS)

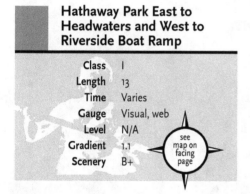

Hathaway Park East to Headwaters and West to Riverside Boat Ramp

Class	I
Length	13
Time	Varies
Gauge	Visual, web
Level	N/A
Gradient	1.1
Scenery	B+

see map on facing page

68 DESCRIPTION Most paddlers will head upstream from Hathaway Park. Leave the small canoe/kayak launch (there is a boat ramp here at the first entrance to Hathaway Park) in a dug pond to quickly emerge onto 80-foot-wide Shell Creek. Head right, then pass under Washington Loop Road Bridge. Upstream from here is a no-wake zone for motorboaters. Houses will be seen here. The downstream dam keeps the current mild. Rich, high banks are draped in live oaks. Palms rise above cypresses. Epiphytes find their places on the trees.

You will pass under a power line 1.5 miles from Hathaway Park. Enter Shell Creek Preserve at 2.0 miles. Here, the preserved banks provide 5.0 miles of river frontage (counting both sides of the stream) as well as deliver drinking water for the locality and provide a wildlife corridor.

Downstream from Hathaway Park, houses and motorboats become common. Enter the 150-acre watershed lake after 4.0 miles. Below the lake dam, Shell Creek breaks into channels. Below US 17, the waterway is tidal. If taking out at Riverside Park, stay on the main (southern) channel.

◇ **SHUTTLE** To reach the Riverside boat ramp from Exit 164 off I-75 near Punta Gorda, take US 17 East 4.3 miles to Riverside Drive, on your left just before the bridge over Shell Creek. Follow Riverside Drive 0.4 mile and look for the brown RIVERSIDE BOAT RAMP sign on your right; the ramp is a short distance ahead, tucked between two houses.

To reach the Hathaway Park access from Riverside Drive, backtrack south on US 17 for 0.2 mile, then turn left on Washington Loop Road/County Road 764. Follow it for 4.5 miles to the *second* entrance into Hathaway Park, on your left.

◇ **GAUGE** Prairie Creek is paddleable year-round, but a relevant gauge is Shell Creek near Punta Gorda, Florida.

SHELL CREEK IS A CHARLOTTE COUNTY BLUEWAY.

69 CALOOSAHATCHEE RIVER AND HICKEYS CREEK

✧ **OVERVIEW** This adventure combines paddling on the big Caloosahatchee River and small, intimate Hickeys Creek, a state-designated paddling trail and tributary of the Caloosahatchee. It is possible to launch directly on Hickeys Creek at Hickeys Creek Mitigation Park, but this involves a 0.4-mile carry from the parking area to the canoe/kayak launch. Furthermore, if you do this, it eliminates the Caloosahatchee River experience and the savoring of varied waterways.

Instead, I recommend starting at Caloosahatchee Regional Park. You must call ahead to access the launch, but it opens directly onto the Caloosahatchee River. From here, follow the regional-park shoreline downstream, then cross over to Hickeys Creek. Trace the winding, wooded waterway upstream to Hickeys Creek Mitigation Park and then make a return trip, totaling 7–8 miles, depending on how far up uppermost Hickeys Creek you can get.

A wind forecast for the Caloosahatchee River will aid your paddle. This paddle can also be executed from Franklin Lock, downstream of Hickeys Creek on the Caloosahatchee, but is a little longer to reach the mouth of Hickeys Creek. Finally, Caloosahatchee Regional Park also features an excellent hiking trail system as well as a fine, shaded walk-in tent campground.

✧ **MAPS** CALOOSAHATCHEE REGIONAL PARK MAP;
HICKEYS CREEK MITIGATION PARK MAP; OLGA (USGS)

Caloosahatchee Regional Park to Hickeys Creek Mitigation Park and Back

Class	I
Length	7 (out-and-back)
Time	Varies
Gauge	Visual
Level	N/A
Gradient	N/A
Scenery	B

69 **DESCRIPTION** After arranging access with Caloosahatchee Regional Park, launch from a metal dock or gravel shore. The Caloosahatchee stretches several hundred feet wide here, making it a fairway for winds. Head west, downstream on the Caloosahatchee, staying alongside the natural shoreline of the park. Houses stand across the river. Pass an observation deck and fishing dock before leaving the park shores at 1.3 miles. From here, angle over to the left (south) bank.

At 1.6 miles, find the mouth of Hickeys Creek between two residences. Hickeys Creek immediately curves right (west), then passes under the FL 80 bridge at 1.9 miles. From here, the stream winds its way past wooded enclaves, flowing clear. It reaches Hickeys Creek Mitigation Park at 3.2 miles, and the stream's windings increase. Briefly follow a canal, then reach a fishing platform and canoe/kayak launch for this park at 3.5 miles.

Leave left from the canal, reentering Hickeys Creek. Shortly pass under a hiking trail bridge. Then comes paddling Southwest Florida at its finest, as a natural shoreline envelops the creek, with overhanging live oaks forming a canopy.

The creek narrows until an inevitable fallen tree blocks the way. Savor your return

Caloosahatchee River and Hickeys Creek:
Caloosahatchee Regional Park to
Hickeys Creek Mitigation Park and Back

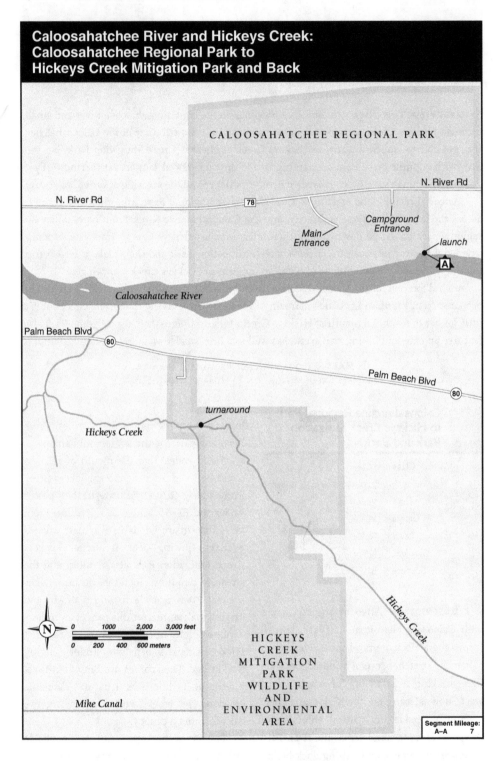

CALOOSAHATCHEE REGIONAL PARK

N. River Rd

N. River Rd

78

Campground
Entrance

Main
Entrance

launch

A

Caloosahatchee River

Palm Beach Blvd

80

Palm Beach Blvd

80

turnaround

Hickeys Creek

Hickeys Creek

N

0   1000   2,000   3,000 feet

0   200   400   600 meters

HICKEYS
CREEK
MITIGATION
PARK
WILDLIFE
AND
ENVIRONMENTAL
AREA

Mike Canal

Segment Mileage:
A–A   7

journey down Hickeys Creek as well as experiencing the big waters of the Caloosahatchee.

◇ **DIRECTIONS** From Exit 141 off I-75 near Fort Myers, take FL 80 East for 2.8 miles to FL 31. Turn left and take FL 31 North for 2.7 miles to County Road 78/North River Road. You'll pass a left turn for CR 78 just after bridging the Caloosahatchee River—ignore that left turn and keep straight (north) on FL 31, passing the Lee County Civic Center; then turn right on CR 78 and follow it 7.8 miles to the Caloosahatchee Regional Park campground entrance, on your right. The first park entrance will be the North Side Trails parking area, on the left. Then you'll pass the day-use area entrance, on your right. The third entrance will be the campground and paddle-access entrance, on your right. Call ahead at 239-694-0398 for information on day-use fees and arranging launch access.

◇ **GAUGE** The Caloosahatchee River and Hickeys Creek are paddleable year-round, but a relevant gauge is Caloosahatchee River at S-79, near Olga, Florida.

THE CALOOSAHATCHEE RIVER CAN BE WIDE BUT SCENIC.

70   COMMODORE CREEK CANOE TRAIL

◇ **OVERVIEW** Sanibel and Captiva Islands, in the Gulf of Mexico across San Carlos Bay from Fort Myers, are reached via the busy Sanibel Causeway. Believe it or not, at one time these barrier islands were relatively undeveloped, providing a quiet refuge for those seeking solitude or a shell-hunting excursion along the now well-known beaches.

Alas, development finally came to the islands, and rustic terrain gradually gave way to condominiums, hotels, and apartments. In 1976, however, a large swath of the islands was designated as the J. N. "Ding" Darling National Wildlife Refuge and protected from future encroachment.

Vegetated with mangrove and sawgrass, the refuge is home to a variety of animals, including ospreys, moorhens, brown pelicans, and alligators. Winter migration brings an abundance of northern visitors, such as blue-winged teals, pintails, mergansers, and Yankees, to name a few. The Commodore Creek Canoe Trail offers an excellent way to tour the refuge.

◇ **MAPS** NAUTICAL CHART 11427, SANIBEL (USGS)

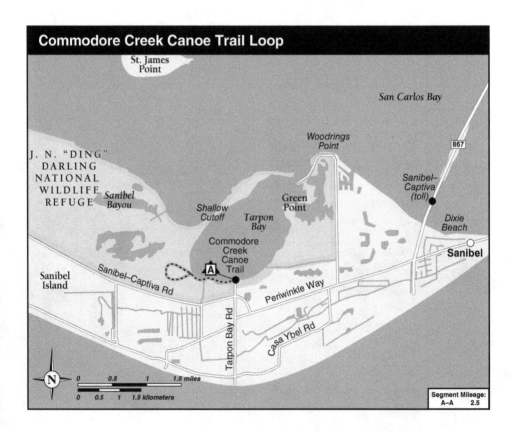

Commodore Creek Canoe Trail Loop

St. James Point

San Carlos Bay

Woodrings Point

867

J. N. "DING" DARLING NATIONAL WILDLIFE REFUGE

Sanibel Bayou

Sanibel–Captiva (toll)

Shallow Cutoff

Green Point

Tarpon Bay

Dixie Beach

Commodore Creek Canoe Trail

Sanibel

Sanibel Island

Sanibel–Captiva Rd

A

Periwinkle Way

Tarpon Bay Rd

Casa Ybel Rd

N

| 0 | 0.5 | 1 | 1.5 miles |

| 0 | 0.5 | 1 | 1.5 kilometers |

Segment Mileage:
A–A   2.5

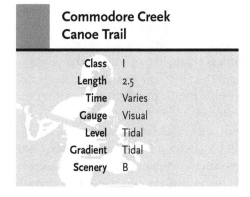

Commodore Creek Canoe Trail

Class	I
Length	2.5
Time	Varies
Gauge	Visual
Level	Tidal
Gradient	Tidal
Scenery	B

70 DESCRIPTION Located at the southeast corner of Tarpon Bay, the Commodore Creek Canoe Trail snakes through tidal mud flats and stands of red mangrove. It offers excellent views of wading birds and small marine animals scurrying along the seabed. The trailhead is reached by paddling 0.75 mile west of the Tarpon Bay Marina along the south shore of the bay. An official refuge concessionaire rents kayaks.

◇ DIRECTIONS From Exit 131 off I-75, take Daniels Parkway/County Road 876 west 2.7 miles to Six Mile Cypress Parkway/CR 865. Turn left (south) on CR 865, which becomes Gladiolus Drive, and in 4.1 miles bear left to merge onto Summerlin Road/CR 869, heading southwest. Follow CR 869 11.2 miles to Sanibel Island—en route, CR 869 becomes McGregor Boulevard/CR 867, then the Sanibel Causeway. Once on the island, take Causeway Boulevard 0.5 mile to Periwinkle Way; turn right on Periwinkle and, in 2.5 miles, turn right on Palm Ridge Road, then right again on Tarpon Bay Road. In 0.2 mile, bear left at the fork to reach Tarpon Bay Explorers and a pay launch leading into Tarpon Bay; for information on rentals, call 239-472-8900 or visit tarpon bayexplorers.com.

◇ GAUGE Visual. Try to catch the trail on a rising or high falling tide.

71 ESTERO RIVER

◇ OVERVIEW Located in a once-quiet area now being overwhelmed by Fort Myers to the north and Naples to the south lies the community of Estero. Bounded on the west by Estero Bay and on the east by the Corkscrew Swamp, Estero was established in 1894 by a religious visionary from Chicago, Dr. Cyrus Reed Teed.

Teed was the founder of a religion that advocated communal living, communal ownership of property, and celibacy. He called this new religion Koreshanity, which is derived from *Koresh*, the Hebrew version of the name Cyrus. Among this religion's most unique beliefs was the theory that the earth was a hollow sphere. Life existed on the inner surface and overlooked the sun, stars, and universe in the center. In 1896, Teed even conducted an experiment with a simple device, known as a "rectilineator," which proved to him that the earth's surface was indeed concave—a central feature of his theory.

The bulk of the Koreshan settlement was built on the Estero River, about 5 miles upstream from Estero Bay. Although the movement declined after Teed's death in 1908, many of the buildings remain intact and are preserved as part of Koreshan State Historic Area. This park, which extends for a mile along the Estero River, has a beautifully wooded camping area, nature trails, a concrete boat ramp, and, of course, the historic Koreshan settlement.

Estero, Spanish for "estuary," was first applied long ago by explorers as they sailed into the bay. Estero Bay is an ecologically rich area in which red mangrove and turtle grass provide a continuous food supply for the large fish population. This productive area has been designated as a state aquatic preserve, and much of the land within 2 miles south of the Estero River and extending through the park is state owned and protected.

The section of the Estero River covered here, part of the official state paddling trail, extends for 5 miles from the point where it passes beneath US 41 until it flows into Estero Bay. Along this course, the character of the river changes dramatically. Beginning as a narrow waterway channeled by limestone and shaded by large oaks, it eventually broadens as it flows through the spartina grass and mangrove of the tidal marsh.

The flow of the river is affected by the tides, so paddlers may want to check local tide tables while planning a trip. Because of extensive powerboat traffic on weekends, the ideal time to paddle this river is during the week. However, it is definitely worth a trip into Estero Bay to visit Mound Key State Archaeological Preserve. Mound Key was the site of Calos, capital city of the fierce Calusa tribe, who ruled South Florida. A walking trail and interpretive information on the island cap a fine paddle on the Estero River.

MAPS KORESHAN STATE HISTORIC AREA MAP, ESTERO (USGS)

US 41 to Mound Key and Back

Class	I
Length	11 (out-and-back)
Time	Varies
Gauge	Visual
Level	Tidal
Gradient	Tidal
Scenery	B+

71 **DESCRIPTION** This is an out-and-back paddle, 5.5 miles each way. From the launch point, paddle to the west under the US 41 bridge. Along the first mile, the south shore is in the state park, and for the first 0.25 mile, several buildings of the historic Koreshan settlement can be seen through the woods on the left.

Although the north shore is developed, with several trailer parks, their associated docks, and boat slips, the scenery is still quite nice. Large oaks draped with Spanish moss

and bromeliads shade most of the river area, and the lush shore vegetation is highlighted with an occasional wild hibiscus. Layers of limestone, stained green in irregular patterns by fungi and dripping wet from the damp mosses that cling to it, protrude from the riverbanks. It is not uncommon to see an alligator resting on a submerged log or outcropping, its body partially obscured by the dark, tannin-stained water.

The state-park boat ramp is concrete and has stone retaining walls. It is on the south side of the river and very easy to find. This is a good starting point if you want to shave a mile off your trip.

Beyond the state-park boat ramp, proceed left (west) toward Estero Bay. Within 2.0 miles of the put-in, the river passes a large trailer park and another residential area, both on river right. The channel is about 60 yards wide here, and the south shore is lined with tall Australian pine trees. At 2.5 miles, Halfway Creek enters from the south. This lovely

Estero River: US 41 to Mound Key and Back

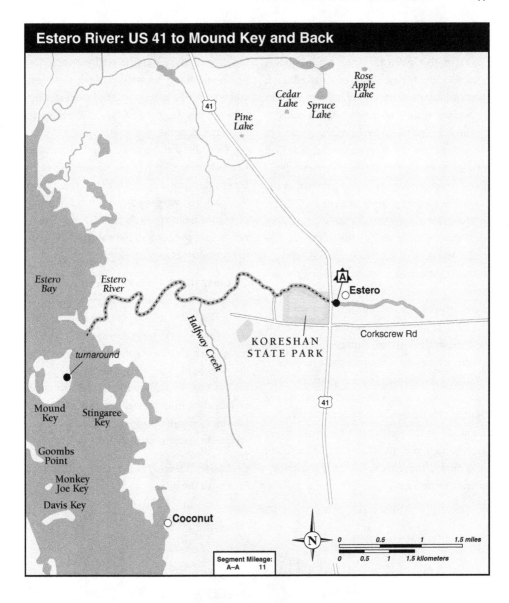

little waterway meanders through a brackish marsh and, in places, separates into multiple channels that weave their way through mangrove and turtle grass. All the vegetation looks alike, so it's easy to become confused, but with a compass or GPS unit and knowledge of the current direction at the mouth of the creek, you can eventually find the main channel. Mangrove is the predominant vegetation from Halfway Creek to Estero Bay, although there

is also a lot of spartina grass and, on the high ground, some Australian and sand pines.

A quarter mile past Halfway Creek, a long, narrow bay protrudes to the south-southeast; at its mouth lies the wreckage of a sunken boat. The wheelhouse is always visible, and at low tide the bow can be seen angling out of the water. For safety reasons, the hulk should not be approached too closely. The dark, tannin-stained water obscures the view, making it difficult to see pieces of hull wreckage that may obstruct the paddler.

From this point on, the river meanders gently to Estero Bay, past a number of small bays and side streams that are interesting areas to explore in their own right. At 3.6 miles, a channel enters the river from the northeast. This side creek winds its way through a thick mangrove forest, and the observant paddler is likely to see herons and egrets perched in the roots or an osprey soaring overhead.

Just past 4.0 miles, the river enters Estero Bay, and the influence of the tides becomes quite pronounced. Paddlers should exercise caution in this area, because moderate chop—enough to swamp a canoe or kayak—can develop quickly in the bay. (Kayakers with covered hatches will have no problems.) Oyster beds, with their sharp, damaging shells, are located near some of the mangrove thickets.

Horseshoe crabs can be seen in the water and scurrying along the sand on mangrove islands. Mullets may surprise you as they jump out of the water next to your boat and arc through the air. Occasionally paddlers may notice the ghostly form of a stingray passing underneath.

Paddlers should then aim for Mound Key, the biggest island in the center of the bay. The island's walking trail connects the north and south landings. Stretch your legs and explore the mounds of the island and the water courts dug by the Calusa. Then return the way you came.

The official state paddling trail extends to Lovers Key State Park, but if you want to paddle Lovers Key, you're better off launching from that park and winding among the dug canals of a failed housing development–turned–park rather than paddling all the way from US 41 or the Koreshan State Historic Site.

✧ **DIRECTIONS** From Exit 123 off I-75, travel west on Corkscrew Road/County Road 853 for 2.0 miles to US 41, the Tamiami Trail. Turn right (north) and proceed 0.25 mile to the bridge over the Estero River. Estero River Outfitters is located on the northeast side of the bridge. There is ample parking, and boats may be launched from a small wooden dock for a nominal fee (call 239-992-4050 or visit esteroriveroutfitters.com for more information).

✧ **GAUGE** Visual. Try to time your out-and-back with the tides.

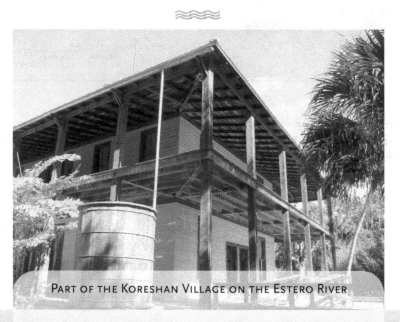

PART OF THE KORESHAN VILLAGE ON THE ESTERO RIVER

PADDLERS PLY THE MANGROVE-LINED SHORES OF THE ESTERO RIVER.

The Everglades

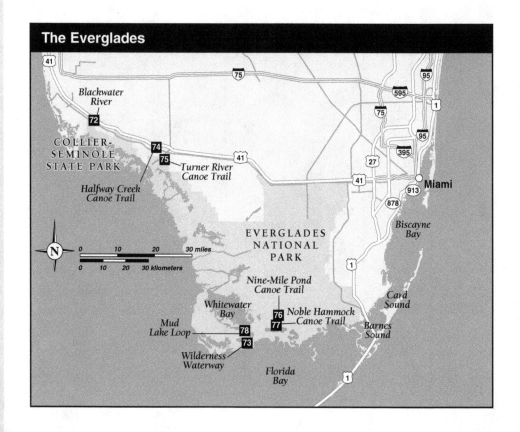

The Everglades

72 BLACKWATER RIVER AT COLLIER-SEMINOLE STATE PARK

◆ **OVERVIEW** The Blackwater River is part of a 13.5-mile paddling circuit that winds through Collier-Seminole State Park. This wilderness preserve at the western extreme of the Everglades features a prime example of the mangrove forest that forms the outer rim of South Florida. The paddling circuit described here includes tidal creeks and bays as well as the Blackwater River. A diverse community of wildlife, including roseate spoonbills and manatees, inhabits the preserve. The tides add another dimension to paddling in the preserve. Current in the creeks becomes moderately swift during tidal change, and even the Blackwater River reverses flow on the incoming tide.

◆ **MAPS** COLLIER-SEMINOLE STATE PARK PADDLE MAP; NOAA NAUTICAL CHART 11430, LOSTMANS RIVER TO WIGGINS PASS; ROYAL PALM HAMMOCK (USGS)

Collier-Seminole State Park Loop

Class	I
Length	13.5 (loop)
Time	6
Gauge	Visual
Level	Tidal
Gradient	Tidal
Scenery	A

72 **DESCRIPTION** Paddlers have special requirements to ply the waters at Collier-Seminole. All paddlers must file a float plan at the entrance station. This requirement is dictated by the high potential for getting lost among the myriad mangrove islands. The rangers will brief all paddlers on the tide situation and stress the necessity for a compass and map (a nautical chart is recommended).

Blackwater River at Collier-Seminole State Park: Collier-Seminole State Park Loop

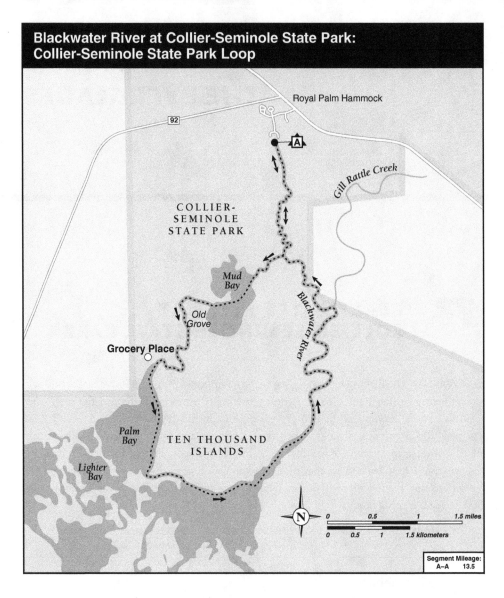

All paddlers who do the entire loop must travel counterclockwise through Mud Bay to Palm Bay and then up the Blackwater River. Be prepared to start your trip early in the morning, as you must return to the ranger station by a specific time unless you are staying at the Grocery Place backcountry campsite, which also requires a permit. *Note:* Check with the office at Blackwater River State Park for the latest tides in Mud Bay.

The trip begins at the Collier-Seminole boat ramp. The first 0.5 mile is on a wide man-made channel to the Blackwater River. The upper river is narrow and winds through a mangrove forest. The red mangrove, with its characteristic prop roots, forms the first echelon of mangrove. The black mangrove, with its hundreds of pencil-like pneumatophore roots sticking out of the muck, is back on higher ground.

PADDLERS STOP AT THE GROCERY PLACE CAMPSITE.

The trail leaves the Blackwater River at 1.8 miles, where a sign directs paddlers to turn right into a tidal creek. This narrow creek almost forms a tunnel through the mangrove. A small bay marks the 2.0-mile point, and Mud Bay is close at hand.

Those arriving at Mud Bay at low tide will soon discover the source of its name, as there are areas where canoes and kayaks must be pulled over mud bars. Bear to the left toward the large island upon entering the bay. Keep to the left side of the island and head into Royal Palm Hammock Creek. West Palm Run comes in on the right as Royal Palm Hammock Creek turns to the south. The Old Grove, one of only two spots of high ground on this trip, is passed on the left at 3.5 miles.

Grocery Place, the other high point and the designated camping area, is on the right, at the mouth of a stream at 4.5 miles. Early settlers arranged for supply boats to cache provisions on this spot, hence the name. Royal Palm Hammock Creek enters the open expanse of Palm Bay downstream of Grocery Place. Paddlers should stick to the left bank

from this point until they reenter the Blackwater River.

You will enter the Ten Thousand Islands region at 6.0 miles. Be aware that it is very easy to get lost here among the numerous look-alike mangrove islands. For this reason, it is essential to keep the mainland to the immediate left of your boat.

After another mile of paddling, you enter Blackwater Bay. Continue bearing left and go into the mouth of the Blackwater River. Channel markers are spaced at intervals going up the river. A branch of Gill Rattle Creek is passed on the right at 7.5 miles, as is another side stream at 10.0 miles.

◆ **DIRECTIONS** From Exit 101 off I-75, drive south on FL 951/Collier Boulevard and follow it 6.8 miles to US 41, the Tamiami Trail. Turn left on US 41, heading southeast; the state park will be 8.4 miles ahead on the right, just past County Road 92. An entrance fee applies (see "Fees and Permits," page 6).

◆ **GAUGE** Visual. Try to time your trip with the tides.

73 EVERGLADES NATIONAL PARK AND THE WILDERNESS WATERWAY

◆ **OVERVIEW** Mention the Everglades, and both water and vegetation come to mind. After all, it is known as the River of Grass. The Everglades is actually a mosaic of numerous ecosystems, from sawgrass plains to pinelands to tropical hardwood hammocks to coastal prairies to sandy islands in the Gulf of Mexico. Paddlers will find themselves plying the brackish, mangrove-bordered waters and the coastal areas along the Gulf.

Simply put, Everglades National Park is one of the best paddling destinations in America, with the most extensive warm-water-paddling area in the United States. Outings can range from 2 hours to 2 weeks. Settings range from the ultranarrow Hells Bay Canoe Trail to miles-wide Florida Bay and the even-more-open Gulf of Mexico.

Fifty-two designated backcountry campsites scattered among the islands, beaches, rivers, and bays of the Everglades allow for years of paddling trips without repeating yourself. (See page 6 for more information about backcountry permits.) Day paddlers have several excellent designated routes that will give them a good taste of what watery adventures the Glades have to offer.

◇ **MAPS** Everglades National Park map;
NOAA Nautical Charts 11430, 11432, and 11433; Waterproof Charts 39 and 41

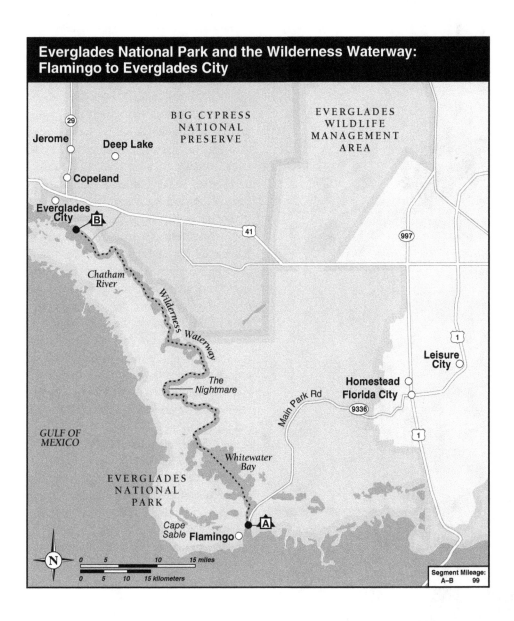

Everglades National Park and the Wilderness Waterway: Flamingo to Everglades City

Flamingo to Everglades City

Class	I
Length	99
Time	Varies
Gauge	Visual
Level	Tidal
Gradient	Tidal
Scenery	A+

THE WILDERNESS WATERWAY IS
MARKED WITH SIGNS LIKE THIS ONE.

73 **DESCRIPTION** There are hundreds of potential routes, and describing them would take a book all by itself. As the author of *A Paddler's Guide to Everglades National Park,* I know that exploring both the "inside" and the "outside" of the Everglades paddling area will enhance your appreciation of this unique ecosystem. The "inside" is the area of rivers, creeks, and bays between the freshwater river of grass, and the "outside" is the waters of the Gulf of Mexico that are pocked by mangrove islands, coastline, and beaches. The outside is better suited for sea kayaks, with so much open water subject to unpredictable winds.

The Wilderness Waterway, a 99-mile marked path maintained by the National Park Service, starts in Flamingo and leads to Everglades City. Most paddlers, however, travel north to south to avoid facing strong north winds that occasionally penetrate the Glades. From Flamingo, paddlers follow the Coast Guard markers to 48, just north of Whitewater Bay, and then follow the rectangular brown signs erected by the park service. These signs are numbered, increasing toward Everglades City, and have an arrow pointing on one side or the other. Be aware, though, that this arrow does not always point you in the right direction. So double-check your chart and don't blindly follow the arrows of the Wilderness Waterway. Although the Wilderness Waterway is the most well-known paddle trail in the park, it is far from the best or most interesting travel route.

◆ **SHUTTLE** To reach Flamingo from the intersection of FL 997 and US 41 in Miami, take FL 997 South 21.7 miles, then turn right (west) on West Palm Drive/FL 9336 in Florida City. In 1.5 miles, turn left (south) to stay on FL 9336; then, in 2.0 miles, turn right (west) to continue on FL 9336. Follow the road 6.1 miles into Everglades National Park to the entrance station and then another 37.4 miles (on the Main Park Road) to the Flamingo Visitor Center.

To reach the north end of the Wilderness Waterway in Everglades City, backtrack on FL 997 to US 41, the Tamiami Trail. Turn left (west) on US 41 and drive 57.9 miles. Turn left on CR 29 and follow it south 3.9 miles to Everglades City. Turn right on East Broadway Avenue and, in two blocks, bear right around the traffic circle to head left (south)

on Copeland Avenue. In 0.7 mile, turn right on Oyster Bar Lane to reach the Gulf Coast Visitor Center.

An entrance fee applies at Flamingo but not Everglades City. Call 305-242-7700 or visit nps.gov/ever/planyourvisit/fees.htm for the latest information.

⟡ GAUGE Visual. The Wilderness Waterway and the paddling area of Everglades National Park are tidally affected.

74 HALFWAY CREEK CANOE TRAIL

⟡ OVERVIEW This route is a microcosm of South Florida in many ways. It reveals human hands on the landscape and offers a good view of the beauty left under park protection. First, you paddle down a man-made canal, definitely a part of modern South Florida. You come to an attractive habitat of sawgrass, cattails, and tree islands. Then you enter a strange and wonderful mangrove tunnel that turns into a brackish stream beneath a taller shady forest. Leave the park boundary, pass by houses, then go under the bridge of an artificial causeway to emerge in busy, wide-open Chokoloskee Bay, ending your paddle at the Gulf Coast Visitor Center.

Consider paying for a shuttle from an outfitter to make this a one-way day paddle. This creek is not on the waterproof charts, but the route is marked most of the way, and Big Cypress National Preserve's visitor centers offer GPS tracks available for download to make your paddling less of a navigational challenge. The preserve has also marked a loop off Halfway Creek, making a shuttle unnecessary.

⟡ MAPS Big Cypress National Preserve map; Everglades National Park map; Ochopee, Chokoloskee, Everglades City (USGS)

Tamiami Trail to Gulf Coast Ranger Station

Class	I
Length	7.5
Time	4
Gauge	Visual, phone
Level	Tidal
Gradient	Tidal
Scenery	A

74 DESCRIPTION Start your trip on US 41, the Tamiami Trail, at Big Cypress National Preserve. Put in to the canal and begin paddling southwesterly. Note the limestone banks here. The water is crystal-clear and bordered by sawgrass, cattails, and occasional mangroves. Other freshwater plants adorn the higher dry land of the south bank.

Halfway Creek Canoe Trail: Tamiami Trail to Gulf Coast Ranger Station

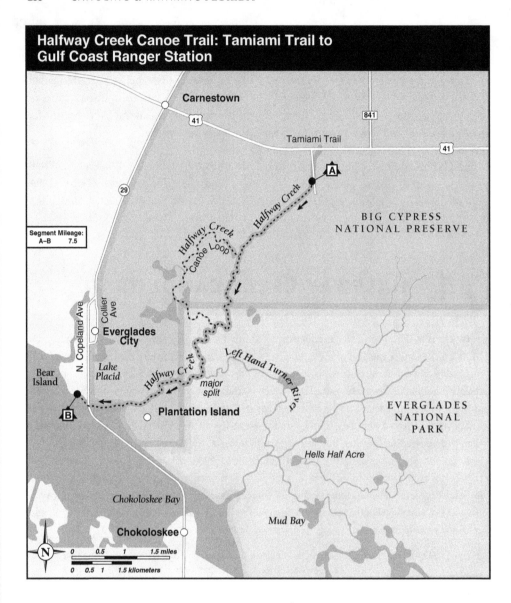

Carnestown

41

841

Tamiami Trail

41

A

Halfway Creek

Halfway Creek

BIG CYPRESS
NATIONAL PRESERVE

29

Segment Mileage:
A–B   7.5

Halfway Creek

Canoe Loop

N. Copeland Ave

Collier
Ave

Everglades
City

Halfway Creek

Left Hand Turner River

Bear
Island

Lake
Placid

Halfway Creek

*major
split*

Plantation Island

EVERGLADES
NATIONAL
PARK

B

Hells Half Acre

Chokoloskee Bay

Mud Bay

Chokoloskee

N

0   0.5   1   1.5 miles

0   0.5   1   1.5 kilometers

Soon pass the markers of an airboat trail crossing the canal. Leave the 40-foot-wide canal and come to the first lake at mile 1. Keep southwest.

Pass marker 1 toward the end of the lake, which meanders, and keep west past marker 2. A beautiful variety of South Florida vegetation is all around. This is some of the most scenic paddling in this entire guidebook. Paddlers headed toward the Gulf will be looking at the green side of these markers. Paddlers heading away from the Gulf will be seeing the red side of these same markers.

The trail alternates between small lakes and narrower creeks, keeping a generally southwesterly direction. Stay with the markers. Past marker 6, arms of trees crowd the slender creek until the trees eventually form a tunnel that continues for a good distance.

Keep a reasonable pace, not going too fast among the twists and turns of the tunnel. The water here is plenty deep, but at times you'll have to duck your head under vegetation. Watch for a bit of land on creek right where you can get out and take a break.

Farther down the tunnel, Halfway Creek takes on a murky, pungent aspect. More fallen trees and brush lie in the water. The canopy rises as you proceed downstream. Tidal influence increases. Come to a major split in the creek at 5.5 miles. To your left (east), a creek leads toward Turner Lake and Left Hand Turner River. To your right (west), Halfway Creek widens and continues toward Chokoloskee Bay. Stay with Halfway Creek.

Leave the Everglades National Park boundary and pass a few houses on your right. Notice the Australian pine, Brazilian pepper, and other exotic vegetation. The Plantation Island community is on your right before the creek opens into a bay. Keep southwest to reach the Halfway Creek bridge. Watch for strong tides flowing through here. Once through the bridge, turn northwest, passing a tour boat landing and two brown National Park Service buildings, to

Everglades National Park's Gulf Coast Visitor Center, ending your route.

⟡ SHUTTLE To reach the take-out from the intersection of FL 997 and US 41 in Miami, drive west on US 41 for 57.9 miles. Turn left on CR 29 and follow it south 3.9 miles to Everglades City. Turn right on East Broadway Avenue and, in two blocks, bear right around the traffic circle to head left (south) on Copeland Avenue. In 0.7 mile, turn right on Oyster Bar Lane to reach the Gulf Coast Visitor Center.

To reach the put-in from Everglades City, backtrack on CR 29 to US 41. Turn right (east) on US 41 and drive 2.5 miles to Sea Grape Drive. Turn right on Sea Grape Drive, adjacent to the Big Cypress Swamp Welcome Center at Big Cypress National Preserve, and follow it a short distance to the Halfway Creek landing. No entrance fee is charged at Big Cypress National Preserve or the Gulf Coast Visitor Center.

⟡ GAUGE Visual, phone. If in doubt, check with the rangers at Big Cypress National Preserve at 239-695-4758 or 239-695-1201 for the latest creek conditions.

75 TURNER RIVER CANOE TRAIL

⟡ OVERVIEW This may be the most biologically diverse paddle in the Everglades. It starts on the Tamiami Trail in Big Cypress National Preserve, amid a freshwater environment dominated by towering cypress trees. It opens into sawgrass broken with occasional tree islands, makes a tight squeeze through eerie tree tunnels, and then transforms to classic mangrove-zone environment before reaching Hurddles Creek. You continue down the Turner River as it opens up and passes a tall historic Calusa Indian mound before arriving at civilized Chokoloskee Island.

Be apprised that the paddling on this trail can be tough. At, first shallow water and hydrilla, an underwater plant, combine for slow going. Next, the tunnels are very constricted, making steering and paddling difficult at best. Kayaks are untenable here; a double-bladed paddle simply can't work in the tight tunnels and sharp turns. To best enjoy this trail, take a canoe or kayak and consider getting one of the many local outfitters to provide a shuttle for a one-way trip. The preserve has a downloadable GPS track for this paddle. Note that water levels can become excessively low by mid-February, causing the preserve to close the trail to outfitters.

✧ **MAPS** Big Cypress National Preserve map; Everglades National Park map; Ochopee, Chokoloskee (USGS)

US 41 to Chokoloskee Island

Class	I
Length	8.5
Time	5
Gauge	Visual, phone
Level	Mostly tidal
Gradient	Mostly tidal
Scenery	A

75 **DESCRIPTION** Put in at the landing adjacent to the bridge over the Turner River, and begin paddling south. The channel soon constricts to less than 15 feet. Your immediate surroundings are marked by freshwater plant species: cypresses, cattails, and willows. The sawgrass-displacing cattails have made a recent appearance due to fertilizer runoff from the farming region north of Everglades National Park.

This river was named for a guide, Richard B. Turner, who led American forces up the waterway in search of Seminole Indians in 1857. The force, commanded by John Parkhill, went upriver and destroyed some native villages. Later, Parkhill was killed in an ambush, and the bluecoats retreated to the Gulf.

Come to the first mangrove tunnel just a short distance into the paddle—here, the roots of red mangrove form a gauntlet for your craft. Overhead the leaves and branches of the trees crowd out the sun, leaving scanty room for your boat. Notice the profusion of epiphytes, or air plants, that grow on the mangrove branches. The water is shallow and crystalline. The going is slow. Briefly emerge

into a pond. Stay right and reenter the mangrove tunnel finally to enter another environment; here, cattails, sawgrass, and willows provide an open and bright contrast to the cool, shady tunnel.

Intersect an old canal and turn right; the canal is blocked off to the left. Continue in the open, occasionally passing sawgrass-ringed tree islands. One of these islands of palm, on river left, provides a dry spot to take a break. The river here varies in width, but stays deep enough to paddle with ease as you enter a very brief second mangrove tunnel. There will be mangrove on river right and sawgrass on the left. Pay close attention here and look for another tunnel diverging right. This tunnel is marked by an orange stake.

Take this tunnel to the right, soon passing an EVERGLADES NATIONAL PARK boundary sign at 3.5 miles. This third tunnel is a little roomier than the first but is still a challenging paddle. After this tunnel opens, the vegetation becomes more typical of the park paddling zone: red and black mangrove, buttonwood, with a few palms thrown in. The Turner twists and turns and continues to vary in width. Keep your eyes peeled for orange tape tied to tree branches to help distinguish the main river from side streams. Otherwise, watch for the stronger tidal flow.

The banks become higher as you come to a large bay on river left; stay right and paddle a bit farther to intersect Hurddles Creek on your left. To your right the Turner River becomes much wider.

Paddle west on the Turner River, passing Left Hand Turner River on your right.

Turner River Canoe Trail: US 41 to Chokoloskee Island

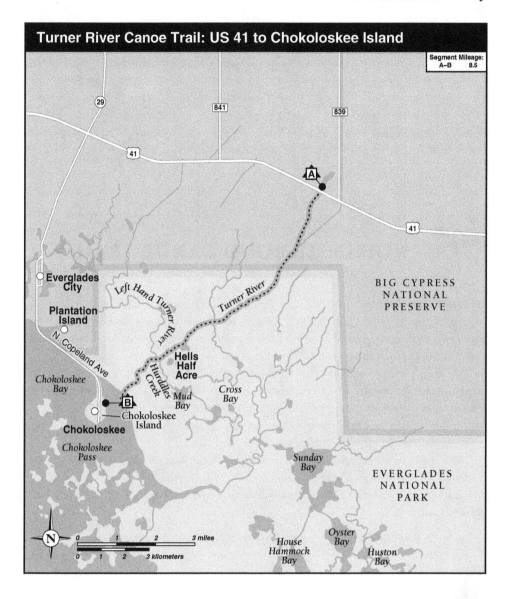

Segment Mileage:
A–B   8.5

Stay with the left-hand bank, looking for the nearly vertical bank of shell, indicating a Calusa shell mound reaching 19 feet at its highest point. Come to the mouth of the Turner River. The mouth is guarded by a few mangrove isles near Wilderness Waterway marker 129. Paddle westerly toward the park-service boat ramp on the north end of Chokoloskee Island, near the Outdoor Resorts, ending your route at 8.5 miles. If you don't wish to pay the access fee, paddle 3.0 miles farther north along the County Road 29 causeway to the Gulf Coast Visitor Center at Everglades National Park.

✧ **SHUTTLE** The take-out is on Chokoloskee Island, 2.7 miles south of Everglades City on CR 29. Outdoor Resorts has a private landing with a fee access. To avoid this fee, you can paddle on the east side of the CR 29 causeway and through the Halfway Creek bridge and take out at the Gulf Coast Visitor Center in Everglades City, adding 3.0 miles to your route.

To access the put-in from the Gulf Coast Visitor Center in Everglades City, drive north on CR 29 for 4.6 miles to US 41. Turn right (east) on US 41 and drive 6.2 miles to the Turner River.

◆ **GAUGE** Visual, phone. If in doubt, check either with the rangers at the Gulf Coast Visitor Center in Everglades City or with the rangers at the Big Cypress Swamp Welcome Center at Big Cypress National Preserve on US 41. Or call the preserve at 239-695-4758 or 239-695-1201 for the latest river conditions.

76 NINE-MILE POND CANOE TRAIL

◆ **OVERVIEW** This loop trail lies within Everglades National Park. The name "Nine-Mile Pond" leads you to believe this paddle is 9 miles, but it is actually 5 miles of multiple Everglades environments packed into one loop. It received its name because the pond was 9 miles from the original park visitor center at Coot Bay Pond.

This trail is marked with sequentially numbered poles to help you navigate among the mangrove islands, prairies, and tree islands of the region. Prairies here are vastly different from those in the Midwest: the Everglades' prairies are open, treeless wetlands, with sawgrass emerging from atop the water. The water levels of these prairies change, depending on the wet or dry season, and can dry up completely at times.

The water here is clear and very shallow; check with the park visitor center to see if there is enough water to float your boat. In some areas you will be paddling through sawgrass that can slow your craft down a bit. Be advised that there is no easily accessible dry land on which to stretch your legs.

◆ **MAPS** Everglades National Park map; Mahogany Hammock (USGS)

Nine-Mile Pond Loop

Class	I
Length	5 (loop)
Time	3.5
Gauge	Phone
Level	N/A
Gradient	None
Scenery	A

76 DESCRIPTION Start your trip at Nine-Mile Pond and head directly across the water from the parking area to the farthest inlet of the pond. This inlet lies east and is between two sawgrass stands. Here begin sequentially numbered poles that mark the paddling trail. Keep your eyes peeled, because Nine-Mile Pond is a good place to see alligators. Pass through a mangrove tunnel and emerge

Nine-Mile Pond Canoe Trail: Nine-Mile Pond Loop

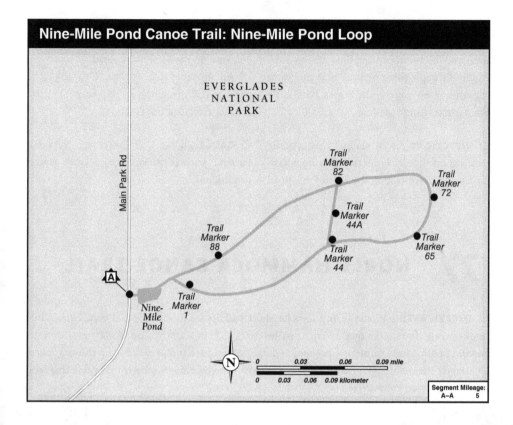

EVERGLADES
NATIONAL
PARK

Main Park Rd

Trail Marker 82

Trail Marker 72

Trail Marker 44A

Trail Marker 88

Trail Marker 44

Trail Marker 65

Trail Marker 1

Nine-Mile Pond

A

N

0   0.03   0.06   0.09 mile

0   0.03   0.06   0.09 kilometer

Segment Mileage:
A–A   5

onto a small prairie. The mud bottom gives a brownish cast to the otherwise clear water, where you can see small fish and minnows darting from your path.

The mangrove-and-sawgrass environments alternate. Here, the sawgrass on the trail is sparse and doesn't affect your travel. Enter a wide-open prairie of sawgrass just beyond marker 42. Sawgrass is the most common plant in the Everglades—to many people, it *is* the Everglades. Across the prairie are palm-topped tree islands, also known as bay heads.

Just after entering the prairie, follow the numbered poles sharply to the right into a mangrove tunnel to continue the entire loop. If you want to shorten your loop, do not take the sharp right turn, but continue forward past marker 44 to 44A and across the prairie to marker 82. Then turn left to complete the shortened loop.

The complete trail opens into another prairie where the sawgrass is thicker and can slow you down. Take time to examine the microcosm of life that flourishes below you. Your direction has been primarily east and north until marker 73. Here, the trail turns sharply to the left and heads westward back toward Nine-Mile Pond. Tall hammocks tinged with palm extend beyond the sawgrass on both sides of the trail, though you'll pass closely by a few palms at marker 80. Leave the sawgrass behind and enter small mangrove islands leading to a few dense palm patches.

Emerge onto a murky alligator pond and veer left through an opening in a line of sawgrass onto another pond. Beyond this pond is yet another opening in the sawgrass through which you can see the parking area. Paddle through this opening, and the parking area is on your right across Nine-Mile Pond, completing your loop.

◇ DIRECTIONS As a loop, this paddle requires no shuttle. From the Flamingo Visitor Center, drive east on the Main Park Road

for 11.2 miles to the Nine-Mile Pond parking area. This loop is 27.0 miles east of the park entrance on the Main Park Road.

An entrance fee applies. Call 305-242-7700 or visit nps.gov/ever/planyourvisit/fees.htm for the latest information.

◇ GAUGE Phone. Call Everglades National Park at 305-242-7700 for the latest water conditions.

77   NOBLE HAMMOCK CANOE TRAIL

◇ OVERVIEW This is one of my favorite short paddles in Everglades National Park. This marked trail offers quiet quality once you leave Main Park Road behind. A narrow, intimate paddling path winds through a mangrove maze, looping around past Noble Hammock, once a haven for moonshiners in the early 20th century. You will also encounter many fish that will stir the waters on your arrival.

THE AUTHOR STOPS AT NOBLE HAMMOCK.

Noble Hammock Canoe Trail Loop

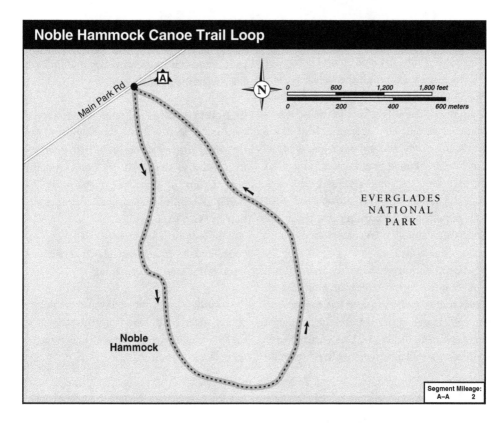

Take this trail if the wind is howling or if you have time for only a short trip. And paddle slowly here—the sudden twists and turns of the trail demand it. Full-size sea kayaks are not maneuverable enough to enjoy this trail. A canoe and excellent cooperation between bow and stern paddlers will maximize your pleasure here. Bring insect repellent along in these covered waters.

◇ **MAPS** EVERGLADES NATIONAL PARK MAP; WEST LAKE (USGS)

Noble Hammock Canoe Trail Loop

Class	I
Length	2 (loop)
Time	2
Gauge	Visual, phone
Level	N/A
Gradient	None
Scenery	A

77 **DESCRIPTION** Depart from the small dock away from Main Park Road and shortly turn right, following the first of 124 sequentially numbered poles. Don't let these poles detract from the scenery, for you would soon be lost if it weren't for the upright white PVC pipes. The waters of the Noble Hammock Trail have a coffee-colored tint to them due to the decomposition of plant matter at its bottom.

Passageways barely wide enough for a canoe or kayak give way to tiny bays where openings draw you toward them—but don't go in them, follow the poles. Then just as quickly the trail leads into tiny creeks over which hang shade-giving mangroves. And so it goes. After marker 45, pass a clump of paurotis palms where you can get out and stand for a moment. There is very little dry land around here.

Continue on through the dense growth. Soon on your right is a sign marking Noble Hammock. There is a small landing where you can get out, but exploring Noble Hammock and maybe finding the remains of Bill Noble's Prohibition-era moonshining brick furnace requires some serious bushwhacking. But it was this very growth and available buttonwood for burning that led to this tree island, among many others, becoming a moonshiner's asylum.

Don't be surprised when the water stirs as you round a corner on this trail. Many fish ply these waters, including such native species as bluegill, largemouth bass, and the distinctive long-snouted Florida gar. Unfortunately, you will also see tilapia, a nonnative breamlike

fish that is successfully reproducing here, crowding out the native species. The circuit paddle ends up a little ways down Main Park Road from the put-in.

✧ **DIRECTIONS** As a loop, this paddle requires no shuttle. From the Flamingo Visitor Center, drive east on Main Park Road for 10.0 miles to the Noble Hammock put-in/take-out, on the right side of the road. The trail is 28.0 miles from the park entrance station on Main Park Road.

An entrance fee applies. Call 305-242-7700 or visit nps.gov/ever/planyourvisit/fees.htm for the latest information.

✧ **GAUGE** Visual, phone. If you are in doubt, obtain water conditions from the rangers at the Flamingo Visitor Center. The number there is 237-695-2945.

78 MUD LAKE LOOP TRAIL

✧ **OVERVIEW** This loop paddle inside Everglades National Park gives you a good sampling of open water, confined water, and, most important, quietwater.

Four miles of this loop are for hand-propelled craft only. There is a price to pay for this solitude, however: one leg of your loop requires a portage between waterways. I recommend this route for canoeists only—the narrow creeks, downed trees, and the portage make sea kayaking downright troublesome.

The following description starts at Coot Bay Pond on Main Park Road, but if you want to shorten the loop, begin at the end of Bear Lake Road, making it a 4.8-mile adventure. Also be apprised that insects can be troublesome, especially on the Bear Lake Canoe Trail portion of this paddle.

✧ **MAPS** Everglades National Park map; Waterproof Chart 39; NOAA Nautical Chart 11433; Flamingo (USGS)

Mud Lake Loop Trail from Coot Bay Pond

Class	I
Length	7 (loop)
Time	4
Gauge	Phone
Level	Tidal
Gradient	Tidal
Scenery	A

78 **DESCRIPTION** Start your paddle on Coot Bay Pond and then pass beneath a mangrove tunnel to Coot Bay. Connect briefly to the Wilderness Waterway and the Buttonwood Canal Route before paddling a small creek to Mud Lake, which is more appealing than its name suggests. Enjoy the quiet of Mud Lake, then take another creek to the Bear Lake Canoe Trail, where you will trace an old drainage canal to the newer Buttonwood Canal. But getting to Buttonwood Canal requires a portage of 160 yards. Head back to Coot Bay Pond via the Buttonwood Canal and Coot Bay.

Set out from one of the small landings on Coot Bay Pond, paddling north to a small, tunnel-like opening. From a distance, it seems there is no passage, but this man-made cut barely wide enough for a canoe or kayak will lead you to Coot Bay. The spoils of the cut create land areas on which grow drier plant species, such as palm.

Open up into Coot Bay and paddle west for Coast Guard marker 3 and the Buttonwood Canal Route. Continue to follow the channel markers north for the shortcut to Whitewater Bay, but for this loop stay with

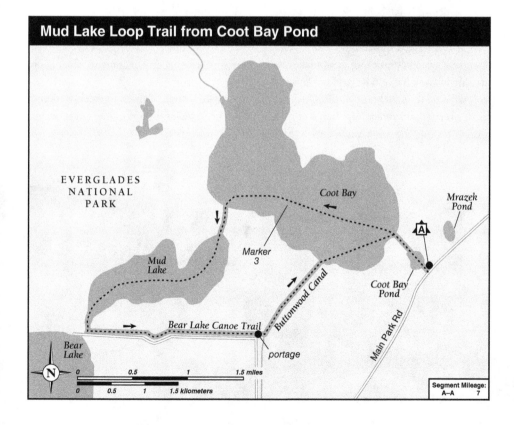

Mud Lake Loop Trail from Coot Bay Pond

EVERGLADES NATIONAL PARK

Coot Bay

Mrazek Pond

Marker 3

Mud Lake

Buttonwood Canal

Coot Bay Pond

Bear Lake Canoe Trail

Main Park Rd

Bear Lake

portage

N

0   0.5   1   1.5 miles
0   0.5   1   1.5 kilometers

Segment Mileage:	
A–A	7

the south shore of Coot Bay to a PVC pipe marker at 2.0 miles, signaling the creek leading to Mud Lake.

Enter a shady, slender waterway, which is made even more closed-in by hundreds of fallen trees, sawn just enough for your passage. Expect to slide over a few logs. Live mangrove hovers over you until emerging onto Mud Lake and a group of small circular islands. Follow the PVC pipe markers south and west across the lake. Its pretty, reddish-copper–colored waters contrast nicely with the green shores. The markers lead to the most southwesterly corner and a short creek connecting to the Bear Lake Canoe Trail. Follow this short creek to the Bear Lake Canoe Trail.

Once on the canoe trail, make sure to turn left (east). The pungent waters here are rich with the smell of decay as the vegetation continues its never-ending cycle of life and death. It is about 200 yards west to Bear Lake. The Bear Lake Canoe Trail traces the old Homestead Canal, built in the 1920s alongside a road attempting to connect Florida City to Cape Sable. The road has reverted to a trail, and the canal is now silting in, making for very shallow paddling. Roots of mangrove grow into the water and branches hang overhead. Insects can be bothersome on the nearly 2.0 miles of paddling until the dock and ground landing at the portage.

Once you arrive at the portage, take out and carry your boat on the foot trail to your left; then head left again toward two wooden posts to a landing on the Buttonwood Canal where you'll put in again.

Head left (north) up the waterway, which will seem like the Mississippi River after the Bear Lake Canoe Trail. Come to Coot Bay at mile 6 and paddle east toward a PVC pipe marker to the small channel to Coot Bay Pond. Head back through the tunnel to Coot Bay Pond, completing your loop at mile 7.

◆ **DIRECTIONS** As a loop, this paddle requires no shuttle. Coot Bay Pond is 34.0 miles east of the main park entrance in Florida City and 4.0 miles west of the Flamingo Visitor Center on Main Park Road.

An entrance fee applies. Call 305-242-7700 or visit nps.gov/ever/planyourvisit/fees.htm for the latest information.

◆ **GAUGE** Phone. Call Everglades National Park at 305-242-7700 for the latest water conditions.

CAMPSITES LIKE THIS AWAIT EVERGLADES PADDLERS.

APPENDIX A: OUTFITTERS

THE WESTERN PANHANDLE
ADVENTURES UNLIMITED

8974 Tomahawk Landing Road
Milton, FL 32570
800-239-6864; adventuresunlimited.com

This group has an elaborate outpost that serves Coldwater, Sweetwater, and Juniper Creeks as well as the Blackwater and Perdido Rivers. They provide shuttle service, canoe and kayak rentals, catered meals, cabins, campsites for individuals and large groups, and outdoor-challenge courses.

BLACKWATER CANOE OUTPOST
AND RENTAL

6974 Deaton Bridge Road
Milton, FL 32583
850-623-0235; blackwatercanoe.com

This outfit, located near Blackwater River State Park, is open year-round and rents canoes, kayaks, and tubes for use on the Blackwater River. They also provide shuttles for private boats. Reservations are recommended. In addition, they run a camp store.

BOB'S CANOE RENTAL AND SALES

7525 Munson Highway
Milton, FL 32570
850-623-5457

In business since 1971, Bob's operates exclusively on Coldwater Creek. They offer shuttle services and rent canoes and kayaks. Call ahead for reservations between October 1 and April 1.

HOLMES CREEK CANOE LIVERY

2899 FL 79
Vernon, FL 32462
850-210-7001; holmescreekcanoelivery.com

Situated on upper Holmes Creek near Vernon, they offer canoe and kayak rentals as well as shuttle services, whether you rent a boat or bring your own.

SCOTTS FERRY GENERAL STORE
AND CAMPGROUND

6648 FL 71 South
Blountstown, FL 32424
850-674-2900
facebook.com/scottsferrycampground

This store rents canoes on the lower Chipola River and has cabins and a campground. They do not provide shuttles, however.

THE CENTRAL PANHANDLE
ECONFINA CANOE LIVERY

5641-A Porter Pond Road
Youngstown, FL 32466
850-722-9032; canoeeconfinacreek.net

Based on beautiful Econfina Creek, this friendly group rents canoes and kayaks and provides shuttles for their boats and private boats as well. Reservations are recommended.

APPENDIX A: OUTFITTERS

THE BIG BEND

RIVER HAVEN MARINA & HOTEL

1110 River Side Drive
Steinhatchee, FL 32359
352-498-0709; riverhavenmarine.com

This outfit rents kayaks and canoes and provides shuttle service for trips on the Steinhatchee River.

THE WILDERNESS WAY

4901 Woodville Highway
Tallahassee, FL 32305
850-877-7200; thewildernessway.net

Rents canoes and kayaks and leads trips on the St. Marks and Wakulla Rivers.

THE NORTHERN PENINSULA

AMERICAN CANOE ADVENTURES

10610 Bridge St.
White Springs, FL 32095
386-397-1309; aca1.com

This outfit operates primarily on the upper Suwannee River but serves the entire Suwannee from the Okefenokee Swamp to the Gulf of Mexico. They also sell and service canoes. Reservations are recommended.

GINNIE SPRINGS OUTDOORS

5000 NE 60th Ave.
High Springs, FL 32643
386-454-7188; ginniespringsoutdoors.com

This group operates on the Santa Fe. They rent canoes, kayaks, and tubes.

ICHETUCKNEE FAMILY CANOE & CABINS

8587 Southwest Elim Church Road
Fort White, FL 32038
866-224-2064
ichetuckneecanoeandcabins.com

Located near the Ichetucknee River, they rent tubes, canoes, and kayaks and offer shuttle service to and from the Ichetucknee, Santa Fe, and Suwannee Rivers. They also have cabins and a campground for overnighting.

ST. MARYS RIVER FISH CAMP AND CANOE COUNTRY OUTPOST

29506 Scotts Landing Road
Hilliard, FL 32046
904-845-4440; stmarysriverfishcamp.com

Located on the St. Marys River off US 1, this outfit rents canoes and provides shuttles.

SANTA FE CANOE OUTPOST

PO Box 592
High Springs, FL 32655
386-454-2050; santaferiver.com

Jim Wood and company are located on the Santa Fe River near US 441. They rent canoes and kayaks and offer shuttles for private boats. They also work the Ichetucknee and Suwannee.

SUWANNEE CANOE OUTPOST

2461 95th Drive
Live Oak, FL 32060
800-428-4147; suwanneeoutpost.com

This group rents canoes and kayaks, and shuttles private boats and backpackers hiking nearby portions of the Florida Trail. They service not only the Suwannee but also the Withlacoochee North and the Alapaha.

THE CENTRAL PENINSULA

KING'S LANDING CANOE RENTAL

5722 Baptist Camp Road
Apopka, FL 32712
407-886-0859; kingslandingfl.com

Conveniently located at the head of Rock Springs Run and the Wekiva River, these folks rent canoes and kayaks and provide shuttles for private boat owners.

NOBLETON OUTPOST

29295 Lake Lindsay Road
Nobleton, FL 34661
800-783-5284; nobletonoutpost.com

Located on the middle portion of the Withlacoochee River (South), this outfit rents canoes, pontoon boats, and fishing boats. They also rent bikes and provide shuttles for private boats.

OCKLAWAHA CANOE OUTPOST & RESORT

15260 NE 152nd Place
Fort McCoy, FL 32134
352-236-4606; outpostresort.com

This outfit rents canoes and kayaks and offers overnight trips. They have a campground and cabins for rent. They also shuttle private boats.

RAINBOW RIVER KAYAK AND BOAT RENTALS

19783 E. Pennsylvania Ave.
Dunnellon, FL 34432
352-643 0524
aquaticwildernessadventures.com

These very friendly folks rent stand-up paddleboards (SUPs), kayaks, and tubes and provide shuttles for runs on the Rainbow River.

WEKIVA ISLAND

1014 Miami Springs Road
Longwood, FL 32779
407-862-1500; wekivaisland.com

This group, located on the Wekiva River, rents canoes and kayaks.

WEKIWA SPRINGS STATE PARK NATURE ADVENTURES

1800 Wekiwa Circle
Apopka, FL 32712
407-884-4311; canoewekiva.com

This concessionaire rents canoes and kayaks and offers overnight rentals.

WITHLACOOCHEE RIVER RV PARK AND CANOE RENTAL

PO Box 114
Lacoochee, FL
352-583-4778; canoegatorstyle.com

On the upper part of the Withlacoochee River (South), this friendly outfit rents canoes as well as shuttles private vehicles. They have a campground that caters to RVs and tents.

THE CENTRAL HIGHLANDS

CANOE OUTPOST–PEACE RIVER

2816 NW County Road 661
Arcadia, FL 34266
800-268-0083; canoeoutpost.com

This outfit rents canoes and kayaks, shuttles private boats, and has a campground. They are located near Arcadia but service the entire Peace.

FISHEATING CREEK OUTFITTERS

7555 US 27 Northwest
Palmdale, FL 33944
863-675-4467; fisheatingcreekoutpost.com

These folks are the concessionaires for the state-owned campground and outfitter on Fisheating Creek. They rent boats and provide shuttle service for paddlers on the entire creek. You must use these outfitters to access certain parts of the river. Reservations are required.

THE PADDLING CENTER AT SHINGLE CREEK

4266 W. Vine St. (US 192)
Kissimmee, FL 34741
407-343-7740; paddlingcenter.com

The official paddling concessionaire for Shingle Creek Regional Park, this outfit rents canoes, kayaks, and SUPs, as well as provides shuttles for trips along fascinating Shingle Creek.

SEMINOLE PADDLING ADVENTURES

Chuluota, FL 32766
407-925-7896; seminole-paddle-adventures.com

Offers kayak and canoe rentals as well as shuttles on the Econlockhatchee River.

THE ATLANTIC COAST

CANOE OUTFITTERS OF FLORIDA

9060 W. Indiantown Road
Jupiter, FL 33478
561-746-7053; canoeoutfittersofflorida.com

These folks have been in business for more than 20 years and offer canoe and kayak rentals and sales on the Loxahatchee River. Reservations are recommended.

APPENDIX A: OUTFITTERS

THE ATLANTIC COAST

(continued)

SOUTH RIVER OUTFITTERS

7647 SE Lost River Road
Stuart, FL 34997
772-223-1500
southriveroutfitters.com

Located on the South Fork St. Lucie River, this
is the official concessionaire for Halpatiokee
Regional Park. They rent and sell kayaks,
canoes, and SUPs and lots of other cool gear.
They are situated at the primary launch for
the South Fork St. Lucie River.

THE SOUTHWEST GULF COAST

ALAFIA RIVER CANOE RENTALS

4419 River Drive
Valrico, FL 33594
813-689-8645

This outfitter, the oldest livery on the Alafia,
primarily runs trips on the Alafia River between
Alderman's Ford Park and Lithia–Pinecrest Road.
They rent boats and will shuttle private boats.

CANOE ESCAPE

12702 US 301
Thonotosassa, FL 33592
813-986-2067; canoeescape.com

Located at John B. Sargent Park, Canoe Escape
operates on and offers trips of varying lengths
down the Hillsborough River. They also rent
canoes and kayaks and provide shuttles for
private boats.

CANOE OUTPOST–LITTLE MANATEE RIVER

18001 US 301 South
Wimauma, FL 33596
813-634-2228; canoeoutpost.com

This outfit offers trips of varied lengths along
the Little Manatee River, including canoe
camping. They rent canoes and kayaks; they
also shuttle private boats. A camp store is
conveniently located on site in case you forgot
anything.

ESTERO RIVER OUTFITTERS

20991 S. Tamiami Trail (US 41)
Estero, FL 33928
239-992-4050
esteroriveroutfitters.com

Rents canoes and kayaks for use both on and off
the Estero River, offers guided tours and local
trip information, sells saltwater bait and tackle,
and leads monthly moonlight paddles.

PADDLING ADVENTURES AT WEEKI WACHEE SPRINGS STATE PARK

6131 Commercial Way
Spring Hill, FL 34606
352-597-8484; paddlingadventures.com

Rents canoes and kayaks and provides shuttles
for private boats on the Weeki Wachee River.

RAY'S CANOE HIDEAWAY AND KAYAK CENTER

1289 Hagle Park Road
Bradenton, FL 34212
941-747-3909; rayscanoehideaway.com

Tucked away on the upper Manatee River,
Ray's offers canoe and kayak rentals as well as
boat launching from their facility. They also
have a camp store.

THE EVERGLADES

EVERGLADES INTERNATIONAL HOSTEL

20 SW Second Ave.
Florida City, FL 33034
305-248-1122; evergladeshostel.com

This outfit provides inexpensive lodging and
kayak and canoe rentals for Everglades National
Park and the Wilderness Waterway. It's only
15 minutes from the east entrance to Everglades
National Park.

NORTH AMERICAN CANOE TOURS

PO Box 5038
Everglades City, FL 34139
239-695-3299; evergladesadventures.com

These folks rent canoes and kayaks, lead tours,
and provide shuttles at Everglades National
Park, Wilderness Waterway, Turner River, and
Halfway Creek. They also offer lodging at the
adjacent Ivey House Inn in Everglades City.

APPENDIX B: SAFETY CODE OF AMERICAN WHITEWATER

CHARLIE WALBRIDGE *Safety Chairman* | **MARK SINGLETON** *Executive Director*

© 1999–2016 American Whitewater, PO Box 1540, Cullowhee, NC 28723;
866-BOAT-4-AW; info@amwhitewater.org

INTRODUCTION

This code has been prepared using the best available information and has been reviewed by a broad cross section of whitewater experts. The code, however, is only a collection of guidelines; attempts to minimize risks should be flexible, not constrained by a rigid set of rules. Varying conditions and group goals may combine with unpredictable circumstances to require alternate procedures. This code is not intended to serve as a standard of care for commercial outfitters or guides.

I. PERSONAL PREPAREDNESS AND RESPONSIBILITY

1. Be a competent swimmer, with the ability to handle yourself under water.

2. Wear a life jacket. A snugly fitting vest-type life preserver offers back and shoulder protection as well as the flotation needed to swim safely in whitewater.

3. Wear a solid, correctly fitted helmet when upsets are likely. This is essential in kayaks or covered canoes, and recommended for open canoeists using thigh straps and rafters running steep drops.

4. Do not boat out of control. Your skills should be sufficient to stop or reach shore before reaching danger. Do not enter a rapid unless you are reasonably sure that you can run it safely or swim it without injury.

5. Whitewater rivers contain many hazards that are not always easily recognized. The following are the most frequent killers:

    A. *High water.* The river's speed and power increase tremendously as the flow increases, raising the difficulty of most rapids. Rescue becomes progressively harder as the water rises, adding to the danger. Floating debris and strainers make even an easy rapid quite hazardous. It is often misleading to judge the river level at the put-in, since a small rise in a wide, shallow place will be multiplied many times where the river narrows. Use reliable gauge information whenever possible, and be aware that sun on snowpack, hard rain, and upstream dam releases may greatly increase the flow.

    B. *Cold.* Cold drains your strength and robs you of the ability to make sound decisions on matters affecting your survival. Cold-water immersion, because of the initial shock and the rapid heat loss that follows, is especially dangerous. Dress appropriately for bad weather or sudden immersion in the water. When the water temperature is less than 50°F, a wetsuit or drysuit is essential for protection if you swim. Next best is wool or pile clothing under a waterproof shell. In this case, you should also carry waterproof matches and a change of clothing in a waterproof bag. If, after prolonged exposure, a person experiences uncontrollable shaking, loss of coordination, or difficulty speaking, he or she is hypothermic and needs your assistance.

    C. *Strainers.* Brush, fallen trees, bridge pilings, undercut rocks, or anything else that allows river current to sweep through can pin boats and boaters against the obstacle. Water pressure on anything trapped this way can be overwhelming. Rescue is often extremely difficult. Pinning may occur in fast current, with little or no whitewater to warn of the danger.

D. *Dams, weirs, ledges, reversals, holes, and hydraulics.* When water drops over an obstacle, it curls back on itself, forming a strong upstream current that may be capable of holding a boat or swimmer. Some holes make for excellent sport; others are proven killers. Paddlers who cannot recognize the difference should avoid all but the smallest holes. Hydraulics around man-made dams must be treated with utmost respect regardless of their height or the level of the river. Despite their seemingly benign appearance, they can create an almost escape-proof trap. The swimmer's only exit from the "drowning machine" is to dive below the surface when the downstream current is flowing beneath the reversal.

E. *Broaching.* When a boat is pushed sideways against a rock by strong current, it may collapse and wrap. This is especially dangerous to kayak and decked-canoe paddlers; these boats will collapse, and the combination of indestructible hulls and tight outfitting may create a deadly trap. Even without entrapment, releasing pinned boats can be extremely time-consuming and dangerous. To avoid pinning, throw your weight downstream toward the rock. This allows the current to slide harmlessly underneath the hull.

6. Boating alone is discouraged. The minimum party is three people or two craft.

7. Have a frank knowledge of your boating ability, and don't attempt rivers or rapids that lie beyond that ability.

8. Be in good physical and mental condition, consistent with the difficulties that may be expected. Make adjustments for loss of skills due to age, health, fitness. Any health limitations must be explained to your fellow paddlers prior to starting the trip.

9. Be practiced in self-rescue, including escape from an overturned craft. The Eskimo roll is strongly recommended for decked boaters who run rapids Class IV or greater, or who paddle in cold environmental conditions.

10. Be trained in rescue skills, CPR, and first aid, with special emphasis on recognizing and treating hypothermia. It may save your friend's life.

11. Carry equipment needed for unexpected emergencies, including footwear that will protect your feet when walking out, a throw rope, knife, whistle, and waterproof matches. If you wear eyeglasses, tie them on and carry a spare pair on long trips. Bring cloth repair tape on short runs and a full repair kit on isolated rivers. Do not wear bulky jackets, ponchos, heavy boots, or anything else that could reduce your ability to survive a swim.

12. Despite the mutually supportive group structure described in this code, individual paddlers are ultimately responsible for their own safety and must assume sole responsibility for the following decisions:

A. *The decision to participate on any trip.* This includes an evaluation of the expected difficulty of the rapids under the conditions existing at the time of the put-in.

B. *The selection of appropriate equipment,* including a boat design suited to their skills and the appropriate rescue and survival gear.

C. *The decision to scout any rapid, and to run or portage according to their best judgment.* Other members of the group may offer advice, but paddlers should resist pressure from anyone to paddle beyond their skills. It is also their responsibility to decide whether to pass up any walkout or takeout opportunity.

D. *All trip participants should consistently evaluate their own and their group's safety,* voicing their concerns when appropriate and following what they believe to be the best course of action. Paddlers are encouraged to speak with anyone whose actions on the water are dangerous, whether they are a part of your group or not.

II. BOAT AND EQUIPMENT PREPAREDNESS

1. Test new and different equipment under familiar conditions before relying on it for difficult runs. This is especially true when adopting a new boat design or outfitting system. Low-volume craft may present additional hazards to inexperienced or poorly conditioned paddlers.

2. Be sure your boat and gear are in good repair before starting a trip. The more isolated and difficult the run, the more rigorous this inspection should be.

3. Install flotation bags in noninflatable craft, securely fixed in each end and designed to displace as much water as possible. Inflatable boats should have multiple air chambers and be test-inflated before launching.

4. Have strong, properly sized paddles or oars for controlling your craft. Carry sufficient spares for the length and difficulty of the trip.

5. Outfit your boat safely. The ability to exit your boat quickly is an essential component of safety in rapids. It is your responsibility to see that there is absolutely nothing to cause entrapment when coming free of an upset craft, such as the following:

   A. *Spray covers that won't release reliably* or that release prematurely.

   B. *Boat outfitting too tight to allow a fast exit,* especially in low-volume kayaks or decked canoes. This includes low-hung thwarts in canoes lacking adequate clearance for your feet and kayak footbraces which fail or allow your feet to become wedged under them.

   C. *Inadequately supported decks* that collapse on a paddler's legs when a decked boat is pinned by water pressure. Inadequate clearance with the deck because of your size or build.

   D. *Loose ropes that cause entanglement.* Beware of any length of loose line attached to a whitewater boat. All items must be tied tightly and excess line eliminated; painters, throw lines, and safety-rope systems must be completely and effectively stored. Do not knot the end of a rope, as it can get caught in cracks between rocks.

6. Provide ropes that permit you to hold on to your craft so that it may be rescued. The following methods are recommended:

   A. *Kayaks and covered canoes* should have grab loops of one-quarter-inch-plus rope or equivalent webbing sized to admit a normal-sized hand. Stern painters are permissible if properly secured.

B. *Open canoes* should have securely anchored bow and stern painters consisting of eight to ten feet of one-quarter-inch-plus line. These must be secured in such a way that they are readily accessible but cannot come loose accidentally. Grab loops are acceptable but are more difficult to reach after an upset.

C. *Rafts and dories* may have taut perimeter lines threaded through the loops provided. Footholds should be designed so that a paddler's feet cannot be forced through them, causing entrapment. Flip lines should be carefully and reliably stowed.

7. Know your craft's carrying capacity and how added loads affect boat handling in whitewater. Most rafts have a minimum crew size that can be added to on day trips or in easy rapids. Carrying more than two paddlers in an open canoe when running rapids is not recommended.

8. Car-top racks must be strong and attach positively to the vehicle. Lash your boat to each crossbar, then tie the ends of the boats directly to the bumpers for added security. This arrangement should survive all but the most violent vehicle accident.

III. GROUP PREPAREDNESS AND RESPONSIBILITY

1. **ORGANIZATION.** A river trip should be regarded as a common adventure by all participants, except on instructional or commercially guided trips as defined below. Participants share the responsibility for the conduct of the trip, and each participant is individually responsible for judging his or her own capabilities and for his or her own safety as the trip progresses. Participants are encouraged (but are not obligated) to offer advice and guidance for the independent consideration and judgment of others.

2. **RIVER CONDITIONS.** The group should have a reasonable knowledge of the difficulty of the run. Participants should evaluate this information and adjust their plans accordingly. Maps and guidebooks, if available, should be examined if the run is exploratory or no one is familiar with the river. The group should secure accurate flow information; the more difficult the run, the more important this will be. Be aware of possible changes in river level and how this will affect the difficulty of the run. If the trip involves tidal stretches, secure appropriate information on tides.

3. **GROUP EQUIPMENT SHOULD BE SUITED TO THE DIFFICULTY OF THE RIVER.** The group should always have a throw line available, and one line per boat is recommended on difficult runs. The list may include: carabiners, prussic loops, first-aid kit, flashlight, folding saw, fire starter, guidebooks, maps, food, extra clothing, and any other rescue or survival items suggested by conditions. Each item is not required on every run, and this list is not meant to be a substitute for good judgment.

4. **KEEP THE GROUP COMPACT, BUT MAINTAIN SUFFICIENT SPACING TO AVOID COLLISIONS.** If the group is large, consider dividing into smaller groups or using the "buddy system" as an additional safeguard. Space yourselves closely enough to permit good communication, but not so close as to interfere with one another in rapids.

A. *A point paddler sets the pace.* When in front, do not get in over your head. Never run drops when you cannot see a clear route to the bottom or, for advanced paddlers, a sure route to the next eddy. When in doubt, stop and scout.

B. *Keep track of all group members.* Each boat keeps the one behind it in sight, stopping if necessary. Know how many people are in your group, and take head counts regularly. No one should paddle ahead or walk out without first informing the group. Paddlers requiring additional support should stay at the center of a group and not allow themselves to lag behind in the more difficult rapids. If the group is large and contains a wide range of abilities, a "sweep boat" may be designated to bring up the rear.

C. *Courtesy.* On heavily used rivers, do not cut in front of a boater running a drop. Always look upstream before leaving eddies to run or play. Never enter a crowded drop or eddy when no room for you exists. Passing other groups in a rapid may be hazardous: it's often safer to wait upstream until the group ahead has passed.

5. **FLOAT PLAN.** If the trip is into a wilderness area or for an extended period, plans should be filed with a responsible person who will contact the authorities if you are overdue. It may be wise to establish checkpoints along the way where civilization could be contacted if necessary. Knowing the location of possible help and preplanning escape routes can speed rescue.

6. **DRUGS.** The use of alcohol or mind-altering drugs before or during river trips is not recommended. These substances dull reflexes, reduce decision-making ability, and may interfere with important survival reflexes.

7. **INSTRUCTIONAL OR COMMERCIALLY GUIDED TRIPS.** In contrast to the common adventure-trip format, these trip formats involve a boating instructor or commercial guide who assumes some of the responsibilities normally exercised by the group as a whole, as appropriate under the circumstances. These formats recognize that instructional or commercially guided trips may involve participants who lack significant experience in whitewater. However, as a participant acquires experience, he or she takes on increasing responsibility for his or her own safety, in accordance with what he or she knows or should know as a result of that increased experience. Also, as in all trip formats, every participant must realize and assume the risks associated with the serious hazards of whitewater rivers. It is advisable for instructors and commercial guides or their employers to acquire trip or personal liability insurance:

A. An *"instructional trip"* is characterized by a clear teacher–pupil relationship, where the primary purpose of the trip is to teach boating skills, and which is conducted for a fee.

B. A *"commercially guided trip"* is characterized by a licensed, professional guide conducting trips for a fee.

IV. GUIDELINES FOR RIVER RESCUE

1. Recover from an upset with an Eskimo roll whenever possible. Evacuate your boat immediately if there is imminent danger of being trapped against rocks, brush, or any other kind of strainer.

2. If you swim, hold on to your boat. It has much flotation and is easy for rescuers to spot. Get to the upstream end so that you cannot be crushed between a rock and your boat

by the force of the current. Persons with good balance may be able to climb on top of a swamped kayak or flipped raft and paddle to shore.

3. Release your craft if this will improve your chances, especially if the water is cold or dangerous rapids lie ahead. Actively attempt self-rescue whenever possible by swimming for safety. Be prepared to assist others who may come to your aid.

   A. *When swimming in shallow or obstructed rapids, lie on your back with feet held high and pointed downstream.* Do not attempt to stand in fast-moving water; if your foot wedges on the bottom, fast water will push you under and keep you there. Get to slow or very shallow water before attempting to stand or walk. Look ahead! Avoid possible pinning situations, including undercut rocks, strainers, downed trees, holes, and other dangers, by swimming away from them.

   B. *If the rapids are deep and powerful, roll over onto your stomach and swim aggressively for shore.* Watch for eddies and slackwater, and use them to get out of the current. Strong swimmers can effect a powerful upstream ferry and get to shore fast. If the shores are obstructed with strainers or undercut rocks, however, it is safer to "ride the rapid out" until a safer escape can be found.

4. If others spill and swim, go after the boaters first. Rescue boats and equipment only if this can be done safely. While participants are encouraged (but not obligated) to assist one another to the best of their ability, they should do so only if they can, in their judgment, do so safely. The first duty of a rescuer is not to compound the problem by becoming another victim.

5. The use of rescue lines requires training; uninformed use may cause injury. Never tie yourself into either end of a line without a reliable quick-release system. Have a knife handy to deal with unexpected entanglement. Learn to place set lines effectively, to throw accurately, to belay effectively, and to properly handle a rope thrown to you.

6. When reviving a drowning victim, be aware that cold water may greatly extend survival time under water. Victims of hypothermia may have depressed vital signs, causing them to look and feel dead. Don't give up; continue CPR for as long as possible without compromising safety.

V. UNIVERSAL RIVER SIGNALS

These signals may be substituted with an alternate set of signals agreed upon by the group.

STOP: *Potential hazard ahead.* Wait for "all clear" signal before proceeding, or scout ahead. Form a horizontal bar with your outstretched arms. Those seeing the signal should pass it back to others in the party.

STOP: *Potential hazard ahead.*

HELP: *Emergency.* Assist the signaler as quickly as possible. Give three long blasts on a police whistle while waving a paddle, helmet or life vest over your head. If a whistle is not available, use the visual signal alone. A whistle is best carried on a lanyard attached to your life vest.

HELP: *Emergency.*

ALL CLEAR: *Come ahead.*

ALL CLEAR: *Come ahead.* In the absence of other directions, proceed down the center. Form a vertical bar with your paddle or one arm held high above your head (see left). Paddle blade should be turned flat for maximum visibility. To signal direction or a preferred course through a rapid around obstruction, lower the previously vertical "all clear" by 45 degrees toward the side of the river with the preferred route (see right). Never point toward the obstacle you wish to avoid (see next page).

I'M OK: *I'm not hurt.* While holding an elbow outward toward your side, repeatedly pat the top of your head.

I'M OK: *I'm not hurt.*

VI. INTERNATIONAL SCALE OF RIVER DIFFICULTY

This is the American version of a rating system used to compare river difficulty throughout the world. This system is not exact: rivers do not always fit easily into one category, and regional or individual interpretations may cause misunderstandings. It is no substitute for a guidebook or accurate first-hand descriptions of a run.

Paddlers attempting difficult runs in unfamiliar areas should act cautiously until they get a feel for the way the scale is interpreted locally. River difficulty may change each year due to fluctuations in water level, downed trees, recent floods, geological disturbances, or bad weather. Stay alert for unexpected problems!

As river difficulty increases, the danger to swimming paddlers becomes more severe. As rapids become longer and more continuous, the challenge increases. There is a difference between running an occasional Class IV rapid and dealing with an entire river of this category. Allow an extra margin of safety between skills and river ratings when the water is cold or if the river itself is remote and inaccessible.

Examples of commonly run rapids that fit each of the classifications are presented in the document "International Scale of River Difficulty: Standard Rated Rapids." This document is available online at **tinyurl.com/awriverdifficultyscale**. Rapids of a difficulty similar to rapids on this list are rated the same. Rivers are also rated using this scale. A river rating should take into account many factors including the difficulty of individual rapids, remoteness, hazards, etc.

The Six Difficulty Classes:

CLASS I: *Easy.* Fast-moving water with riffles and small waves. Few obstructions, all obvious and easily missed with little training. Risk to swimmers is slight; self-rescue is easy.

CLASS II: *Novice.* Straightforward rapids with wide, clear channels that are evident without scouting. Occasional maneuvering may be required, but rocks and medium-size waves are easily missed by trained paddlers. Swimmers are seldom injured, and group assistance, while helpful, is seldom needed. Rapids that are at the upper end of this difficulty range are designated "Class II+."

CLASS III: *Intermediate.* Rapids with moderate, irregular waves that may be difficult to avoid and can swamp an open canoe. Complex maneuvers in fast current and good boat control in tight passages or around ledges are often required; large waves or strainers may be present but are easily avoided. Strong eddies and powerful current effects can be found, particularly on large-volume rivers. Scouting is advisable for inexperienced parties. Injuries while swimming are rare; self-rescue is usually easy, but group assistance may be required to avoid long swims. Rapids that are at the lower or upper end of this difficulty range are designated "Class III–" or "Class III+," respectively.

CLASS IV: *Advanced.* Intense, powerful, but predictable rapids requiring precise boat handling in turbulent water. Depending on the character of the river, it may feature large, unavoidable waves and holes or constricted passages demanding fast maneuvers under pressure. A fast, reliable eddy turn may be needed to initiate maneuvers, scout rapids, or rest. Rapids may require "must" moves above dangerous hazards. Scouting may be necessary the first time down. Risk of injury to swimmers is moderate to high, and water conditions may make self-rescue difficult. Group assistance for rescue is often essential but requires practiced skills. A strong Eskimo roll is highly recommended. Rapids that are at the upper end of this difficulty range are designated "Class IV–" or "Class IV+," respectively.

CLASS V: *Expert.* Extremely long, obstructed, or very violent rapids that expose a paddler to added risk. Drops may contain large, unavoidable waves and holes or steep, congested chutes with complex, demanding routes. Rapids may continue for long distances between pools, demanding a high level of fitness. What eddies exist may be small, turbulent, or difficult to reach. At the high end of the scale, several of these factors may be combined. Scouting is recommended but may be difficult. Swims are dangerous, and rescue is often difficult even for experts. A very reliable Eskimo roll, proper equipment, extensive experience, and practiced rescue skills are essential. Because of the large range of difficulty that exists beyond Class IV, Class 5 is an open-ended, multiple-level scale designated by 5.0, 5.1, 5.2, etc. Each of these levels is an order of magnitude more difficult than the last. Example: increasing difficulty from Class 5.0 to Class 5.1 is a similar order of magnitude as increasing from Class IV to Class 5.0.

CLASS VI: *Extreme and exploratory.* These runs have almost never been attempted and often exemplify extremes of difficulty, unpredictability, and danger. The consequences of errors are very severe, and rescue may be impossible. For teams of experts only, at favorable water levels, after close personal inspection and taking all precautions. After a Class VI rapids has been run many times, its rating may be changed to an appropriate Class 5.x rating.

Boil line Located immediately downstream of a hole (see next page), this is point at which current begins to pass downstream again instead of rushing upstream into the hole.

Boof To launch over and off of a rock at the top lip of a drop. A successful boof lifts the bow so that the angle of the boat is more shallow than the angle of the water falling off the drop.

Bow The forward end of a canoe or kayak.

Brace Paddle stroke used to prevent the boat from flipping over.

Breaking wave A wave that intermittently curls back on itself, falling upstream.

Bypass A channel cut across a meander that creates an island or oxbow lake.

Chock stone A stone onto which the current flowing over a falls lands.

Chute A channel between obstructions that has faster current than the surrounding water.

Curler A wave with a top that is curled over onto the face of the wave.

Deadfall Trees or brush that have fallen into a stream, totally or partially obstructing it.

Decked boat A kayak (usually) or canoe that is completely enclosed and fitted with a spray skirt that keeps the hull from filling with water.

Downstream V A river feature that often marks the best route through obstacles, with the point of the *V* facing downstream. It's formed by the eddy lines resulting from two obstacles bracketing a faster channel of water, or by turbulent water bracketing a smooth tongue.

Drop-and-pool A river characterized by rapids separated with long, placid stretches. The rapids act as natural dams that still the current preceding the drop.

Eddy The water downstream of an obstruction in the current or below a river-bend. The water in the eddy may be relatively calm or boiling, and will flow upstream.

Eddy line The boundary at the edge of an eddy separating two currents of different velocity and direction.

Eddy out To exit the downstream current into an eddy.

Eddy turn Maneuver used to enter or exit an eddy.

Ferry A maneuver for moving laterally across a stream, executed facing up- or downstream.

Flood stage The point at which a river is out of its banks. The level associated with flood stage is location specific and depends on the depth of the riverbed, height of the banks, and flow.

Gradient A river's change in altitude over a fixed distance, usually expressed in feet per mile.

Hair Turbulent, foamy whitewater.

GLOSSARY

Haystack A pyramid-shaped standing wave caused by deceleration of current from underwater resistance, commonly found at the end of a chute where the faster current collides with the slower-moving water pooled below the rapid.

Hole A river feature in which water moves over an obstacle with sufficient flow and velocity to create a wave that violently and continuously breaks (recirculates) upstream against its face.

Hydraulic General term for souse holes and holes.

Keeper Any hole that is difficult to exit. Can take the form of a hole whose right and left edges curve upstream and fold back into itself, or a very large hole whose boil line is more than a boat length downstream.

Ledge The exposed edge of a rock stratum that acts as a low natural dam, creating a falls or rapid as current passes over it.

Line A viable route through a rapid.

Low-head dam A usually man-made obstacle that laterally spans a river from the left to the right bank, creating a pool upstream and a keeper hydraulic immediately below. Grimly referred to as the "perfect killing machine" for its lack of exit points once a boater is caught in the hydraulic.

Meander A large loop in a river's path through a wide floodplain.

Oxbow A U-shaped lake formed when a river's meander is bypassed by the main channel.

Peel-out A maneuver for exiting an eddy and quickly entering the downstream current.

Pencil in To pierce the water below a drop in a vertical position.

PFD Personal flotation device. The US Coast Guard recognizes five classes of PFDs. The American Canoe Association recommends Coast Guard–approved Class III PFDs.

Pile The frothy white water on top of a wave or in a hole.

Pillow Bulge on the surface of a river created by water piling up against an underwater obstruction, usually a rock.

Pinning When an object (usually a boat) is pushed onto an obstacle (usually a rock) and held there forcefully by the pressure of the current.

Pool A section of river where the prevailing current has been stilled and the water is usually deep and quiet.

Portage To avoid an obstacle, hazard, or rapid by exiting the river, carrying boat and gear downstream, and reentering the river below the obstacle.

Pothole Formed by erosion, a depression in the river bed at the base of a steep drop.

Pour-over A sticky hole formed by water flowing over an abrupt drop.

Punch To approach and pass through a hole aggressively, boat perpendicular to the hole, to reach the current moving downstream beyond the boil line.

Rapids Portion of a river where there is appreciable turbulence usually accompanied by obstacles.

Riffles Slight turbulence with or without a few rocks tossed in; usually found where current is swift and very shallow.

River left The left side of the river facing downstream.

River right The right side of the river facing downstream.

Rock garden Rapids that have many exposed or partially submerged rocks, necessitating intricate and technical maneuvering.

Roll The technique of righting a capsized kayak or canoe with the paddler remaining in the paddling position.

Scout To evaluate a rapid (either from the shore or while your boat is in an eddy) to decide whether or not to run it or facilitate selection of a suitable route through it.

Shuttle To use vehicles to transport people and boats on land between river-access points before or after a run.

Sieve A hazard formed by channels of swift water flowing through menacingly tight spaces between and underneath boulders, usually accompanied by undercuts. Water can flow freely through, but debris and paddlers are easily pinned under water by the forceful currents.

Slide rapid An elongated ledge that descends or slopes gradually rather than abruptly, usually covered by shallow water.

Sneak An alternative route through a rapid that avoids the main flow. Usually, but not always, an easier route than the main channel.

Souse hole See *Hole.*

Spray skirt A hemmed piece of neoprene or nylon clothing that resembles a short skirt, with an elastic hem fitted around the boater's waist and an elastic hem fitted around the cockpit of a decked boat.

Standing wave A wave that does not move in relation to the river bed. See *Haystack.*

Stern The rear end of a canoe or kayak.

GLOSSARY

Strainers Branches, trees, or vegetation that is partially or totally submerged in a river's current. Serious hazards for paddlers, strainers allow only water to pass through freely. The current will pull anything else down and plaster it into place, similar to the action of a kitchen colander.

Surfing The technique of situating your boat on the upstream face of a wave.

Swamp To have a canoe or kayak fill with water.

Tongue See *Chute*.

Undercut rock A hazard in which a river has eroded a boulder below the surface of the water, creating a cavity with potential for entrapment not visible above the surface.

INDEX

INDEX

INDEX

INDEX

INDEX

Photo: Keri Anne Molloy

JOHNNY MOLLOY is an outdoors writer based in Johnson City, Tennessee, who spends his winters in Florida. Born in Memphis, he moved to Knoxville in 1980 to attend the University of Tennessee. During his college years, he developed a love of the natural world that has since become the primary focus of his life.

It all started on a backpacking foray into the Great Smoky Mountains National Park. That first trip was a disaster; nevertheless, Johnny discovered a love of the natural world that would lead him to canoe-camp and backpack throughout the United States and abroad over the next 25 years. Today, he averages 150 nights per year camping out.

After graduating from Tennessee in 1987 with a degree in economics, Johnny spent an ever-increasing amount of time in the wild, becoming more skilled in the environment. Friends enjoyed his adventure stories; one even suggested he write a book. He pursued that idea and soon parlayed his love of the outdoors into an occupation.

The results of his efforts are more than 60 books. These include hiking, camping, paddling, and other comprehensive guidebooks, as well as books on true outdoor adventures. In addition to updating and rewriting *Canoeing & Kayaking Florida*, he has written several other Florida-focused outdoors guides, including *A Paddler's Guide to Everglades National Park; Best Tent Camping: Florida; Beach & Coastal Camping in Florida; The Hiking Trails of Florida's National Forests Parks and Preserves; Day Hiking Southwest Florida; Best Easy Day Hikes: Jacksonville; Best Easy Day Hikes: Tallahassee; Best Easy Day Hikes: Tampa Bay;* and two true-adventure stories, *From the Swamp to the Keys: A Paddle Through Florida History* and *Hiking the Florida Trail: 1,100 Miles, 78 Days, Two Pairs of Boots, and One Heck of an Adventure.* His other books primarily cover the Southeast but range over 26 states.

For the latest on Johnny, visit his website, johnnymolloy.com.

CPSIA information can be obtained
at www.ICGtesting.com
Printed in the USA
JSHW031747010920
7575JS00004B/4

9 781634 040303